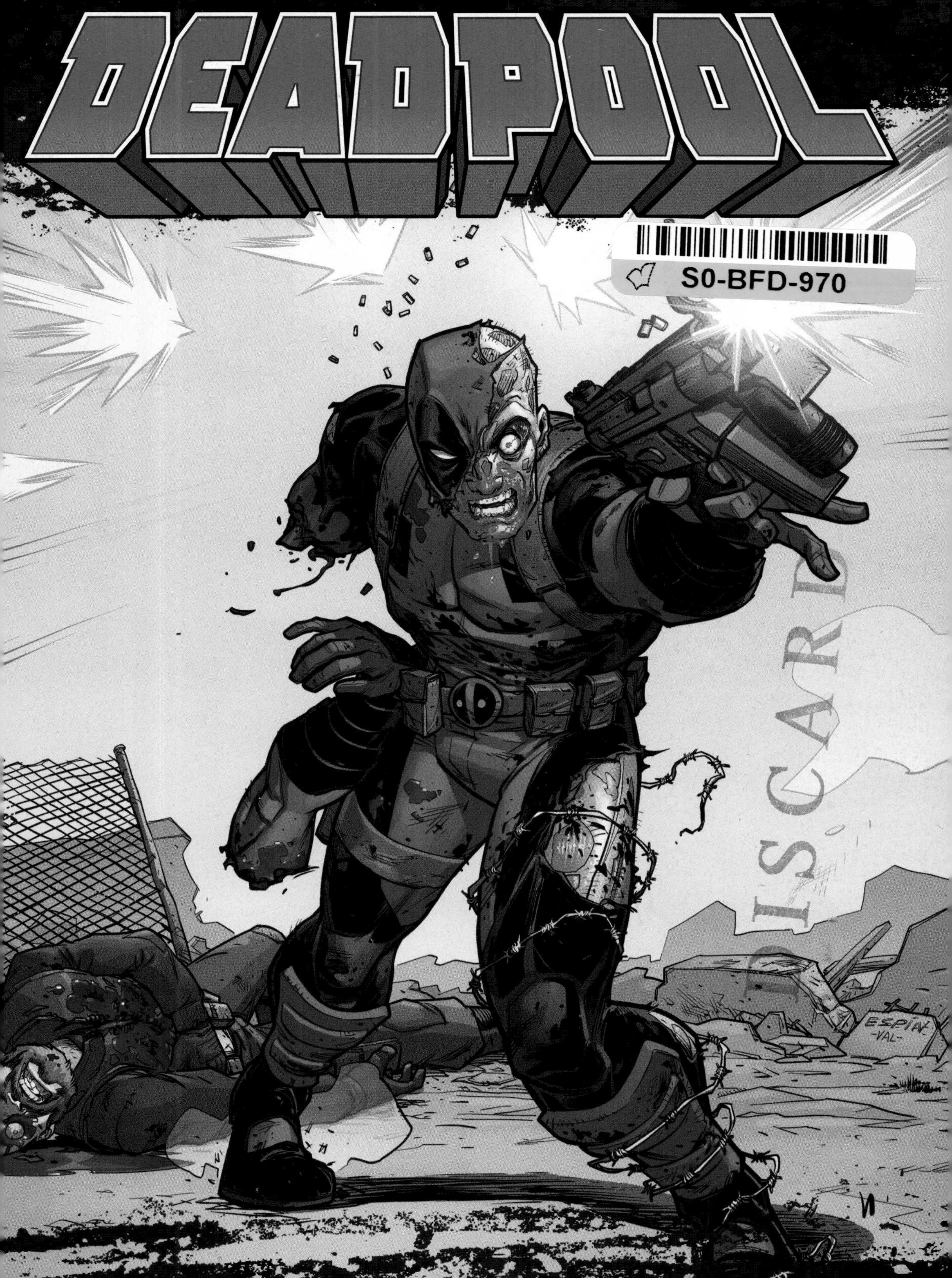
DEADPOOL
ESPIN
-VAL-

LETTERER
VC'S JOE SABINO

ASSISTANT EDITORS
CHARLES BEACHAM
& HEATHER ANTOS

EDITOR
JORDAN D. WHITE

X-MEN GROUP EDITOR
MIKE MARTS

DEADPOOL CREATED BY ROB LIEFELD & FABIAN NICIEZA

Collection Editor: Jennifer Grünwald • Assistant Editor: Sarah Brunstad • Associate Managing Editor: Alex Starbuck
Editor, Special Projects: Mark D. Beazley • Senior Editor, Special Projects: Jeff Youngquist • SVP Print, Sales & Marketing: David Gabriel

Editor in Chief: Axel Alonso • Chief Creative Officer: Joe Quesada • Publisher: Dan Buckley • Executive Producer: Alan Fine

DEADPOOL VOL. 8: ALL GOOD THINGS. Contains material originally published in magazine form as DEADPOOL #41-44 and #250. First printing 2015. ISBN# 978-0-7851-9244-2. Published by MARVEL WORLDWIDE, INC., a subsidiary of MARVEL ENTERTAINMENT, LLC. OFFICE OF PUBLICATION: 135 West 50th Street, New York, NY 10020. Copyright © 2015 MARVEL No similarity between any of the names, characters, persons, and/or institutions in this magazine with those of any living or dead person or institution is intended, and any such similarity which may exist is purely coincidental. Printed in the U.S.A. ALAN FINE, President, Marvel Entertainment; DAN BUCKLEY, President, TV, Publishing and Brand Management; JOE QUESADA, Chief Creative Officer; TOM BREVOORT, SVP of Publishing; DAVID BOGART, SVP of Operations & Procurement, Publishing; C.B. CEBULSKI, VP of International Development & Brand Management; DAVID GABRIEL, SVP Print, Sales & Marketing; JIM O'KEEFE, VP of Operations & Logistics; DAN CARR, Executive Director of Publishing Technology; SUSAN CRESPI, Editorial Operations Manager; ALEX MORALES, Publishing Operations Manager; STAN LEE, Chairman Emeritus. For information regarding advertising in Marvel Comics or on Marvel.com, please contact Jonathan Rheingold, VP of Custom Solutions & Ad Sales, at jrheingold@marvel.com. For Marvel subscription inquiries, please call 800-217-9158. Manufactured between 4/3/2015 and 5/11/2015 by R.R. DONNELLEY,

DEADPOOL

WRITERS
GERRY DUGGAN & BRIAN POSEHN

ISSUES #41-44

ARTIST
SALVA ESPIN

COLORIST
VAL STAPLES

COVER ART
MARK BROOKS (#41-42) AND GIUSEPPE CAMUNCOLI & ISRAEL SILVA (#43-44)

ISSUE #250 (A.K.A. #45)

PENCILER
MIKE HAWTHORNE

INKER
TERRY PALLOT

COLORIST
JORDIE BELLAIRE

COVER ART
SCOTT KOBLISH & RUTH REDMOND

BONUS STORIES
WRITERS: MIKE DRUCKER, BEN ACKER & BEN BLACKER, JASON MANTZOUKAS,
PAUL SCHEER & NICK GIOVANNETTI, SCOTT AUKERMAN, MATT SELMAN AND
GERRY DUGGAN & BRIAN POSEHN
ARTISTS: J.J. KIRBY, NATALIE NOURIGAT, TODD NAUCK, TY TEMPLETON,
MIRKO COLAK, JACOB CHABOT AND SCOTT KOBLISH
COLORISTS: VERONICA GANDINI, NATALIE NOURIGAT, TY TEMPLETON,
RUTH REDMOND, JACOB CHABOT AND VAL STAPLES

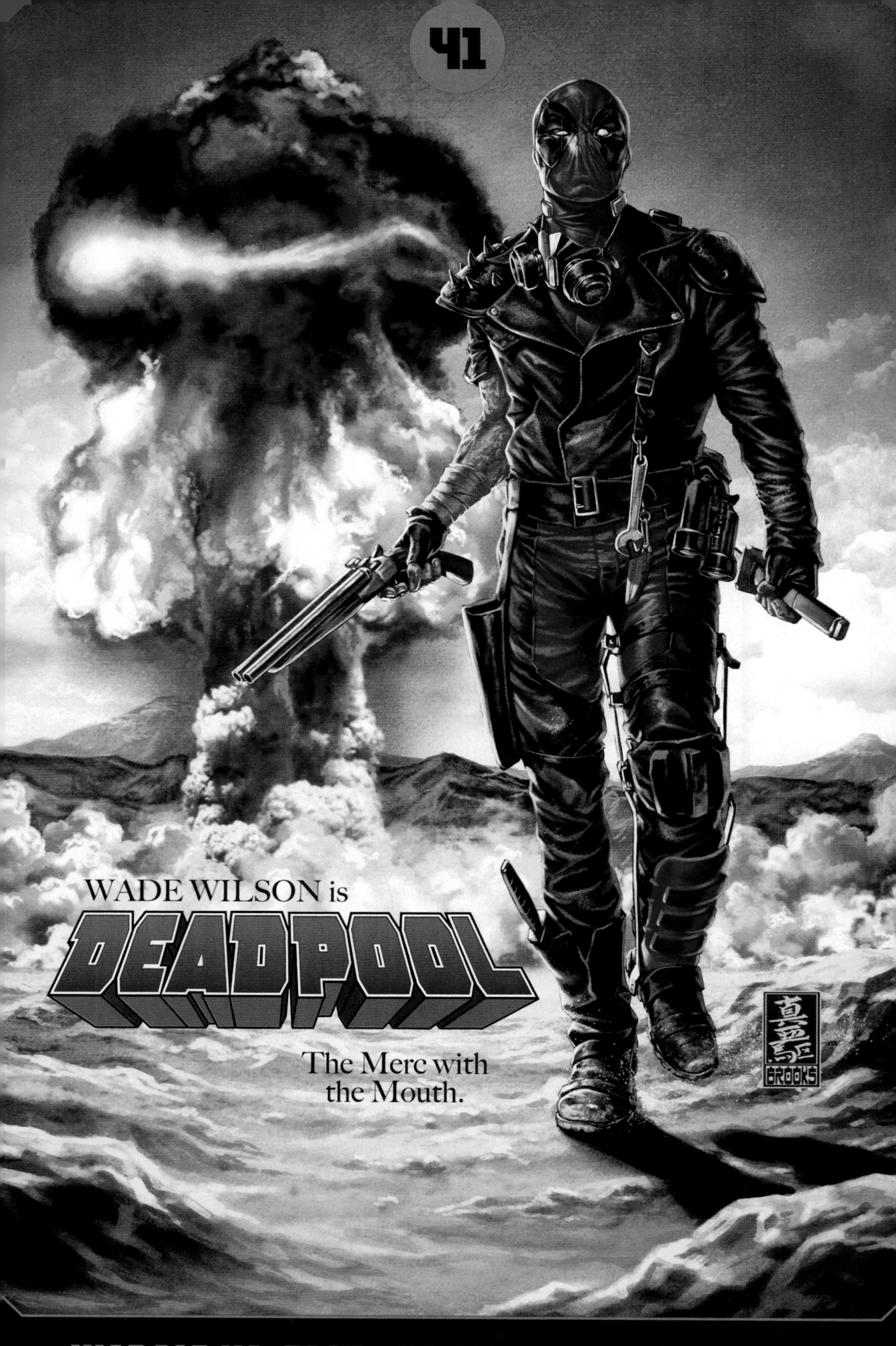
41
WADE WILSON is
DEADPOOL
The Merc with
the Mouth.
BROOKS

ossibly the world's most skilled mercenary, definitely the world's most annoying, /ade Wilson was chosen for a top-secret government program that gave him a ealing factor allowing him to heal from any wound. Now, Wade makes his way as gun for hire, shooting his prey's faces off while talking his friends' ears off. Call him the Merc with the Mouth...call him the Regeneratin' Degenerate...call him...

DEADPOOL

HEY, GUYS.
SO, I'M *DEADPOOL*--THE *MERC* WITH THE *MOUTH.* AND USUALLY, THAT MOUTH IS SMILING. BUT YOU KNOW WHAT? IT'S *FAKE.* I'M NOT REALLY VERY HAPPY.
I JUST WENT THROUGH SOME STUFF. GOT TURNED INTO A DIFFERENT ME-- A ME WHO WAS AT PEACE WITH HIMSELF AND THE WORLD.
BUT THAT'S NOT ME.
I'VE GOT AN AWESOME, GORGEOUS AND POWERFUL *WIFE* WHO LOVES ME.
I'VE GOT *FRIENDS* WHO CARE ABOUT ME.
I'VE GOT A *DAUGHTER* WHO... WHO DOESN'T KNOW ENOUGH TO BE SCARED TO KNOW ME.
I DON'T KNOW. I JUST...
I'VE BEEN TO ASGARD, I'VE BEEN TO THE SAVAGE LAND, I'VE BEEN TO WAKANDA... BUT I'VE NEVER BEEN TO *ME.*
YOU KNOW?

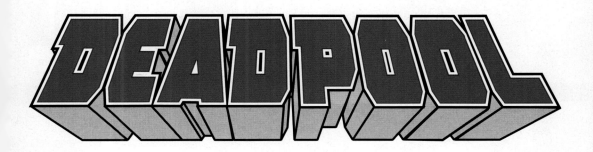

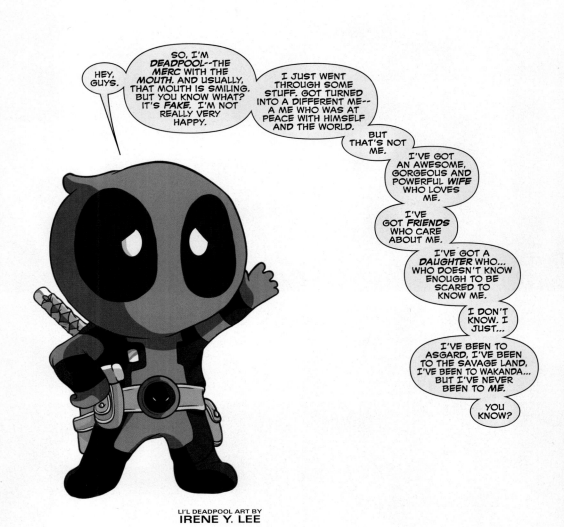

LI'L DEADPOOL ART BY
IRENE Y. LEE

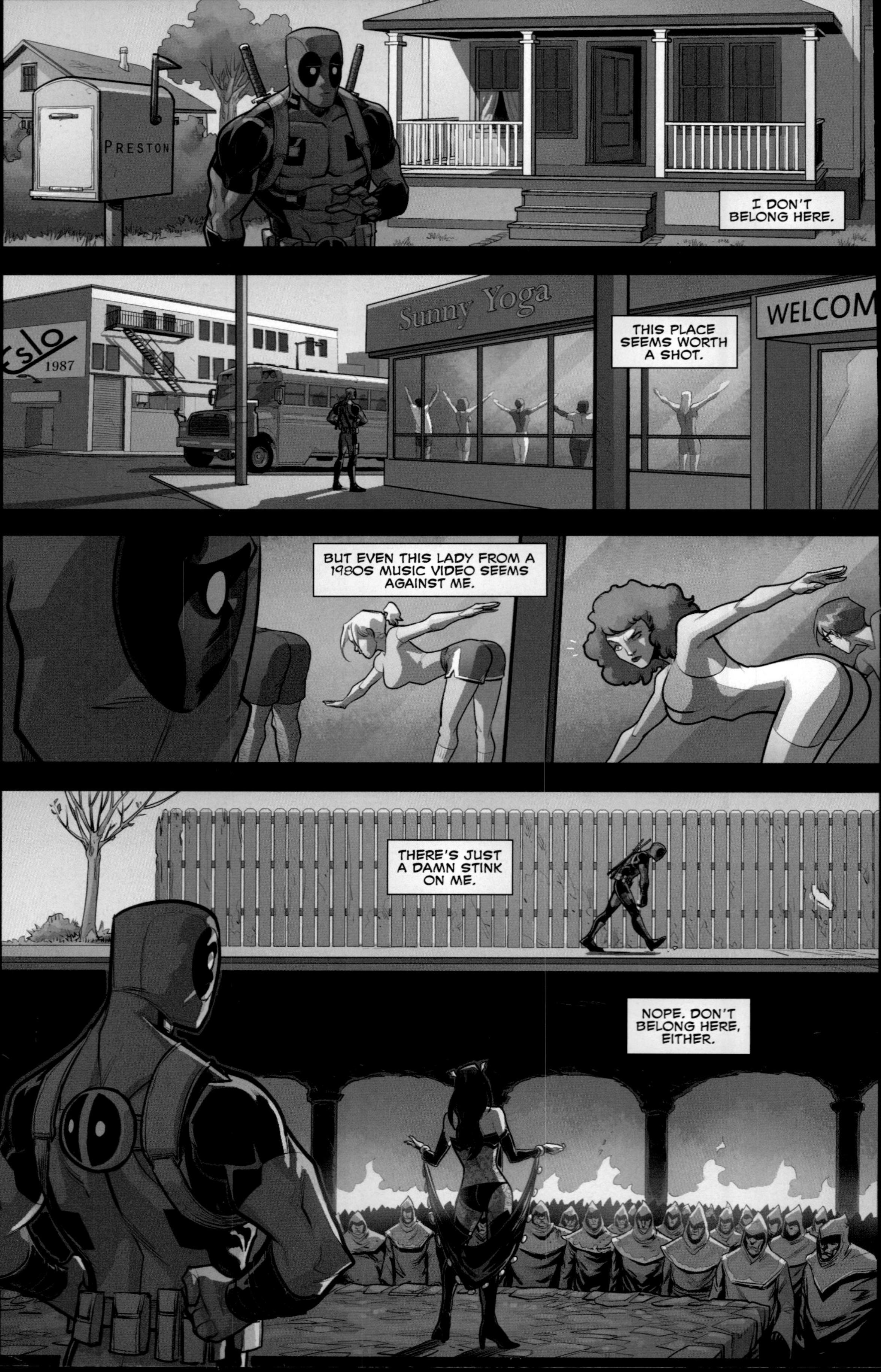
PRESTON
I DON'T BELONG HERE.
Sunny Yoga
WELCOM
1987
THIS PLACE SEEMS WORTH A SHOT.
BUT EVEN THIS LADY FROM A 1980S MUSIC VIDEO SEEMS AGAINST ME.
THERE'S JUST A DAMN STINK ON ME.
NOPE. DON'T BELONG HERE, EITHER.

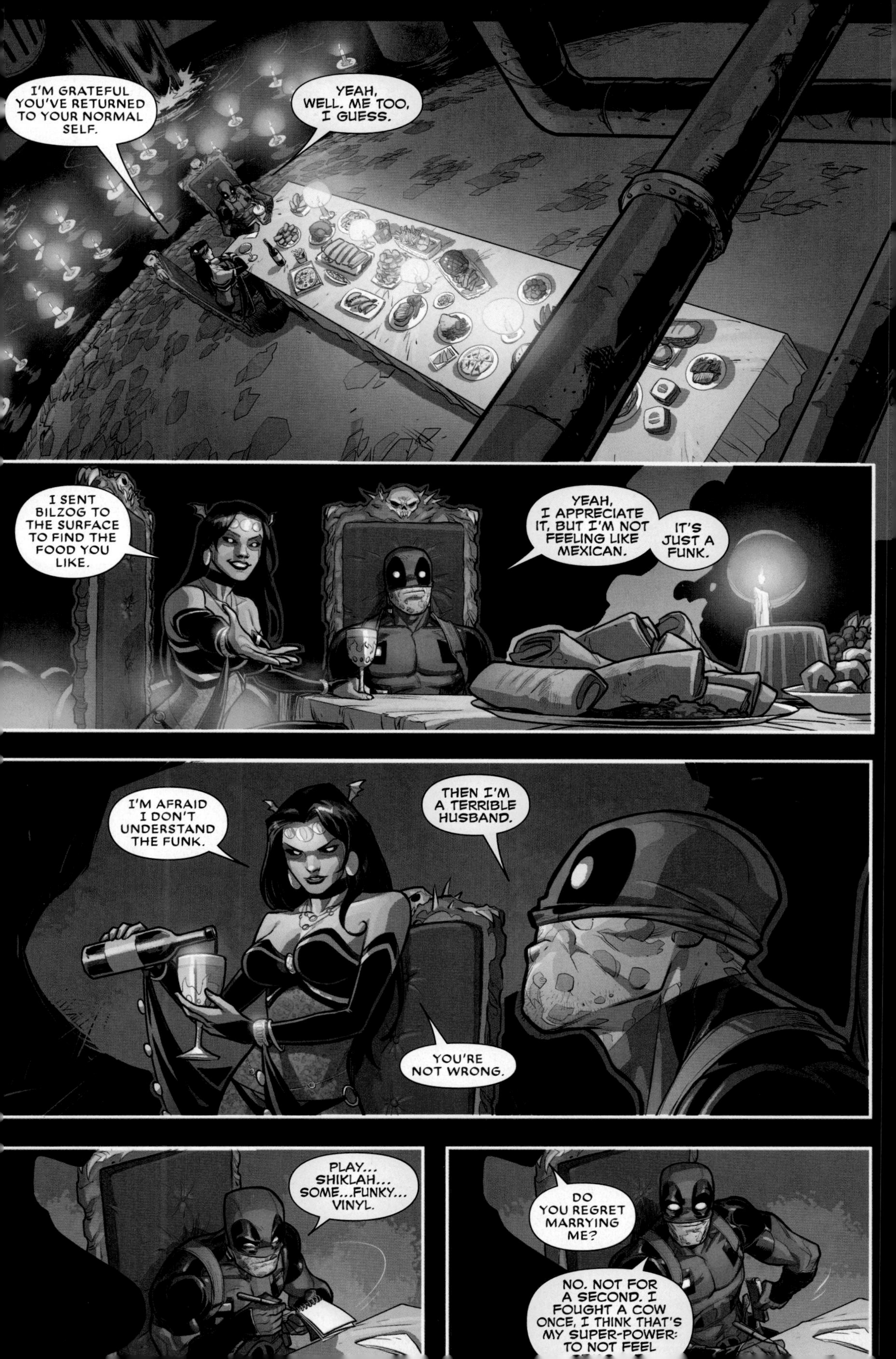
I'M GRATEFUL YOU'VE RETURNED TO YOUR NORMAL SELF.
YEAH, WELL. ME TOO, I GUESS.
I SENT BILZOG TO THE SURFACE TO FIND THE FOOD YOU LIKE.
YEAH, I APPRECIATE IT, BUT I'M NOT FEELING LIKE MEXICAN.
IT'S JUST A FUNK.
I'M AFRAID I DON'T UNDERSTAND THE FUNK.
THEN I'M A TERRIBLE HUSBAND.
YOU'RE NOT WRONG.
PLAY... SHIKLAH... SOME...FUNKY... VINYL.
DO YOU REGRET MARRYING ME?
NO. NOT FOR A SECOND. I FOUGHT A COW ONCE, I THINK THAT'S MY SUPER-POWER: TO NOT FEEL

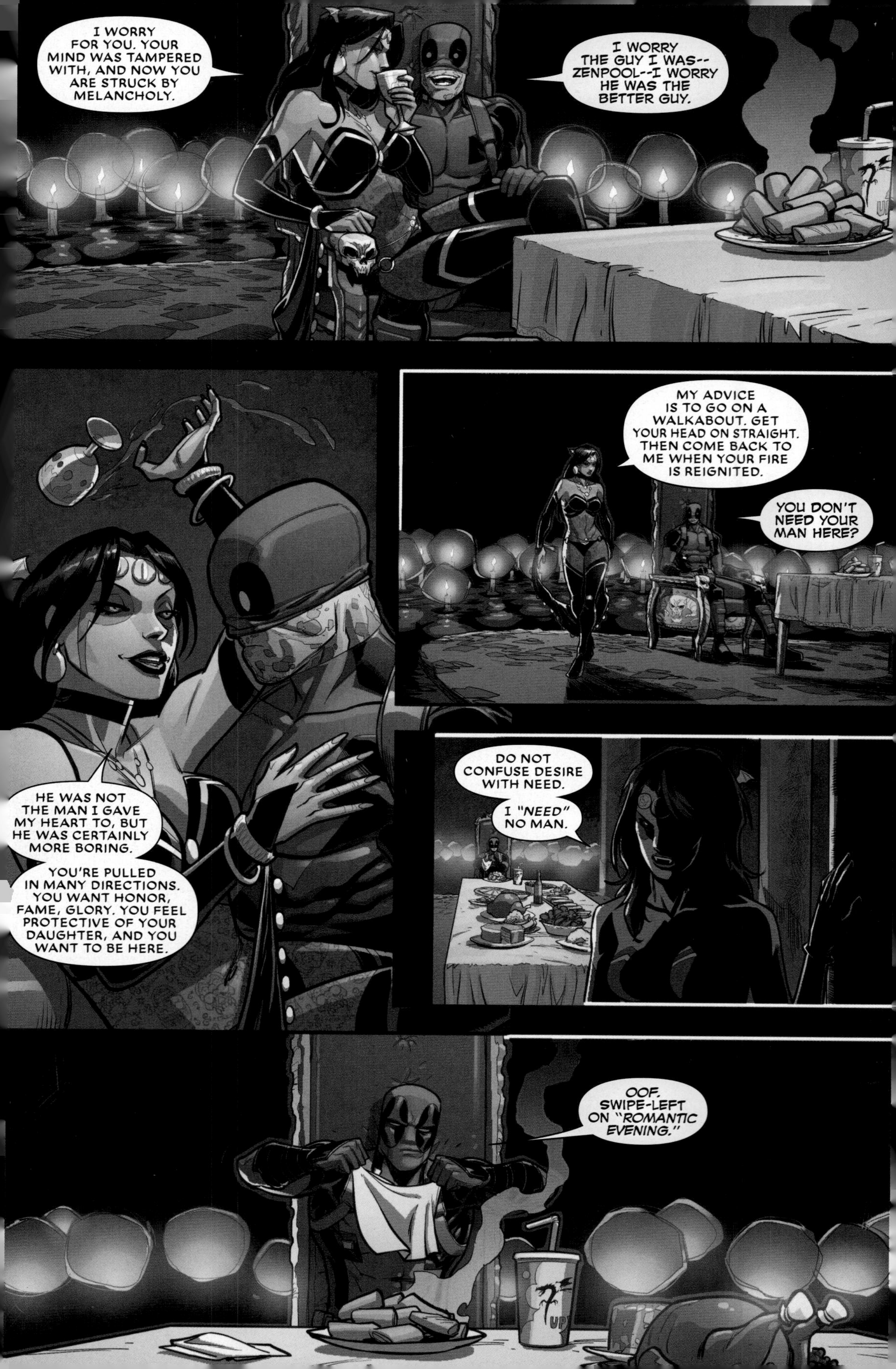
I WORRY FOR YOU. YOUR MIND WAS TAMPERED WITH, AND NOW YOU ARE STRUCK BY MELANCHOLY.
I WORRY THE GUY I WAS--ZENPOOL--I WORRY HE WAS THE BETTER GUY.
UP
HE WAS NOT THE MAN I GAVE MY HEART TO, BUT HE WAS CERTAINLY MORE BORING.
YOU'RE PULLED IN MANY DIRECTIONS. YOU WANT HONOR, FAME, GLORY. YOU FEEL PROTECTIVE OF YOUR DAUGHTER, AND YOU WANT TO BE HERE.
MY ADVICE IS TO GO ON A WALKABOUT. GET YOUR HEAD ON STRAIGHT. THEN COME BACK TO ME WHEN YOUR FIRE IS REIGNITED.
YOU DON'T NEED YOUR MAN HERE?
DO NOT CONFUSE DESIRE WITH NEED.
I "NEED" NO MAN.
OOF. SWIPE-LEFT ON "ROMANTIC EVENING."
UP

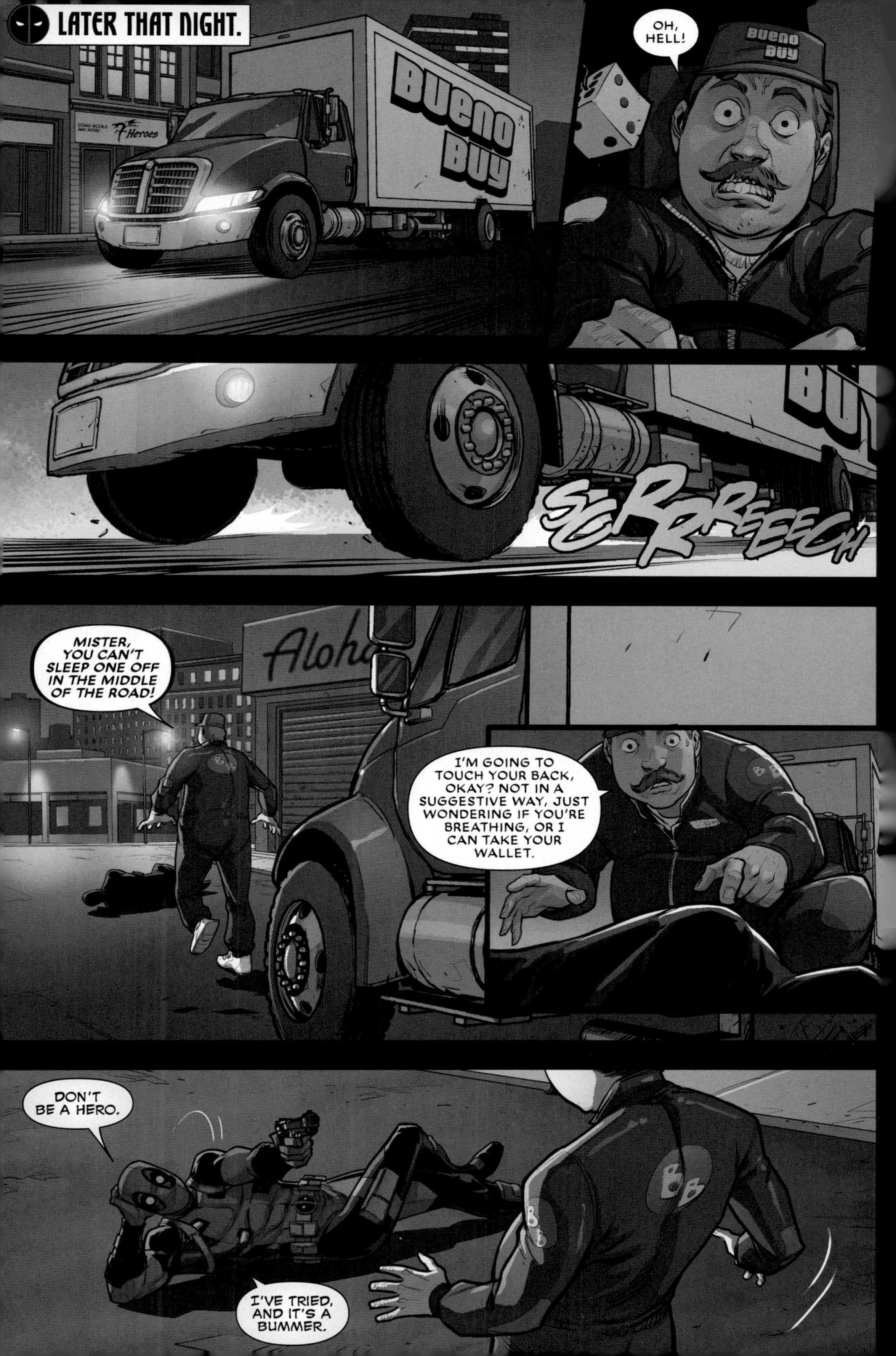
LATER THAT NIGHT.
BUENO BUY
COMIC-BOOKS AND MORE! Heroes
OH, HELL!
BUENO BUY
SCRREEECH
Aloha
MISTER, YOU CAN'T SLEEP ONE OFF IN THE MIDDLE OF THE ROAD!
I'M GOING TO TOUCH YOUR BACK, OKAY? NOT IN A SUGGESTIVE WAY, JUST WONDERING IF YOU'RE BREATHING, OR I CAN TAKE YOUR WALLET.
DON'T BE A HERO.
I'VE TRIED, AND IT'S A BUMMER.

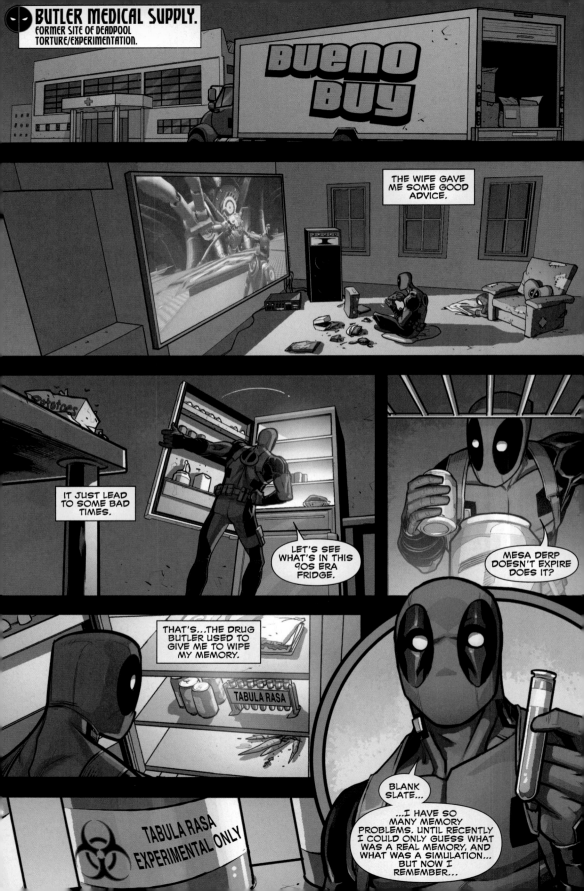

BUTLER MEDICAL SUPPLY.
FORMER SITE OF DEADPOOL TORTURE/EXPERIMENTATION.

BUENO BUY

THE WIFE GAVE ME SOME GOOD ADVICE.

IT JUST LEAD TO SOME BAD TIMES.

LET'S SEE WHAT'S IN THIS 90S ERA FRIDGE.

MESA DERP DOESN'T EXPIRE DOES IT?

THAT'S...THE DRUG BUTLER USED TO GIVE ME TO WIPE MY MEMORY.

TABULA RASA

BLANK SLATE...

...I HAVE SO MANY MEMORY PROBLEMS. UNTIL RECENTLY I COULD ONLY GUESS WHAT WAS A REAL MEMORY, AND WHAT WAS A SIMULATION... BUT NOW I REMEMBER...

TABULA RASA EXPERIMENTAL ONLY

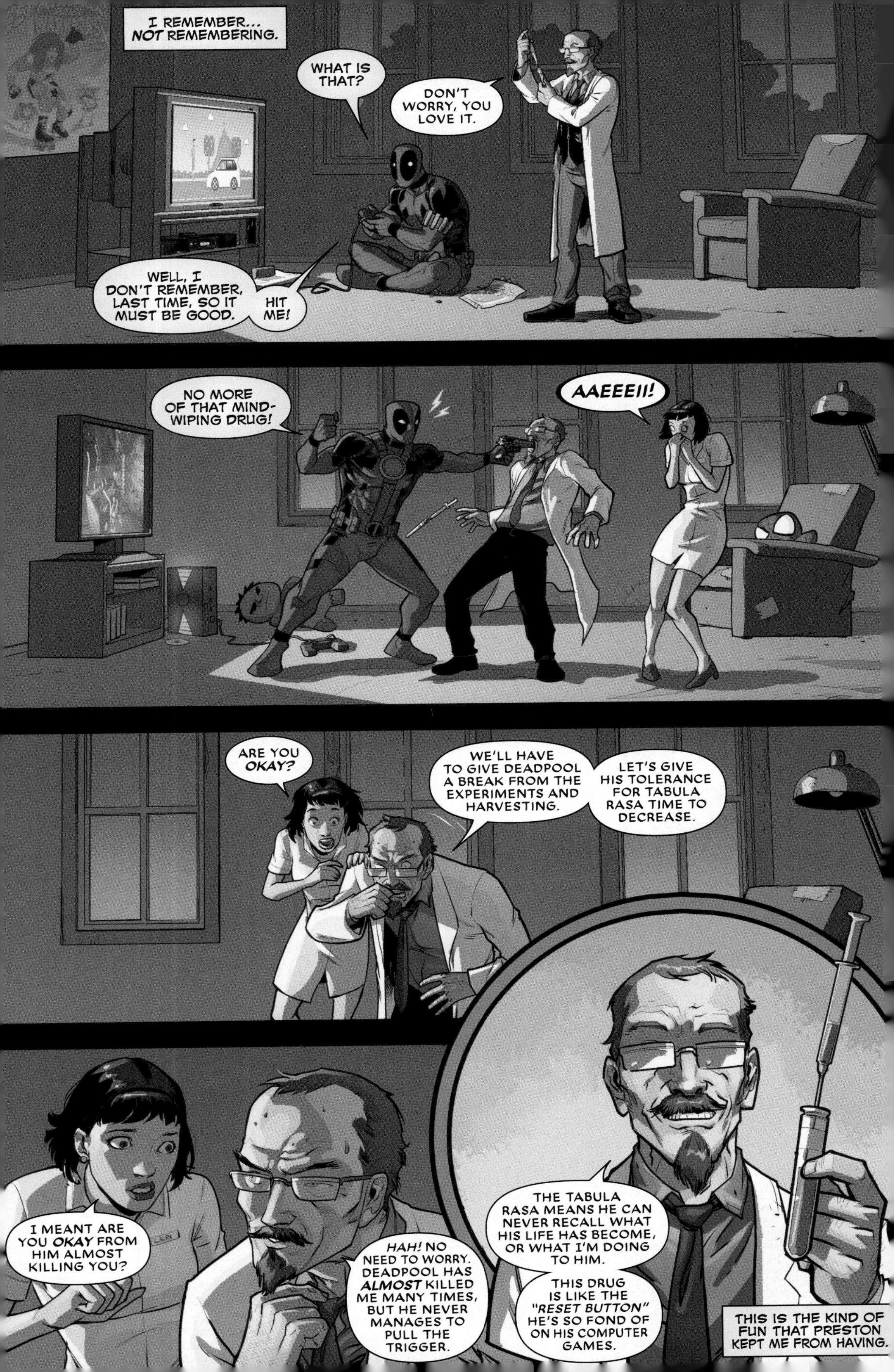
I REMEMBER... *NOT* REMEMBERING.
WHAT IS THAT?
DON'T WORRY, YOU LOVE IT.
WELL, I DON'T REMEMBER, LAST TIME, SO IT MUST BE GOOD.
HIT ME!
NO MORE OF THAT MIND-WIPING DRUG!
AAEEEII!
ARE YOU *OKAY?*
WE'LL HAVE TO GIVE DEADPOOL A BREAK FROM THE EXPERIMENTS AND HARVESTING.
LET'S GIVE HIS TOLERANCE FOR TABULA RASA TIME TO DECREASE.
I MEANT ARE YOU *OKAY* FROM HIM ALMOST KILLING YOU?
HAH! NO NEED TO WORRY. DEADPOOL HAS ***ALMOST*** KILLED ME MANY TIMES, BUT HE NEVER MANAGES TO PULL THE TRIGGER.
THE TABULA RASA MEANS HE CAN NEVER RECALL WHAT HIS LIFE HAS BECOME, OR WHAT I'M DOING TO HIM.
THIS DRUG IS LIKE THE *"RESET BUTTON"* HE'S SO FOND OF ON HIS COMPUTER GAMES.
THIS IS THE KIND OF FUN THAT PRESTON KEPT ME FROM HAVING.

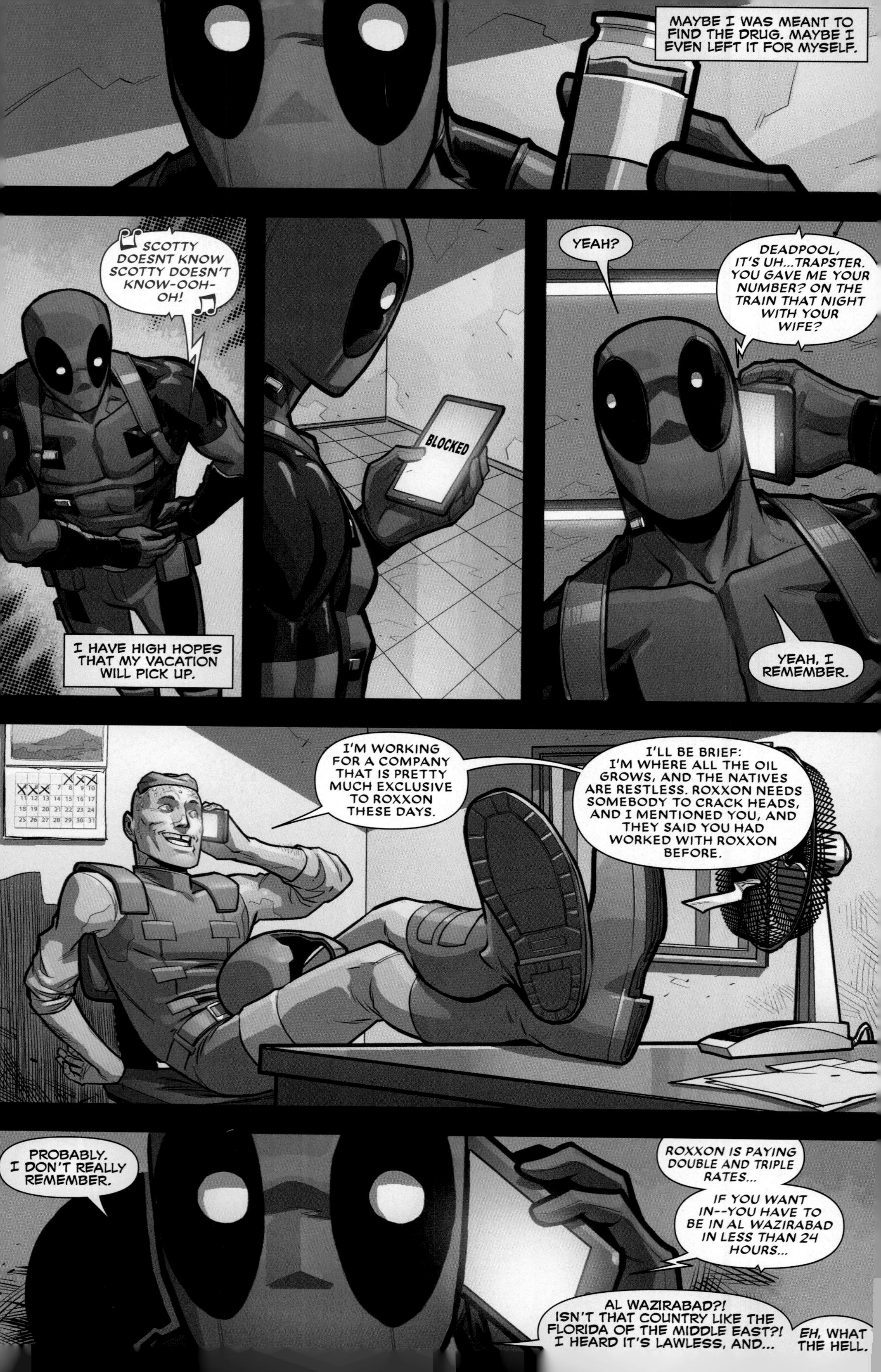
MAYBE I WAS MEANT TO FIND THE DRUG. MAYBE I EVEN LEFT IT FOR MYSELF.
SCOTTY DOESNT KNOW SCOTTY DOESN'T KNOW-OOH-OH!
I HAVE HIGH HOPES THAT MY VACATION WILL PICK UP.
BLOCKED
YEAH?
DEADPOOL, IT'S UH...TRAPSTER. YOU GAVE ME YOUR NUMBER? ON THE TRAIN THAT NIGHT WITH YOUR WIFE?
YEAH, I REMEMBER.
I'M WORKING FOR A COMPANY THAT IS PRETTY MUCH EXCLUSIVE TO ROXXON THESE DAYS.
I'LL BE BRIEF: I'M WHERE ALL THE OIL GROWS, AND THE NATIVES ARE RESTLESS. ROXXON NEEDS SOMEBODY TO CRACK HEADS, AND I MENTIONED YOU, AND THEY SAID YOU HAD WORKED WITH ROXXON BEFORE.
PROBABLY. I DON'T REALLY REMEMBER.
ROXXON IS PAYING DOUBLE AND TRIPLE RATES...
IF YOU WANT IN--YOU HAVE TO BE IN AL WAZIRABAD IN LESS THAN 24 HOURS...
AL WAZIRABAD?! ISN'T THAT COUNTRY LIKE THE FLORIDA OF THE MIDDLE EAST?! I HEARD IT'S LAWLESS, AND...
EH, WHAT THE HELL.

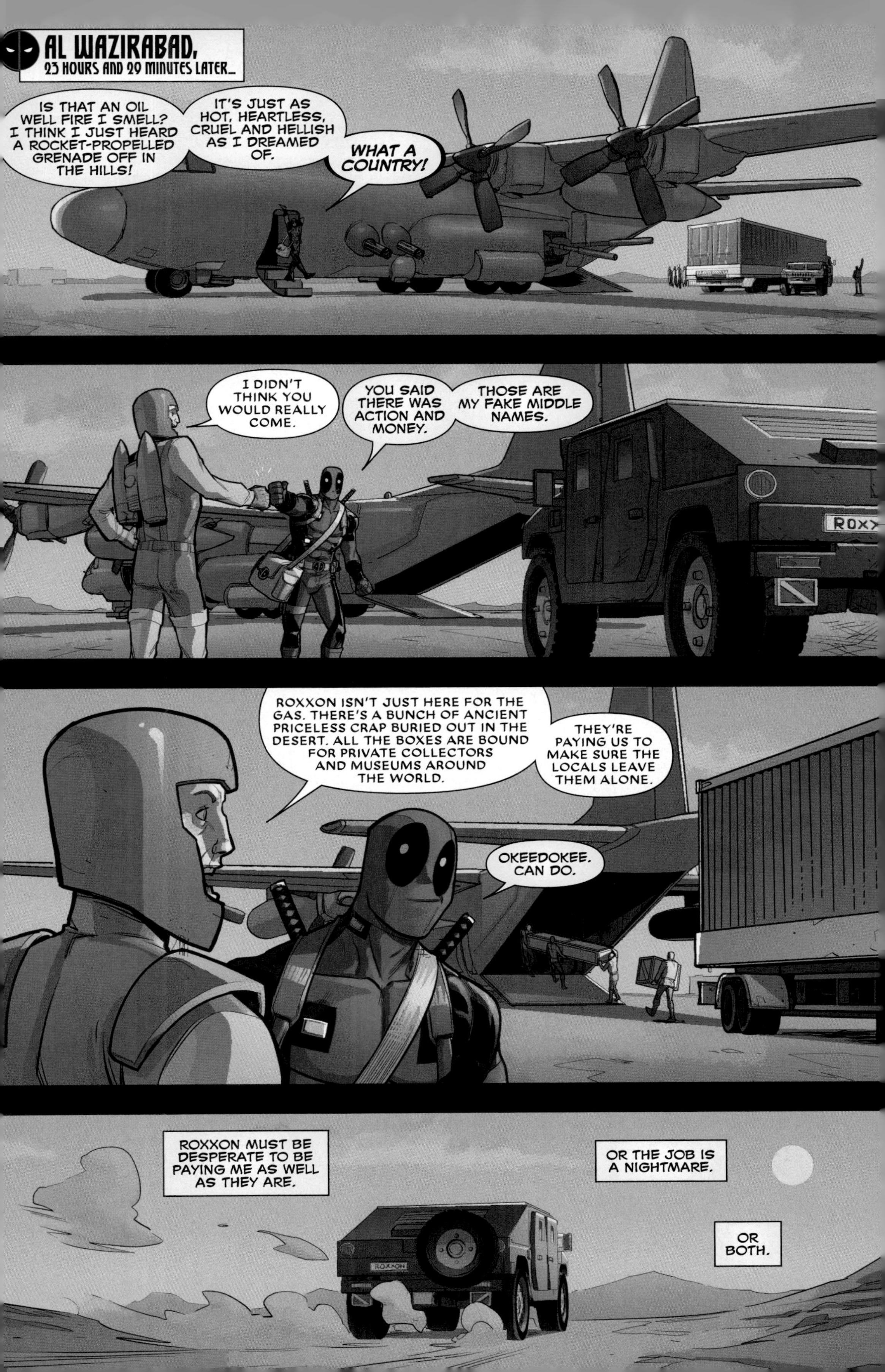
AL WAZIRABAD, 23 HOURS AND 29 MINUTES LATER...
IS THAT AN OIL WELL FIRE I SMELL? I THINK I JUST HEARD A ROCKET-PROPELLED GRENADE OFF IN THE HILLS!
IT'S JUST AS HOT, HEARTLESS, CRUEL AND HELLISH AS I DREAMED OF.
WHAT A COUNTRY!
I DIDN'T THINK YOU WOULD REALLY COME.
YOU SAID THERE WAS ACTION AND MONEY.
THOSE ARE MY FAKE MIDDLE NAMES.
ROXX
ROXXON ISN'T JUST HERE FOR THE GAS. THERE'S A BUNCH OF ANCIENT PRICELESS CRAP BURIED OUT IN THE DESERT. ALL THE BOXES ARE BOUND FOR PRIVATE COLLECTORS AND MUSEUMS AROUND THE WORLD.
THEY'RE PAYING US TO MAKE SURE THE LOCALS LEAVE THEM ALONE.
OKEEDOKEE. CAN DO.
ROXXON MUST BE DESPERATE TO BE PAYING ME AS WELL AS THEY ARE.
OR THE JOB IS A NIGHTMARE.
OR BOTH.

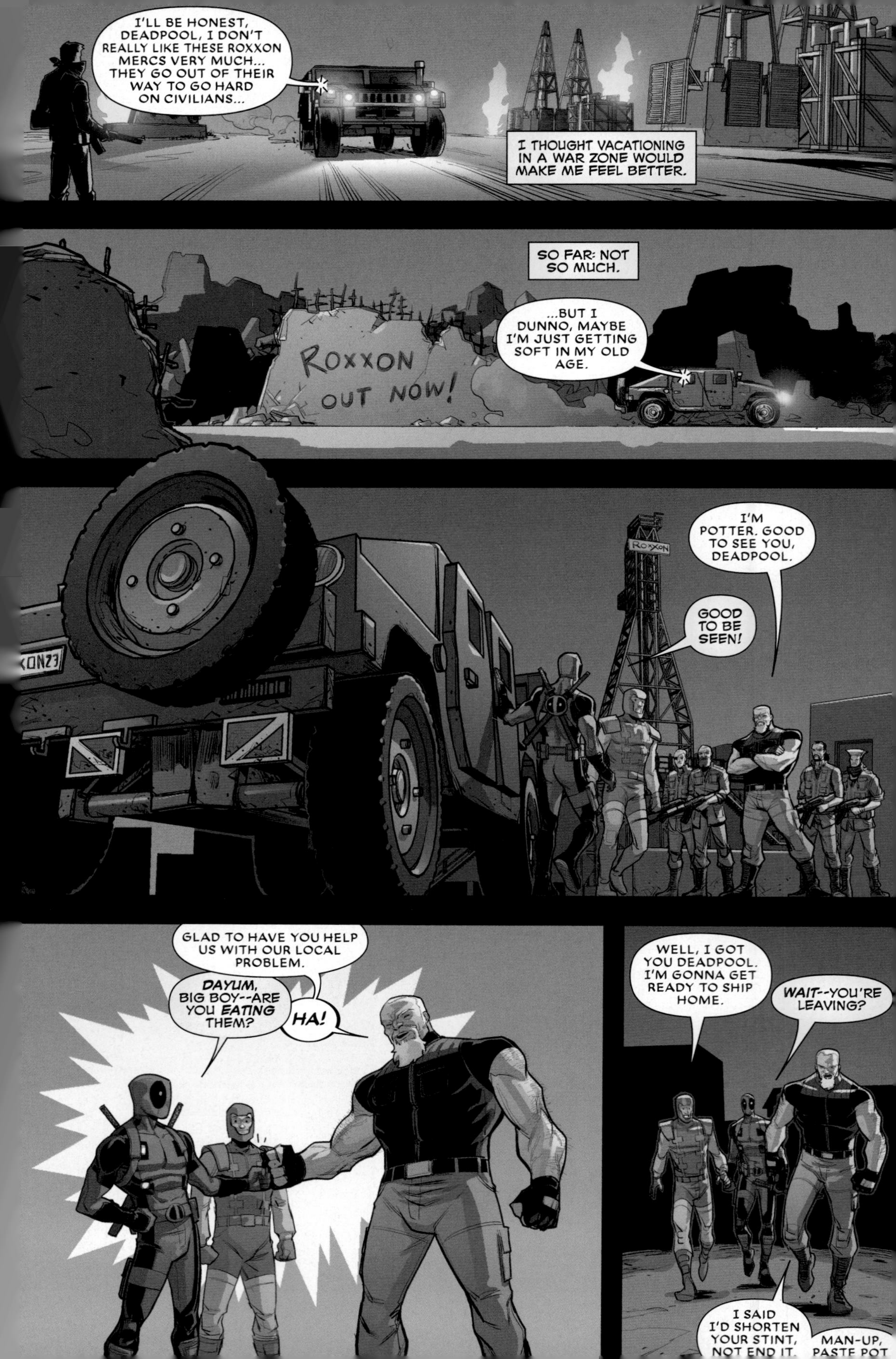
I'LL BE HONEST, DEADPOOL, I DON'T REALLY LIKE THESE ROXXON MERCS VERY MUCH... THEY GO OUT OF THEIR WAY TO GO HARD ON CIVILIANS...
I THOUGHT VACATIONING IN A WAR ZONE WOULD MAKE ME FEEL BETTER.
SO FAR: NOT SO MUCH.
ROXXON OUT NOW!
...BUT I DUNNO, MAYBE I'M JUST GETTING SOFT IN MY OLD AGE.
ROXXON
I'M POTTER. GOOD TO SEE YOU, DEADPOOL.
GOOD TO BE SEEN!
GLAD TO HAVE YOU HELP US WITH OUR LOCAL PROBLEM.
DAYUM, BIG BOY--ARE YOU EATING THEM?
HA!
WELL, I GOT YOU DEADPOOL. I'M GONNA GET READY TO SHIP HOME.
WAIT--YOU'RE LEAVING?
I SAID I'D SHORTEN YOUR STINT, NOT END IT.
MAN-UP, PASTE POT

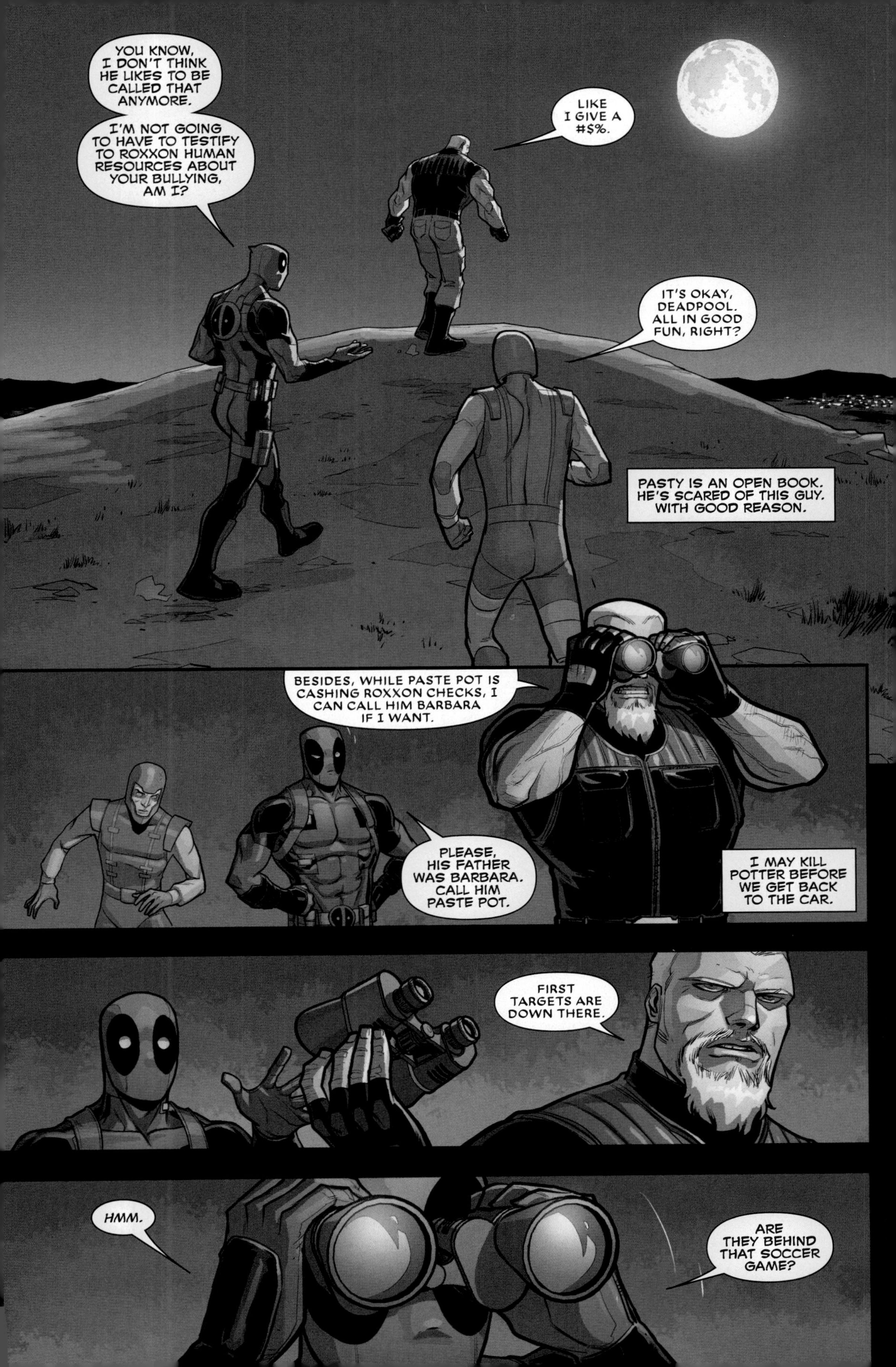
YOU KNOW, I DON'T THINK HE LIKES TO BE CALLED THAT ANYMORE.
I'M NOT GOING TO HAVE TO TESTIFY TO ROXXON HUMAN RESOURCES ABOUT YOUR BULLYING, AM I?
LIKE I GIVE A #$%.
IT'S OKAY, DEADPOOL. ALL IN GOOD FUN, RIGHT?
PASTY IS AN OPEN BOOK. HE'S SCARED OF THIS GUY. WITH GOOD REASON.
BESIDES, WHILE PASTE POT IS CASHING ROXXON CHECKS, I CAN CALL HIM BARBARA IF I WANT.
PLEASE, HIS FATHER WAS BARBARA. CALL HIM PASTE POT.
I MAY KILL POTTER BEFORE WE GET BACK TO THE CAR.
FIRST TARGETS ARE DOWN THERE.
HMM.
ARE THEY BEHIND THAT SOCCER GAME?

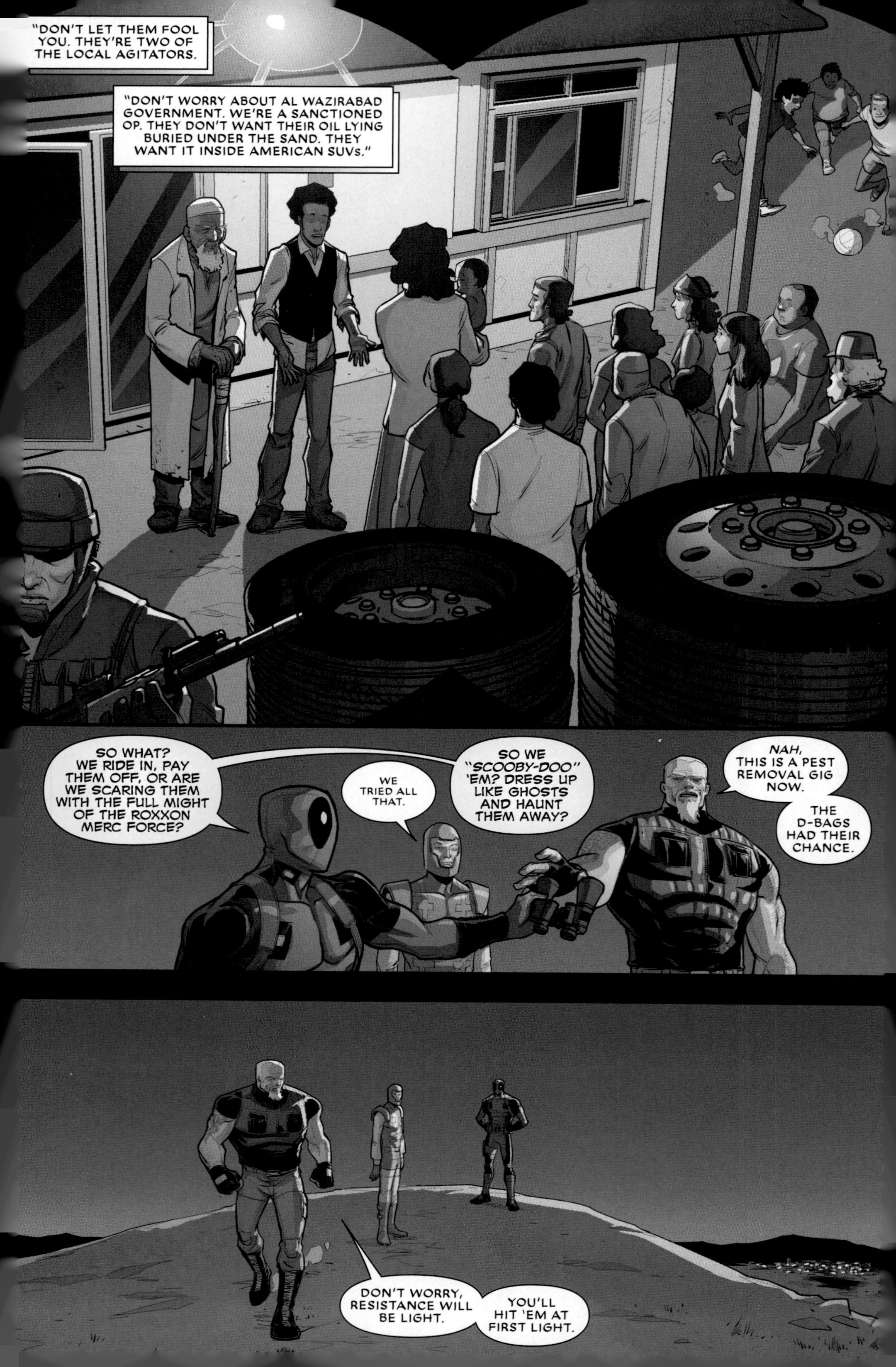
"DON'T LET THEM FOOL YOU. THEY'RE TWO OF THE LOCAL AGITATORS.
"DON'T WORRY ABOUT AL WAZIRABAD GOVERNMENT. WE'RE A SANCTIONED OP. THEY DON'T WANT THEIR OIL LYING BURIED UNDER THE SAND. THEY WANT IT INSIDE AMERICAN SUVs."
SO WHAT? WE RIDE IN, PAY THEM OFF, OR ARE WE SCARING THEM WITH THE FULL MIGHT OF THE ROXXON MERC FORCE?
WE TRIED ALL THAT.
SO WE "SCOOBY-DOO" 'EM? DRESS UP LIKE GHOSTS AND HAUNT THEM AWAY?
NAH, THIS IS A PEST REMOVAL GIG NOW.
THE D-BAGS HAD THEIR CHANCE.
DON'T WORRY, RESISTANCE WILL BE LIGHT.
YOU'LL HIT 'EM AT FIRST LIGHT.

IF THIS WORKS OUT, THERE IS A LOT OF WORK OVER HERE. THE WHOLE COUNTRY IS RISING UP. WE'RE FIGHTING ON ROXXON'S DIME NOW, BUT THE DICTATOR IN CHARGE OF AL WAZIRABAD NEEDS PROPPING UP ALL OVER THE DAMN COUNTRY.

GUYS, MEET DEADPOOL. DEADPOOL, MEET THE CREW.

WHY YOU GOTTA HIDE YOUR FACE?

THE MASK ISN'T FOR ME, IT'S FOR YOU.

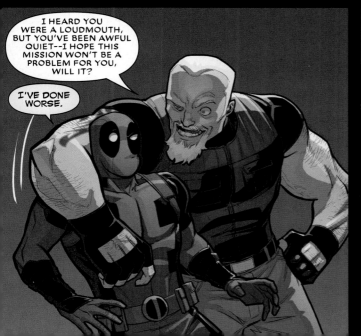

I HEARD YOU WERE A LOUDMOUTH, BUT YOU'VE BEEN AWFUL QUIET--I HOPE THIS MISSION WON'T BE A PROBLEM FOR YOU, WILL IT?

I'VE DONE WORSE.

HA-HA! I BET YOU HAVE.

ONE TIME I EVEN FOUGHT A COW.

GET SOME SLEEP. WE GOT A BUSY DAY TOMORROW.

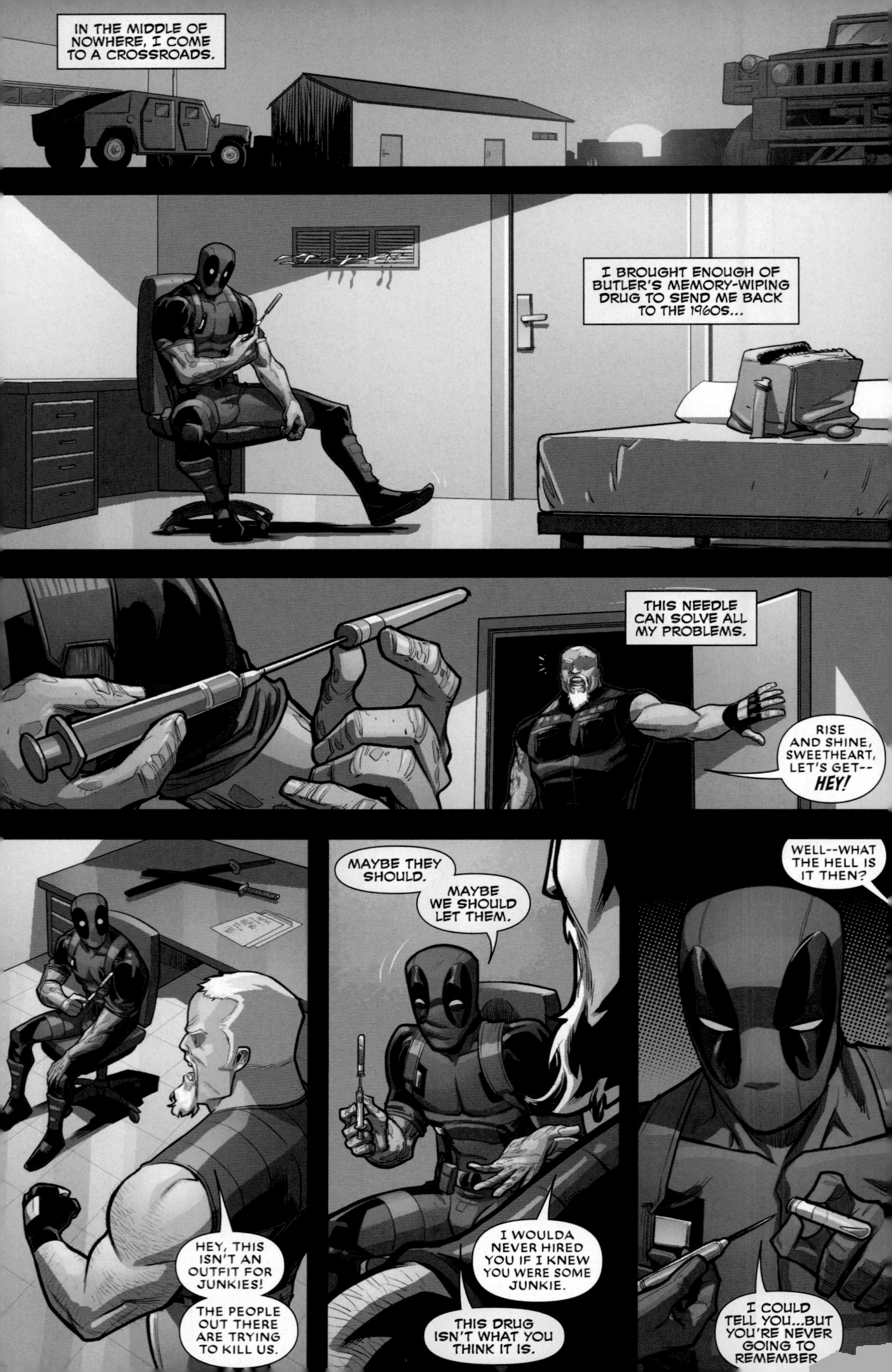
IN THE MIDDLE OF NOWHERE, I COME TO A CROSSROADS.
I BROUGHT ENOUGH OF BUTLER'S MEMORY-WIPING DRUG TO SEND ME BACK TO THE 1960S...
THIS NEEDLE CAN SOLVE ALL MY PROBLEMS.
RISE AND SHINE, SWEETHEART, LET'S GET-- HEY!
HEY, THIS ISN'T AN OUTFIT FOR JUNKIES!
THE PEOPLE OUT THERE ARE TRYING TO KILL US.
MAYBE THEY SHOULD.
MAYBE WE SHOULD LET THEM.
I WOULDA NEVER HIRED YOU IF I KNEW YOU WERE SOME JUNKIE.
THIS DRUG ISN'T WHAT YOU THINK IT IS.
WELL--WHAT THE HELL IS IT THEN?
I COULD TELL YOU...BUT YOU'RE NEVER GOING TO REMEMBER

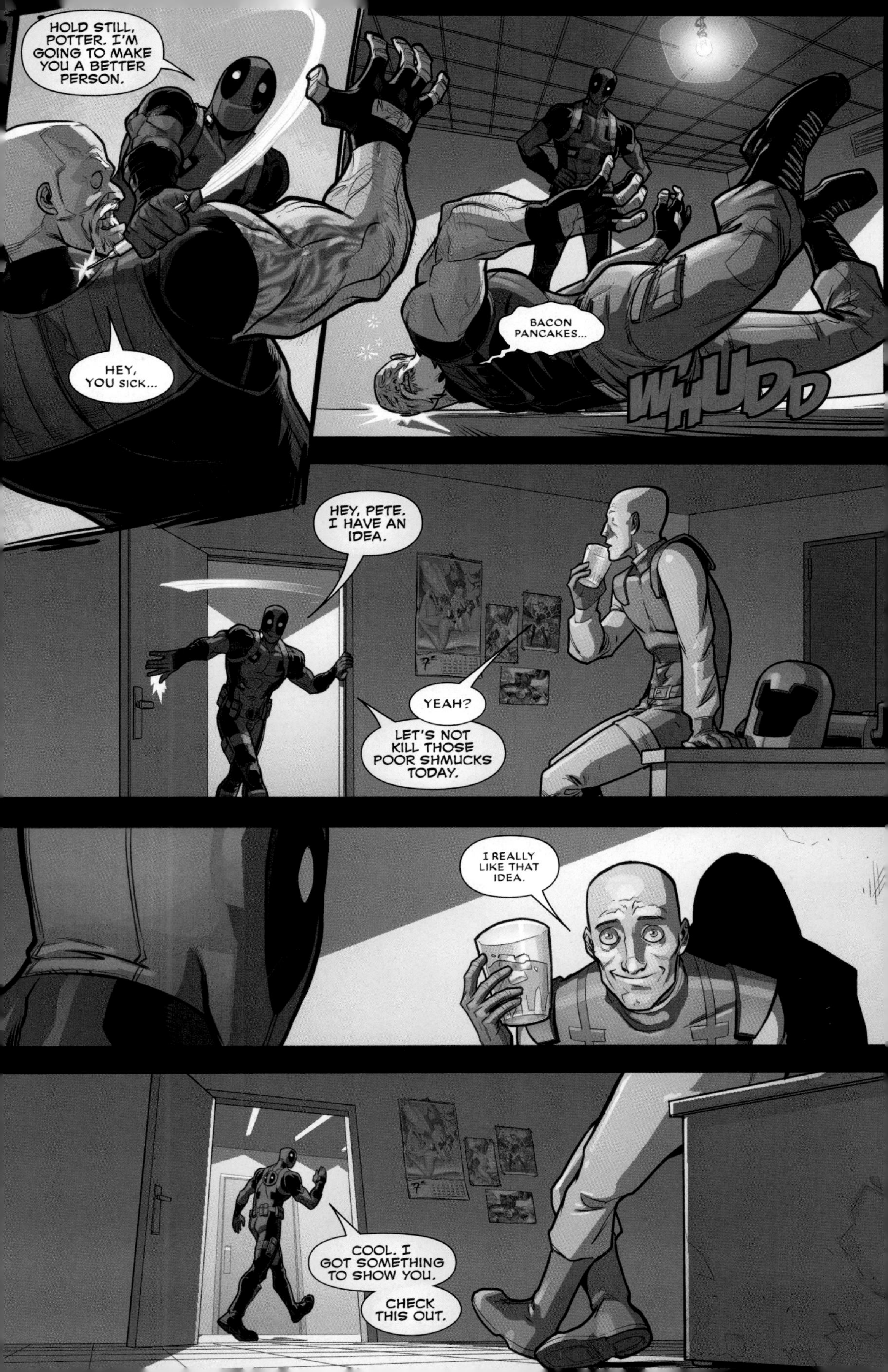
HOLD STILL, POTTER. I'M GOING TO MAKE YOU A BETTER PERSON.
HEY, YOU SICK...
BACON PANCAKES...
WHUDD
HEY, PETE. I HAVE AN IDEA.
YEAH?
LET'S NOT KILL THOSE POOR SHMUCKS TODAY.
I REALLY LIKE THAT IDEA.
COOL. I GOT SOMETHING TO SHOW YOU.
CHECK THIS OUT.

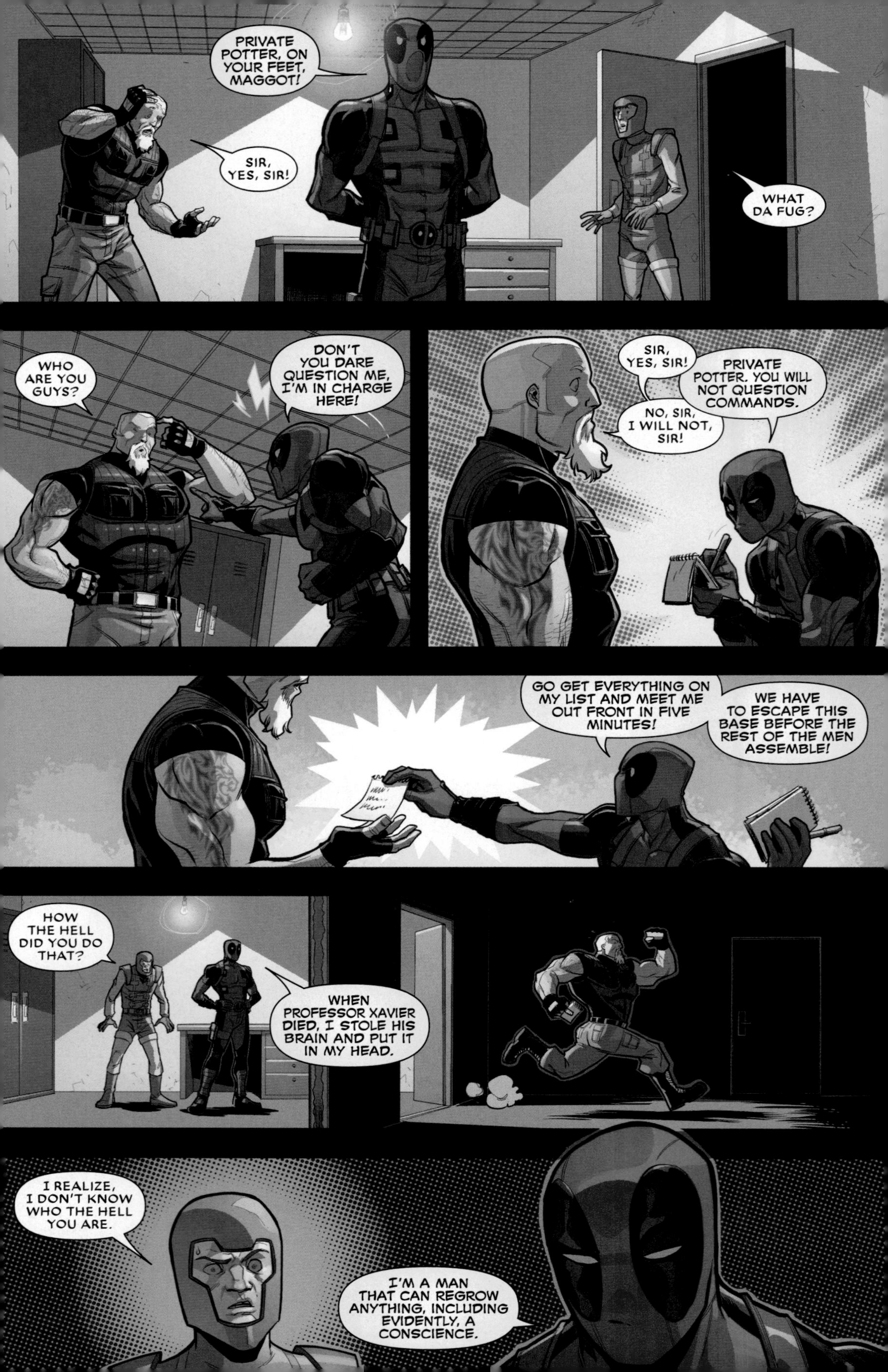
PRIVATE POTTER, ON YOUR FEET, MAGGOT!
SIR, YES, SIR!
WHAT DA FUG?
WHO ARE YOU GUYS?
DON'T YOU DARE QUESTION ME, I'M IN CHARGE HERE!
SIR, YES, SIR!
PRIVATE POTTER. YOU WILL NOT QUESTION COMMANDS.
NO, SIR, I WILL NOT, SIR!
GO GET EVERYTHING ON MY LIST AND MEET ME OUT FRONT IN FIVE MINUTES!
WE HAVE TO ESCAPE THIS BASE BEFORE THE REST OF THE MEN ASSEMBLE!
HOW THE HELL DID YOU DO THAT?
WHEN PROFESSOR XAVIER DIED, I STOLE HIS BRAIN AND PUT IT IN MY HEAD.
I REALIZE, I DON'T KNOW WHO THE HELL YOU ARE.
I'M A MAN THAT CAN REGROW ANYTHING, INCLUDING EVIDENTLY, A CONSCIENCE.

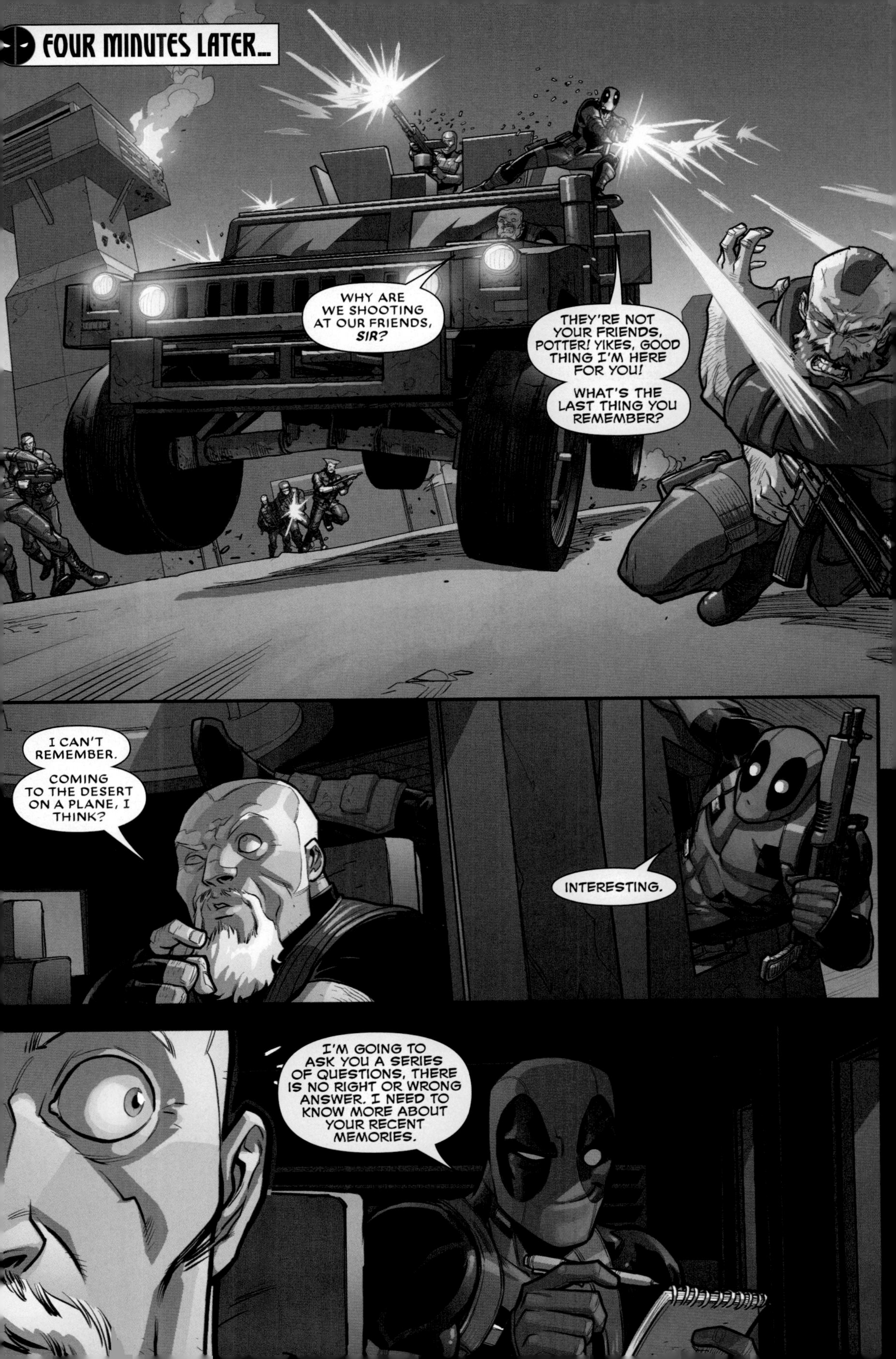
FOUR MINUTES LATER...
WHY ARE WE SHOOTING AT OUR FRIENDS, SIR?
THEY'RE NOT YOUR FRIENDS, POTTER! YIKES, GOOD THING I'M HERE FOR YOU!
WHAT'S THE LAST THING YOU REMEMBER?
I CAN'T REMEMBER.
COMING TO THE DESERT ON A PLANE, I THINK?
INTERESTING.
I'M GOING TO ASK YOU A SERIES OF QUESTIONS, THERE IS NO RIGHT OR WRONG ANSWER. I NEED TO KNOW MORE ABOUT YOUR RECENT MEMORIES.

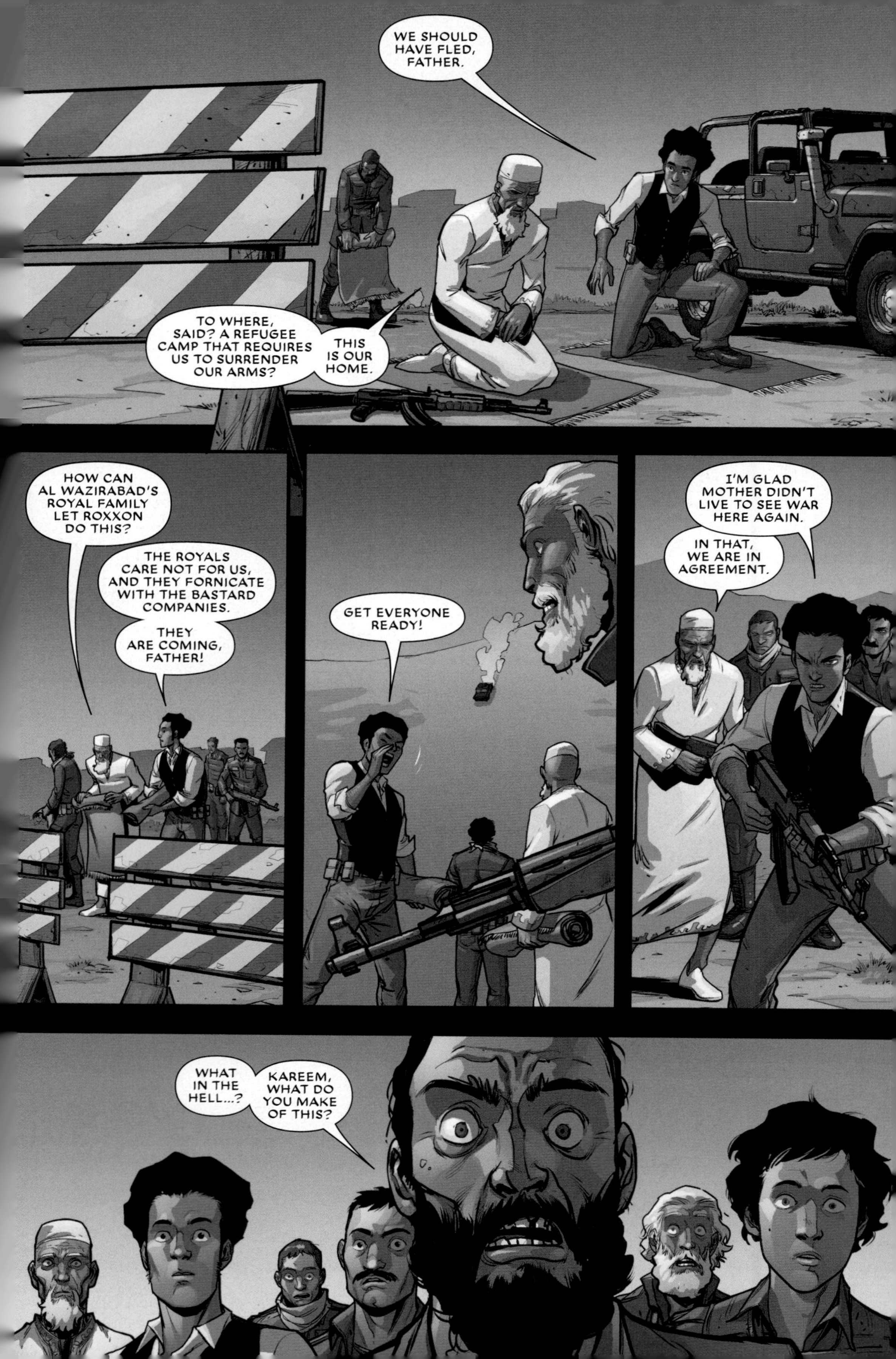
WE SHOULD HAVE FLED, FATHER.
TO WHERE, SAID? A REFUGEE CAMP THAT REQUIRES US TO SURRENDER OUR ARMS?
THIS IS OUR HOME.
HOW CAN AL WAZIRABAD'S ROYAL FAMILY LET ROXXON DO THIS?
THE ROYALS CARE NOT FOR US, AND THEY FORNICATE WITH THE BASTARD COMPANIES.
THEY ARE COMING, FATHER!
GET EVERYONE READY!
I'M GLAD MOTHER DIDN'T LIVE TO SEE WAR HERE AGAIN.
IN THAT, WE ARE IN AGREEMENT.
WHAT IN THE HELL...?
KAREEM, WHAT DO YOU MAKE OF THIS?

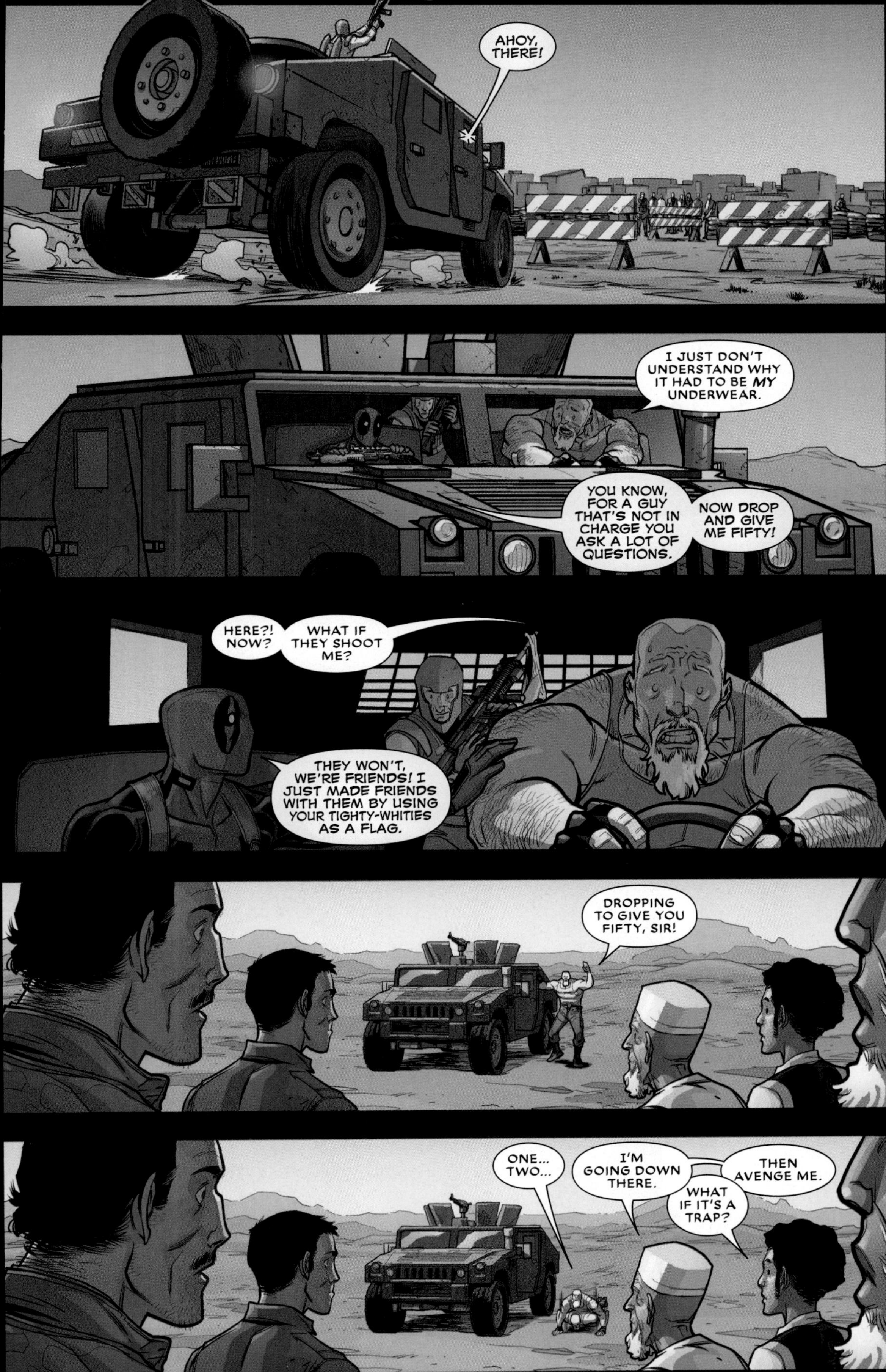
AHOY, THERE!
I JUST DON'T UNDERSTAND WHY IT HAD TO BE MY UNDERWEAR.
YOU KNOW, FOR A GUY THAT'S NOT IN CHARGE YOU ASK A LOT OF QUESTIONS.
NOW DROP AND GIVE ME FIFTY!
HERE?! NOW?
WHAT IF THEY SHOOT ME?
THEY WON'T, WE'RE FRIENDS! I JUST MADE FRIENDS WITH THEM BY USING YOUR TIGHTY-WHITIES AS A FLAG.
DROPPING TO GIVE YOU FIFTY, SIR!
ONE... TWO...
I'M GOING DOWN THERE.
WHAT IF IT'S A TRAP?
THEN AVENGE ME.

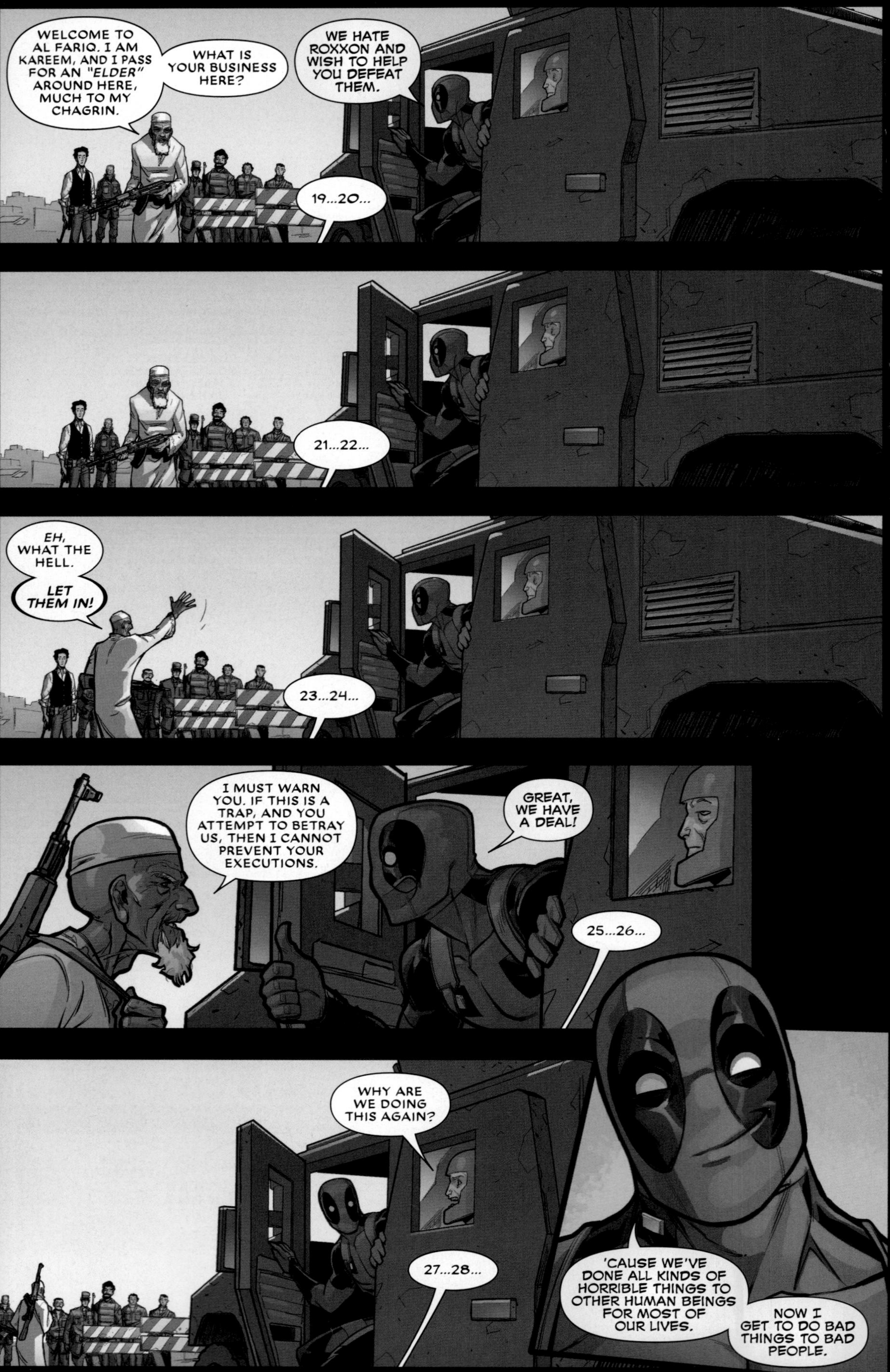

WELCOME TO AL FARIQ. I AM KAREEM, AND I PASS FOR AN "ELDER" AROUND HERE, MUCH TO MY CHAGRIN.
WHAT IS YOUR BUSINESS HERE?
WE HATE ROXXON AND WISH TO HELP YOU DEFEAT THEM.
19...20...
21...22...
EH, WHAT THE HELL.
LET THEM IN!
23...24...
I MUST WARN YOU. IF THIS IS A TRAP, AND YOU ATTEMPT TO BETRAY US, THEN I CANNOT PREVENT YOUR EXECUTIONS.
GREAT, WE HAVE A DEAL!
25...26...
WHY ARE WE DOING THIS AGAIN?
27...28...
'CAUSE WE'VE DONE ALL KINDS OF HORRIBLE THINGS TO OTHER HUMAN BEINGS FOR MOST OF OUR LIVES.
NOW I GET TO DO BAD THINGS TO BAD PEOPLE.

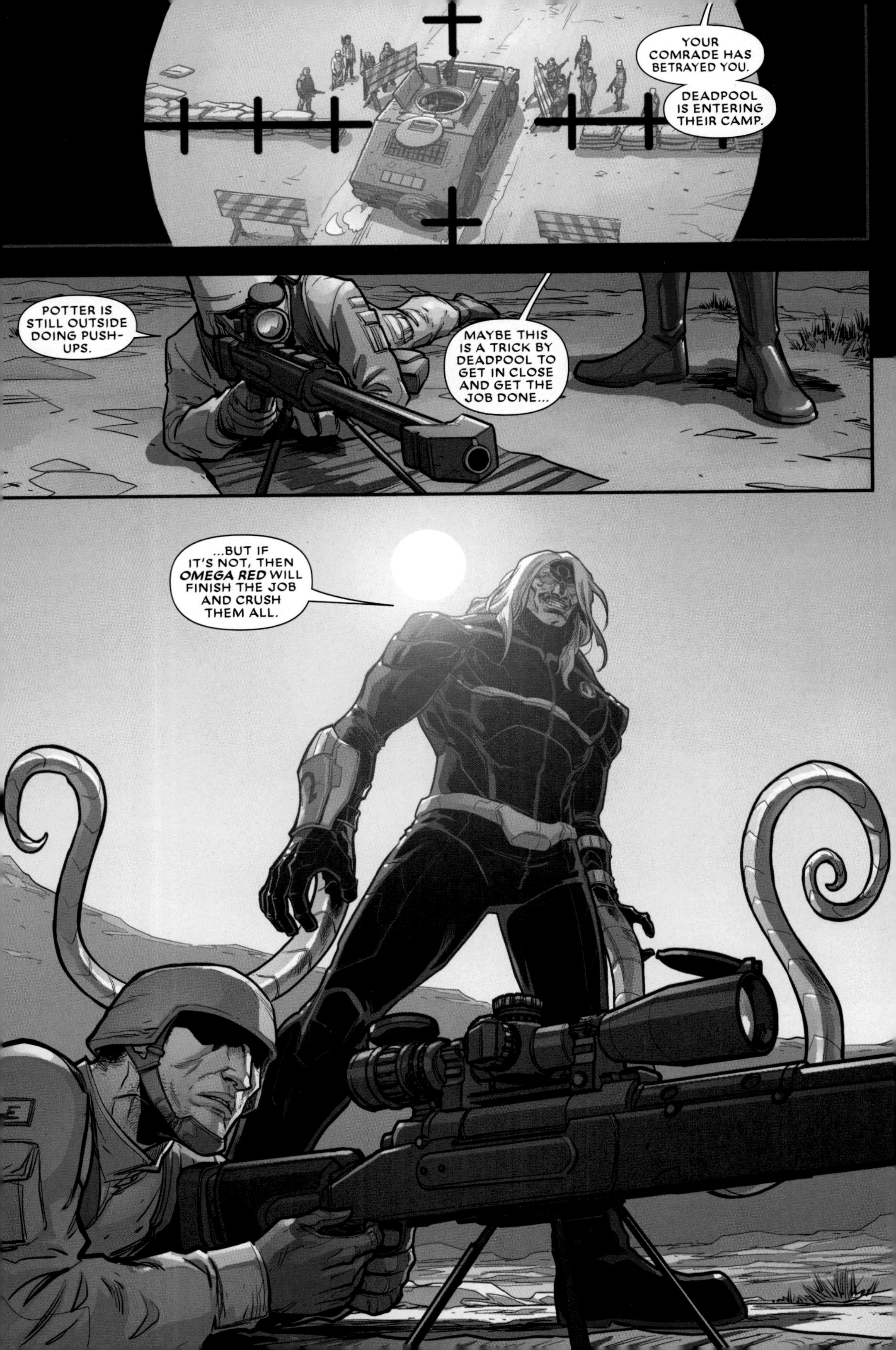
YOUR COMRADE HAS BETRAYED YOU.
DEADPOOL IS ENTERING THEIR CAMP.
POTTER IS STILL OUTSIDE DOING PUSH-UPS.
MAYBE THIS IS A TRICK BY DEADPOOL TO GET IN CLOSE AND GET THE JOB DONE...
...BUT IF IT'S NOT, THEN OMEGA RED WILL FINISH THE JOB AND CRUSH THEM ALL.

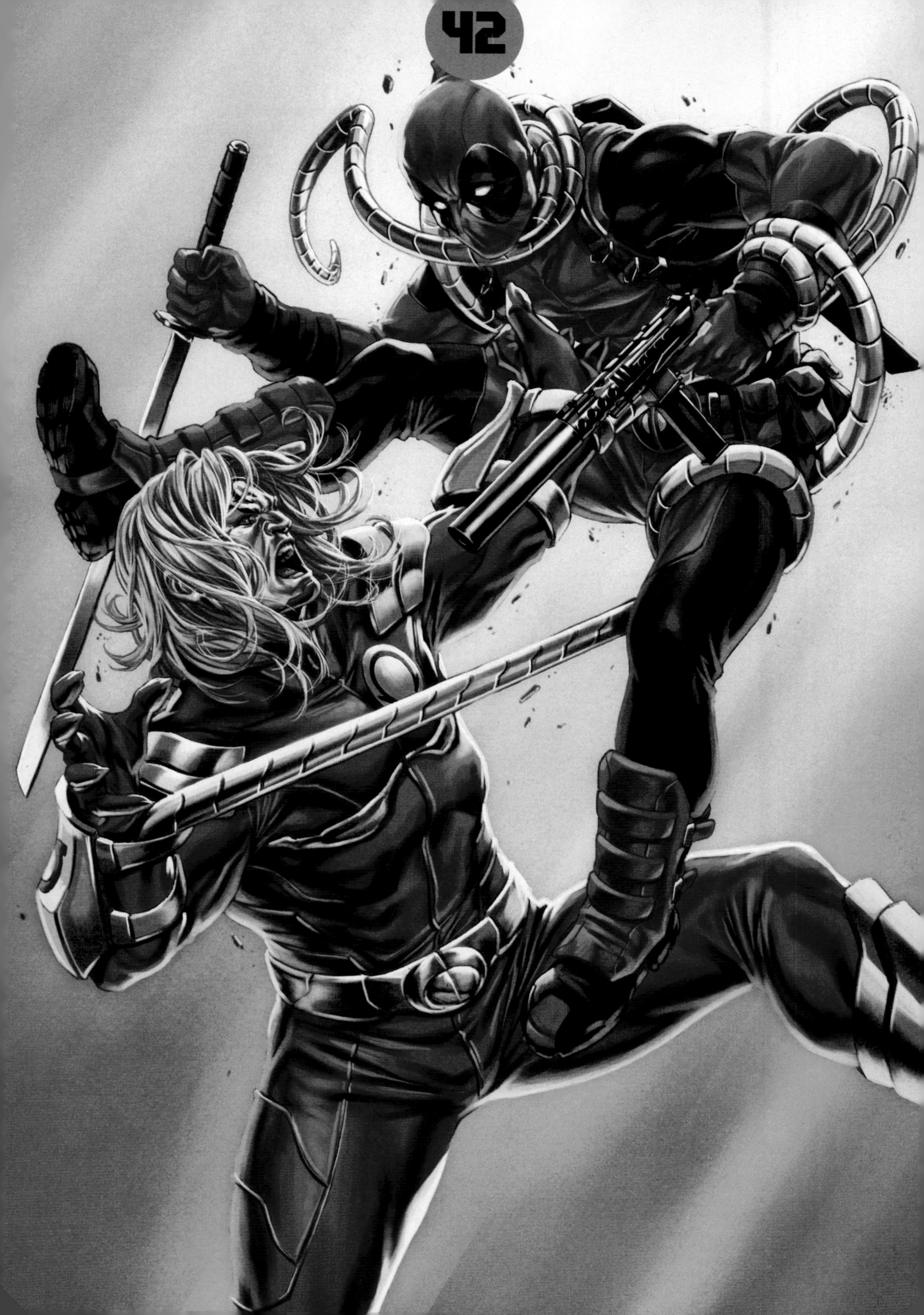
42

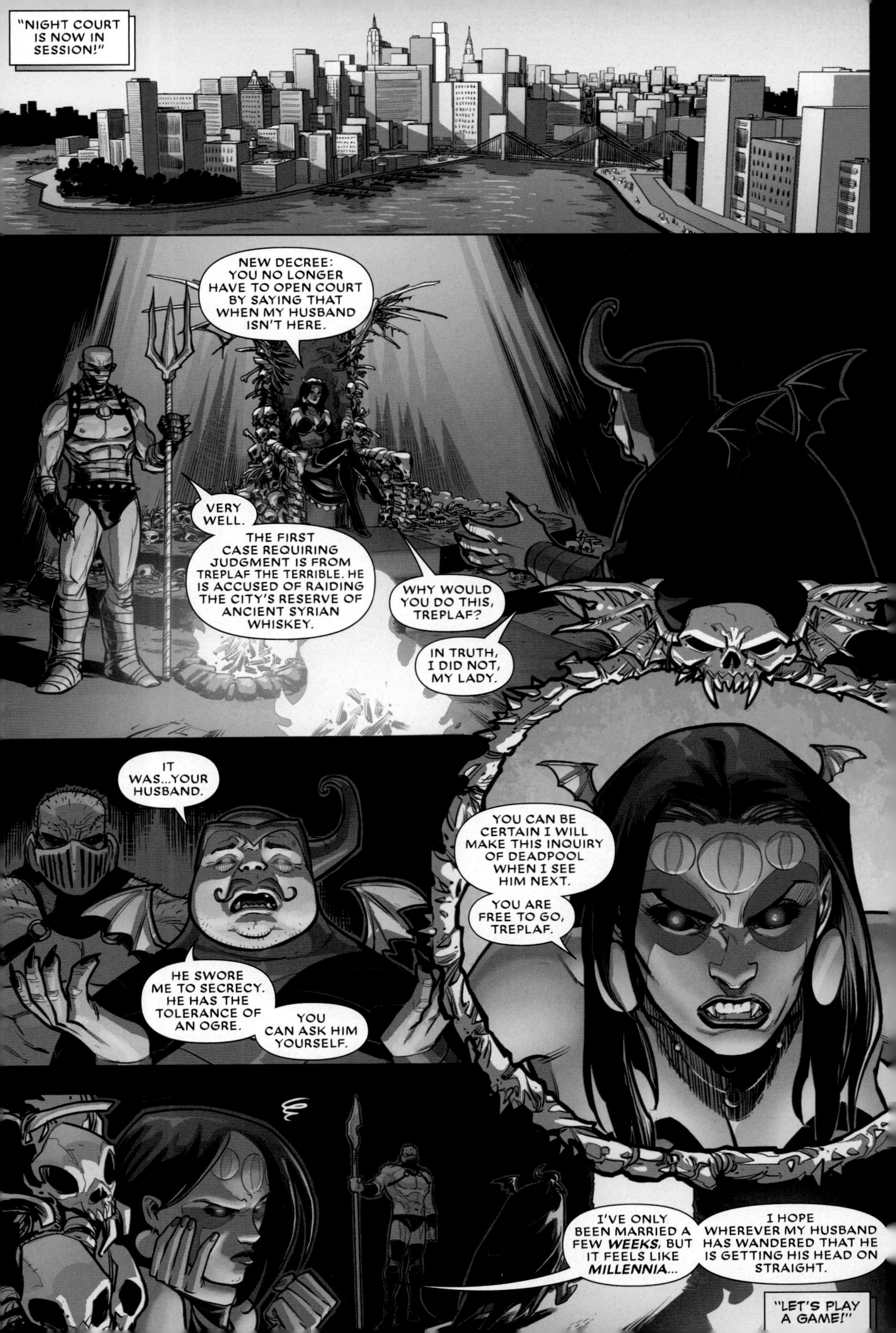
"NIGHT COURT IS NOW IN SESSION!"
NEW DECREE: YOU NO LONGER HAVE TO OPEN COURT BY SAYING THAT WHEN MY HUSBAND ISN'T HERE.
VERY WELL.
THE FIRST CASE REQUIRING JUDGMENT IS FROM TREPLAF THE TERRIBLE. HE IS ACCUSED OF RAIDING THE CITY'S RESERVE OF ANCIENT SYRIAN WHISKEY.
WHY WOULD YOU DO THIS, TREPLAF?
IN TRUTH, I DID NOT, MY LADY.
IT WAS...YOUR HUSBAND.
HE SWORE ME TO SECRECY. HE HAS THE TOLERANCE OF AN OGRE.
YOU CAN ASK HIM YOURSELF.
YOU CAN BE CERTAIN I WILL MAKE THIS INQUIRY OF DEADPOOL WHEN I SEE HIM NEXT.
YOU ARE FREE TO GO, TREPLAF.
I'VE ONLY BEEN MARRIED A FEW *WEEKS*, BUT IT FEELS LIKE *MILLENNIA*...
I HOPE WHEREVER MY HUSBAND HAS WANDERED THAT HE IS GETTING HIS HEAD ON STRAIGHT.
"LET'S PLAY A GAME!"

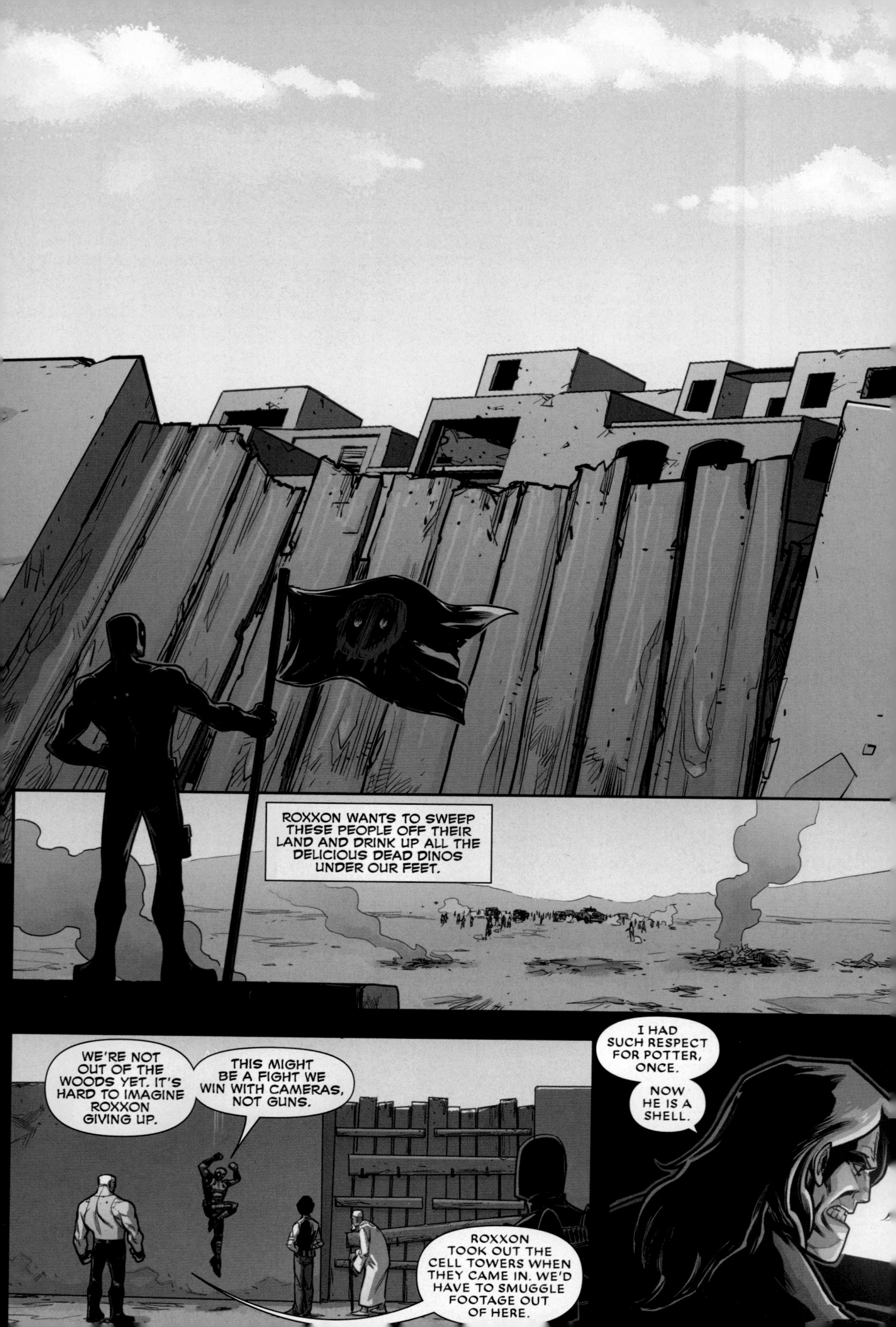

ROXXON WANTS TO SWEEP THESE PEOPLE OFF THEIR LAND AND DRINK UP ALL THE DELICIOUS DEAD DINOS UNDER OUR FEET.
WE'RE NOT OUT OF THE WOODS YET. IT'S HARD TO IMAGINE ROXXON GIVING UP.
THIS MIGHT BE A FIGHT WE WIN WITH CAMERAS, NOT GUNS.
ROXXON TOOK OUT THE CELL TOWERS WHEN THEY CAME IN. WE'D HAVE TO SMUGGLE FOOTAGE OUT OF HERE.
I HAD SUCH RESPECT FOR POTTER, ONCE.
NOW HE IS A SHELL.

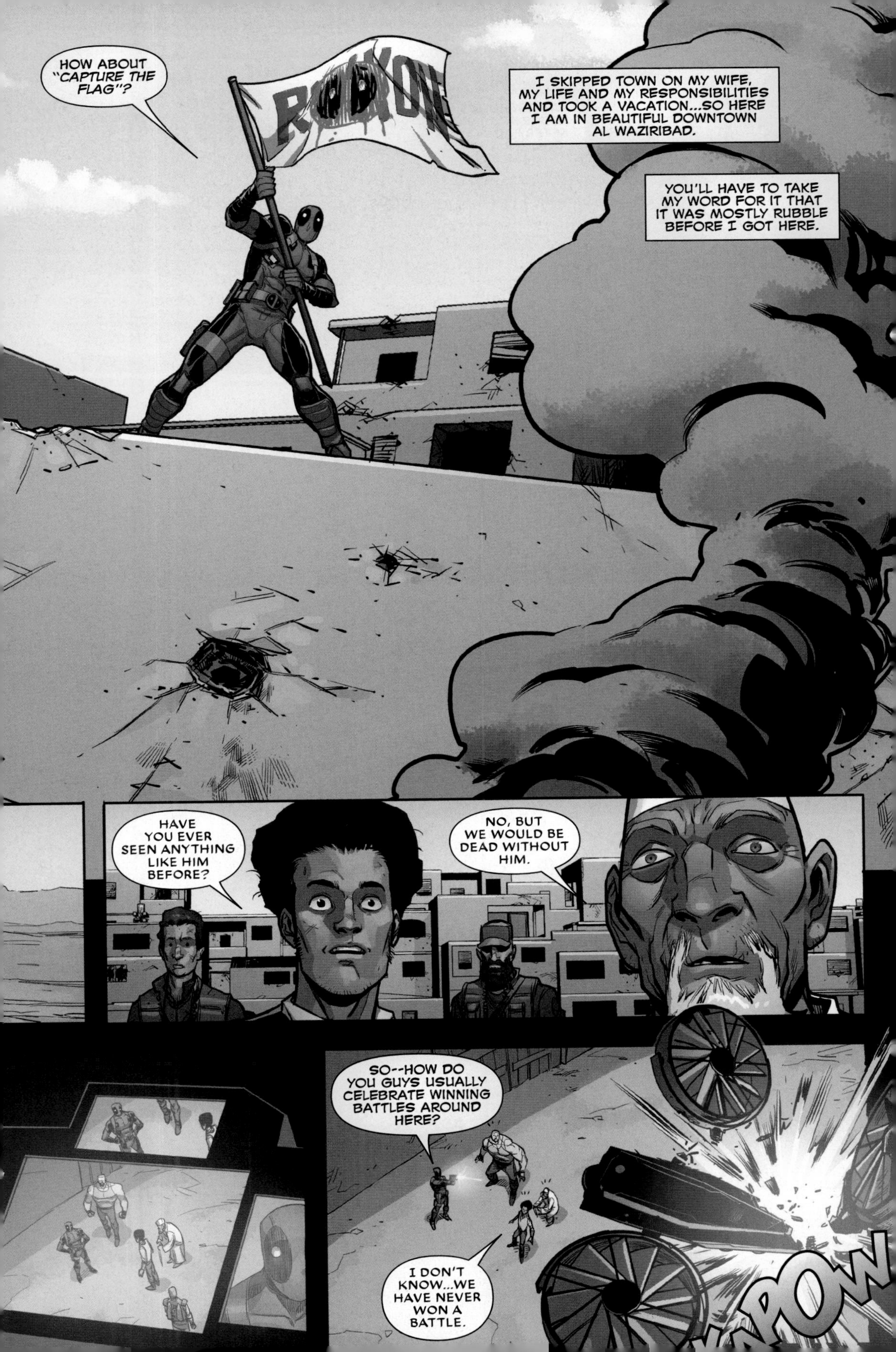
HOW ABOUT "CAPTURE THE FLAG"?
I SKIPPED TOWN ON MY WIFE, MY LIFE AND MY RESPONSIBILITIES AND TOOK A VACATION...SO HERE I AM IN BEAUTIFUL DOWNTOWN AL WAZIRIBAD.
YOU'LL HAVE TO TAKE MY WORD FOR IT THAT IT WAS MOSTLY RUBBLE BEFORE I GOT HERE.
HAVE YOU EVER SEEN ANYTHING LIKE HIM BEFORE?
NO, BUT WE WOULD BE DEAD WITHOUT HIM.
SO--HOW DO YOU GUYS USUALLY CELEBRATE WINNING BATTLES AROUND HERE?
I DON'T KNOW...WE HAVE NEVER WON A BATTLE.

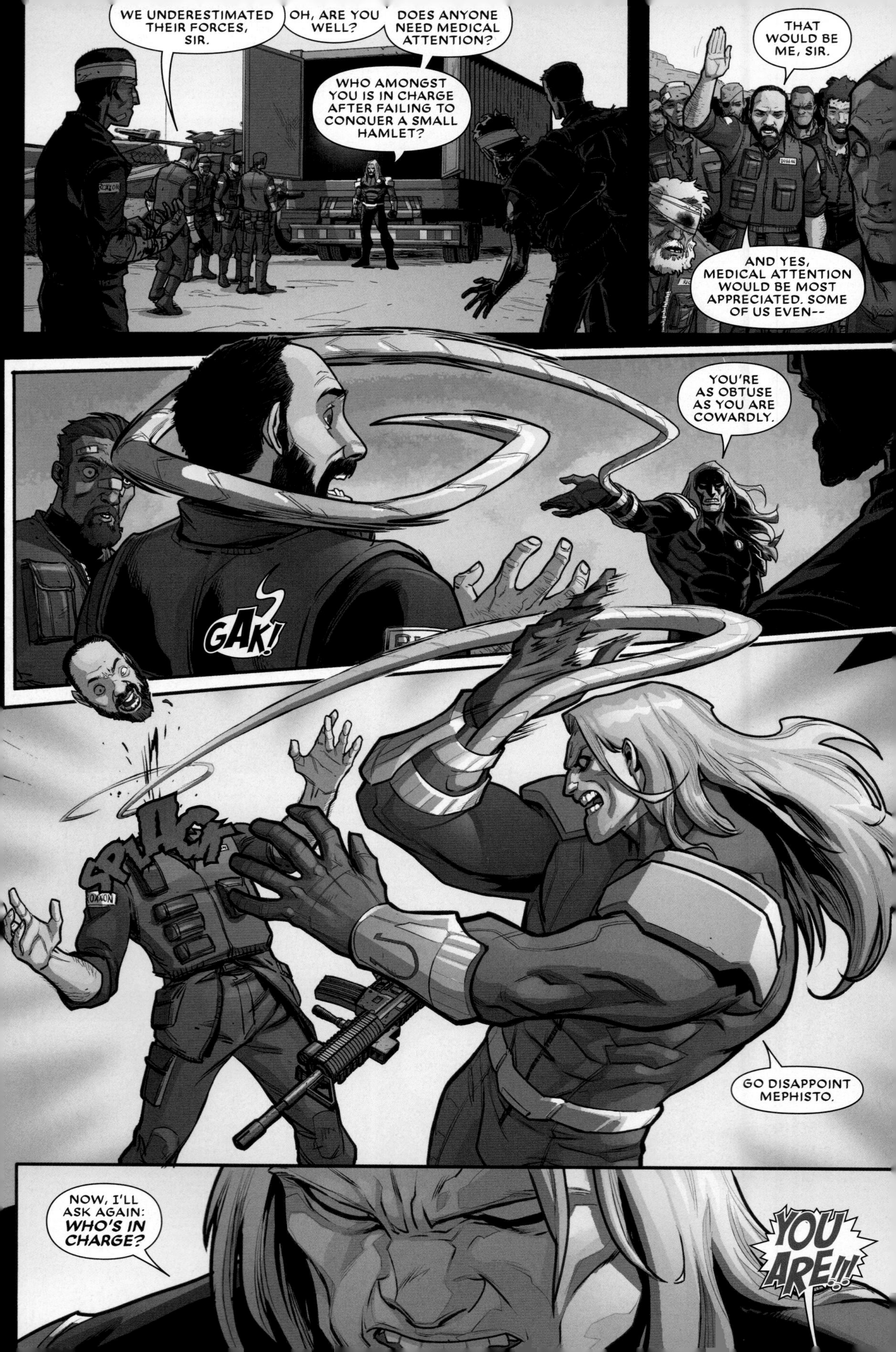
WE UNDERESTIMATED THEIR FORCES, SIR.
OH, ARE YOU WELL?
DOES ANYONE NEED MEDICAL ATTENTION?
WHO AMONGST YOU IS IN CHARGE AFTER FAILING TO CONQUER A SMALL HAMLET?
THAT WOULD BE ME, SIR.
AND YES, MEDICAL ATTENTION WOULD BE MOST APPRECIATED. SOME OF US EVEN--
YOU'RE AS OBTUSE AS YOU ARE COWARDLY.
GAK!
GO DISAPPOINT MEPHISTO.
NOW, I'LL ASK AGAIN: *WHO'S IN CHARGE?*
YOU ARE!!!

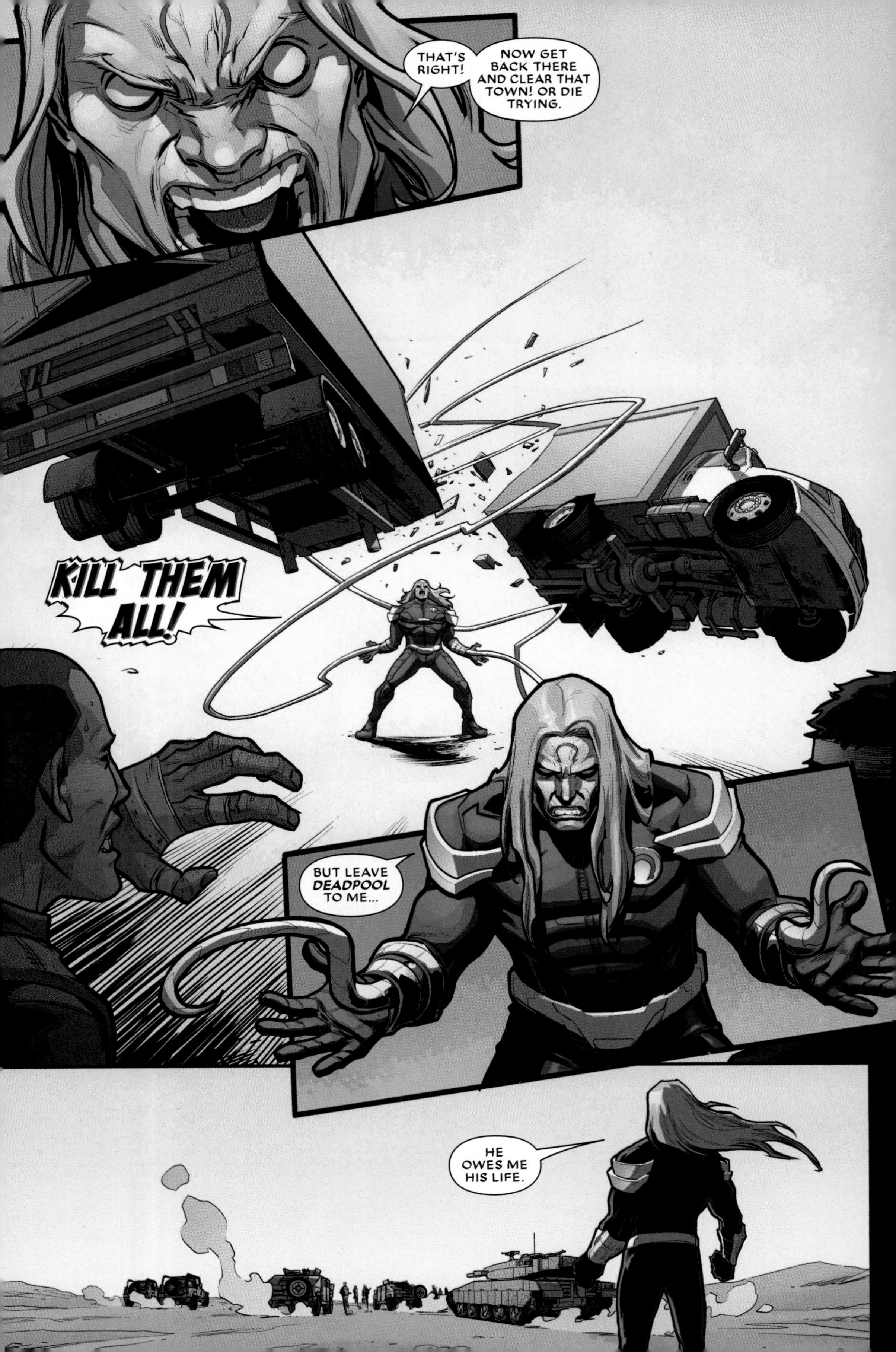
THAT'S RIGHT!
NOW GET BACK THERE AND CLEAR THAT TOWN! OR DIE TRYING.
KILL THEM ALL!
BUT LEAVE DEADPOOL TO ME...
HE OWES ME HIS LIFE.

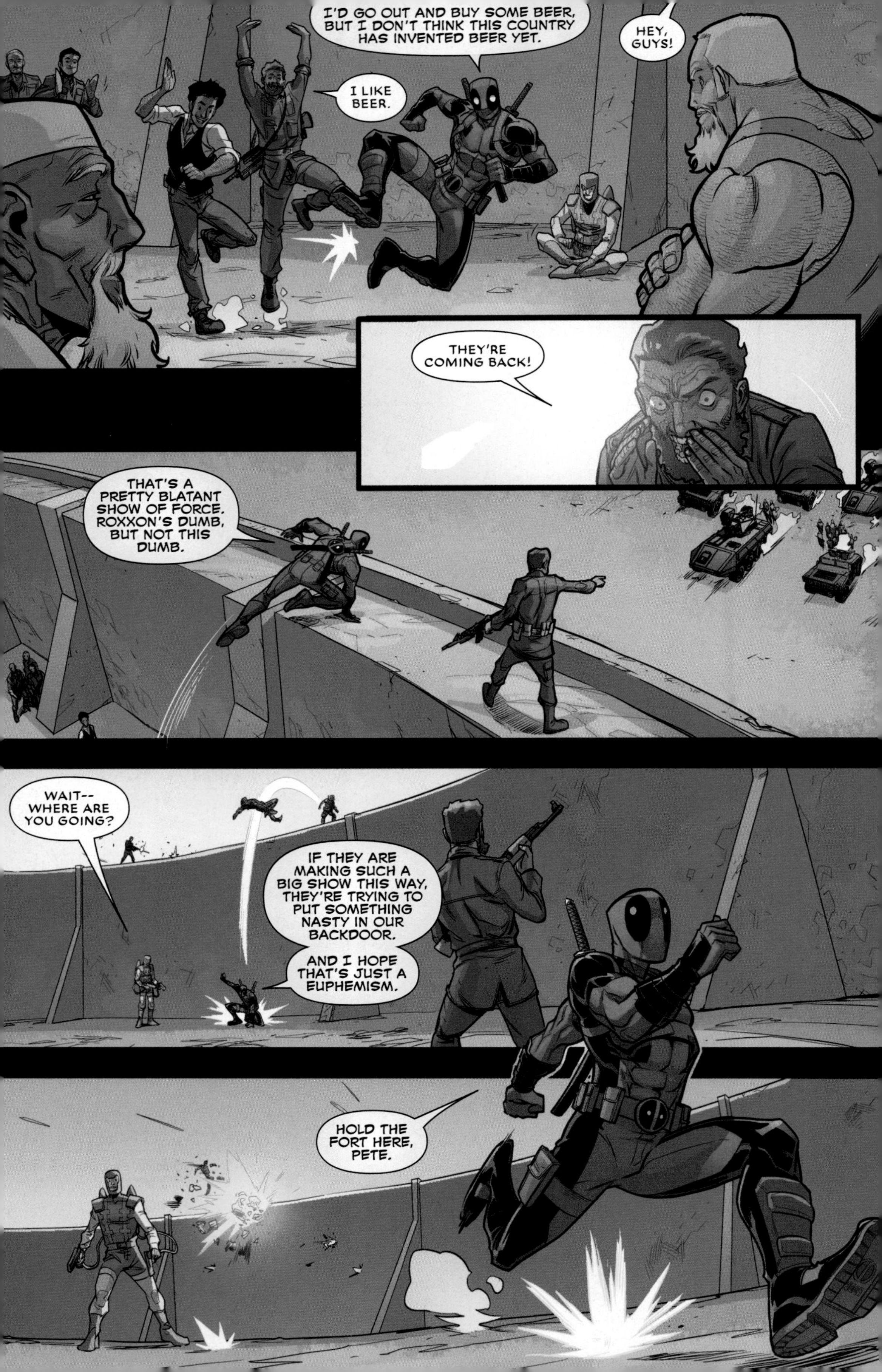
I'D GO OUT AND BUY SOME BEER, BUT I DON'T THINK THIS COUNTRY HAS INVENTED BEER YET.
I LIKE BEER.
HEY, GUYS!
THEY'RE COMING BACK!
THAT'S A PRETTY BLATANT SHOW OF FORCE. ROXXON'S DUMB, BUT NOT THIS DUMB.
WAIT-- WHERE ARE YOU GOING?
IF THEY ARE MAKING SUCH A BIG SHOW THIS WAY, THEY'RE TRYING TO PUT SOMETHING NASTY IN OUR BACKDOOR.
AND I HOPE THAT'S JUST A EUPHEMISM.
HOLD THE FORT HERE, PETE.

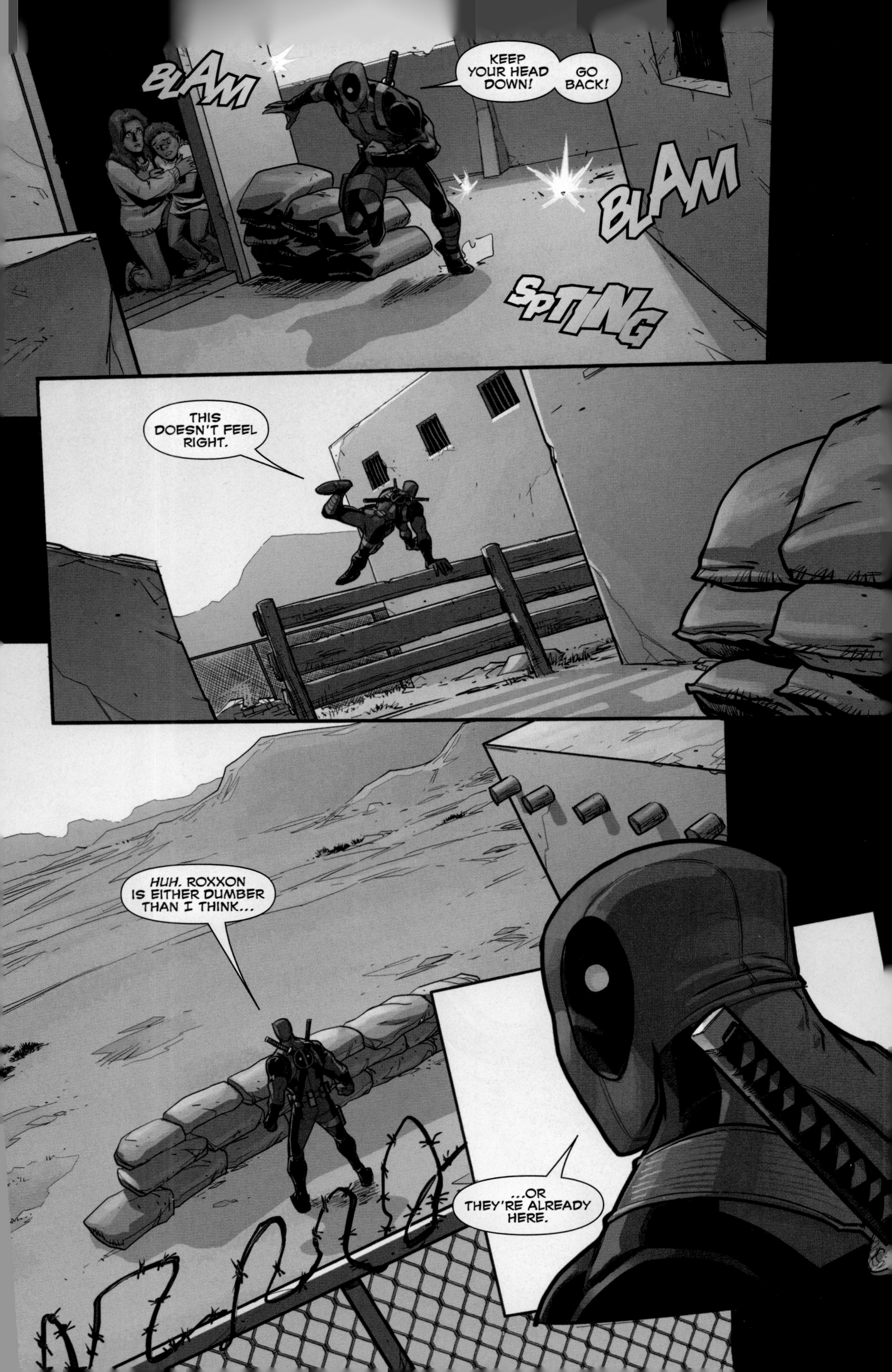
BLAM
KEEP YOUR HEAD DOWN!
GO BACK!
BLAM
SPTING
THIS DOESN'T FEEL RIGHT.
HUH. ROXXON IS EITHER DUMBER THAN I THINK...
...OR THEY'RE ALREADY HERE.

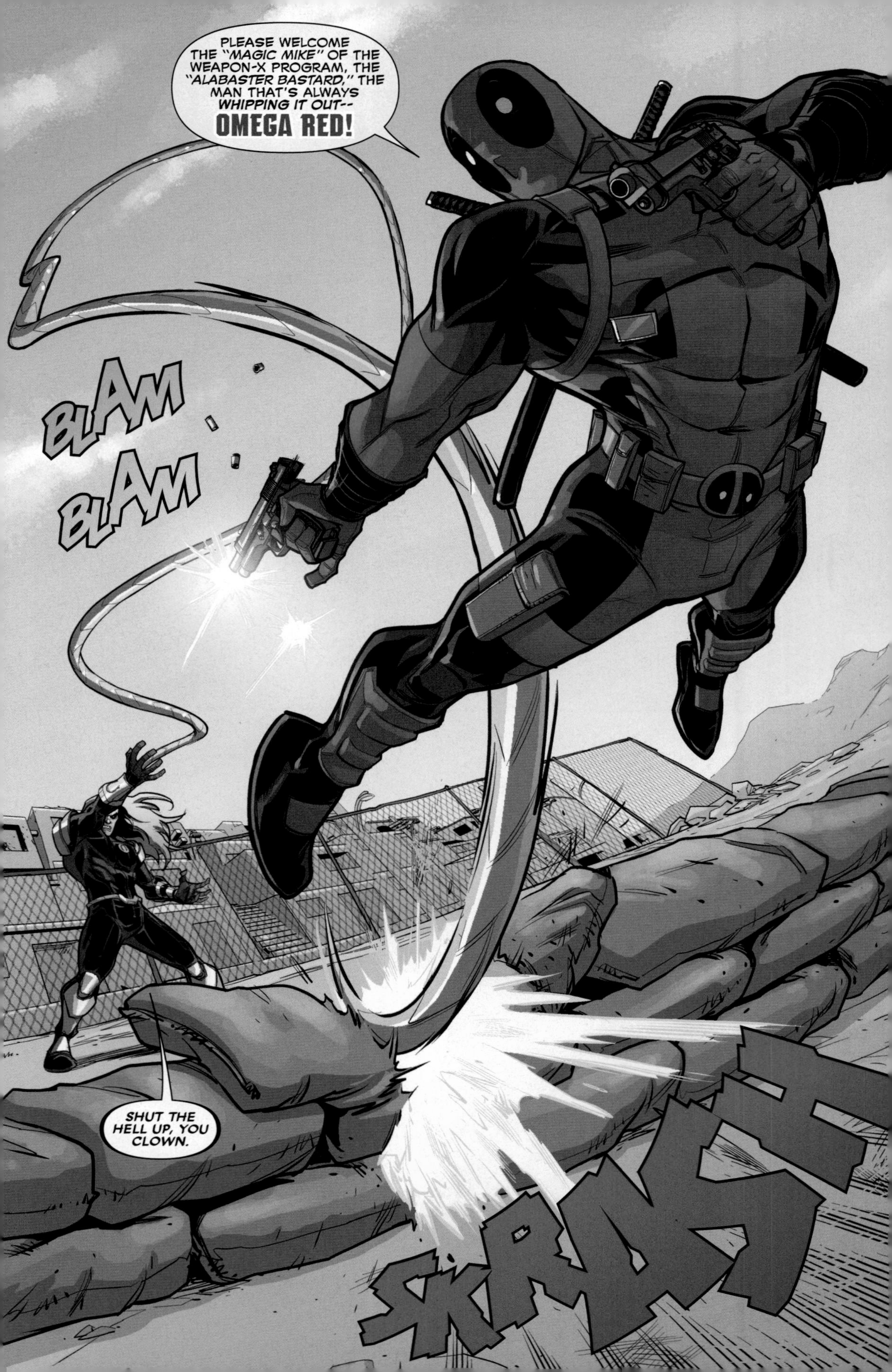
PLEASE WELCOME THE "MAGIC MIKE" OF THE WEAPON-X PROGRAM, THE "ALABASTER BASTARD," THE MAN THAT'S ALWAYS WHIPPING IT OUT-- OMEGA RED!
BLAM
BLAM
SHUT THE HELL UP, YOU CLOWN.
SKRAASH

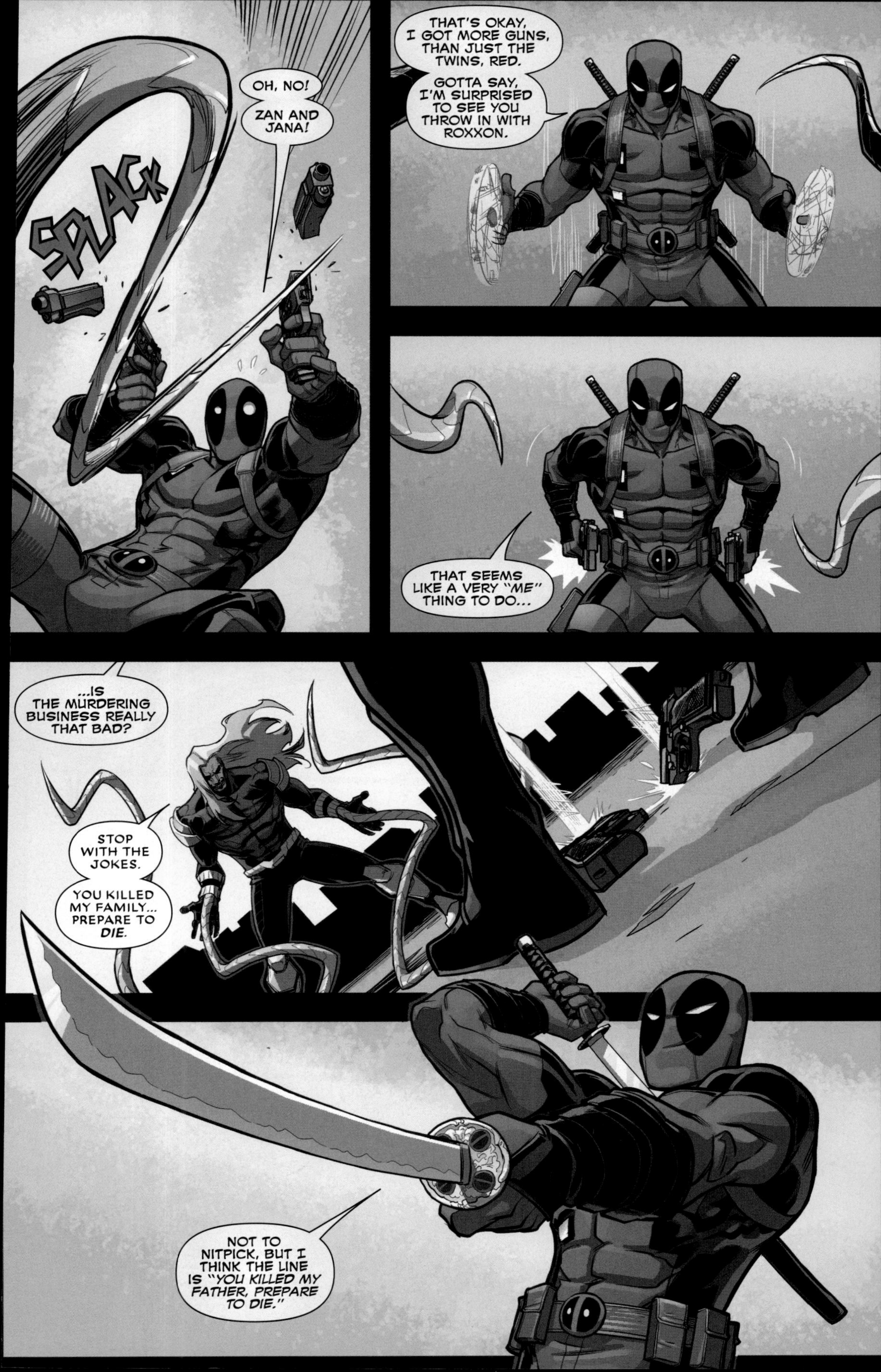
OH, NO!
ZAN AND JANA!
SPLACK
THAT'S OKAY, I GOT MORE GUNS, THAN JUST THE TWINS, RED.
GOTTA SAY, I'M SURPRISED TO SEE YOU THROW IN WITH ROXXON.
THAT SEEMS LIKE A VERY "ME" THING TO DO...
...IS THE MURDERING BUSINESS REALLY THAT BAD?
STOP WITH THE JOKES.
YOU KILLED MY FAMILY... PREPARE TO DIE.
NOT TO NITPICK, BUT I THINK THE LINE IS "YOU KILLED MY FATHER, PREPARE TO DIE."

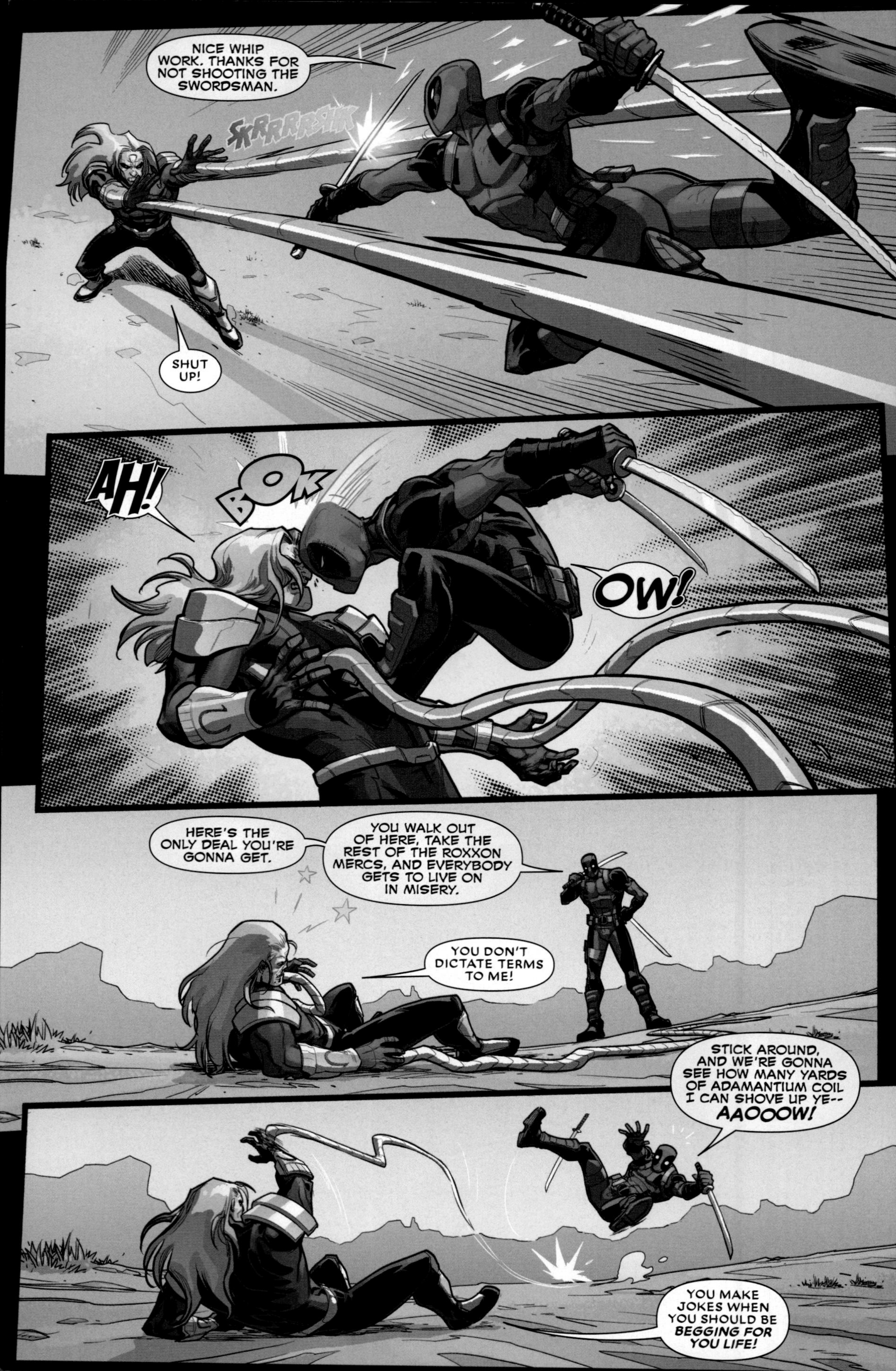
NICE WHIP WORK. THANKS FOR NOT SHOOTING THE SWORDSMAN.
SKRRRRSHK
SHUT UP!
AH!
BOK
OW!
HERE'S THE ONLY DEAL YOU'RE GONNA GET.
YOU WALK OUT OF HERE, TAKE THE REST OF THE ROXXON MERCS, AND EVERYBODY GETS TO LIVE ON IN MISERY.
YOU DON'T DICTATE TERMS TO ME!
STICK AROUND, AND WE'RE GONNA SEE HOW MANY YARDS OF ADAMANTIUM COIL I CAN SHOVE UP YE-- AAOOOW!
YOU MAKE JOKES WHEN YOU SHOULD BE BEGGING FOR YOU LIFE!

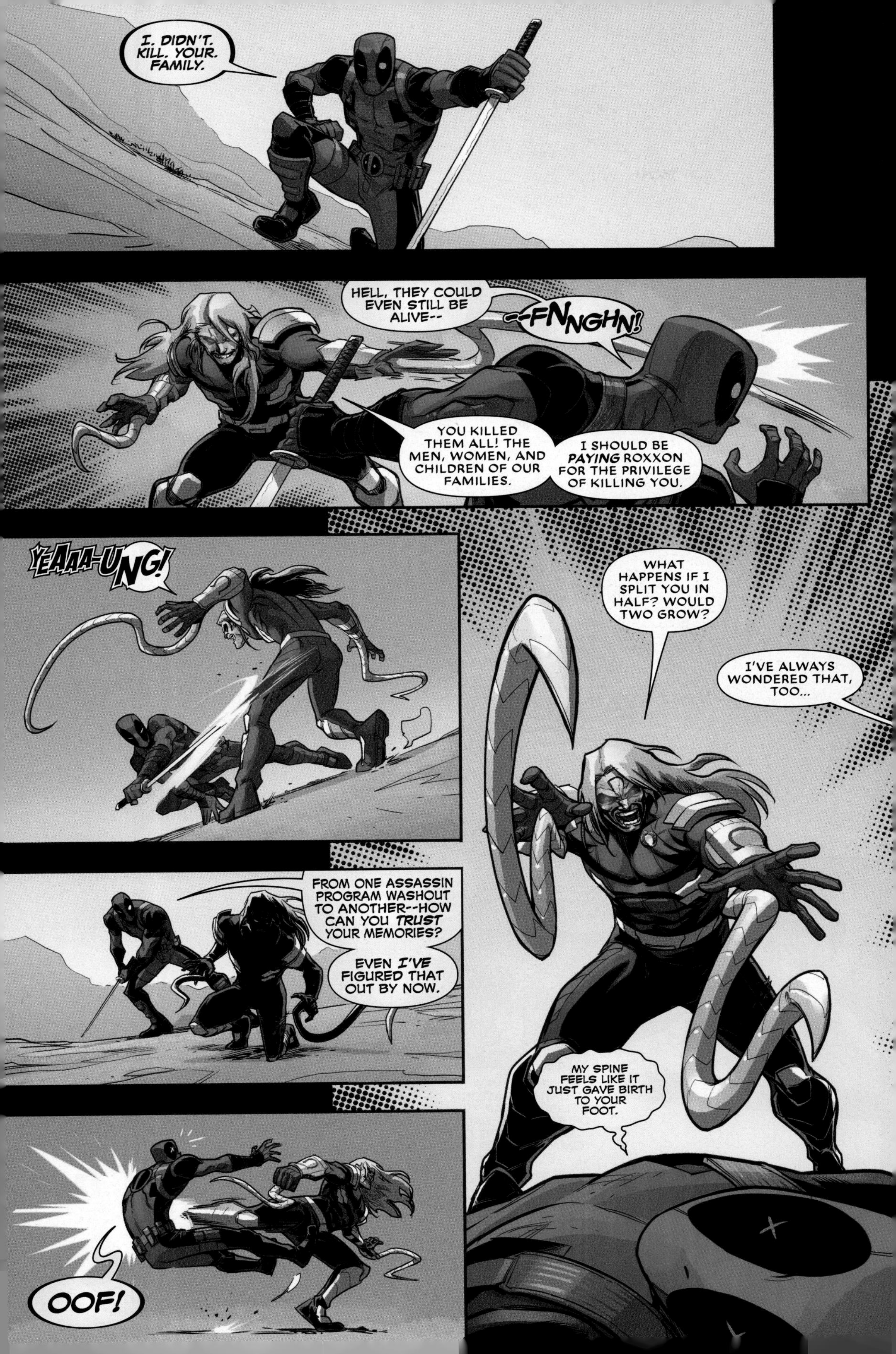
I. DIDN'T. KILL. YOUR. FAMILY.
HELL, THEY COULD EVEN STILL BE ALIVE--
--FNNGHN!
YOU KILLED THEM ALL! THE MEN, WOMEN, AND CHILDREN OF OUR FAMILIES.
I SHOULD BE *PAYING* ROXXON FOR THE PRIVILEGE OF KILLING YOU.
YEAAA-UNG!
WHAT HAPPENS IF I SPLIT YOU IN HALF? WOULD TWO GROW?
I'VE ALWAYS WONDERED THAT, TOO...
FROM ONE ASSASSIN PROGRAM WASHOUT TO ANOTHER--HOW CAN YOU *TRUST* YOUR MEMORIES?
EVEN *I'VE* FIGURED THAT OUT BY NOW.
OOF!
MY SPINE FEELS LIKE IT JUST GAVE BIRTH TO YOUR FOOT.

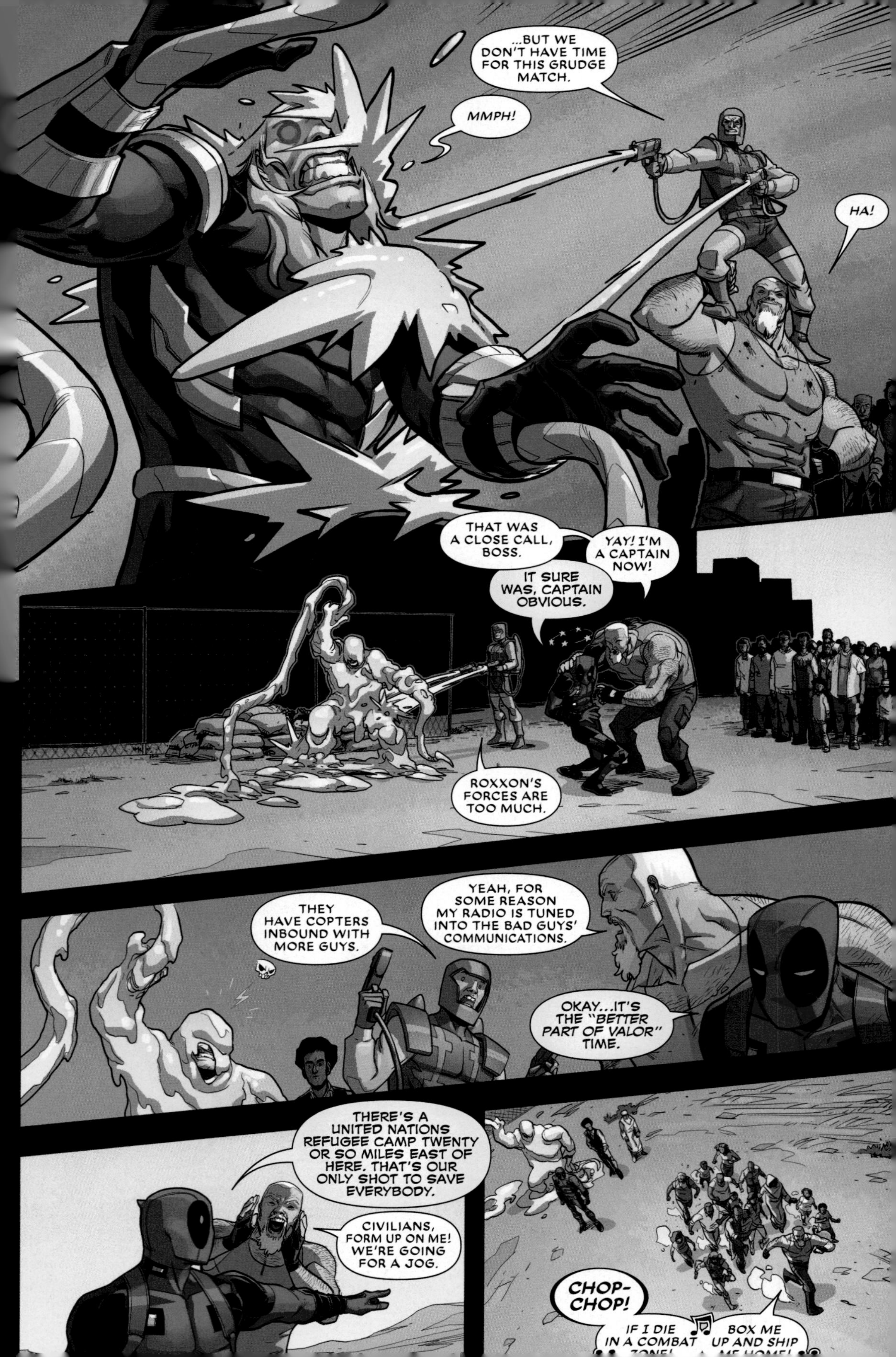
...BUT WE DON'T HAVE TIME FOR THIS GRUDGE MATCH.
MMPH!
HA!
THAT WAS A CLOSE CALL, BOSS.
YAY! I'M A CAPTAIN NOW!
IT SURE WAS, CAPTAIN OBVIOUS.
ROXXON'S FORCES ARE TOO MUCH.
THEY HAVE COPTERS INBOUND WITH MORE GUYS.
YEAH, FOR SOME REASON MY RADIO IS TUNED INTO THE BAD GUYS' COMMUNICATIONS.
OKAY...IT'S THE "BETTER PART OF VALOR" TIME.
THERE'S A UNITED NATIONS REFUGEE CAMP TWENTY OR SO MILES EAST OF HERE. THAT'S OUR ONLY SHOT TO SAVE EVERYBODY.
CIVILIANS, FORM UP ON ME! WE'RE GOING FOR A JOG.
CHOP-CHOP!
IF I DIE IN A COMBAT
BOX ME UP AND SHIP

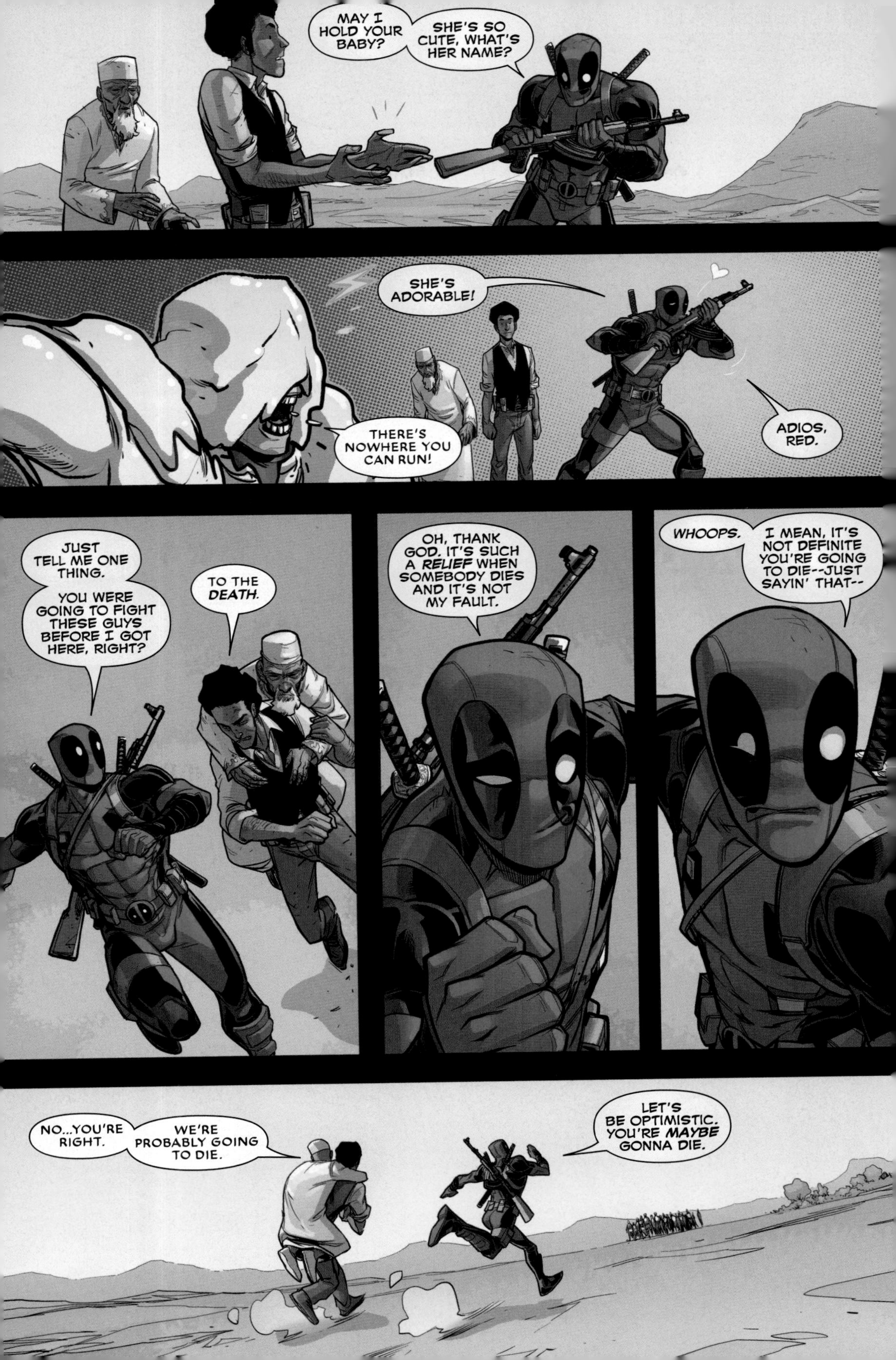
MAY I HOLD YOUR BABY?
SHE'S SO CUTE, WHAT'S HER NAME?
SHE'S ADORABLE!
THERE'S NOWHERE YOU CAN RUN!
ADIOS, RED.
JUST TELL ME ONE THING.
YOU WERE GOING TO FIGHT THESE GUYS BEFORE I GOT HERE, RIGHT?
TO THE DEATH.
OH, THANK GOD. IT'S SUCH A RELIEF WHEN SOMEBODY DIES AND IT'S NOT MY FAULT.
WHOOPS.
I MEAN, IT'S NOT DEFINITE YOU'RE GOING TO DIE--JUST SAYIN' THAT--
NO...YOU'RE RIGHT.
WE'RE PROBABLY GOING TO DIE.
LET'S BE OPTIMISTIC. YOU'RE MAYBE GONNA DIE.

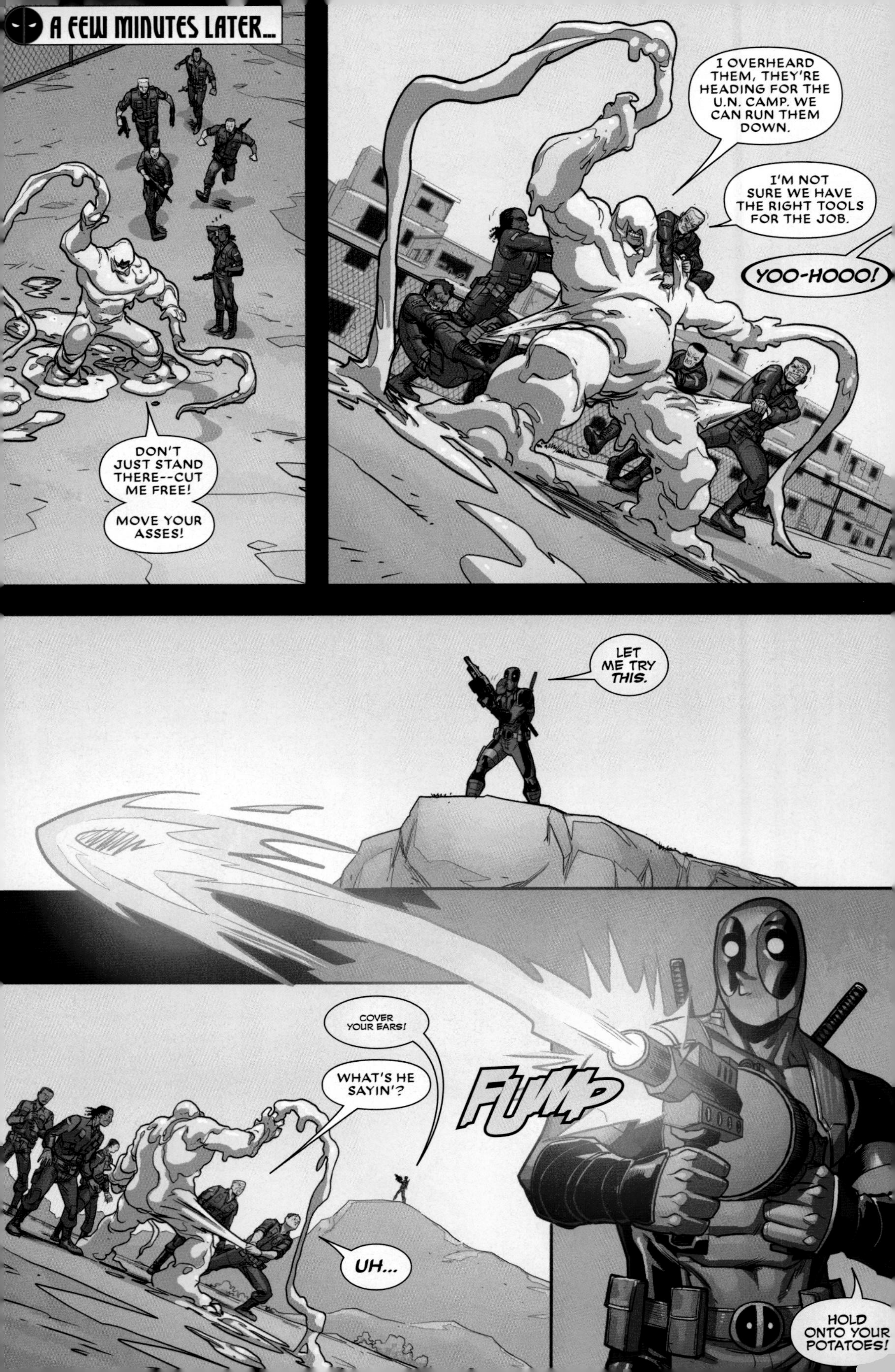
A FEW MINUTES LATER...
DON'T JUST STAND THERE--CUT ME FREE!
MOVE YOUR ASSES!
I OVERHEARD THEM, THEY'RE HEADING FOR THE U.N. CAMP. WE CAN RUN THEM DOWN.
I'M NOT SURE WE HAVE THE RIGHT TOOLS FOR THE JOB.
YOO-HOOO!
LET ME TRY THIS.
COVER YOUR EARS!
WHAT'S HE SAYIN'?
UH...
FUMP
HOLD ONTO YOUR POTATOES!

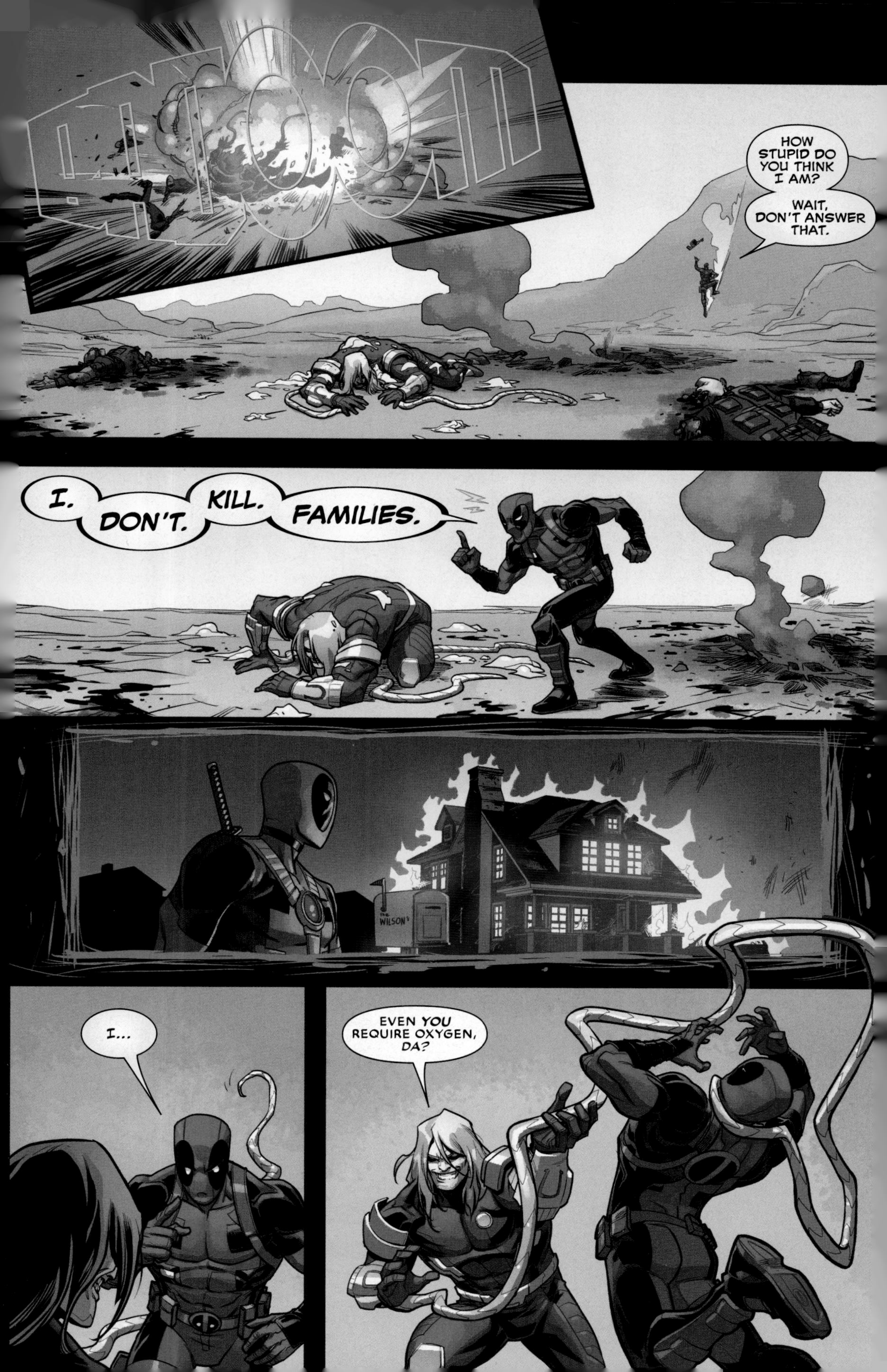
HOW STUPID DO YOU THINK I AM?
WAIT, DON'T ANSWER THAT.
I.
DON'T.
KILL.
FAMILIES.
THE WILSONS
I...
EVEN YOU REQUIRE OXYGEN, DA?

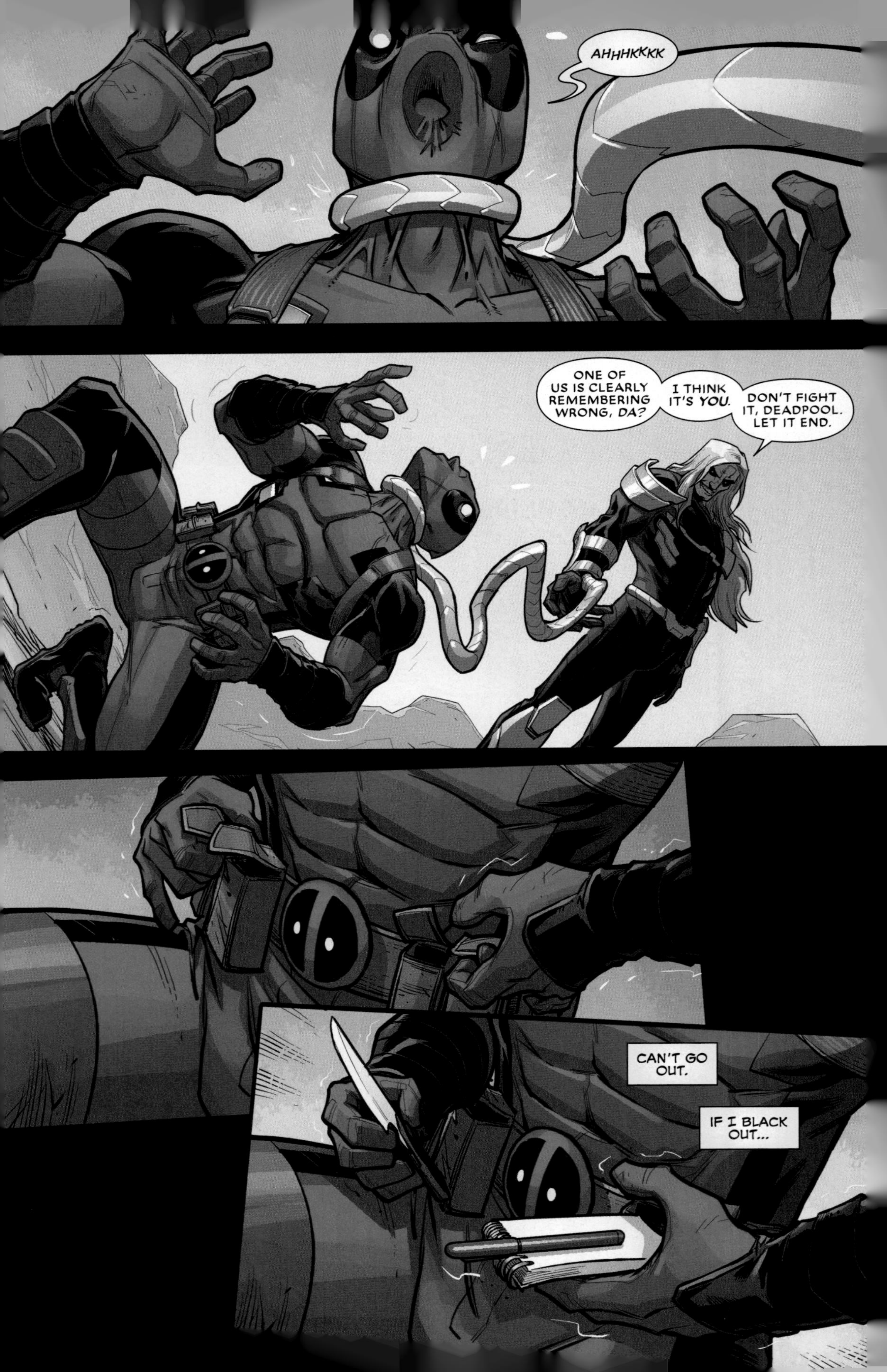
AHHHKKKK
ONE OF US IS CLEARLY REMEMBERING WRONG, DA?
I THINK IT'S YOU.
DON'T FIGHT IT, DEADPOOL. LET IT END.
CAN'T GO OUT.
IF I BLACK OUT...

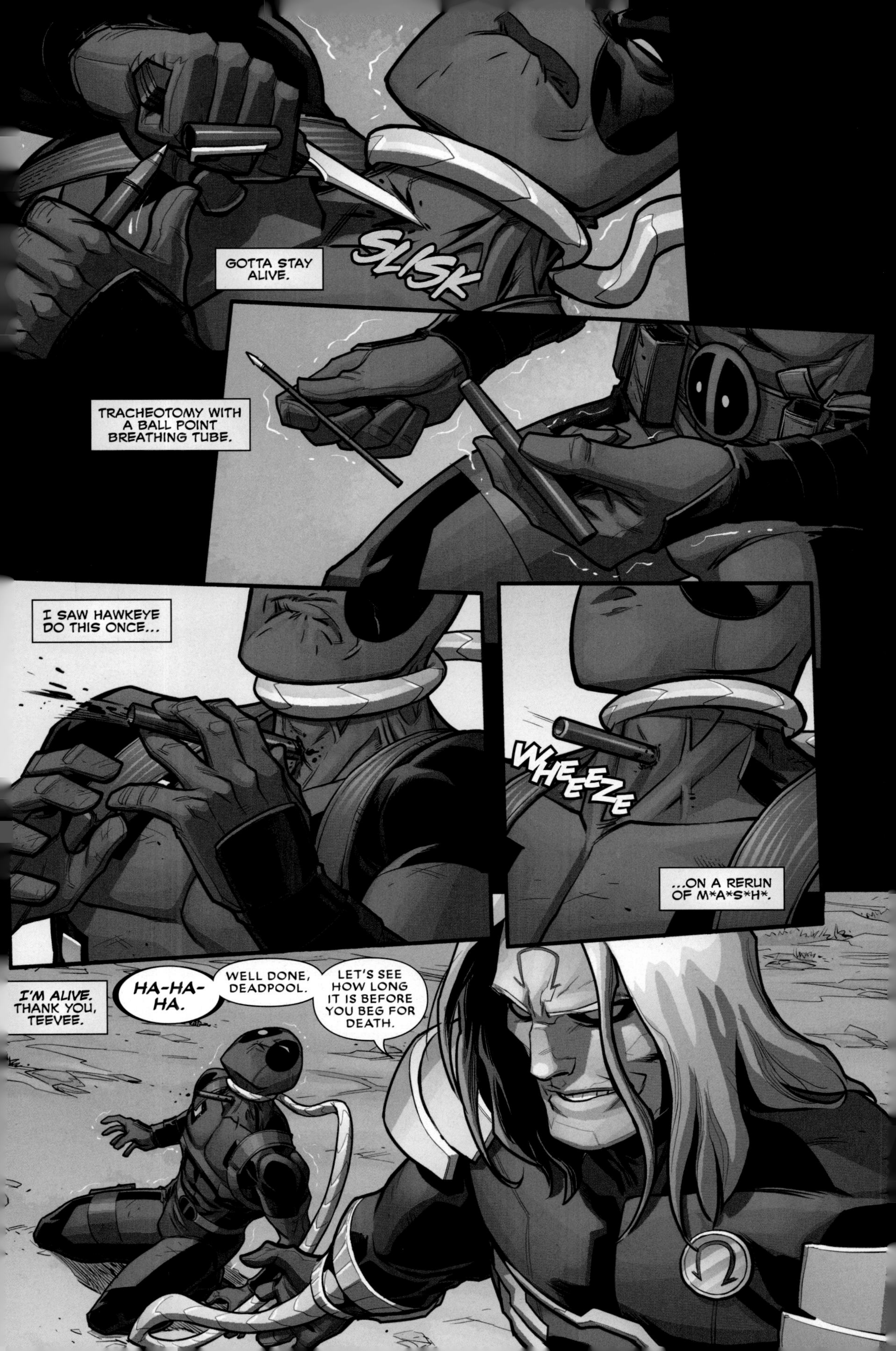
GOTTA STAY ALIVE.
SLISK
TRACHEOTOMY WITH A BALL POINT BREATHING TUBE.
I SAW HAWKEYE DO THIS ONCE...
WHEEEZE
...ON A RERUN OF M*A*S*H*.
I'M ALIVE. THANK YOU, TEEVEE.
HA-HA-HA.
WELL DONE, DEADPOOL.
LET'S SEE HOW LONG IT IS BEFORE YOU BEG FOR DEATH.

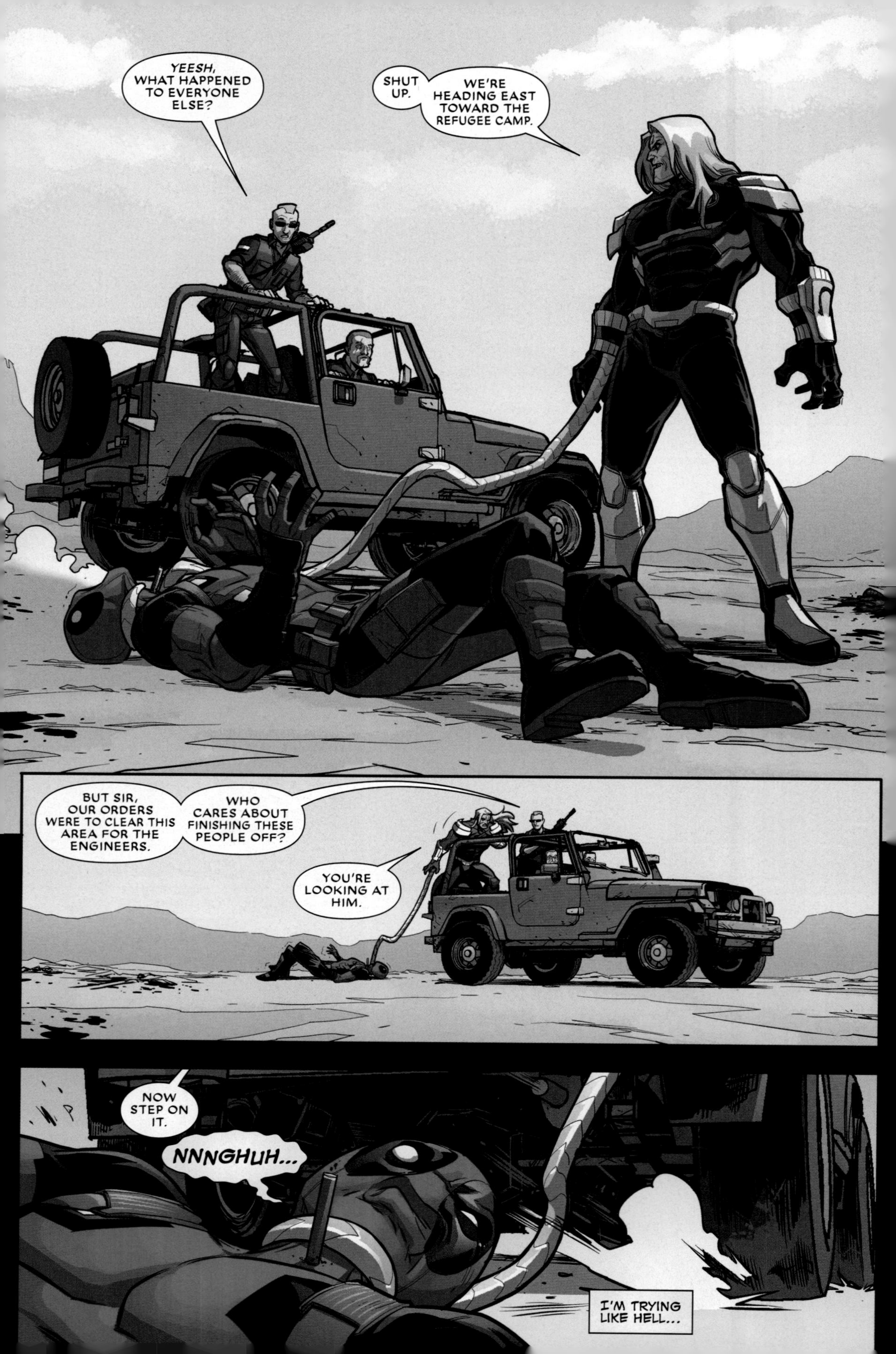
YEESH, WHAT HAPPENED TO EVERYONE ELSE?
SHUT UP.
WE'RE HEADING EAST TOWARD THE REFUGEE CAMP.
BUT SIR, OUR ORDERS WERE TO CLEAR THIS AREA FOR THE ENGINEERS.
WHO CARES ABOUT FINISHING THESE PEOPLE OFF?
YOU'RE LOOKING AT HIM.
NOW STEP ON IT.
NNNGHUH...
I'M TRYING LIKE HELL...

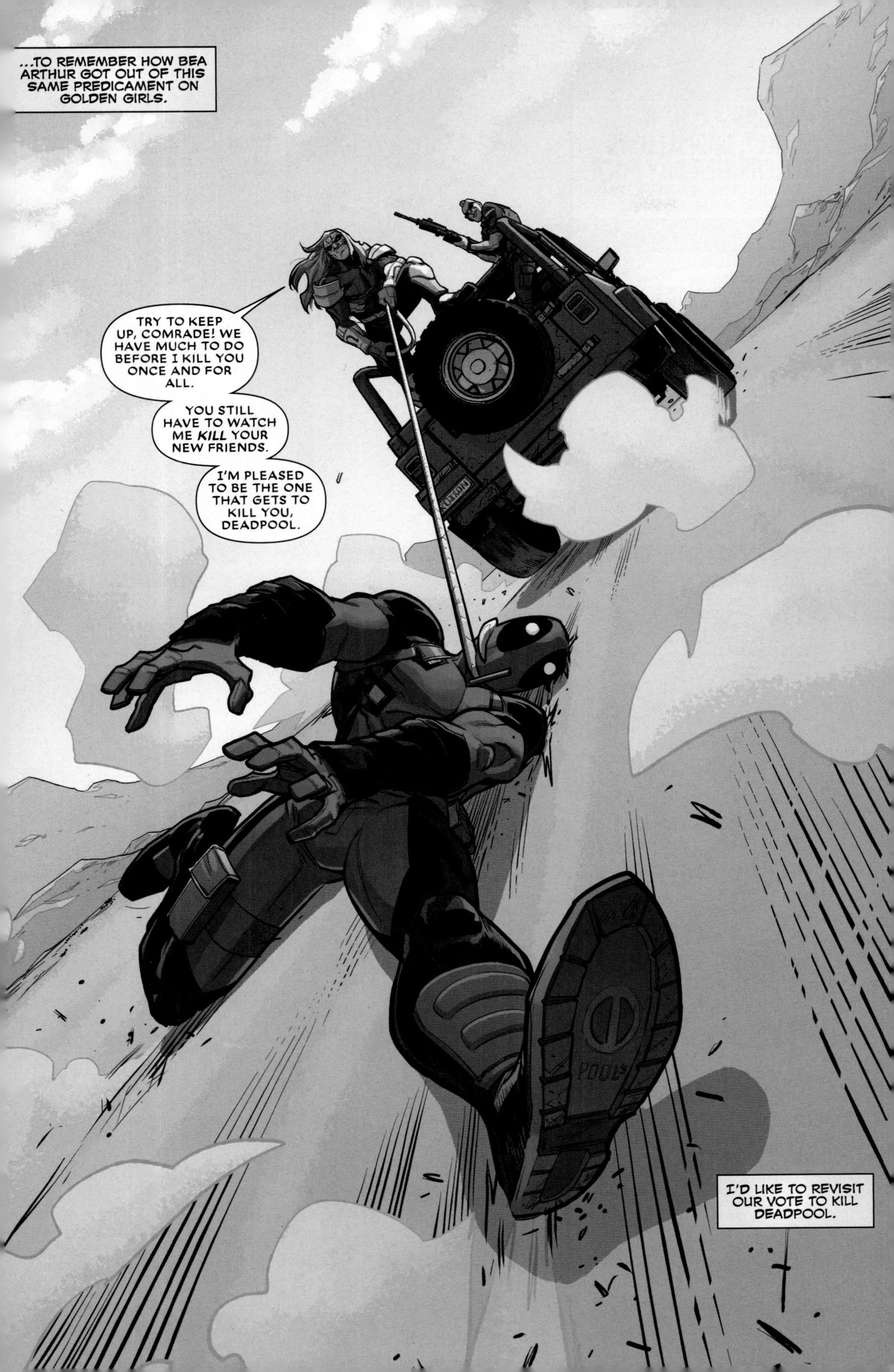
...TO REMEMBER HOW BEA ARTHUR GOT OUT OF THIS SAME PREDICAMENT ON GOLDEN GIRLS.
TRY TO KEEP UP, COMRADE! WE HAVE MUCH TO DO BEFORE I KILL YOU ONCE AND FOR ALL.
YOU STILL HAVE TO WATCH ME *KILL* YOUR NEW FRIENDS.
I'M PLEASED TO BE THE ONE THAT GETS TO KILL YOU, DEADPOOL.
I'D LIKE TO REVISIT OUR VOTE TO KILL DEADPOOL.

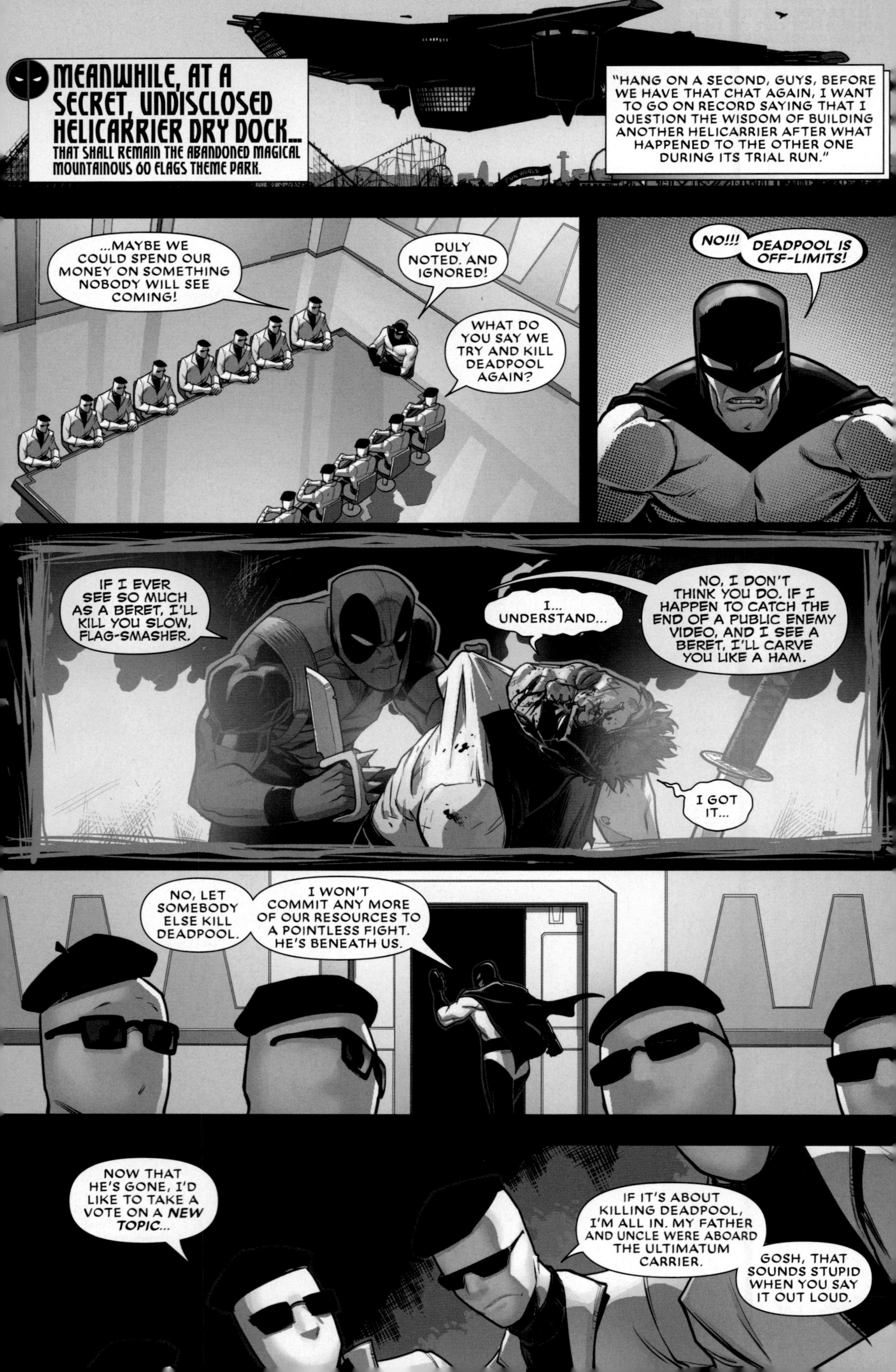

MEANWHILE, AT A SECRET, UNDISCLOSED HELICARRIER DRY DOCK... THAT SHALL REMAIN THE ABANDONED MAGICAL MOUNTAINOUS 60 FLAGS THEME PARK.
"HANG ON A SECOND, GUYS, BEFORE WE HAVE THAT CHAT AGAIN, I WANT TO GO ON RECORD SAYING THAT I QUESTION THE WISDOM OF BUILDING ANOTHER HELICARRIER AFTER WHAT HAPPENED TO THE OTHER ONE DURING ITS TRIAL RUN."
FUN WORLD
...MAYBE WE COULD SPEND OUR MONEY ON SOMETHING NOBODY WILL SEE COMING!
DULY NOTED. AND IGNORED!
WHAT DO YOU SAY WE TRY AND KILL DEADPOOL AGAIN?
NO!!!
DEADPOOL IS OFF-LIMITS!
IF I EVER SEE SO MUCH AS A BERET, I'LL KILL YOU SLOW, FLAG-SMASHER.
I... UNDERSTAND...
NO, I DON'T THINK YOU DO. IF I HAPPEN TO CATCH THE END OF A PUBLIC ENEMY VIDEO, AND I SEE A BERET, I'LL CARVE YOU LIKE A HAM.
I GOT IT...
NO, LET SOMEBODY ELSE KILL DEADPOOL.
I WON'T COMMIT ANY MORE OF OUR RESOURCES TO A POINTLESS FIGHT. HE'S BENEATH US.
NOW THAT HE'S GONE, I'D LIKE TO TAKE A VOTE ON A *NEW TOPIC*...
IF IT'S ABOUT KILLING DEADPOOL, I'M ALL IN. MY FATHER AND UNCLE WERE ABOARD THE ULTIMATUM CARRIER.
GOSH, THAT SOUNDS STUPID WHEN YOU SAY IT OUT LOUD.

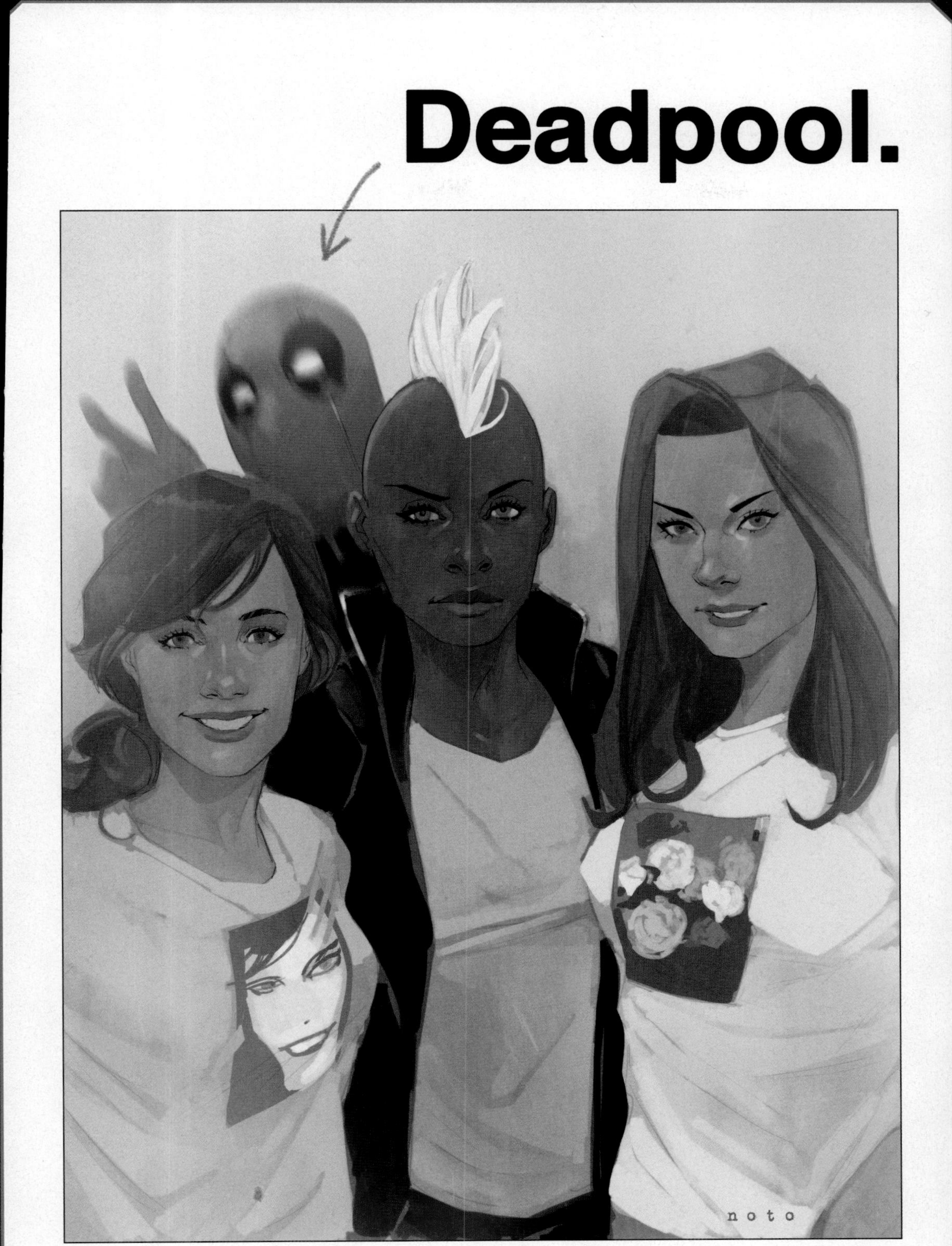
Deadpool.
noto

#42 VARIANT
BY PHIL NOTO

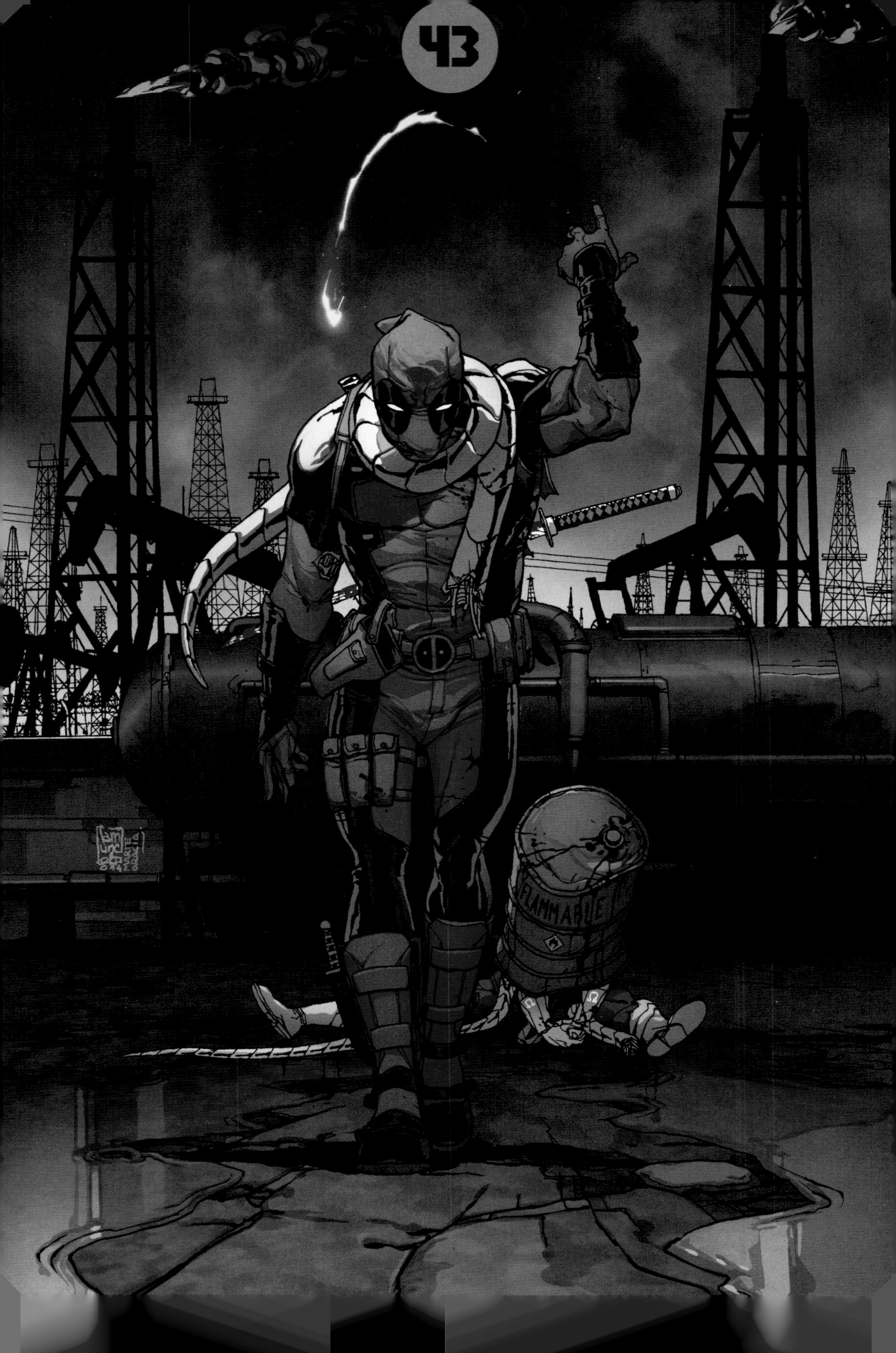
43
FLAMMABLE

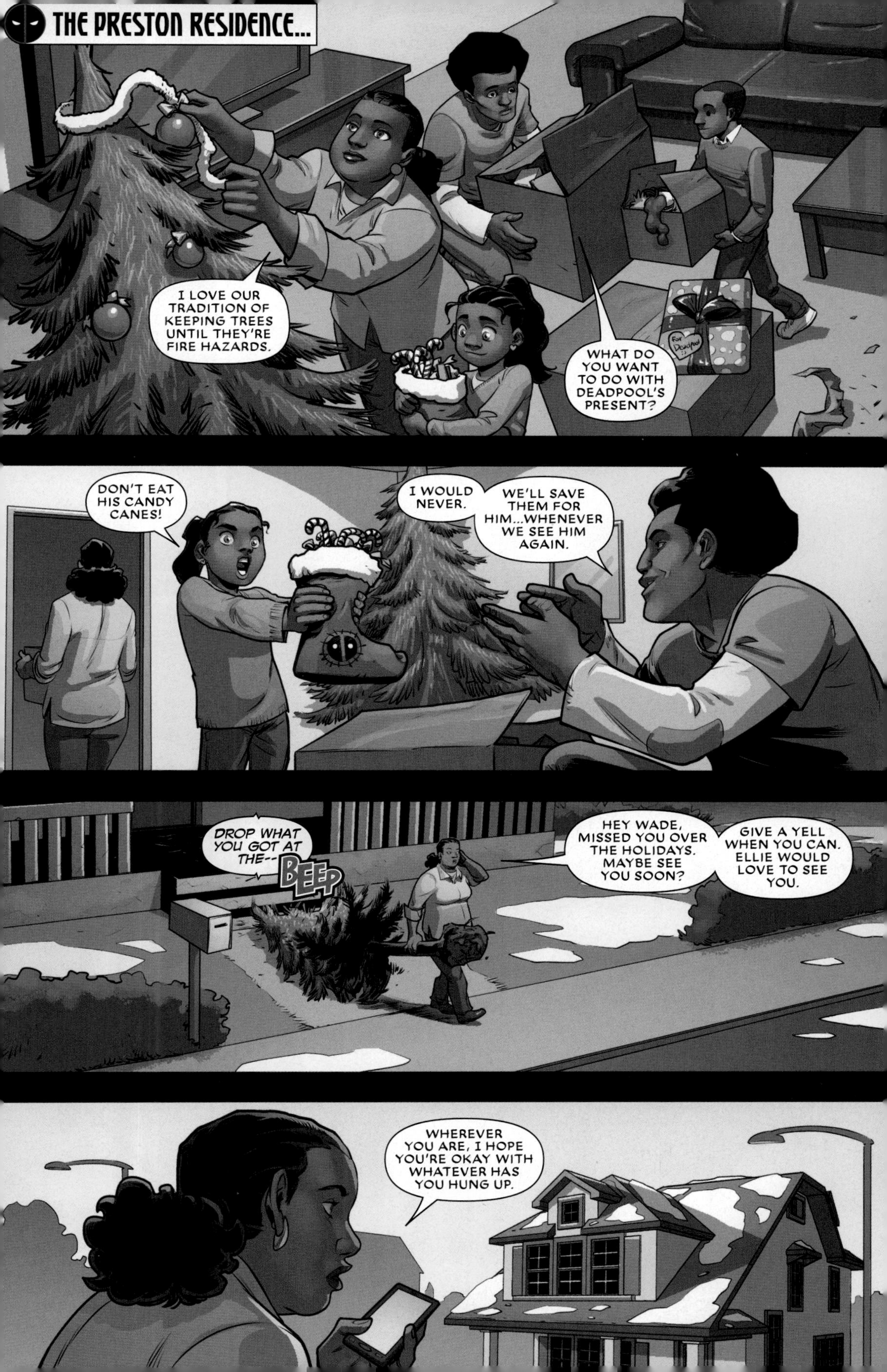
THE PRESTON RESIDENCE...
I LOVE OUR TRADITION OF KEEPING TREES UNTIL THEY'RE FIRE HAZARDS.
WHAT DO YOU WANT TO DO WITH DEADPOOL'S PRESENT?
For Deadpool
DON'T EAT HIS CANDY CANES!
I WOULD NEVER.
WE'LL SAVE THEM FOR HIM...WHENEVER WE SEE HIM AGAIN.
DROP WHAT YOU GOT AT THE--
BEEP
HEY WADE, MISSED YOU OVER THE HOLIDAYS. MAYBE SEE YOU SOON?
GIVE A YELL WHEN YOU CAN. ELLIE WOULD LOVE TO SEE YOU.
WHEREVER YOU ARE, I HOPE YOU'RE OKAY WITH WHATEVER HAS YOU HUNG UP.

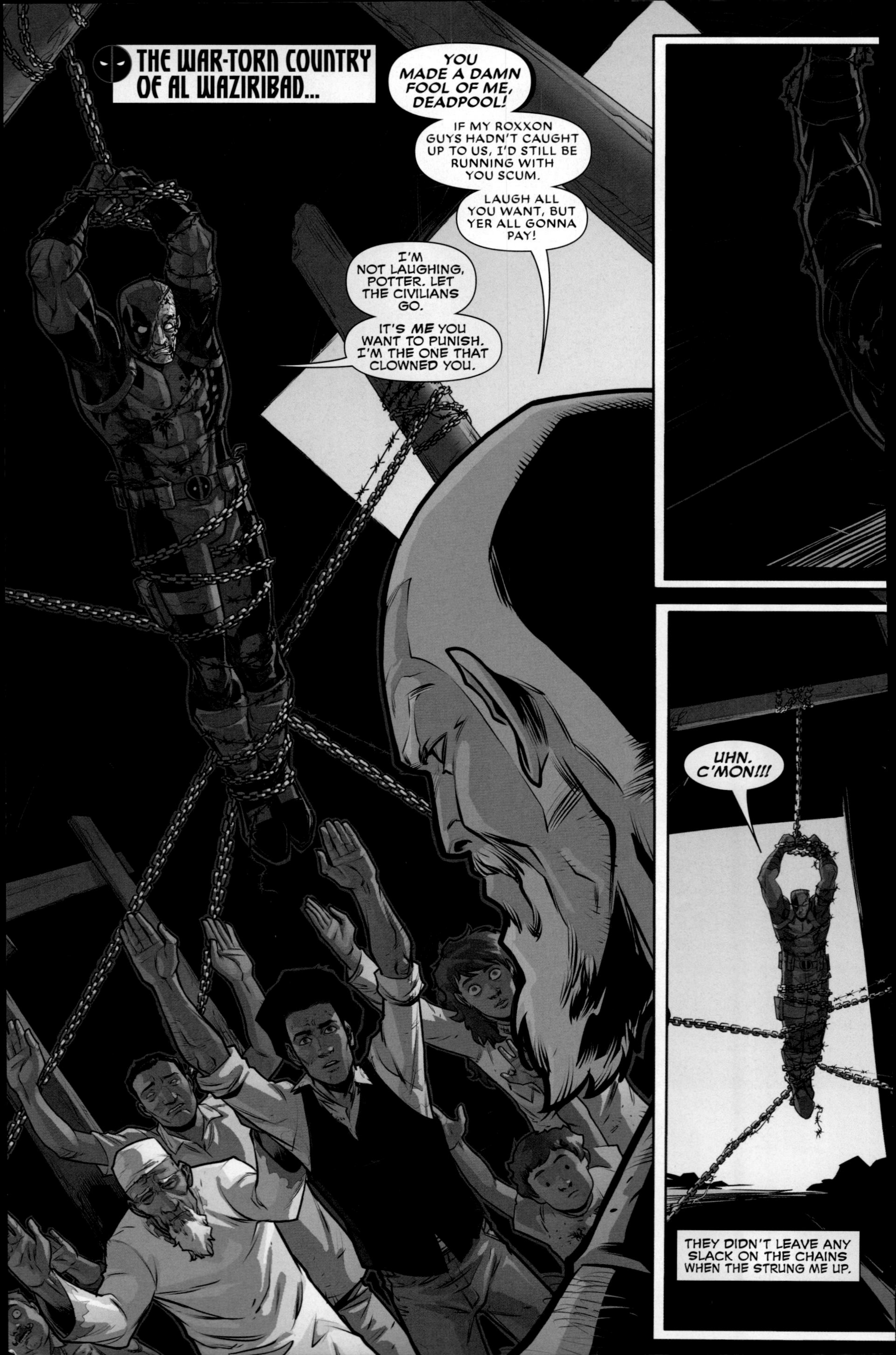
THE WAR-TORN COUNTRY OF AL WAZIRIBAD...
YOU MADE A DAMN FOOL OF ME, DEADPOOL!
IF MY ROXXON GUYS HADN'T CAUGHT UP TO US, I'D STILL BE RUNNING WITH YOU SCUM.
LAUGH ALL YOU WANT, BUT YER ALL GONNA PAY!
I'M NOT LAUGHING, POTTER. LET THE CIVILIANS GO.
IT'S *ME* YOU WANT TO PUNISH. I'M THE ONE THAT CLOWNED YOU.
UHN. C'MON!!!
THEY DIDN'T LEAVE ANY SLACK ON THE CHAINS WHEN THE STRUNG ME UP.

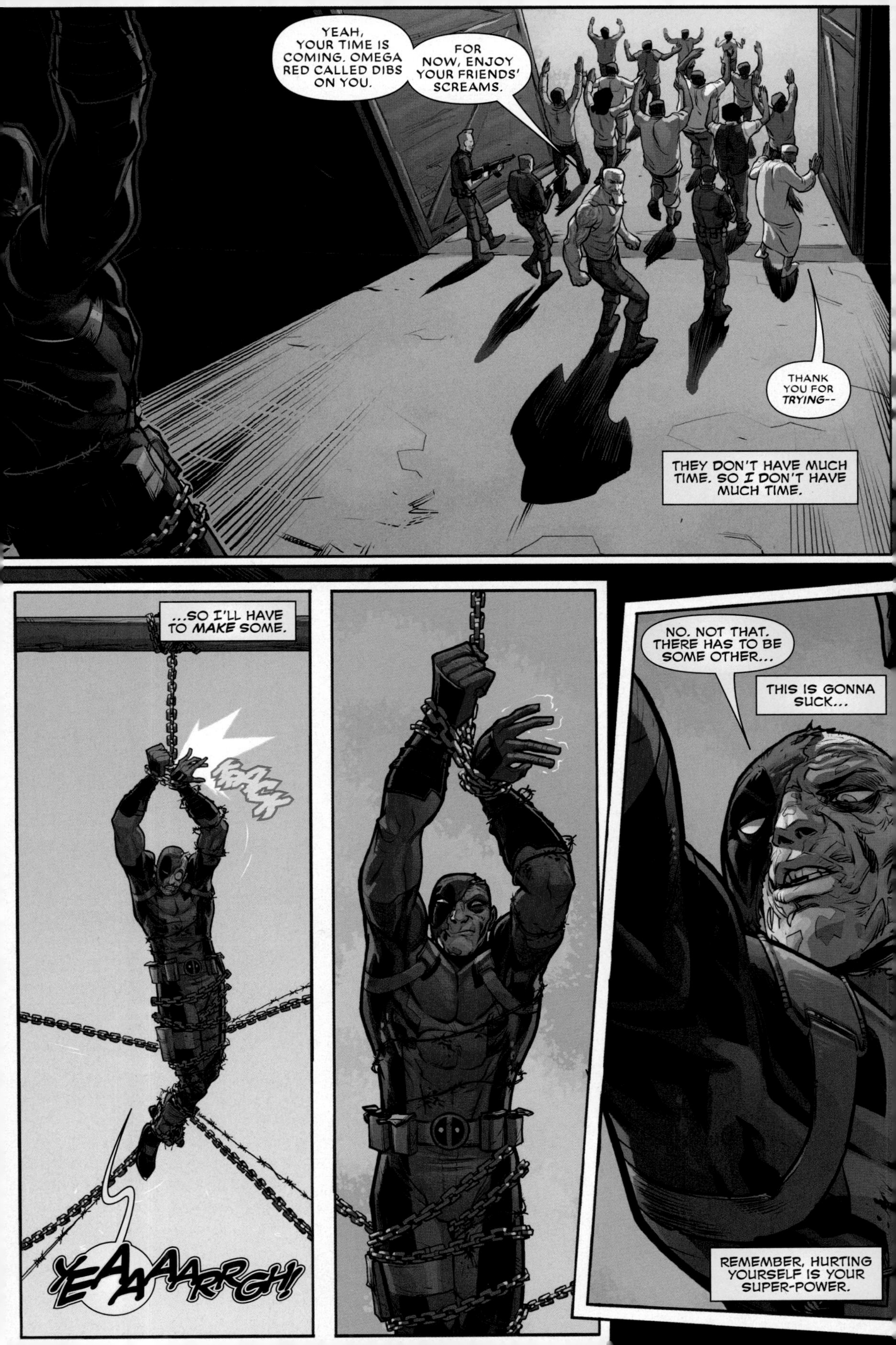
YEAH, YOUR TIME IS COMING. OMEGA RED CALLED DIBS ON YOU.
FOR NOW, ENJOY YOUR FRIENDS' SCREAMS.
THANK YOU FOR *TRYING*--
THEY DON'T HAVE MUCH TIME. SO *I* DON'T HAVE MUCH TIME.
...SO I'LL HAVE TO *MAKE* SOME.
YEAAAARRGH!
NO. NOT THAT. THERE HAS TO BE SOME OTHER...
THIS IS GONNA SUCK...
REMEMBER, HURTING YOURSELF IS YOUR SUPER-POWER.

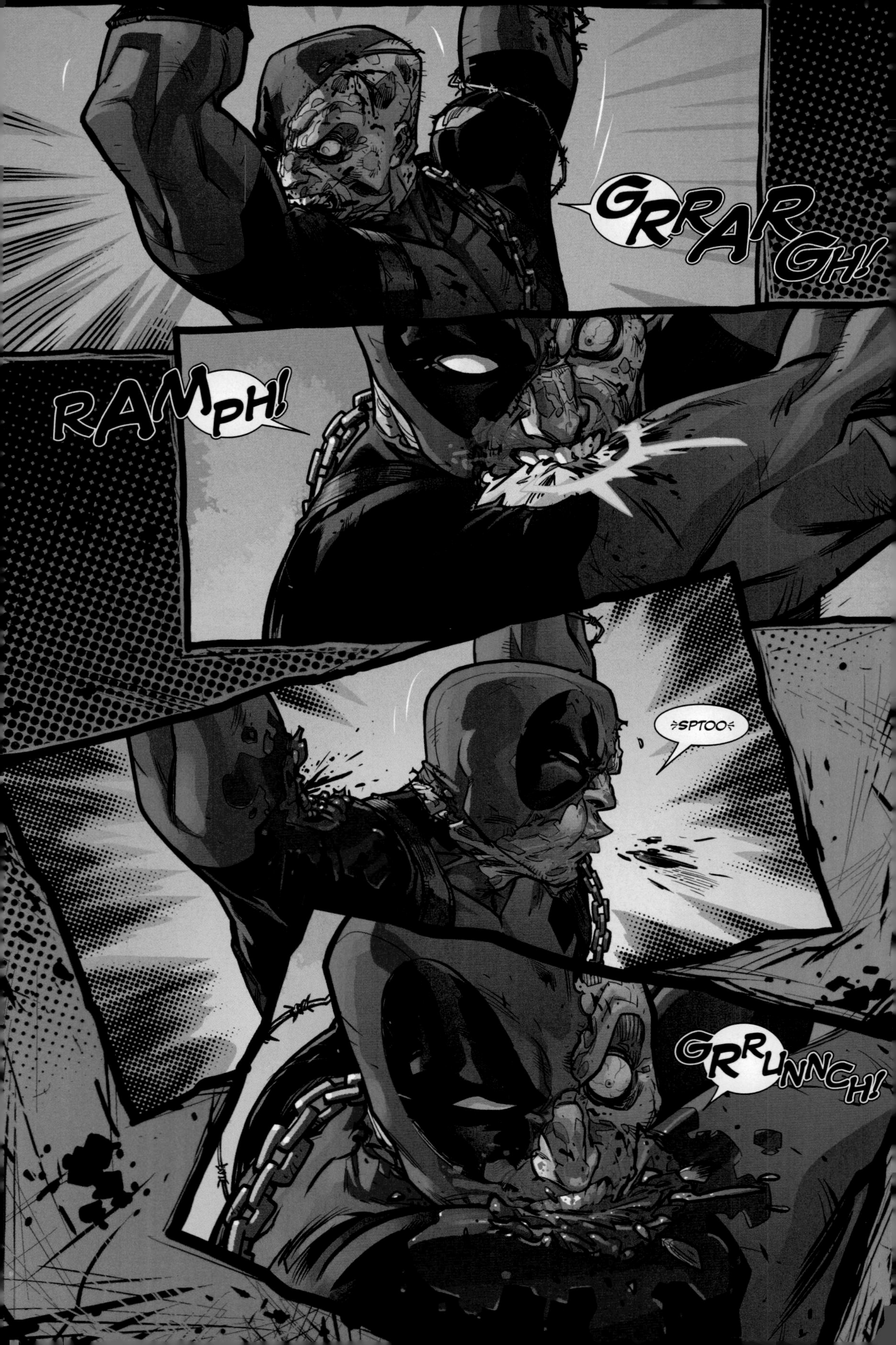
GRRARRGH!
RAMPH!
SPTOO
GRRUNNCH!

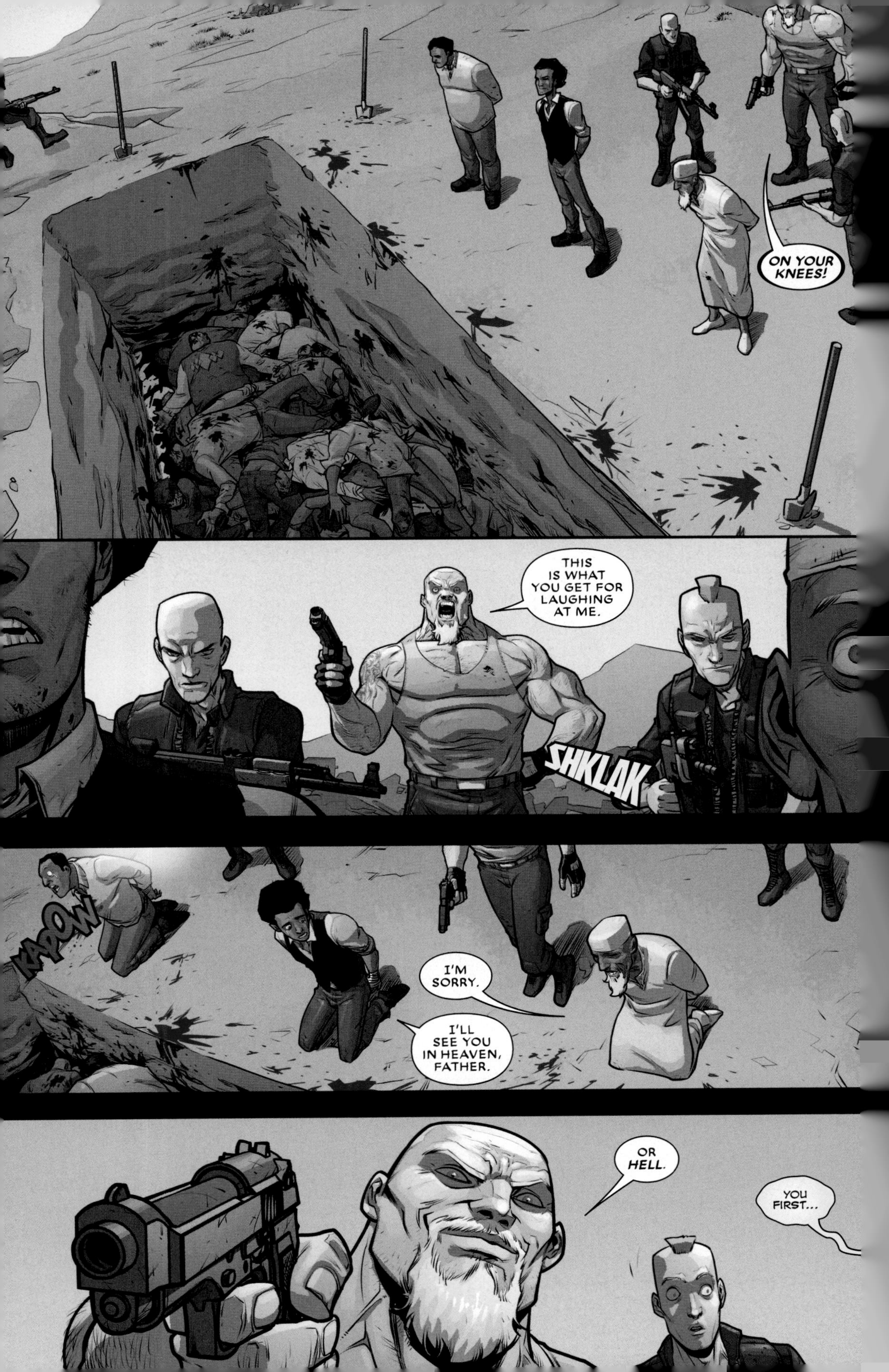
ON YOUR KNEES!
THIS IS WHAT YOU GET FOR LAUGHING AT ME.
SHKLAK
KAPOW
I'M SORRY.
I'LL SEE YOU IN HEAVEN, FATHER.
OR HELL.
YOU FIRST...

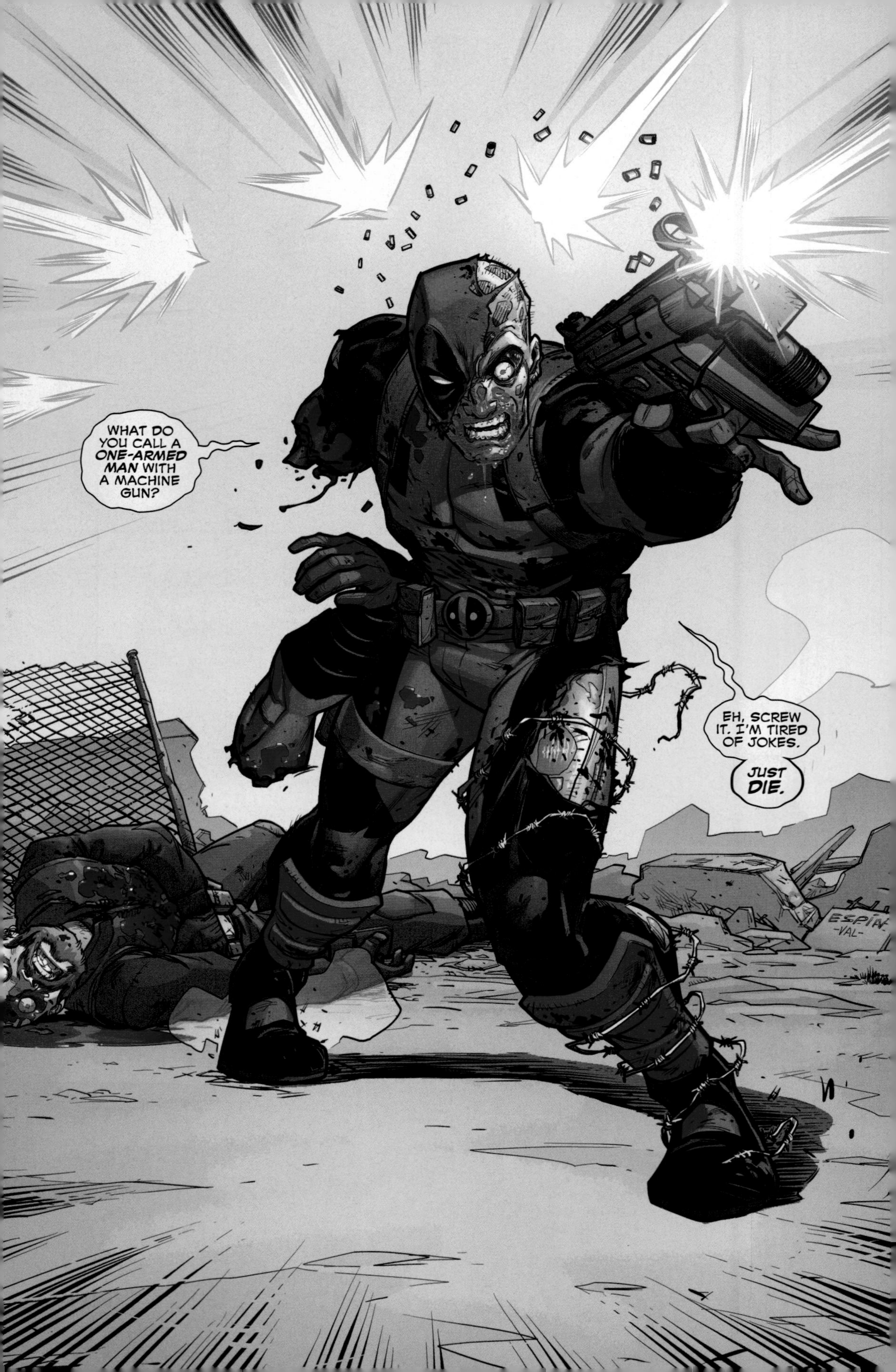
WHAT DO YOU CALL A ONE-ARMED MAN WITH A MACHINE GUN?
EH, SCREW IT. I'M TIRED OF JOKES.
JUST DIE.
ESPIN -VAL-

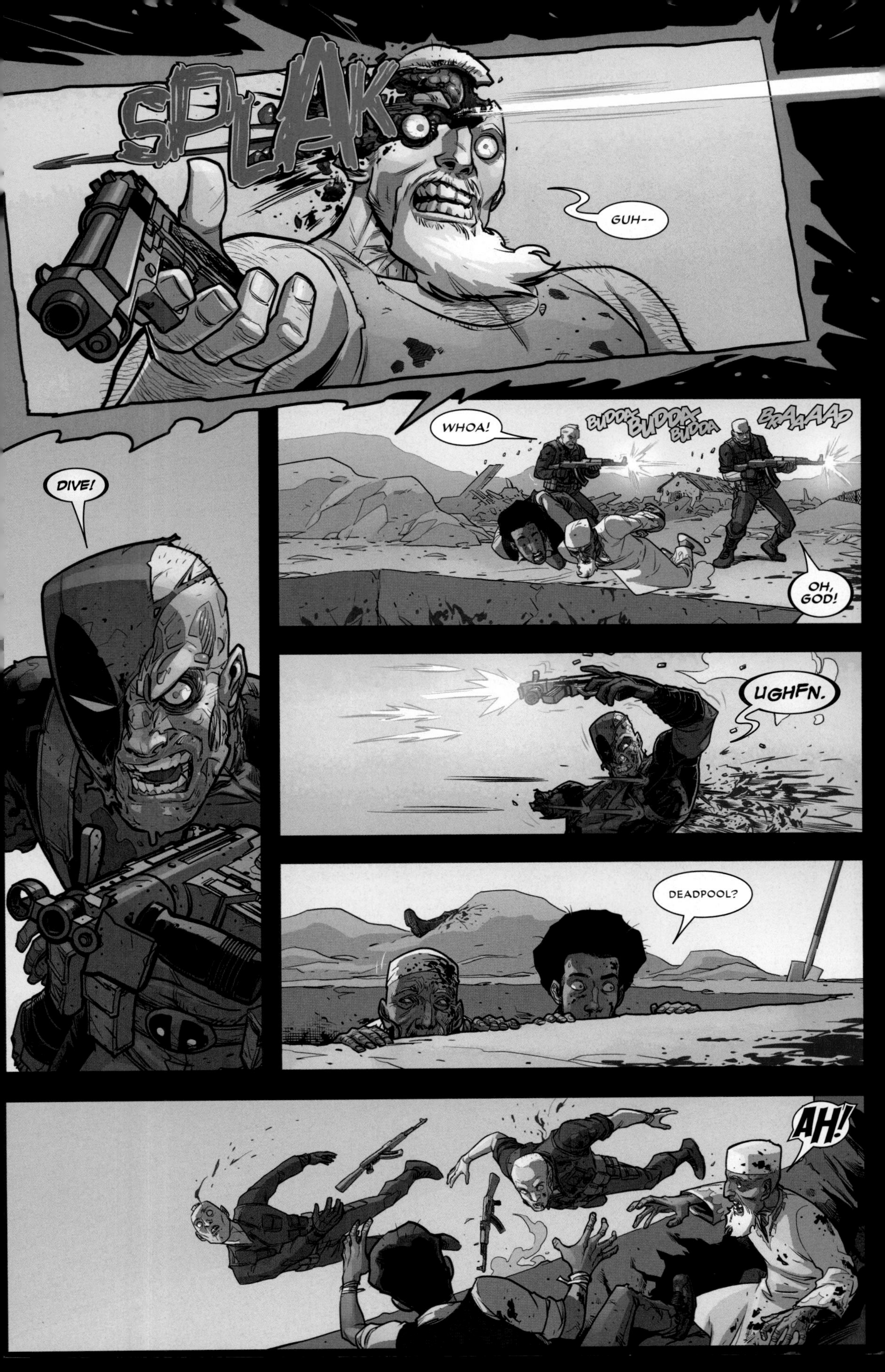
SPLAK
GUH--
DIVE!
WHOA!
BUDDA BUDDA BUDDA
BRAAAAP
OH, GOD!
UGHFN.
DEADPOOL?
AH!

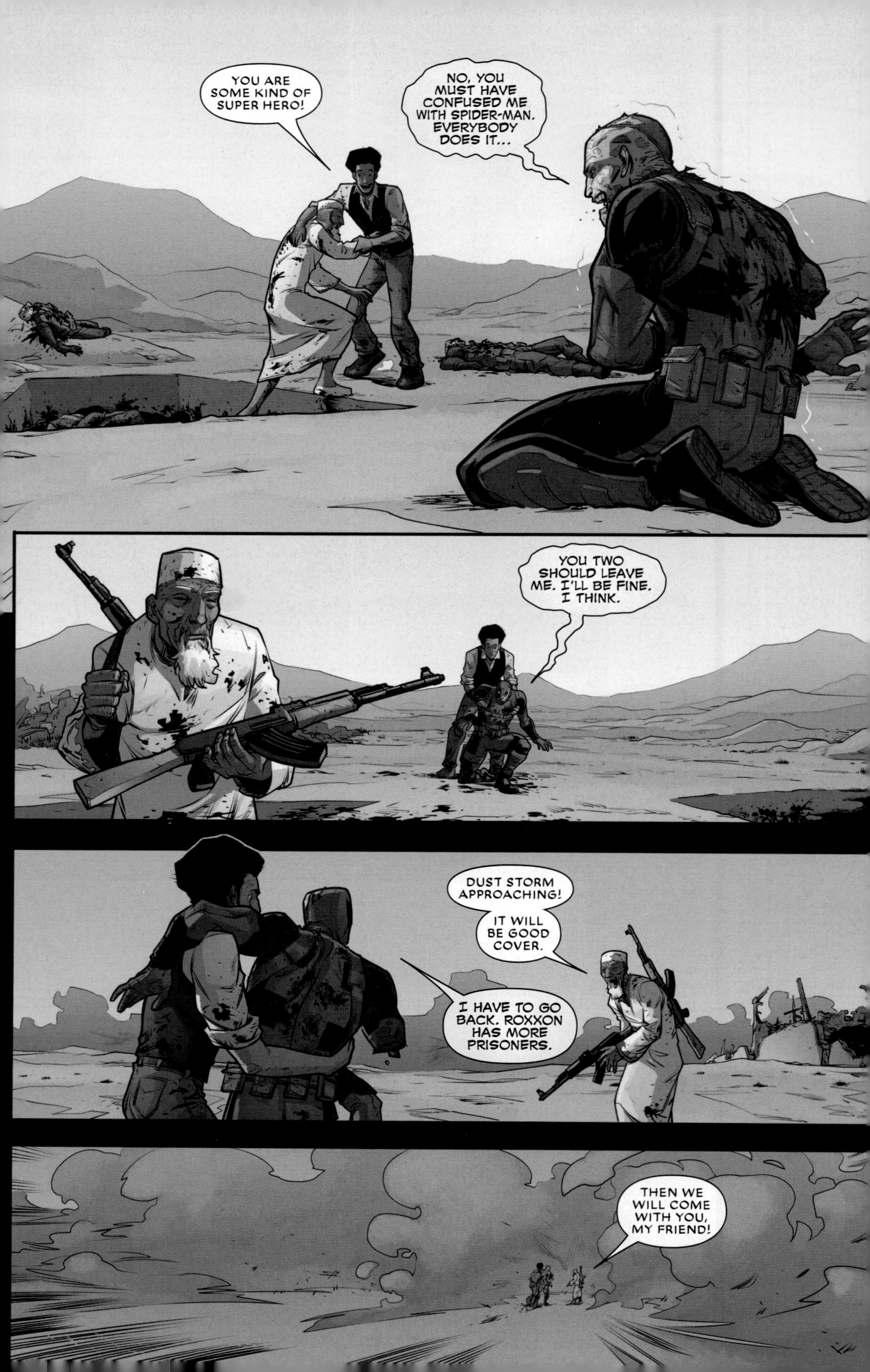
YOU ARE SOME KIND OF SUPER HERO!
NO, YOU MUST HAVE CONFUSED ME WITH SPIDER-MAN. EVERYBODY DOES IT...
YOU TWO SHOULD LEAVE ME. I'LL BE FINE. I THINK.
DUST STORM APPROACHING!
IT WILL BE GOOD COVER.
I HAVE TO GO BACK. ROXXON HAS MORE PRISONERS.
THEN WE WILL COME WITH YOU, MY FRIEND!

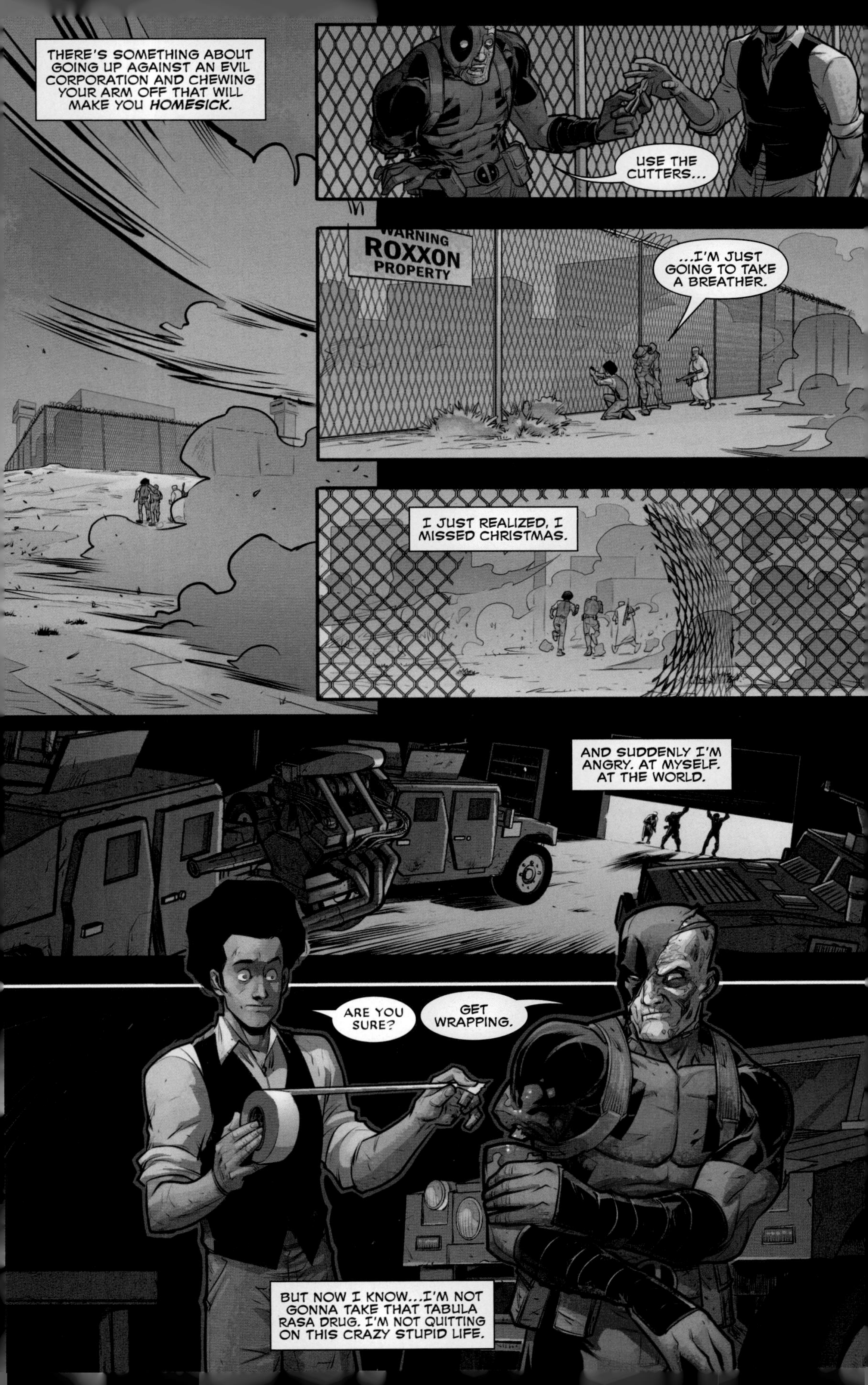
THERE'S SOMETHING ABOUT GOING UP AGAINST AN EVIL CORPORATION AND CHEWING YOUR ARM OFF THAT WILL MAKE YOU *HOMESICK.*
USE THE CUTTERS...
WARNING ROXXON PROPERTY
...I'M JUST GOING TO TAKE A BREATHER.
I JUST REALIZED, I MISSED CHRISTMAS.
AND SUDDENLY I'M ANGRY. AT MYSELF. AT THE WORLD.
ARE YOU SURE?
GET WRAPPING.
BUT NOW I KNOW...I'M NOT GONNA TAKE THAT TABULA RASA DRUG. I'M NOT QUITTING ON THIS CRAZY STUPID LIFE.

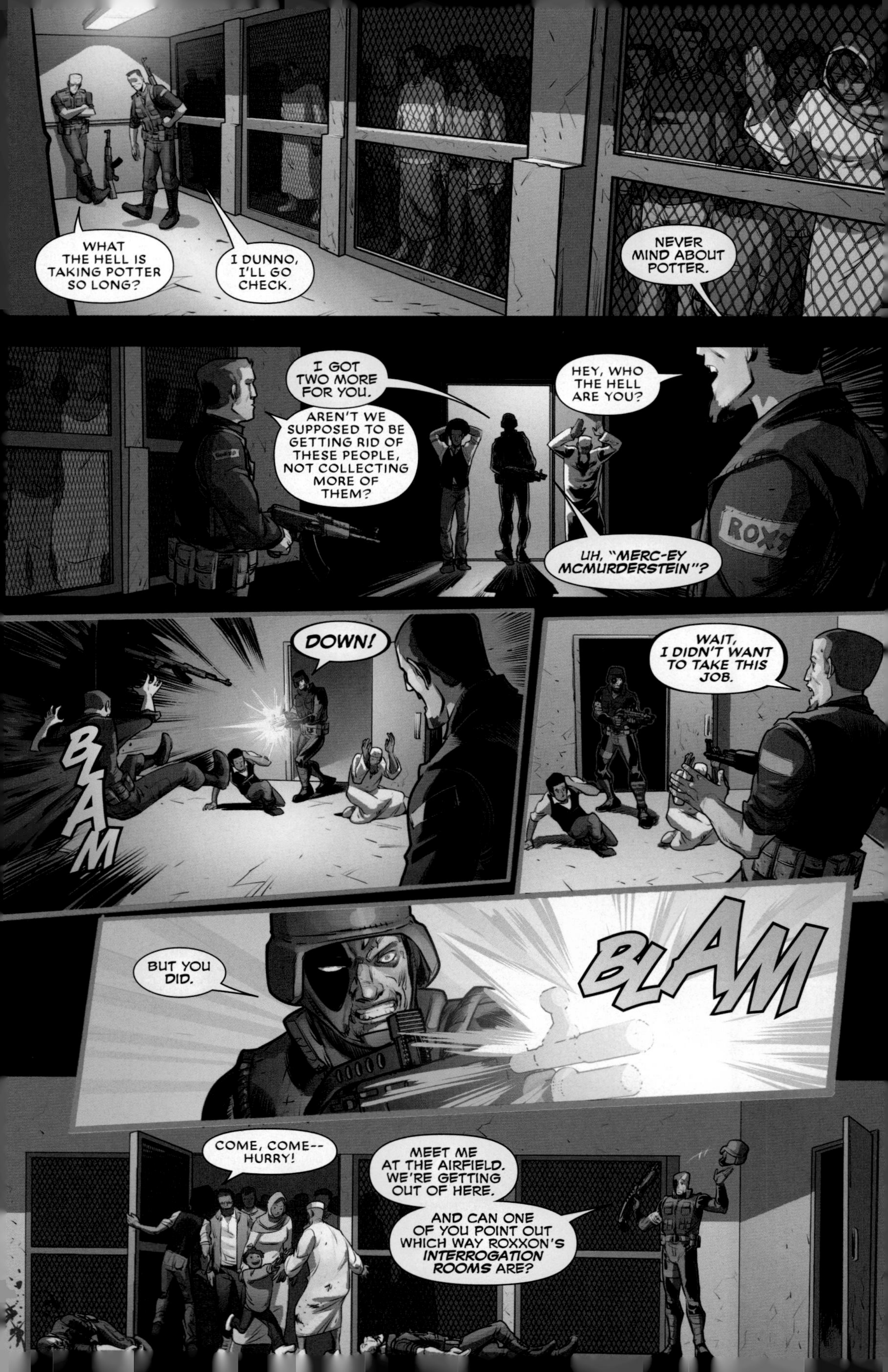
WHAT THE HELL IS TAKING POTTER SO LONG?
I DUNNO, I'LL GO CHECK.
NEVER MIND ABOUT POTTER.
I GOT TWO MORE FOR YOU.
AREN'T WE SUPPOSED TO BE GETTING RID OF THESE PEOPLE, NOT COLLECTING MORE OF THEM?
HEY, WHO THE HELL ARE YOU?
UH, "MERC-EY MCMURDERSTEIN"?
DOWN!
BLAM
WAIT, I DIDN'T WANT TO TAKE THIS JOB.
BUT YOU DID.
BLAM
COME, COME-- HURRY!
MEET ME AT THE AIRFIELD. WE'RE GETTING OUT OF HERE.
AND CAN ONE OF YOU POINT OUT WHICH WAY ROXXON'S *INTERROGATION ROOMS* ARE?

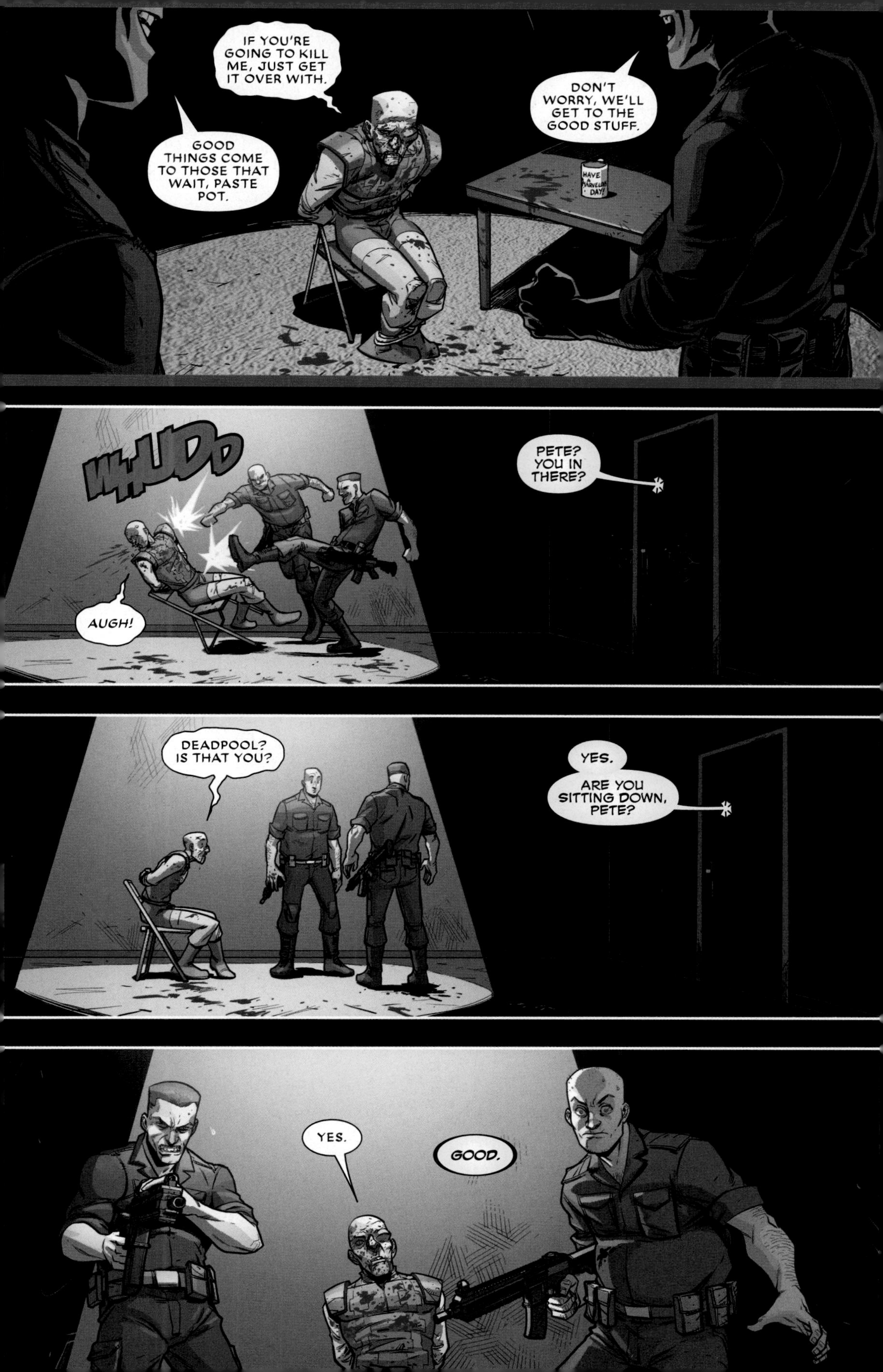
IF YOU'RE GOING TO KILL ME, JUST GET IT OVER WITH.
GOOD THINGS COME TO THOSE THAT WAIT, PASTE POT.
DON'T WORRY, WE'LL GET TO THE GOOD STUFF.
HAVE A MARVELOUS DAY!
WHUDD
AUGH!
PETE? YOU IN THERE?
DEADPOOL? IS THAT YOU?
YES.
ARE YOU SITTING DOWN, PETE?
YES.
GOOD.

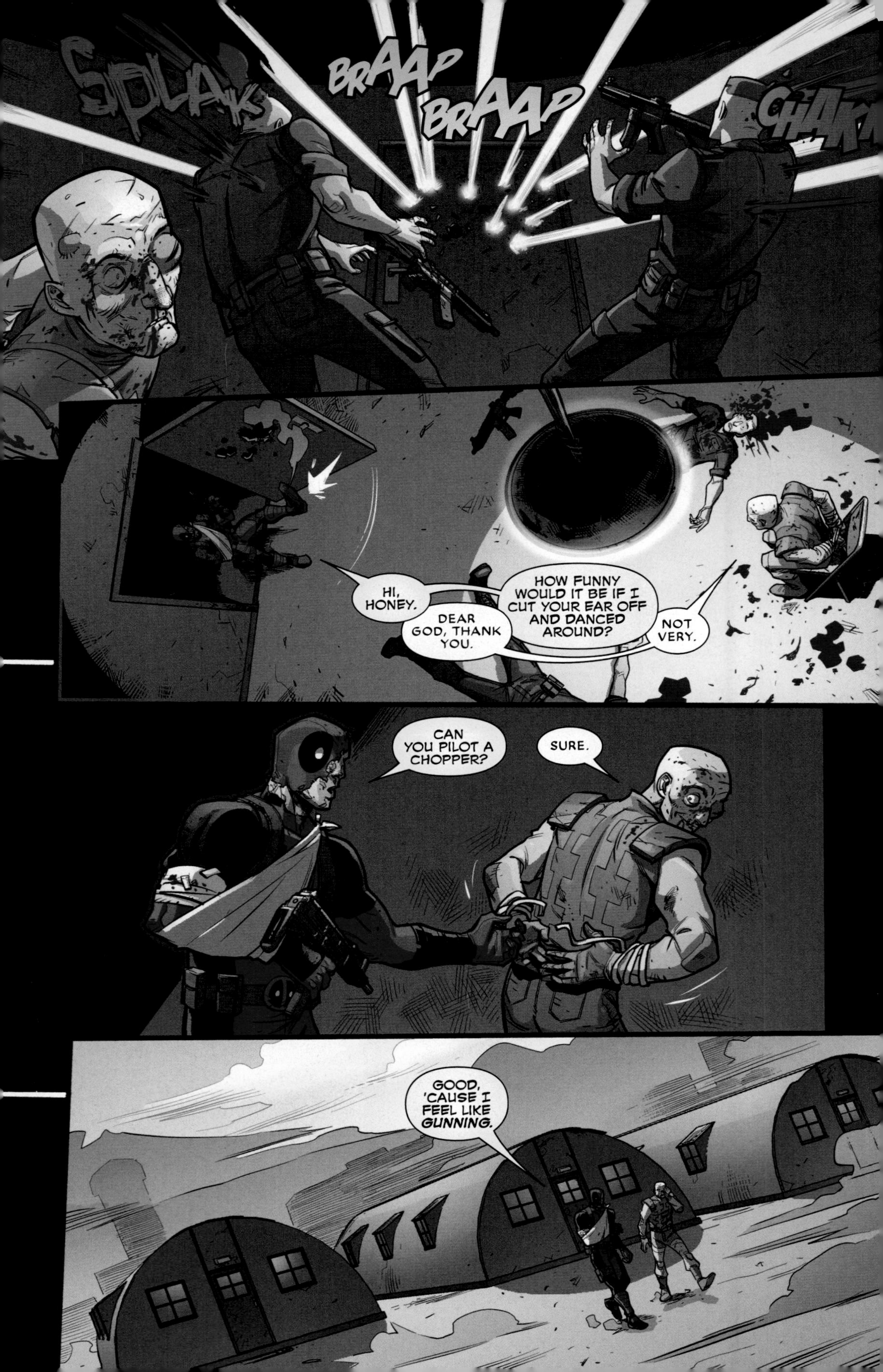
SPLAK
BRAAAP
BRAAAP
HI, HONEY.
HOW FUNNY WOULD IT BE IF I CUT YOUR EAR OFF AND DANCED AROUND?
DEAR GOD, THANK YOU.
NOT VERY.
CAN YOU PILOT A CHOPPER?
SURE.
GOOD, 'CAUSE I FEEL LIKE GUNNING.

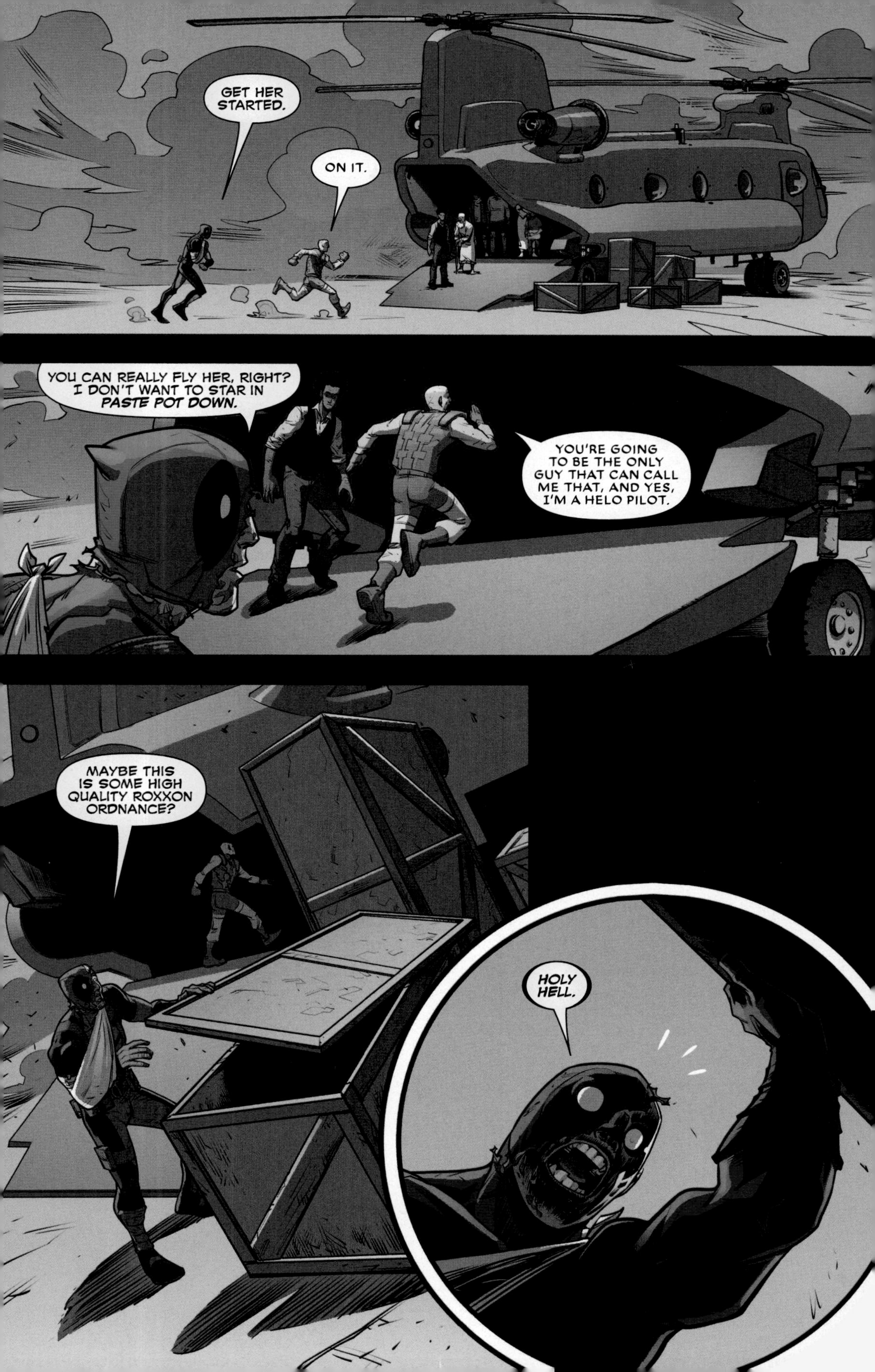
GET HER STARTED.
ON IT.
YOU CAN REALLY FLY HER, RIGHT? I DON'T WANT TO STAR IN *PASTE POT DOWN.*
YOU'RE GOING TO BE THE ONLY GUY THAT CAN CALL ME THAT, AND YES, I'M A HELO PILOT.
MAYBE THIS IS SOME HIGH QUALITY ROXXON ORDNANCE?
HOLY HELL.

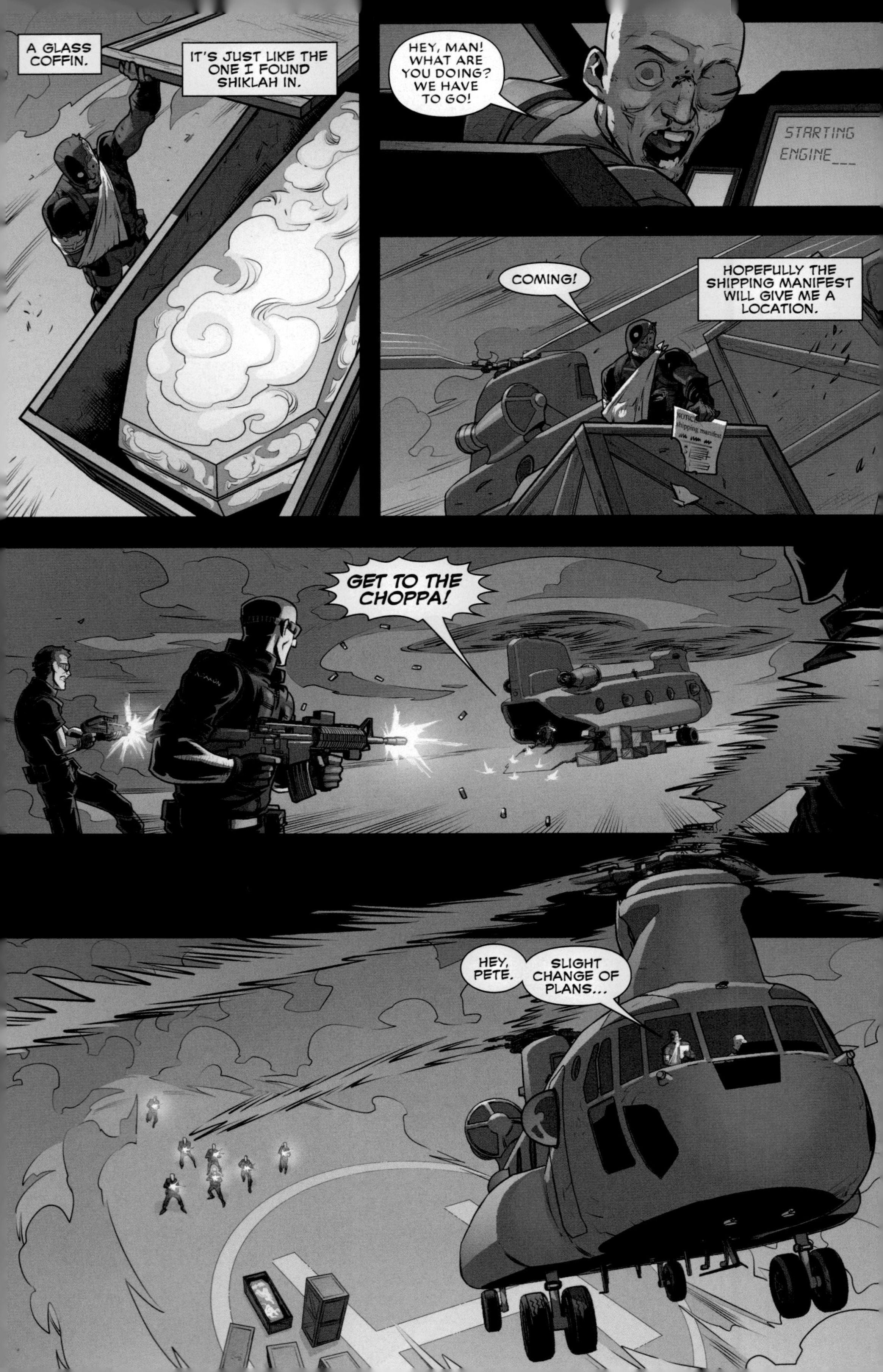
A GLASS COFFIN.
IT'S JUST LIKE THE ONE I FOUND SHIKLAH IN.
HEY, MAN! WHAT ARE YOU DOING? WE HAVE TO GO!
STARTING ENGINE___
COMING!
HOPEFULLY THE SHIPPING MANIFEST WILL GIVE ME A LOCATION.
shipping manifest
GET TO THE CHOPPA!
HEY, PETE.
SLIGHT CHANGE OF PLANS...

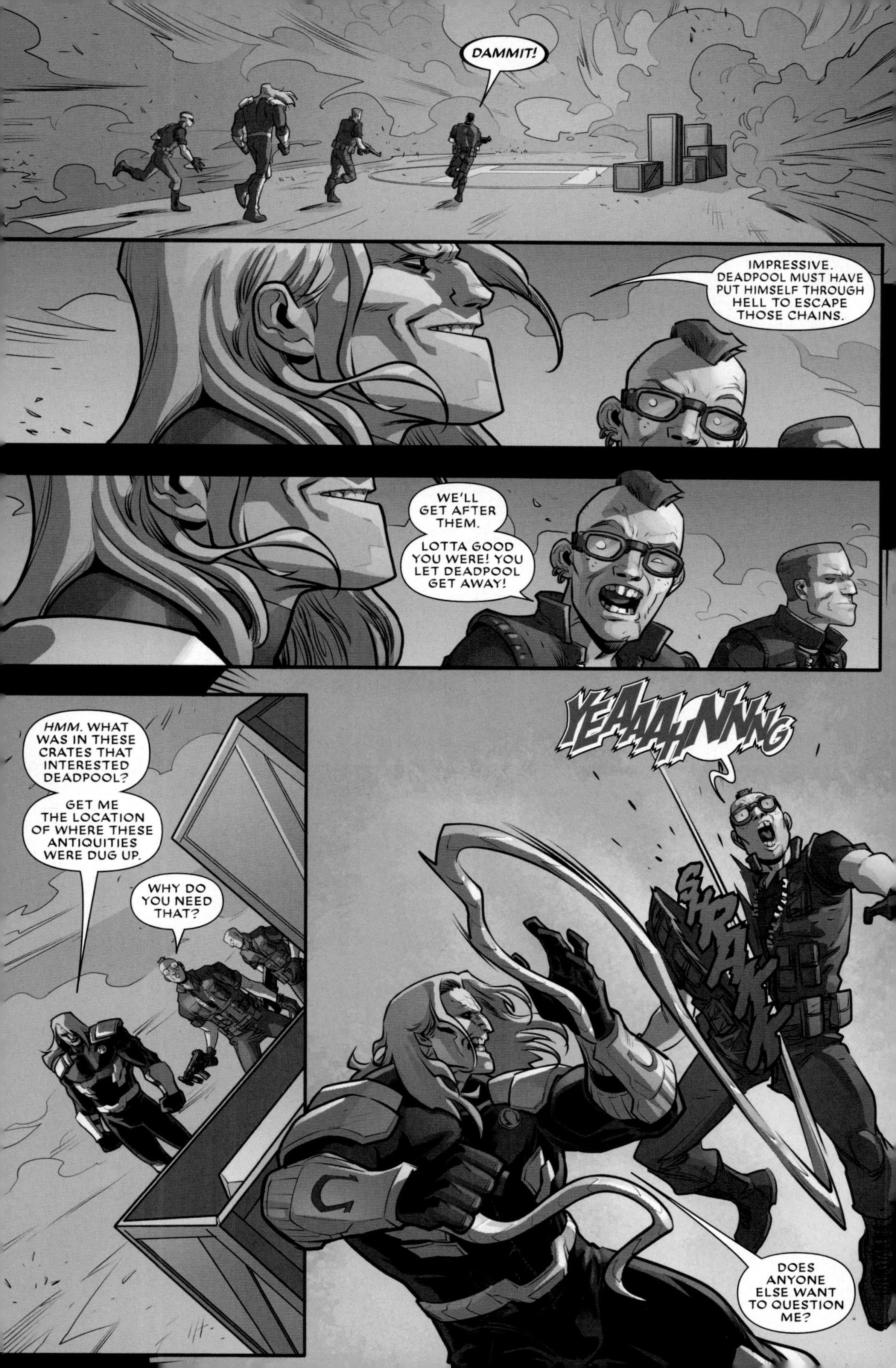
DAMMIT!
IMPRESSIVE. DEADPOOL MUST HAVE PUT HIMSELF THROUGH HELL TO ESCAPE THOSE CHAINS.
WE'LL GET AFTER THEM.
LOTTA GOOD YOU WERE! YOU LET DEADPOOL GET AWAY!
HMM. WHAT WAS IN THESE CRATES THAT INTERESTED DEADPOOL?
GET ME THE LOCATION OF WHERE THESE ANTIQUITIES WERE DUG UP.
WHY DO YOU NEED THAT?
YEAAAHNNNG
SHRAK
DOES ANYONE ELSE WANT TO QUESTION ME?

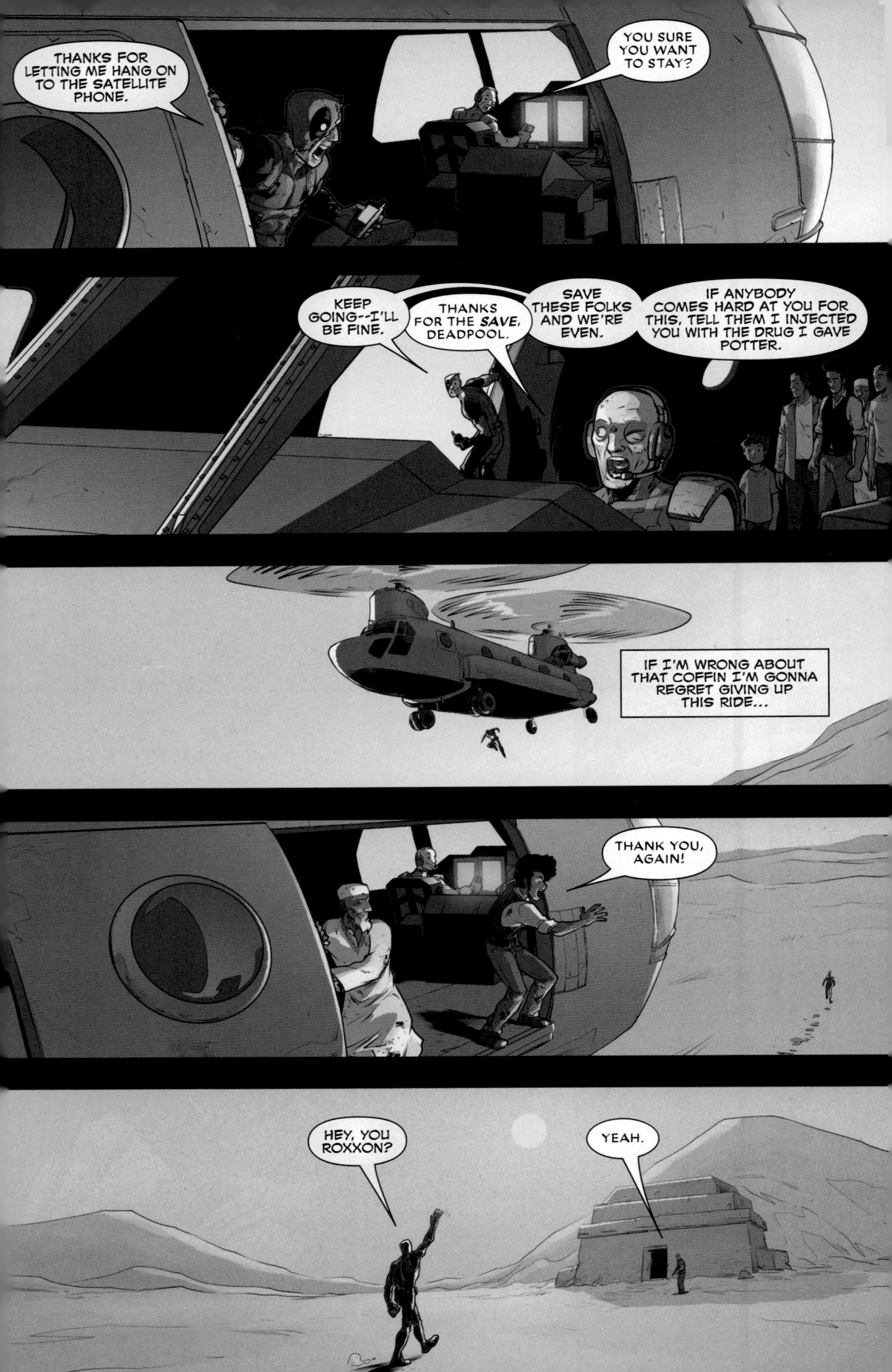
THANKS FOR LETTING ME HANG ON TO THE SATELLITE PHONE.
YOU SURE YOU WANT TO STAY?
KEEP GOING--I'LL BE FINE.
THANKS FOR THE *SAVE*, DEADPOOL.
SAVE THESE FOLKS AND WE'RE EVEN.
IF ANYBODY COMES HARD AT YOU FOR THIS, TELL THEM I INJECTED YOU WITH THE DRUG I GAVE POTTER.
IF I'M WRONG ABOUT THAT COFFIN I'M GONNA REGRET GIVING UP THIS RIDE...
THANK YOU, AGAIN!
HEY, YOU ROXXON?
YEAH.

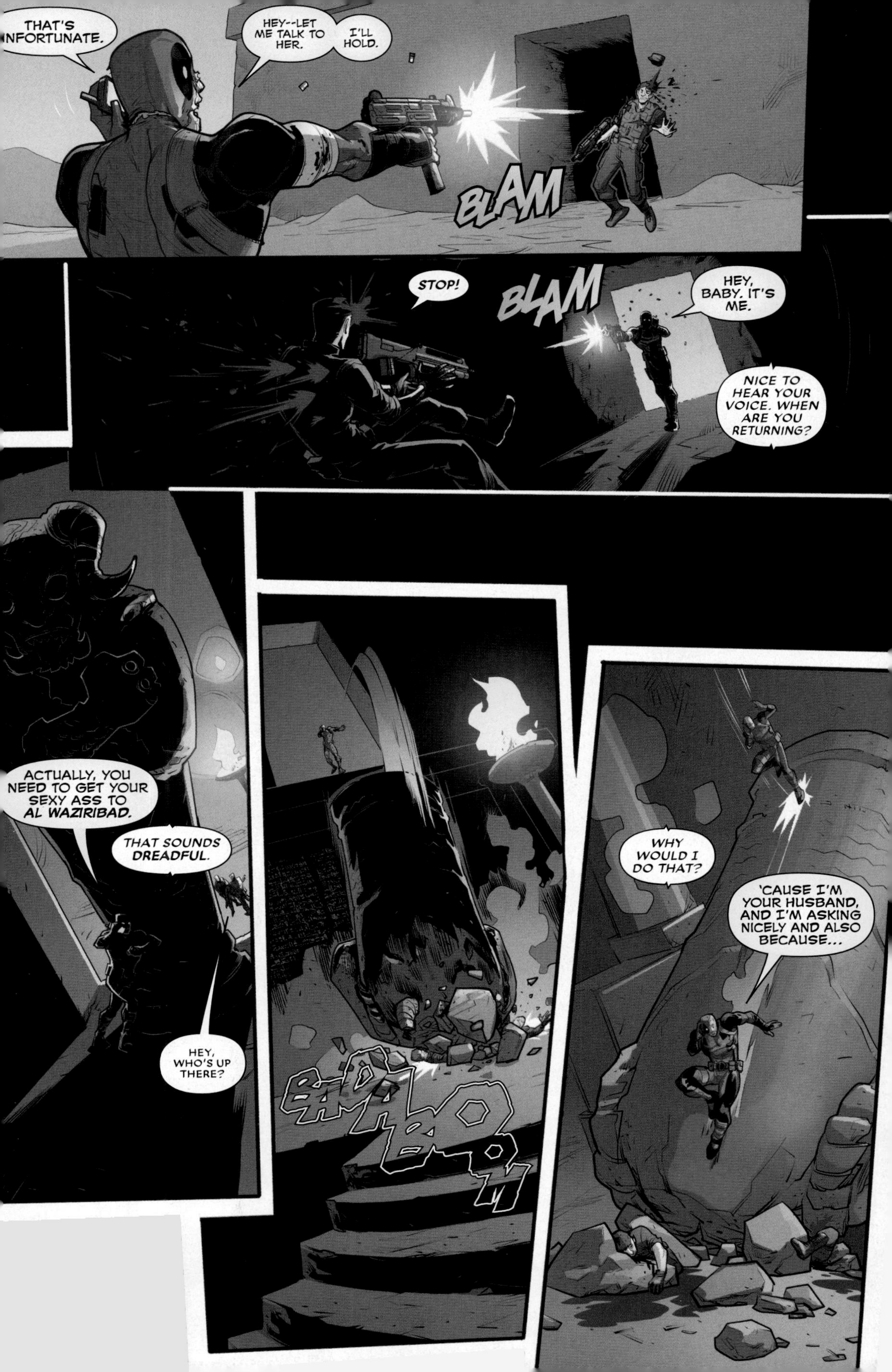

THAT'S UNFORTUNATE.
HEY--LET ME TALK TO HER.
I'LL HOLD.
BLAM
STOP!
BLAM
HEY, BABY. IT'S ME.
NICE TO HEAR YOUR VOICE. WHEN ARE YOU RETURNING?
ACTUALLY, YOU NEED TO GET YOUR SEXY ASS TO AL WAZIRIBAD.
THAT SOUNDS DREADFUL.
HEY, WHO'S UP THERE?
WHY WOULD I DO THAT?
'CAUSE I'M YOUR HUSBAND, AND I'M ASKING NICELY AND ALSO BECAUSE...

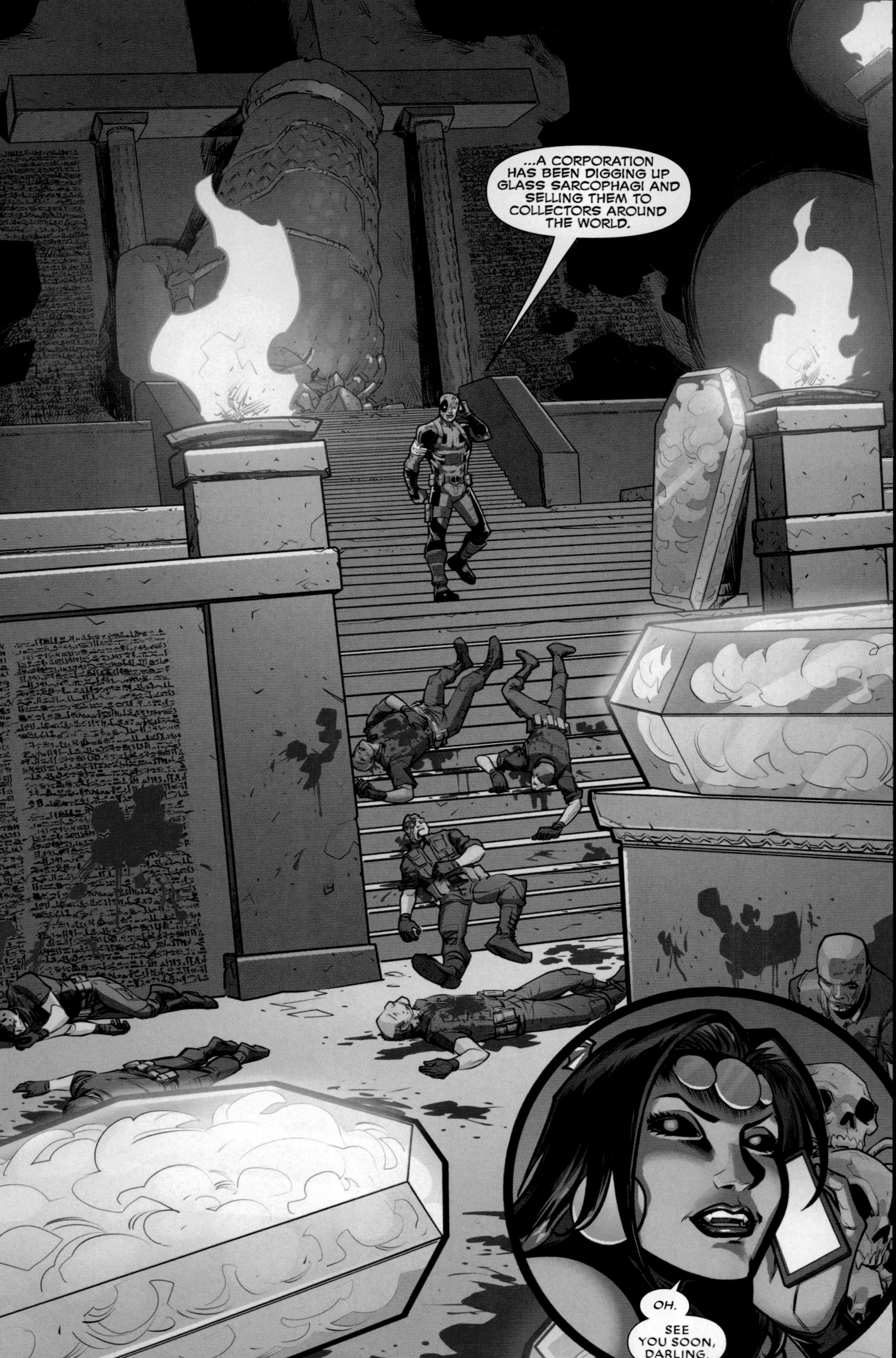
...A CORPORATION HAS BEEN DIGGING UP GLASS SARCOPHAGI AND SELLING THEM TO COLLECTORS AROUND THE WORLD.
OH.
SEE YOU SOON, DARLING.

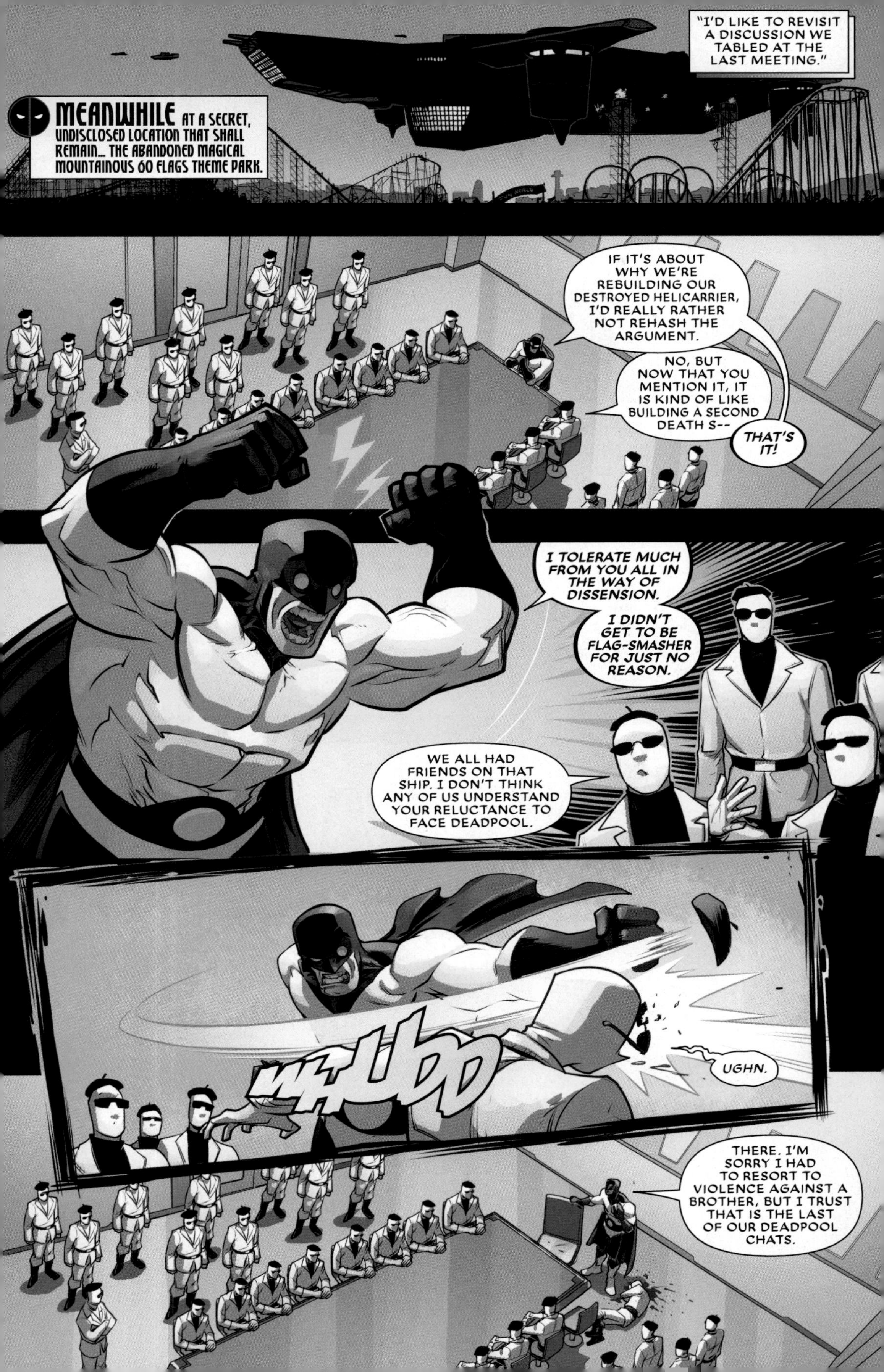
"I'D LIKE TO REVISIT A DISCUSSION WE TABLED AT THE LAST MEETING."
MEANWHILE AT A SECRET, UNDISCLOSED LOCATION THAT SHALL REMAIN... THE ABANDONED MAGICAL MOUNTAINOUS 60 FLAGS THEME PARK.
IF IT'S ABOUT WHY WE'RE REBUILDING OUR DESTROYED HELICARRIER, I'D REALLY RATHER NOT REHASH THE ARGUMENT.
NO, BUT NOW THAT YOU MENTION IT, IT IS KIND OF LIKE BUILDING A SECOND DEATH S--
THAT'S IT!
I TOLERATE MUCH FROM YOU ALL IN THE WAY OF DISSENSION.
I DIDN'T GET TO BE FLAG-SMASHER FOR JUST NO REASON.
WE ALL HAD FRIENDS ON THAT SHIP. I DON'T THINK ANY OF US UNDERSTAND YOUR RELUCTANCE TO FACE DEADPOOL.
WHUDD
UGHN.
THERE. I'M SORRY I HAD TO RESORT TO VIOLENCE AGAINST A BROTHER, BUT I TRUST THAT IS THE LAST OF OUR DEADPOOL CHATS.

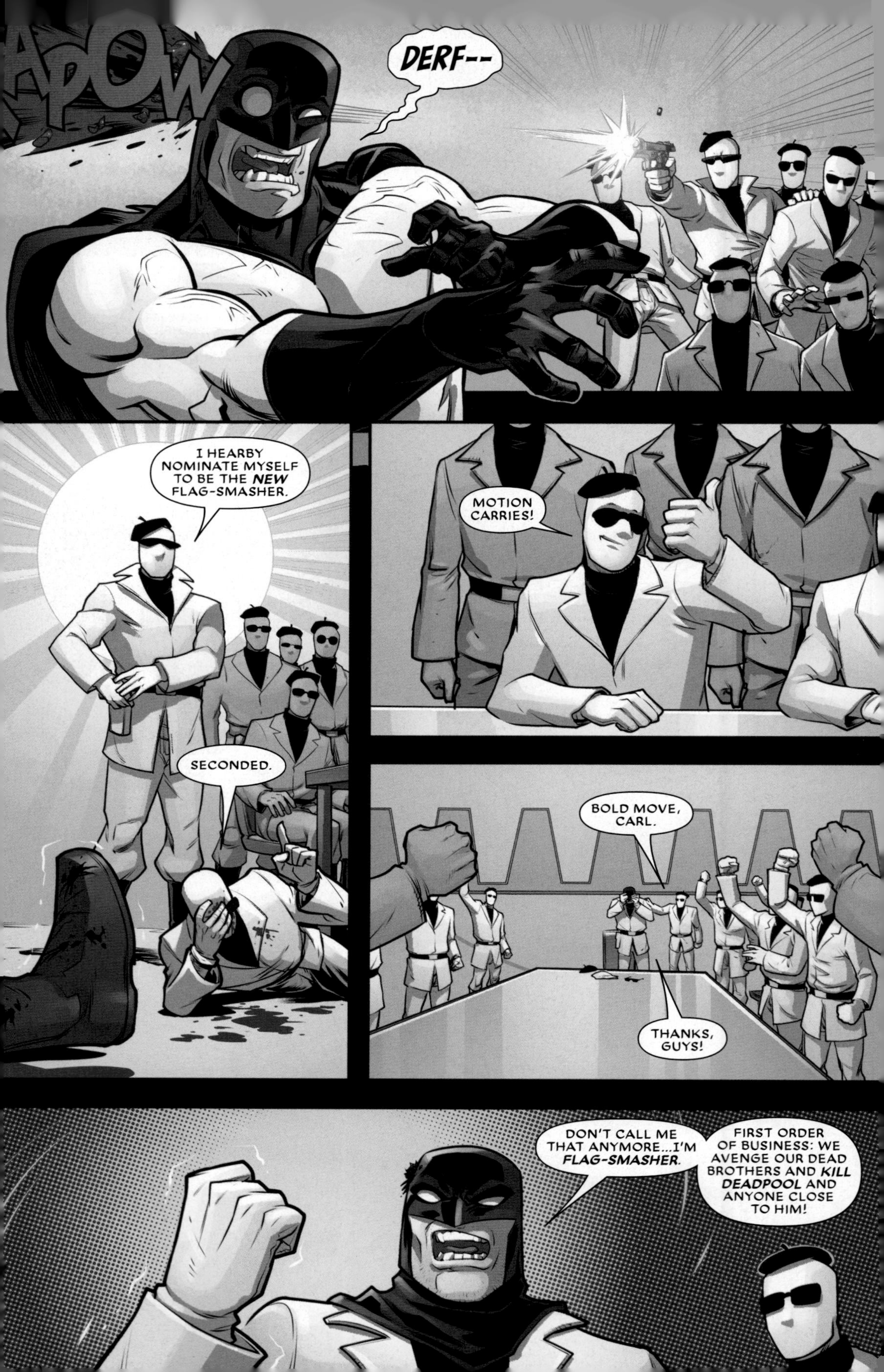
BLAPOW
DERF--
I HEARBY NOMINATE MYSELF TO BE THE NEW FLAG-SMASHER.
SECONDED.
MOTION CARRIES!
BOLD MOVE, CARL.
THANKS, GUYS!
DON'T CALL ME THAT ANYMORE...I'M FLAG-SMASHER.
FIRST ORDER OF BUSINESS: WE AVENGE OUR DEAD BROTHERS AND KILL DEADPOOL AND ANYONE CLOSE TO HIM!

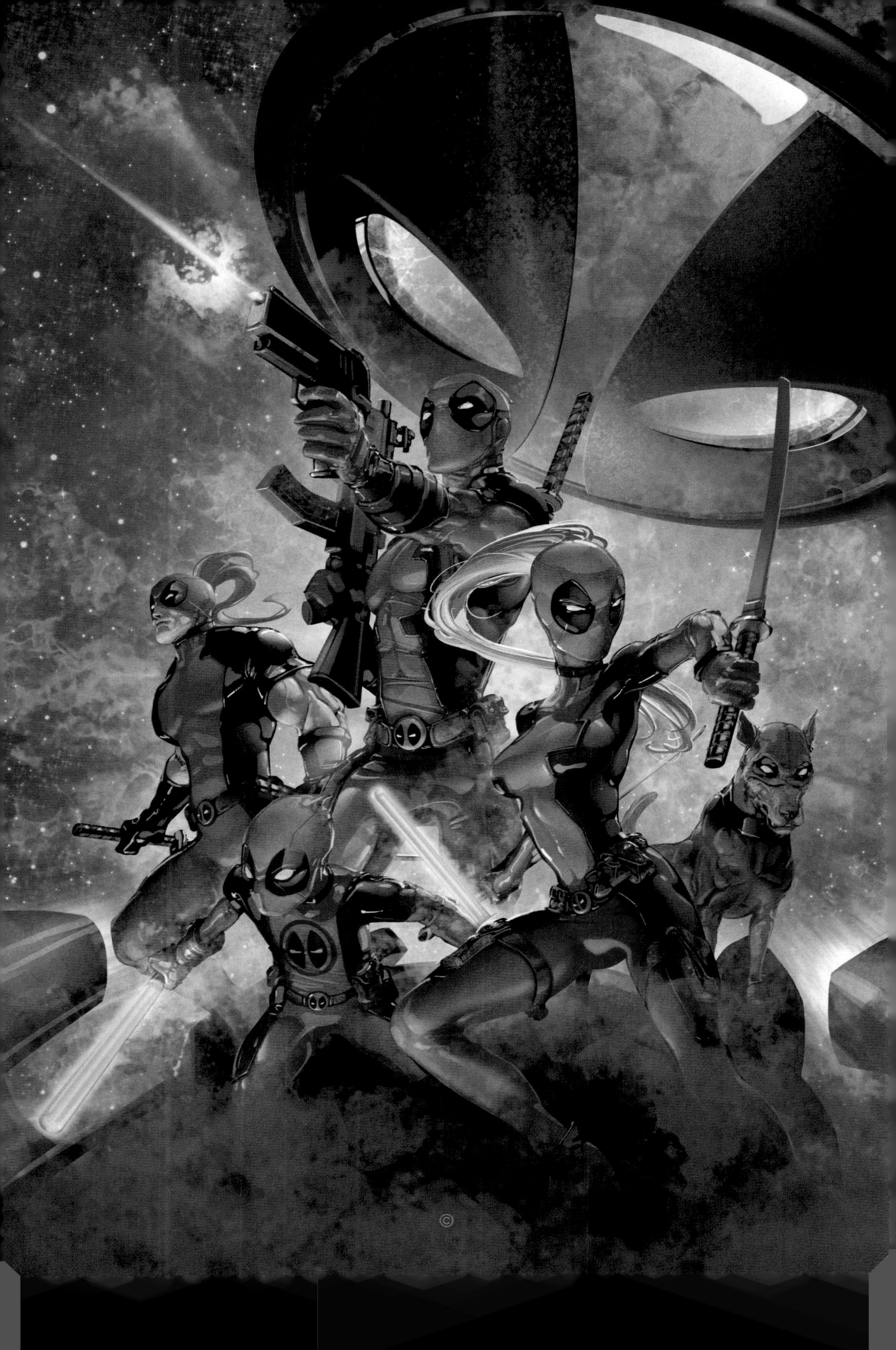

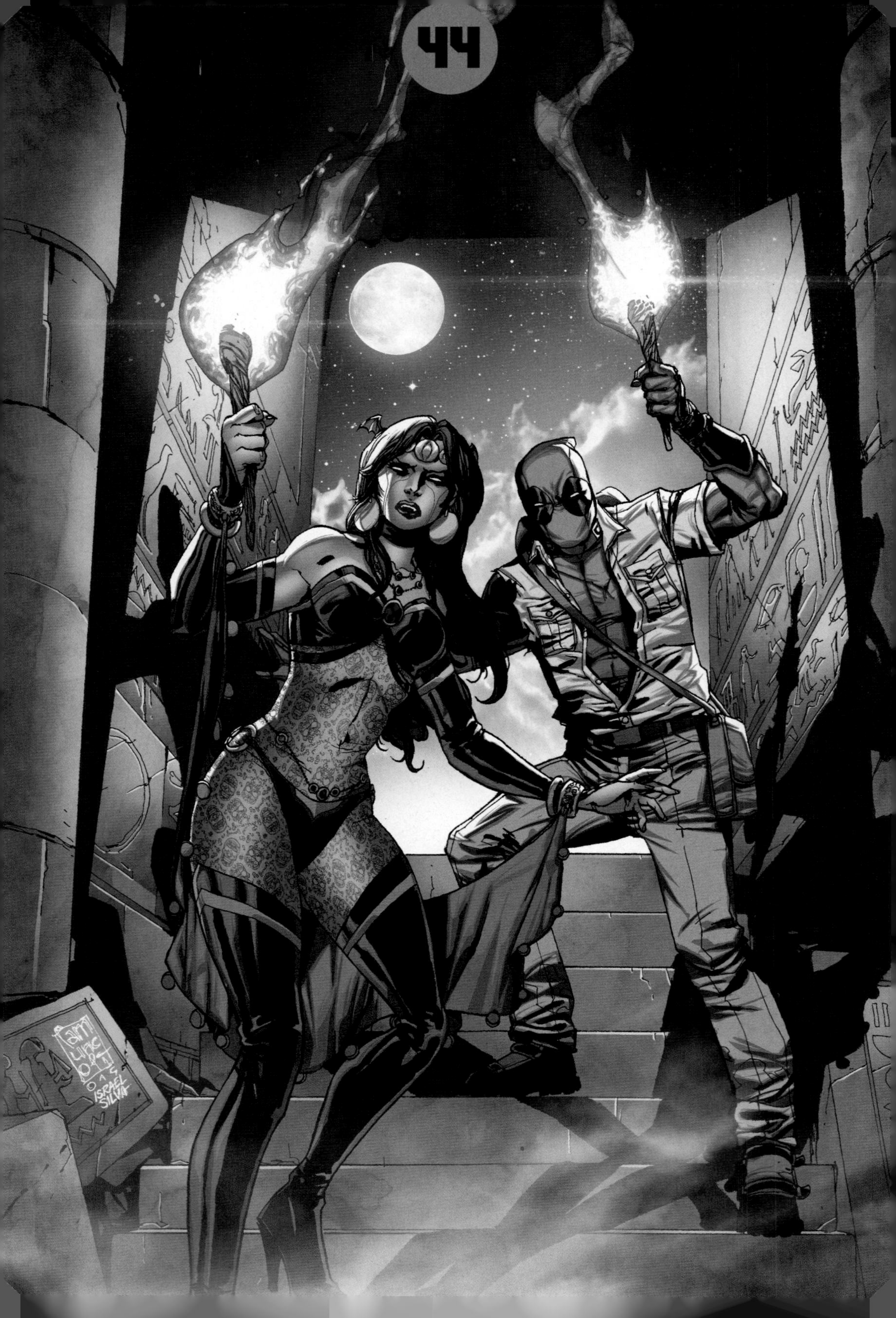
44
ISRAEL SILVA

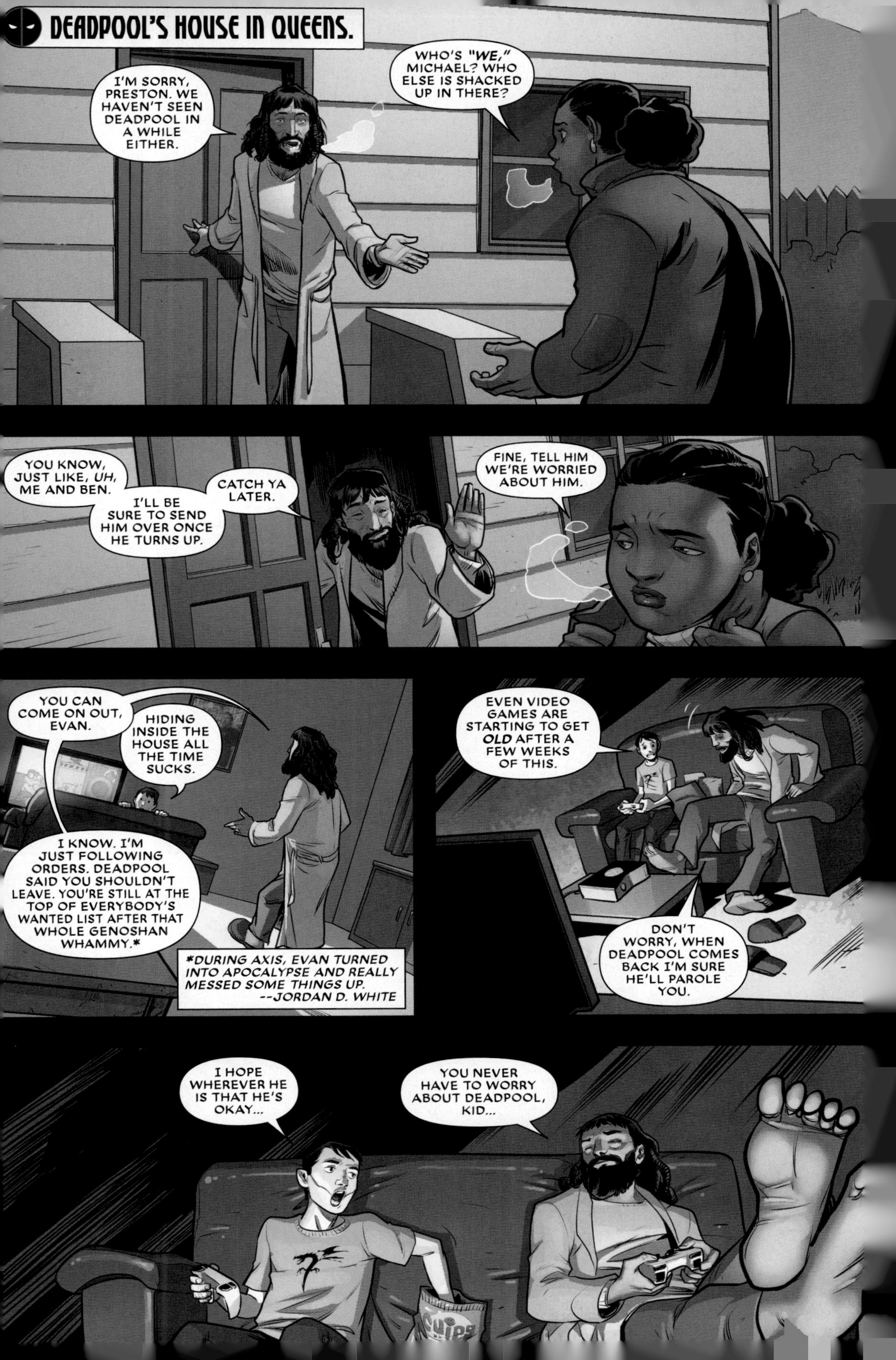
DEADPOOL'S HOUSE IN QUEENS.
I'M SORRY, PRESTON. WE HAVEN'T SEEN DEADPOOL IN A WHILE EITHER.
WHO'S "WE," MICHAEL? WHO ELSE IS SHACKED UP IN THERE?
YOU KNOW, JUST LIKE, UH, ME AND BEN.
I'LL BE SURE TO SEND HIM OVER ONCE HE TURNS UP.
CATCH YA LATER.
FINE, TELL HIM WE'RE WORRIED ABOUT HIM.
YOU CAN COME ON OUT, EVAN.
HIDING INSIDE THE HOUSE ALL THE TIME SUCKS.
I KNOW. I'M JUST FOLLOWING ORDERS. DEADPOOL SAID YOU SHOULDN'T LEAVE. YOU'RE STILL AT THE TOP OF EVERYBODY'S WANTED LIST AFTER THAT WHOLE GENOSHAN WHAMMY.*
*DURING AXIS, EVAN TURNED INTO APOCALYPSE AND REALLY MESSED SOME THINGS UP. --JORDAN D. WHITE
EVEN VIDEO GAMES ARE STARTING TO GET OLD AFTER A FEW WEEKS OF THIS.
DON'T WORRY, WHEN DEADPOOL COMES BACK I'M SURE HE'LL PAROLE YOU.
I HOPE WHEREVER HE IS THAT HE'S OKAY...
YOU NEVER HAVE TO WORRY ABOUT DEADPOOL, KID...
CHIPS

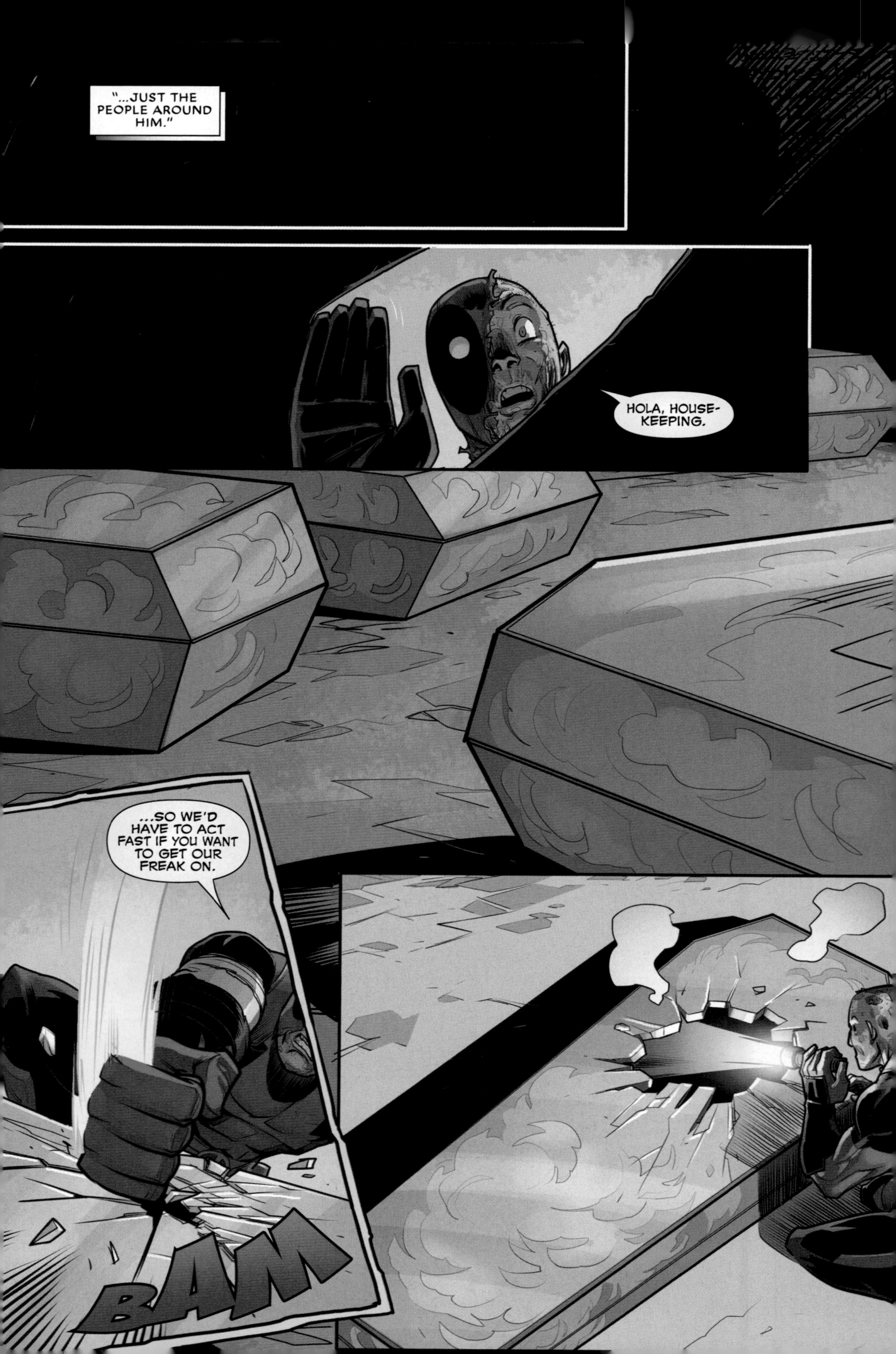
"...JUST THE PEOPLE AROUND HIM."
HOLA, HOUSE-KEEPING.
...SO WE'D HAVE TO ACT FAST IF YOU WANT TO GET OUR FREAK ON.
BAM

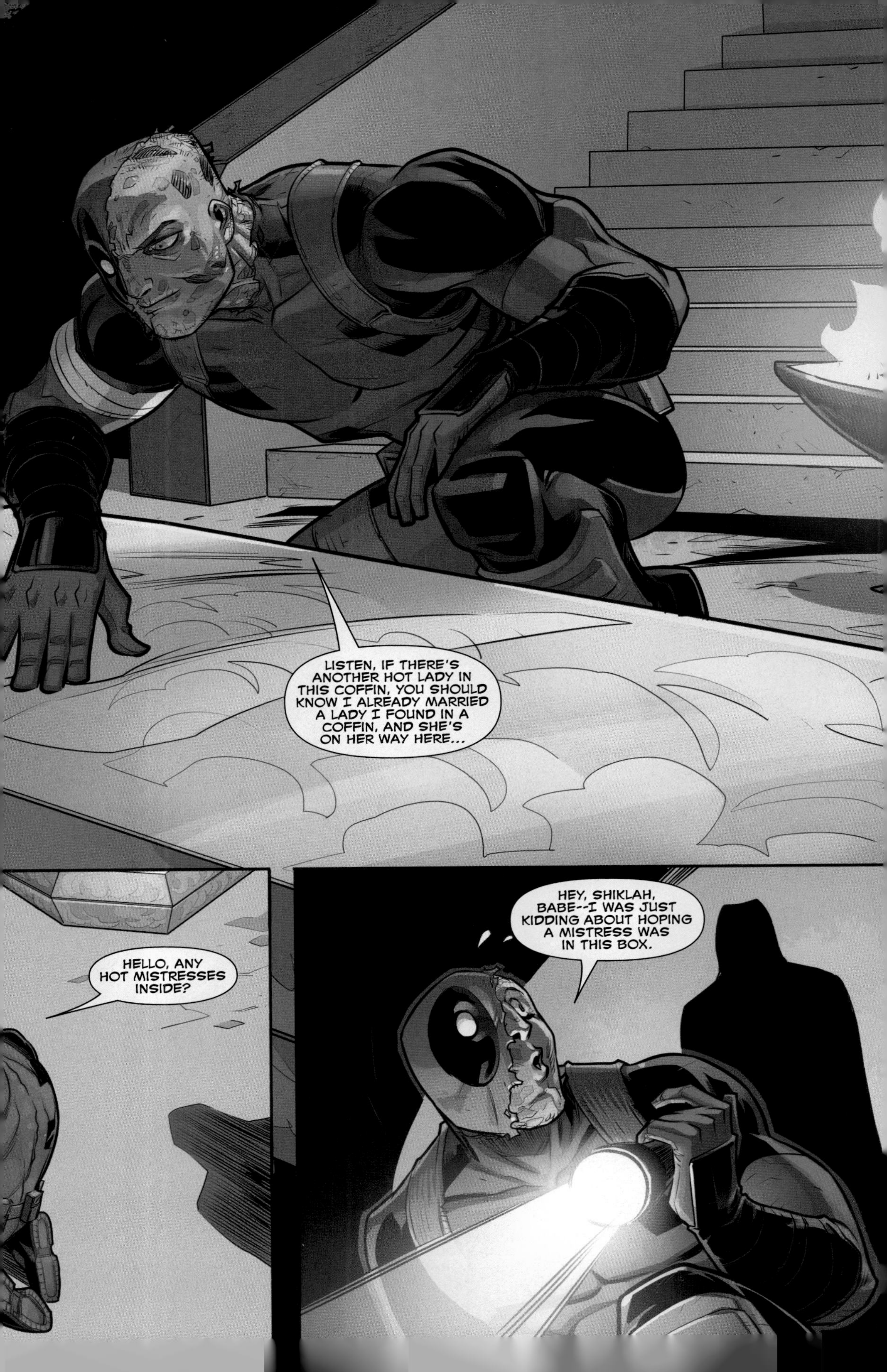
LISTEN, IF THERE'S ANOTHER HOT LADY IN THIS COFFIN, YOU SHOULD KNOW I ALREADY MARRIED A LADY I FOUND IN A COFFIN, AND SHE'S ON HER WAY HERE...
HELLO, ANY HOT MISTRESSES INSIDE?
HEY, SHIKLAH, BABE--I WAS JUST KIDDING ABOUT HOPING A MISTRESS WAS IN THIS BOX.

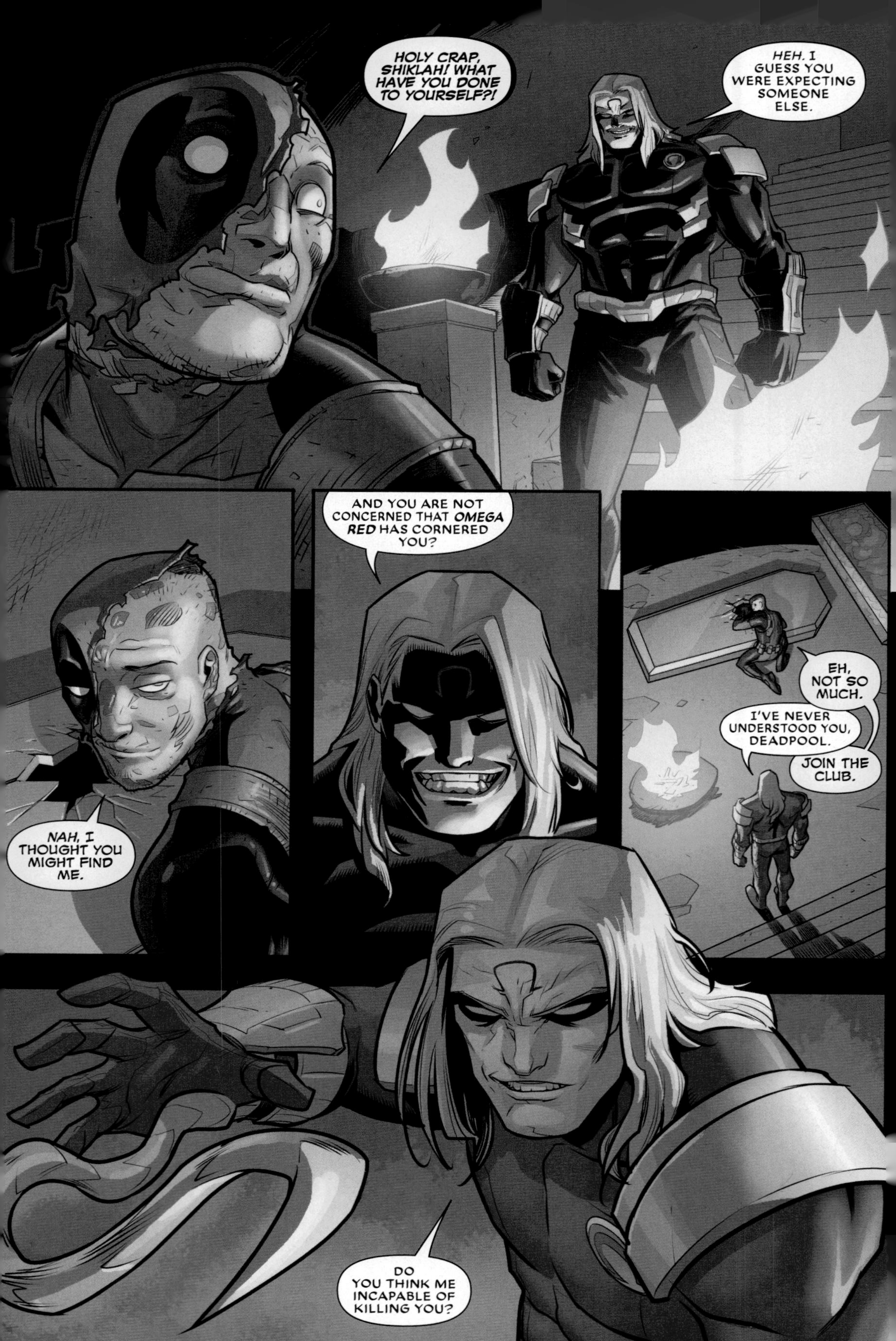
HOLY CRAP, SHIKLAH! WHAT HAVE YOU DONE TO YOURSELF?!
HEH. I GUESS YOU WERE EXPECTING SOMEONE ELSE.
NAH, I THOUGHT YOU MIGHT FIND ME.
AND YOU ARE NOT CONCERNED THAT OMEGA RED HAS CORNERED YOU?
EH, NOT SO MUCH.
I'VE NEVER UNDERSTOOD YOU, DEADPOOL.
JOIN THE CLUB.
DO YOU THINK ME INCAPABLE OF KILLING YOU?

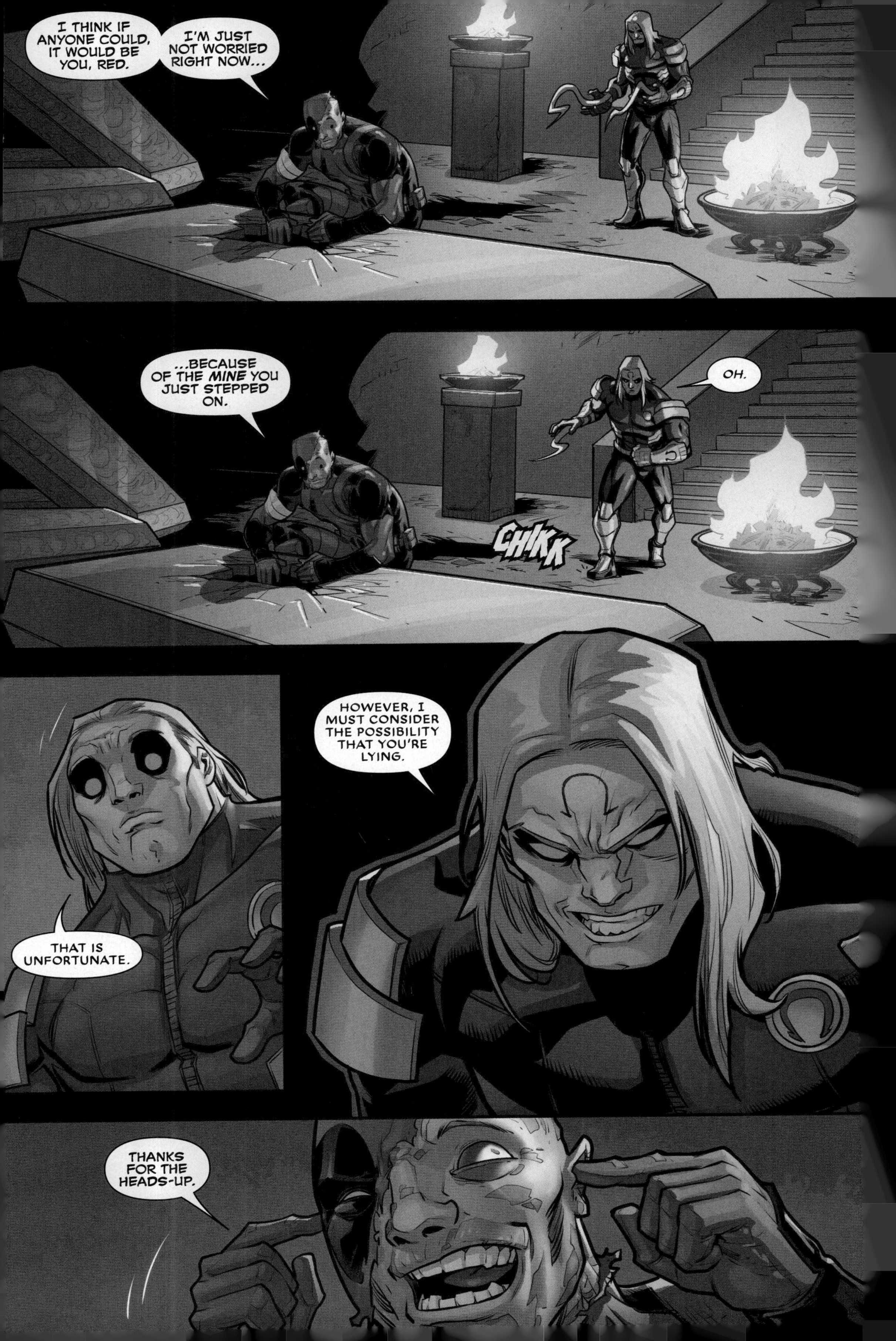
I THINK IF ANYONE COULD, IT WOULD BE YOU, RED.
I'M JUST NOT WORRIED RIGHT NOW...
...BECAUSE OF THE *MINE* YOU JUST STEPPED ON.
OH.
CHIKK
HOWEVER, I MUST CONSIDER THE POSSIBILITY THAT YOU'RE LYING.
THAT IS UNFORTUNATE.
THANKS FOR THE HEADS-UP.

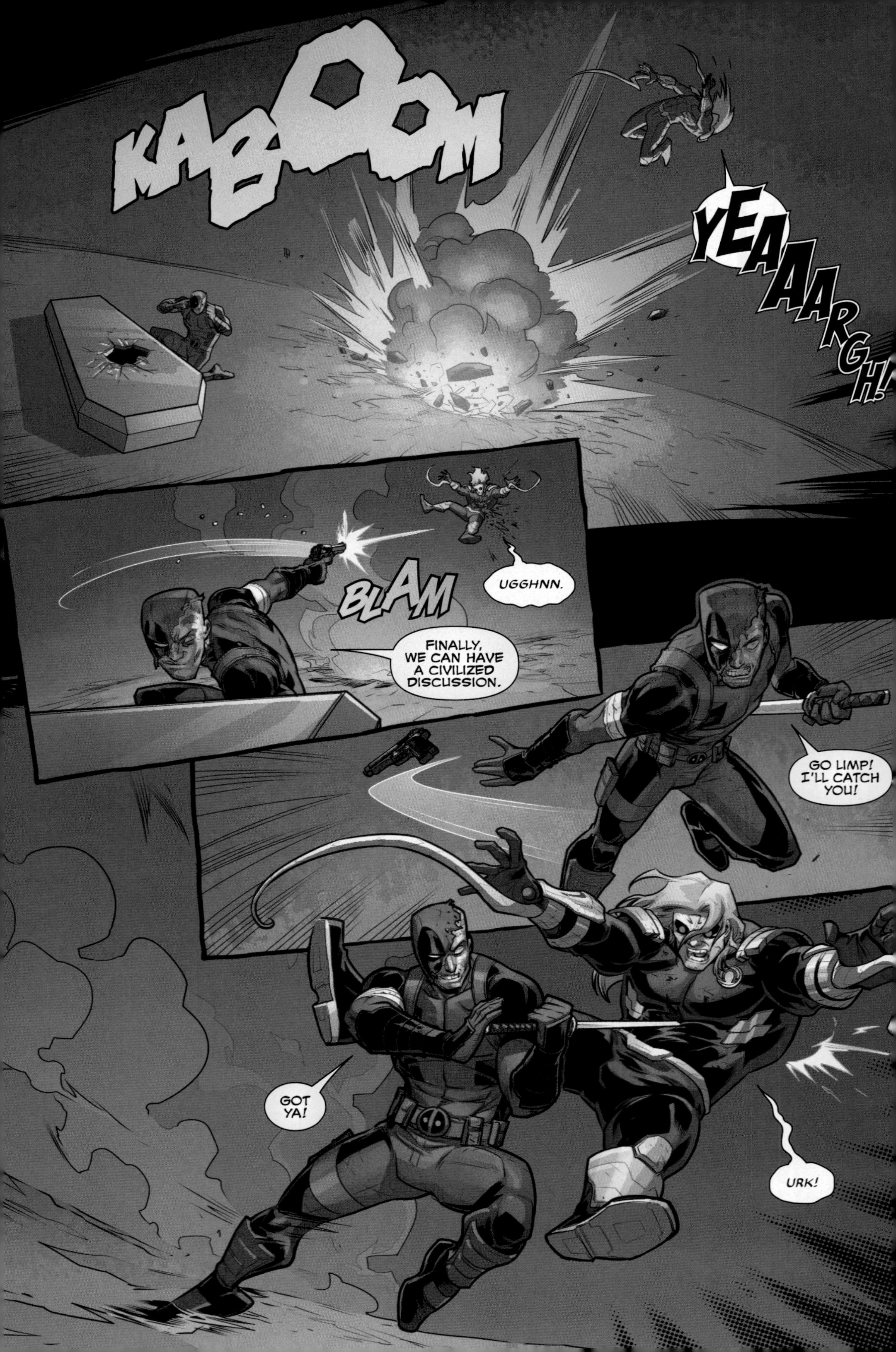
KABOOOM
YEAAAARGH!
BLAM
UGGHNN.
FINALLY, WE CAN HAVE A CIVILIZED DISCUSSION.
GO LIMP! I'LL CATCH YOU!
GOT YA!
URK!

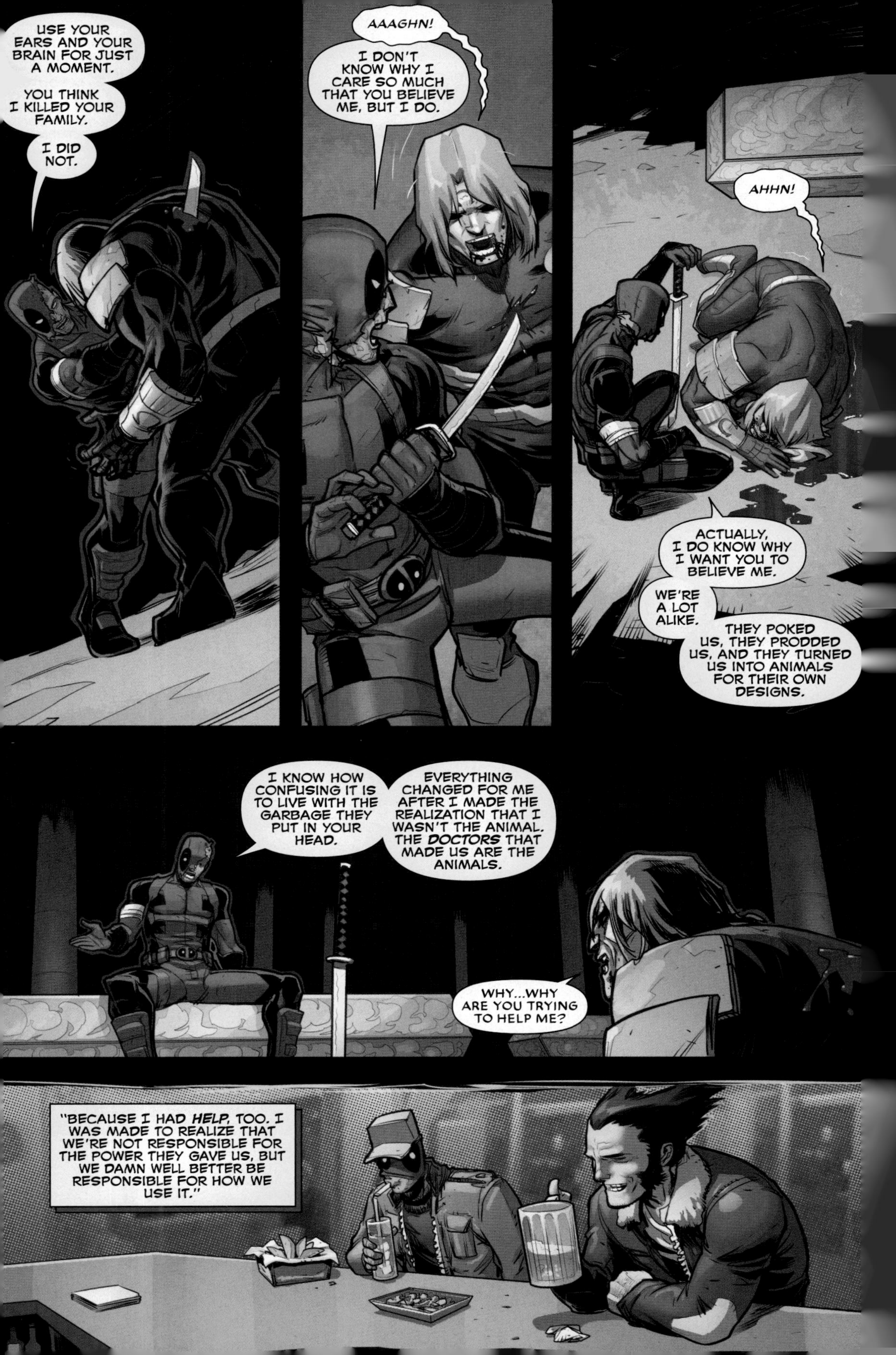
USE YOUR EARS AND YOUR BRAIN FOR JUST A MOMENT.
YOU THINK I KILLED YOUR FAMILY.
I DID NOT.
AAAGHN!
I DON'T KNOW WHY I CARE SO MUCH THAT YOU BELIEVE ME, BUT I DO.
AHHN!
ACTUALLY, I DO KNOW WHY I WANT YOU TO BELIEVE ME.
WE'RE A LOT ALIKE.
THEY POKED US, THEY PRODDED US, AND THEY TURNED US INTO ANIMALS FOR THEIR OWN DESIGNS.
I KNOW HOW CONFUSING IT IS TO LIVE WITH THE GARBAGE THEY PUT IN YOUR HEAD.
EVERYTHING CHANGED FOR ME AFTER I MADE THE REALIZATION THAT I WASN'T THE ANIMAL. THE DOCTORS THAT MADE US ARE THE ANIMALS.
WHY...WHY ARE YOU TRYING TO HELP ME?
"BECAUSE I HAD HELP, TOO. I WAS MADE TO REALIZE THAT WE'RE NOT RESPONSIBLE FOR THE POWER THEY GAVE US, BUT WE DAMN WELL BETTER BE RESPONSIBLE FOR HOW WE USE IT."

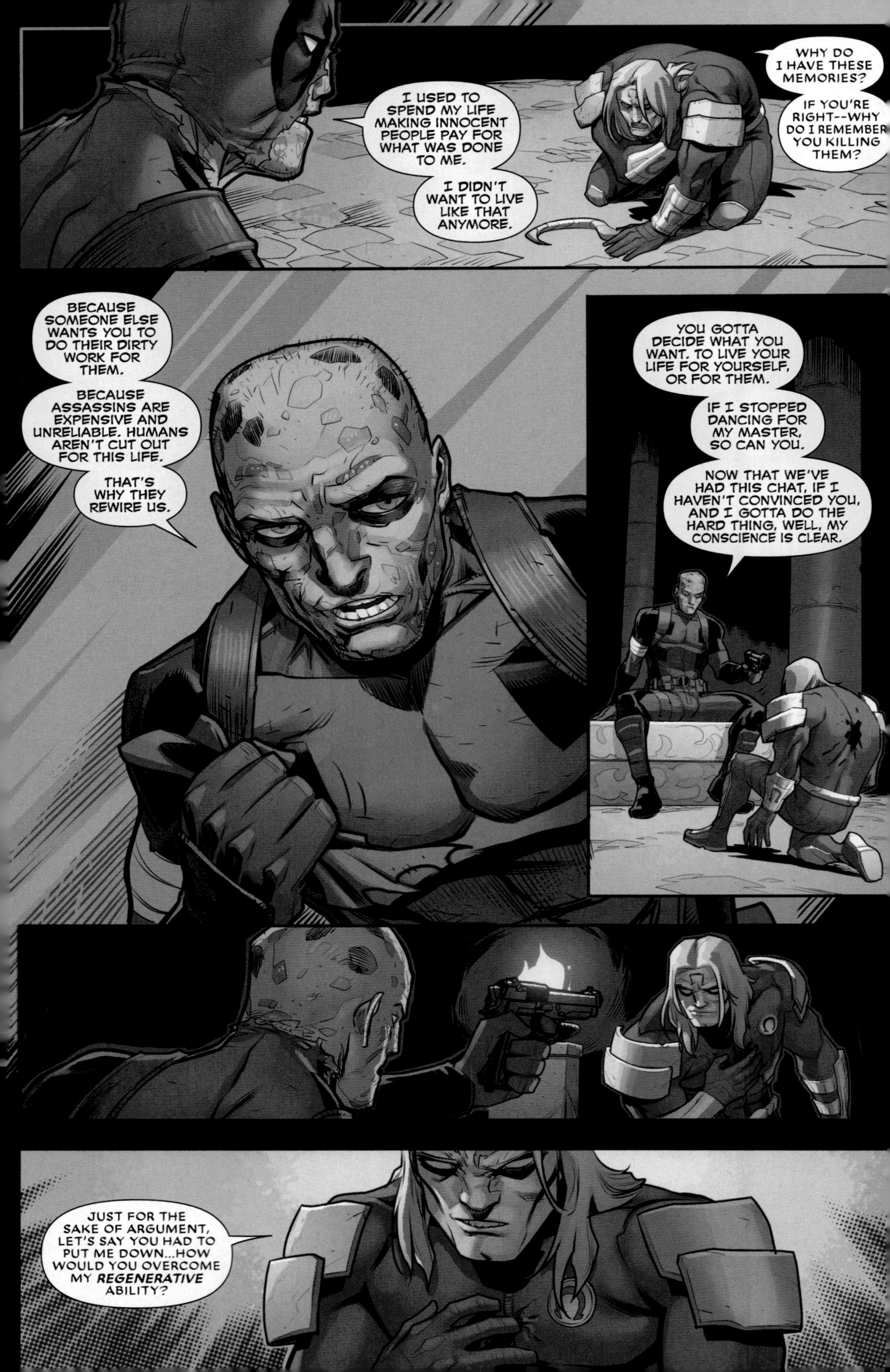
I USED TO SPEND MY LIFE MAKING INNOCENT PEOPLE PAY FOR WHAT WAS DONE TO ME.
I DIDN'T WANT TO LIVE LIKE THAT ANYMORE.
WHY DO I HAVE THESE MEMORIES?
IF YOU'RE RIGHT--WHY DO I REMEMBER YOU KILLING THEM?
BECAUSE SOMEONE ELSE WANTS YOU TO DO THEIR DIRTY WORK FOR THEM.
BECAUSE ASSASSINS ARE EXPENSIVE AND UNRELIABLE. HUMANS AREN'T CUT OUT FOR THIS LIFE.
THAT'S WHY THEY REWIRE US.
YOU GOTTA DECIDE WHAT YOU WANT. TO LIVE YOUR LIFE FOR YOURSELF, OR FOR THEM.
IF I STOPPED DANCING FOR MY MASTER, SO CAN YOU.
NOW THAT WE'VE HAD THIS CHAT, IF I HAVEN'T CONVINCED YOU, AND I GOTTA DO THE HARD THING, WELL, MY CONSCIENCE IS CLEAR.
JUST FOR THE SAKE OF ARGUMENT, LET'S SAY YOU HAD TO PUT ME DOWN...HOW WOULD YOU OVERCOME MY *REGENERATIVE* ABILITY?

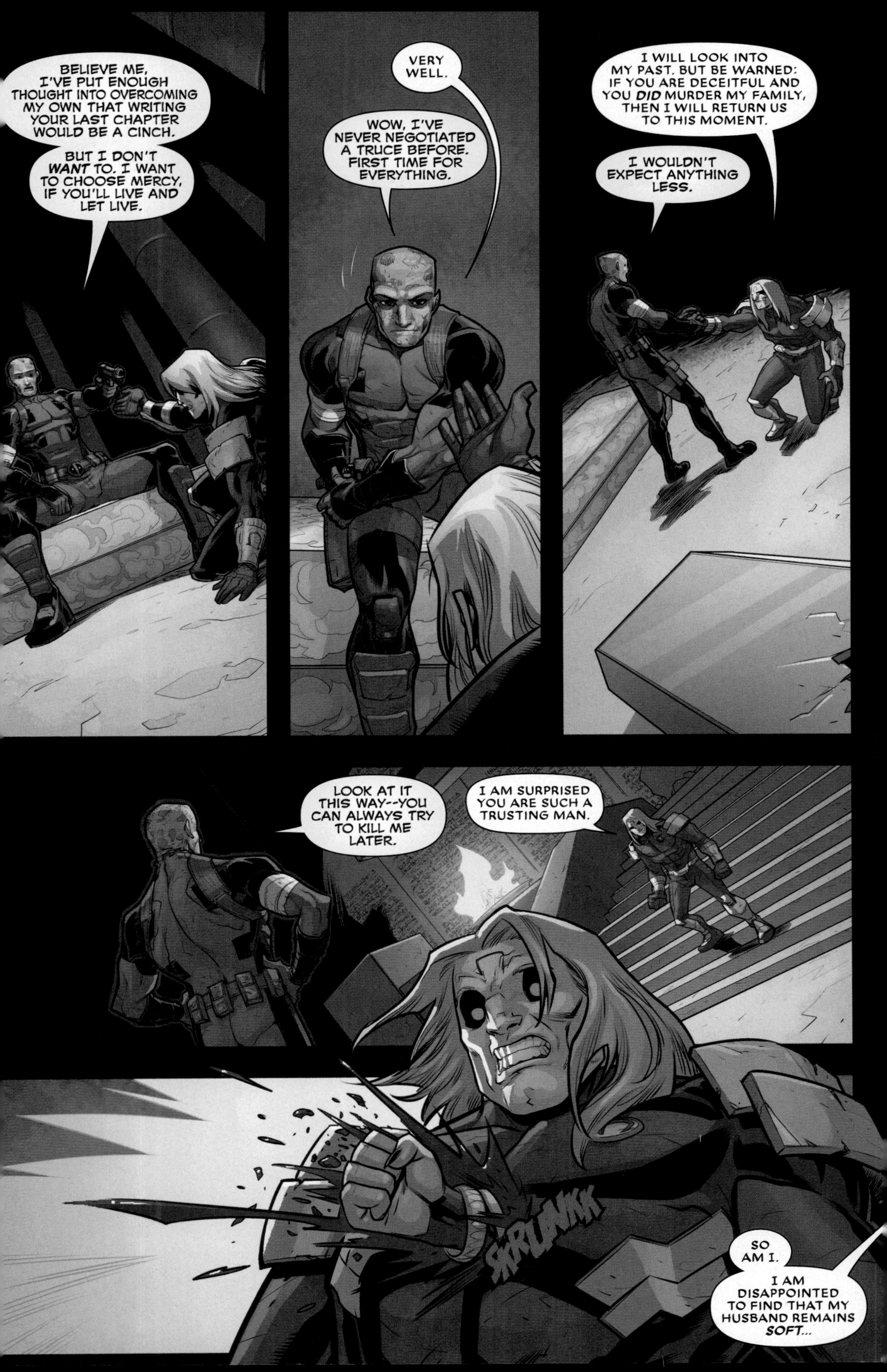
BELIEVE ME, I'VE PUT ENOUGH THOUGHT INTO OVERCOMING MY OWN THAT WRITING YOUR LAST CHAPTER WOULD BE A CINCH.
BUT I DON'T WANT TO. I WANT TO CHOOSE MERCY, IF YOU'LL LIVE AND LET LIVE.
VERY WELL.
WOW, I'VE NEVER NEGOTIATED A TRUCE BEFORE. FIRST TIME FOR EVERYTHING.
I WILL LOOK INTO MY PAST. BUT BE WARNED: IF YOU ARE DECEITFUL AND YOU DID MURDER MY FAMILY, THEN I WILL RETURN US TO THIS MOMENT.
I WOULDN'T EXPECT ANYTHING LESS.
LOOK AT IT THIS WAY--YOU CAN ALWAYS TRY TO KILL ME LATER.
I AM SURPRISED YOU ARE SUCH A TRUSTING MAN.
SKRUNKK
SO AM I.
I AM DISAPPOINTED TO FIND THAT MY HUSBAND REMAINS SOFT...

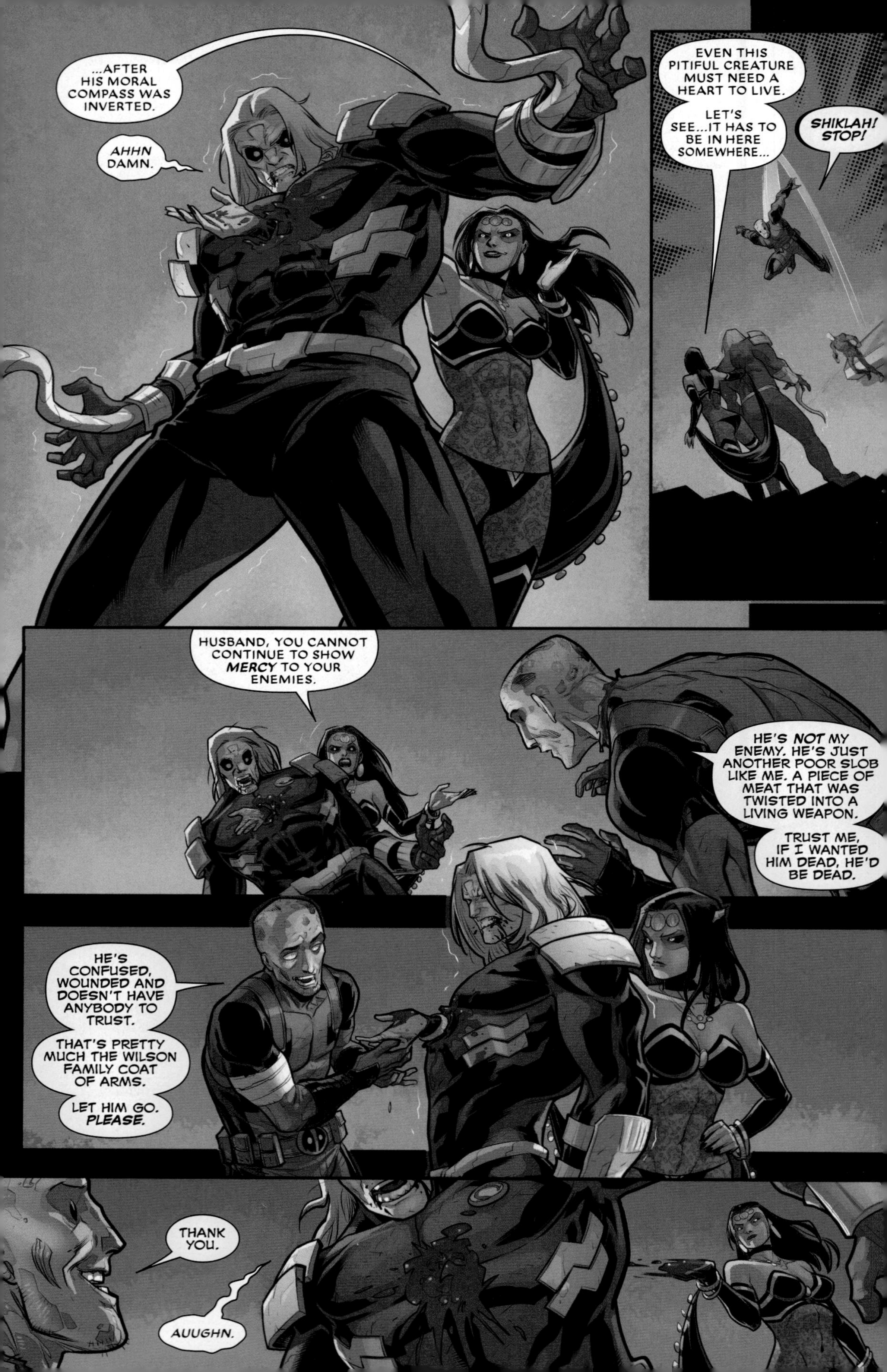
...AFTER HIS MORAL COMPASS WAS INVERTED.
AHHN DAMN.
EVEN THIS PITIFUL CREATURE MUST NEED A HEART TO LIVE.
LET'S SEE...IT HAS TO BE IN HERE SOMEWHERE...
SHIKLAH! STOP!
HUSBAND, YOU CANNOT CONTINUE TO SHOW MERCY TO YOUR ENEMIES.
HE'S NOT MY ENEMY. HE'S JUST ANOTHER POOR SLOB LIKE ME. A PIECE OF MEAT THAT WAS TWISTED INTO A LIVING WEAPON.
TRUST ME, IF I WANTED HIM DEAD, HE'D BE DEAD.
HE'S CONFUSED, WOUNDED AND DOESN'T HAVE ANYBODY TO TRUST.
THAT'S PRETTY MUCH THE WILSON FAMILY COAT OF ARMS.
LET HIM GO. PLEASE.
THANK YOU.
AUUGHN.

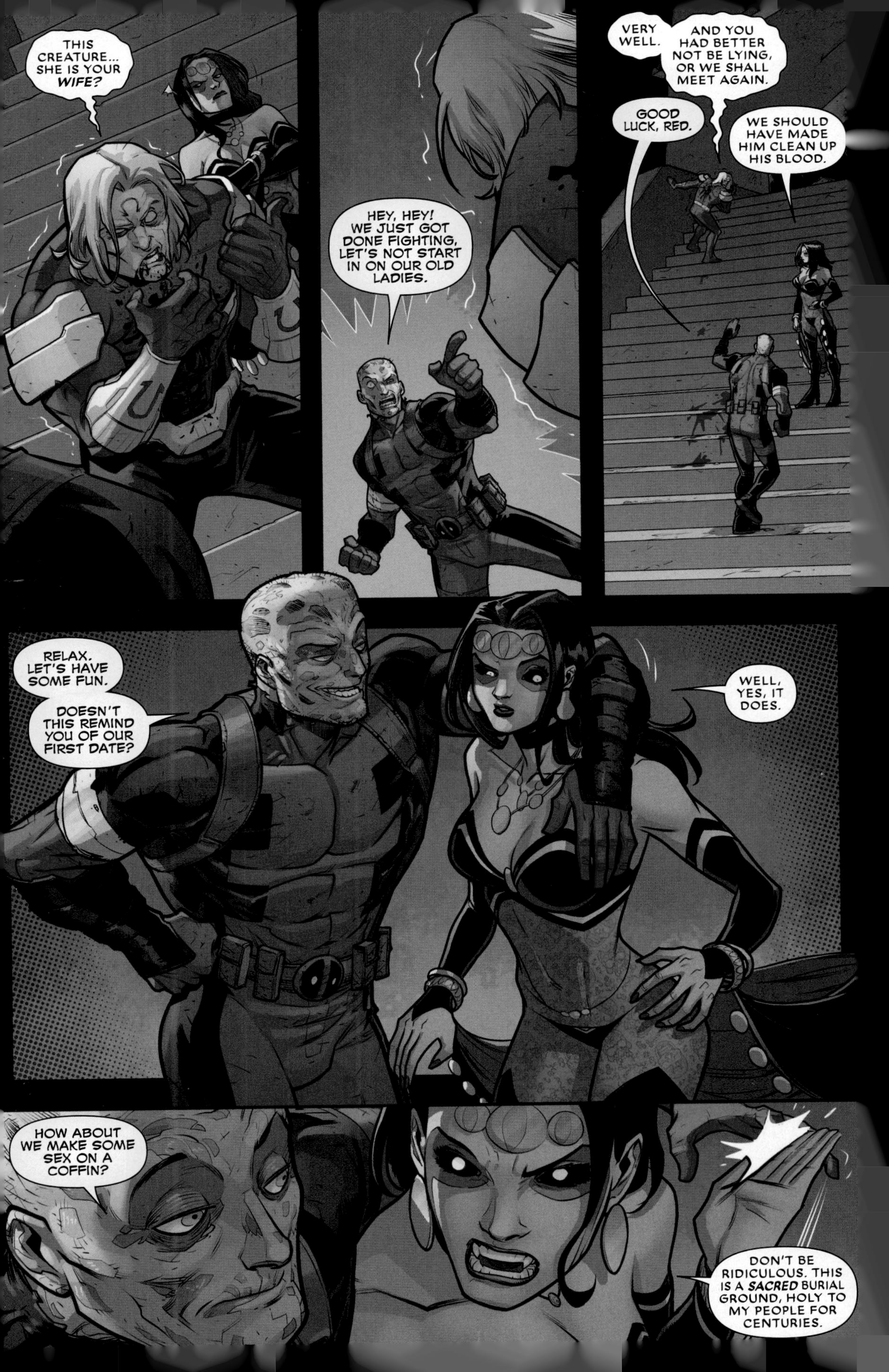
THIS CREATURE... SHE IS YOUR *WIFE*?
HEY, HEY! WE JUST GOT DONE FIGHTING, LET'S NOT START IN ON OUR OLD LADIES.
VERY WELL.
AND YOU HAD BETTER NOT BE LYING, OR WE SHALL MEET AGAIN.
GOOD LUCK, RED.
WE SHOULD HAVE MADE HIM CLEAN UP HIS BLOOD.
RELAX. LET'S HAVE SOME FUN.
DOESN'T THIS REMIND YOU OF OUR FIRST DATE?
WELL, YES, IT DOES.
HOW ABOUT WE MAKE SOME SEX ON A COFFIN?
DON'T BE RIDICULOUS. THIS IS A *SACRED* BURIAL GROUND, HOLY TO MY PEOPLE FOR CENTURIES.

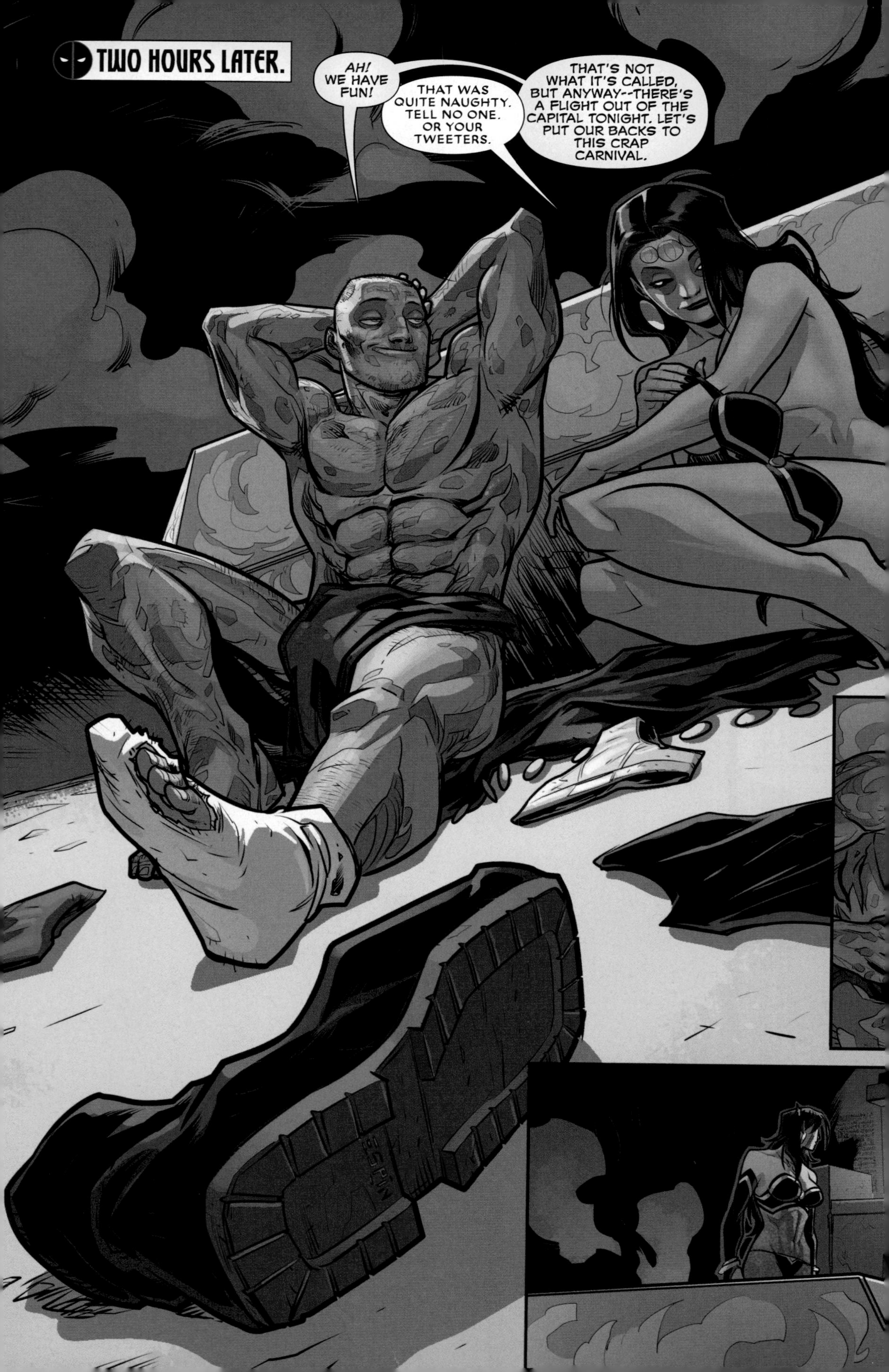
TWO HOURS LATER.
AH! WE HAVE FUN!
THAT WAS QUITE NAUGHTY. TELL NO ONE. OR YOUR TWEETERS.
THAT'S NOT WHAT IT'S CALLED, BUT ANYWAY--THERE'S A FLIGHT OUT OF THE CAPITAL TONIGHT. LET'S PUT OUR BACKS TO THIS CRAP CARNIVAL.

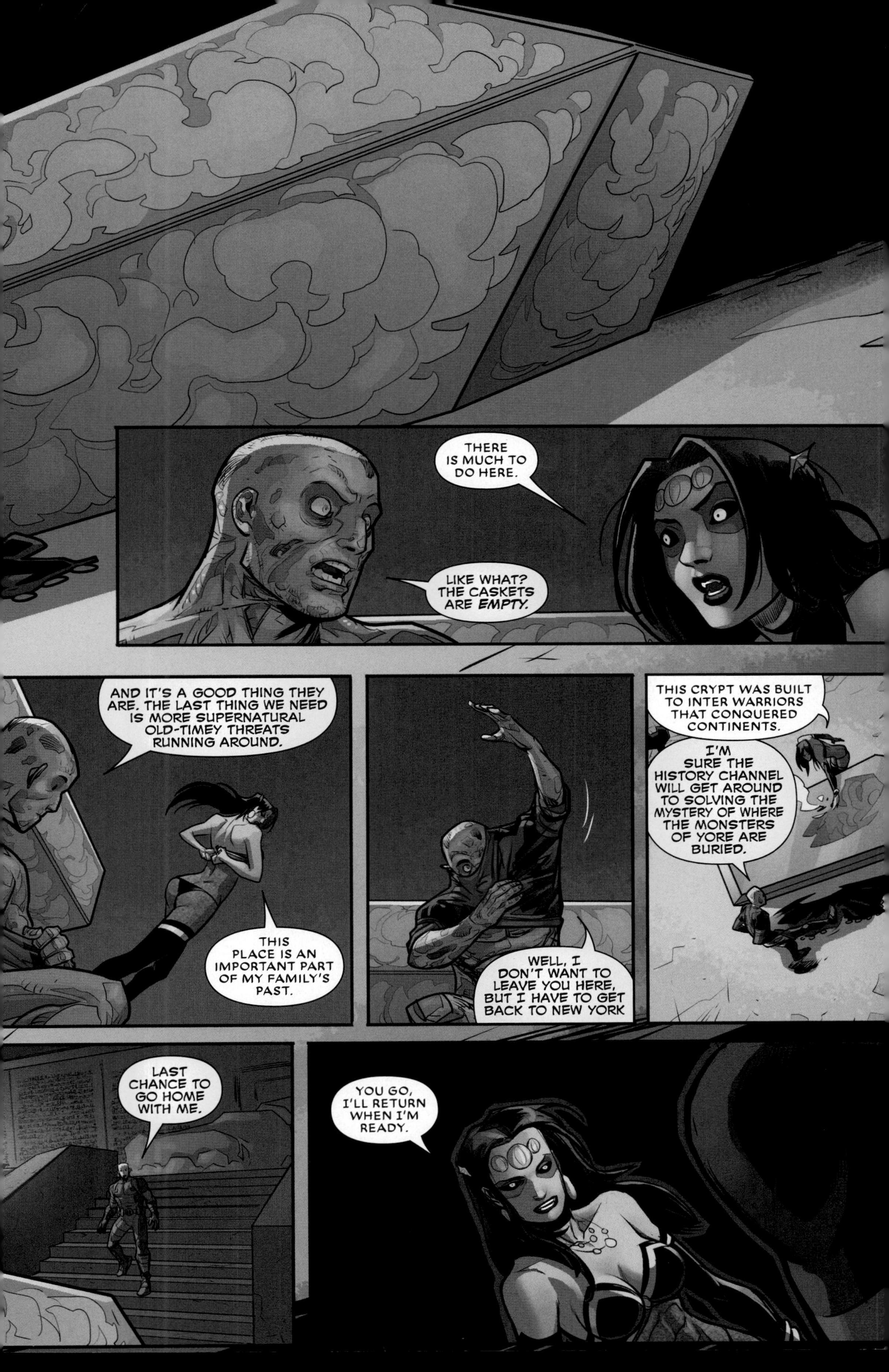
THERE IS MUCH TO DO HERE.
LIKE WHAT? THE CASKETS ARE *EMPTY.*
AND IT'S A GOOD THING THEY ARE. THE LAST THING WE NEED IS MORE SUPERNATURAL OLD-TIMEY THREATS RUNNING AROUND.
THIS PLACE IS AN IMPORTANT PART OF MY FAMILY'S PAST.
WELL, I DON'T WANT TO LEAVE YOU HERE, BUT I HAVE TO GET BACK TO NEW YORK
THIS CRYPT WAS BUILT TO INTER WARRIORS THAT CONQUERED CONTINENTS.
I'M SURE THE HISTORY CHANNEL WILL GET AROUND TO SOLVING THE MYSTERY OF WHERE THE MONSTERS OF YORE ARE BURIED.
LAST CHANCE TO GO HOME WITH ME.
YOU GO, I'LL RETURN WHEN I'M READY.

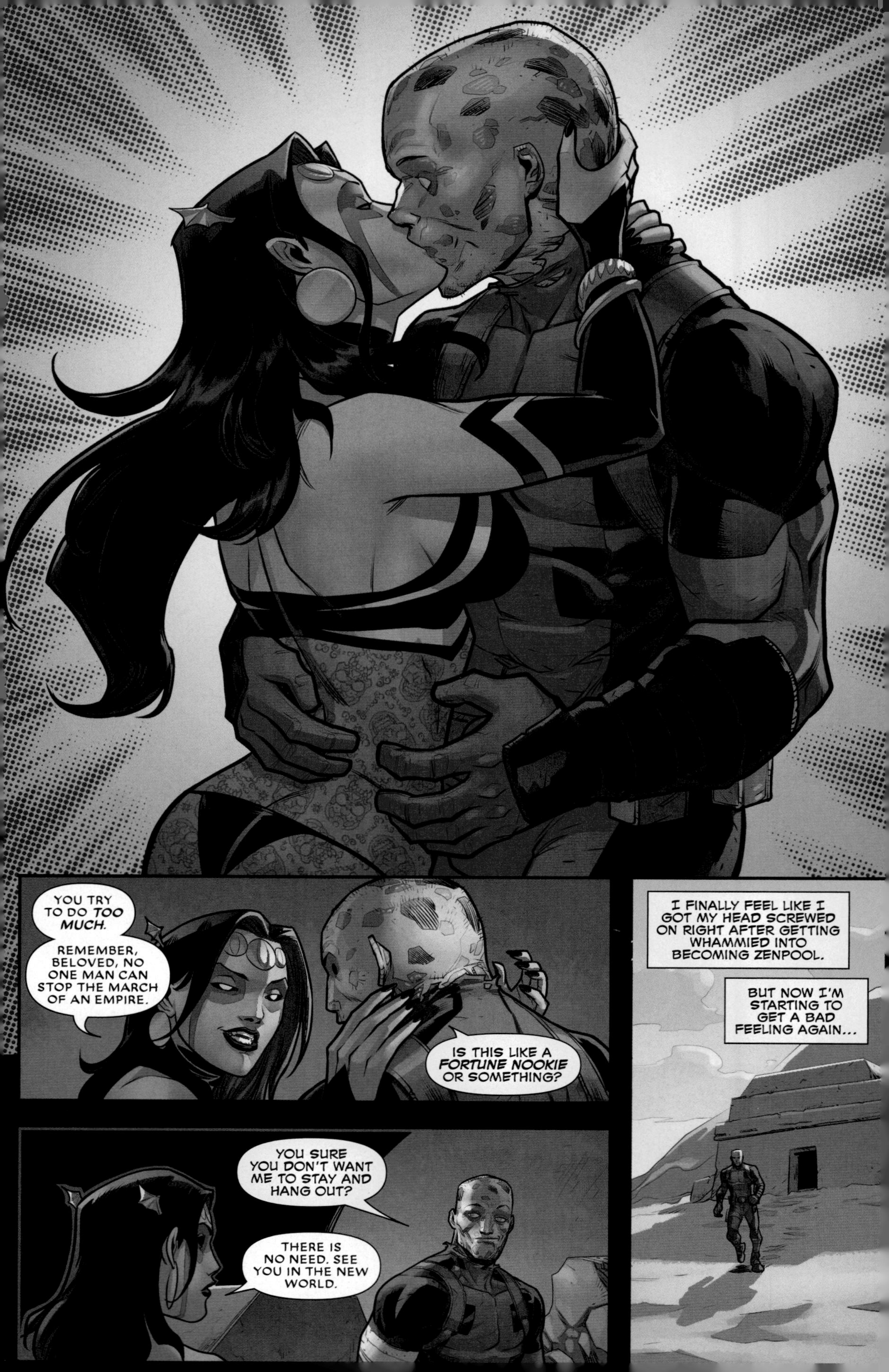

YOU TRY TO DO TOO MUCH.
REMEMBER, BELOVED, NO ONE MAN CAN STOP THE MARCH OF AN EMPIRE.
IS THIS LIKE A FORTUNE NOOKIE OR SOMETHING?
I FINALLY FEEL LIKE I GOT MY HEAD SCREWED ON RIGHT AFTER GETTING WHAMMIED INTO BECOMING ZENPOOL.
BUT NOW I'M STARTING TO GET A BAD FEELING AGAIN...
YOU SURE YOU DON'T WANT ME TO STAY AND HANG OUT?
THERE IS NO NEED. SEE YOU IN THE NEW WORLD.

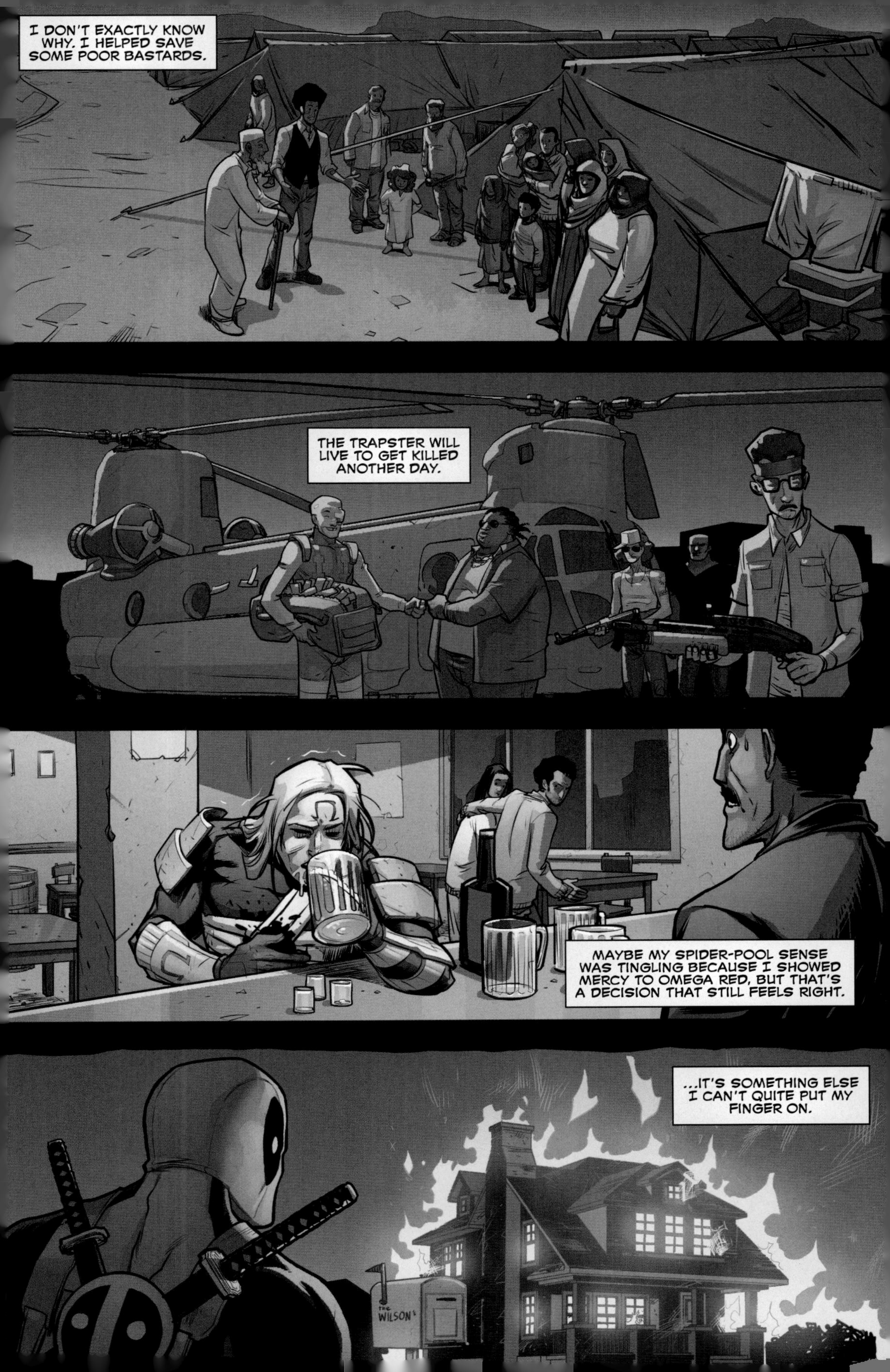
I DON'T EXACTLY KNOW WHY. I HELPED SAVE SOME POOR BASTARDS.
THE TRAPSTER WILL LIVE TO GET KILLED ANOTHER DAY.
MAYBE MY SPIDER-POOL SENSE WAS TINGLING BECAUSE I SHOWED MERCY TO OMEGA RED, BUT THAT'S A DECISION THAT STILL FEELS RIGHT.
...IT'S SOMETHING ELSE I CAN'T QUITE PUT MY FINGER ON.
THE WILSONS

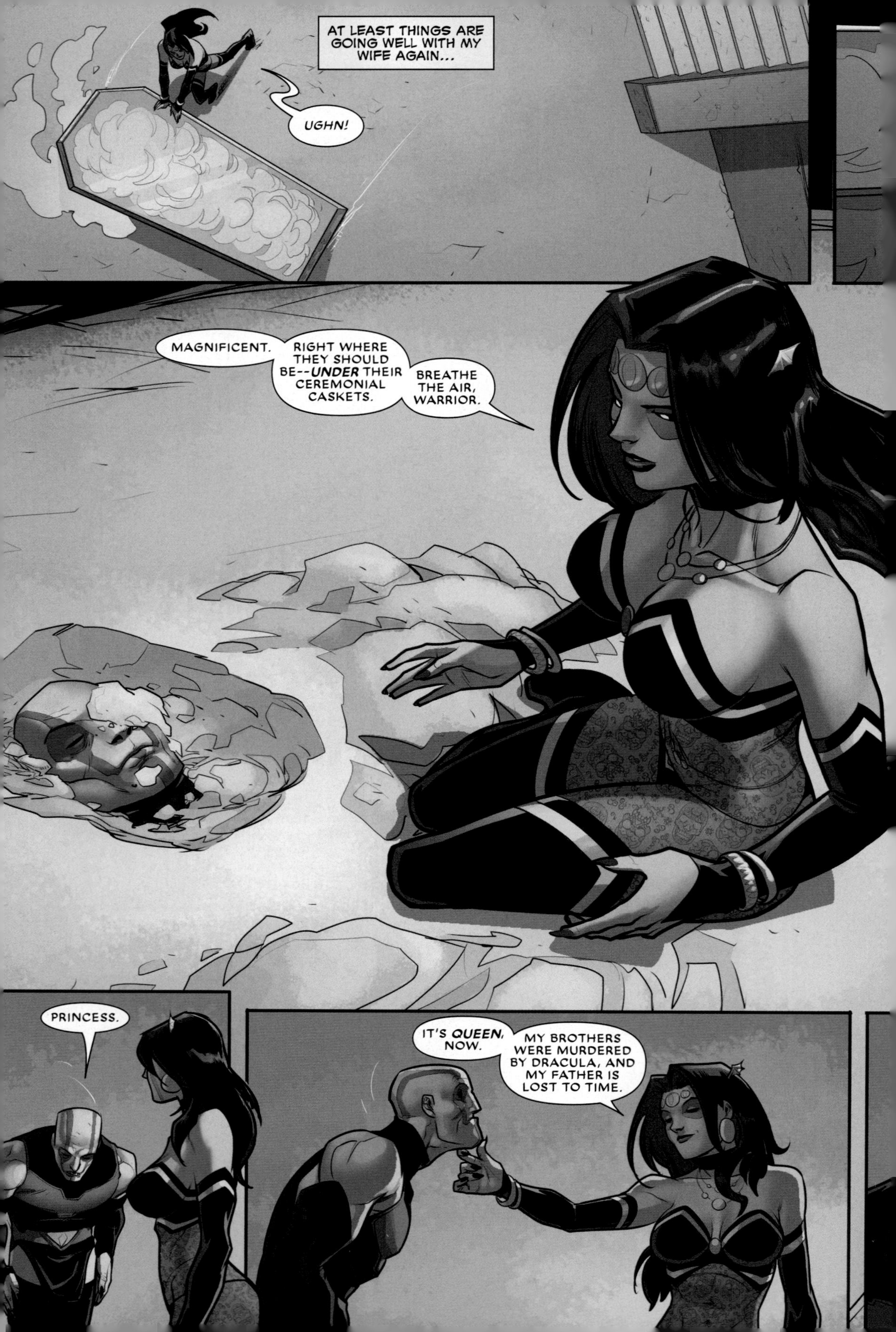
AT LEAST THINGS ARE GOING WELL WITH MY WIFE AGAIN...
UGHN!
MAGNIFICENT.
RIGHT WHERE THEY SHOULD BE--UNDER THEIR CEREMONIAL CASKETS.
BREATHE THE AIR, WARRIOR.
PRINCESS.
IT'S QUEEN, NOW.
MY BROTHERS WERE MURDERED BY DRACULA, AND MY FATHER IS LOST TO TIME.

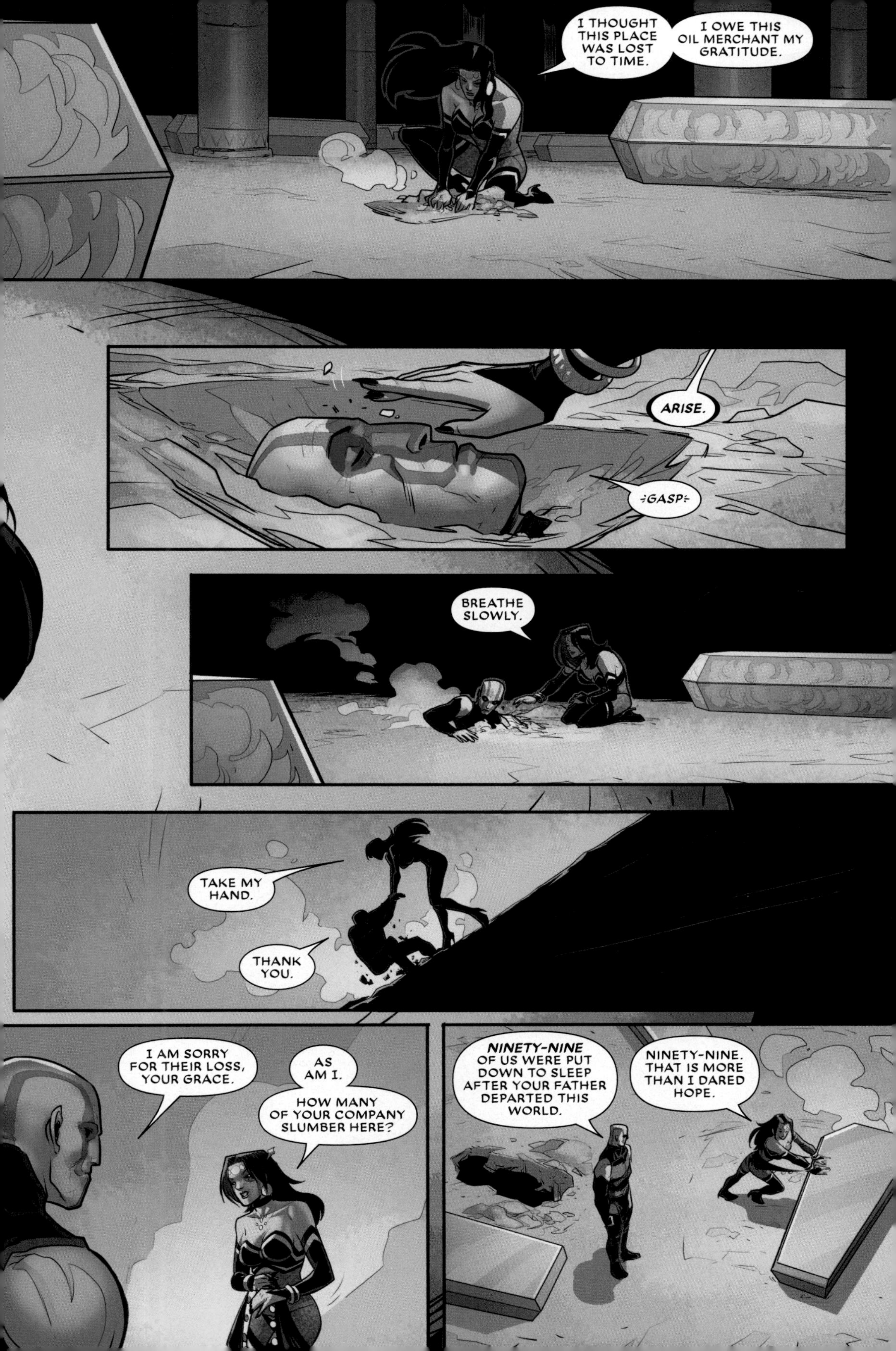
I THOUGHT THIS PLACE WAS LOST TO TIME.
I OWE THIS OIL MERCHANT MY GRATITUDE.
ARISE.
GASP
BREATHE SLOWLY.
TAKE MY HAND.
THANK YOU.
I AM SORRY FOR THEIR LOSS, YOUR GRACE.
AS AM I.
HOW MANY OF YOUR COMPANY SLUMBER HERE?
NINETY-NINE OF US WERE PUT DOWN TO SLEEP AFTER YOUR FATHER DEPARTED THIS WORLD.
NINETY-NINE. THAT IS MORE THAN I DARED HOPE.

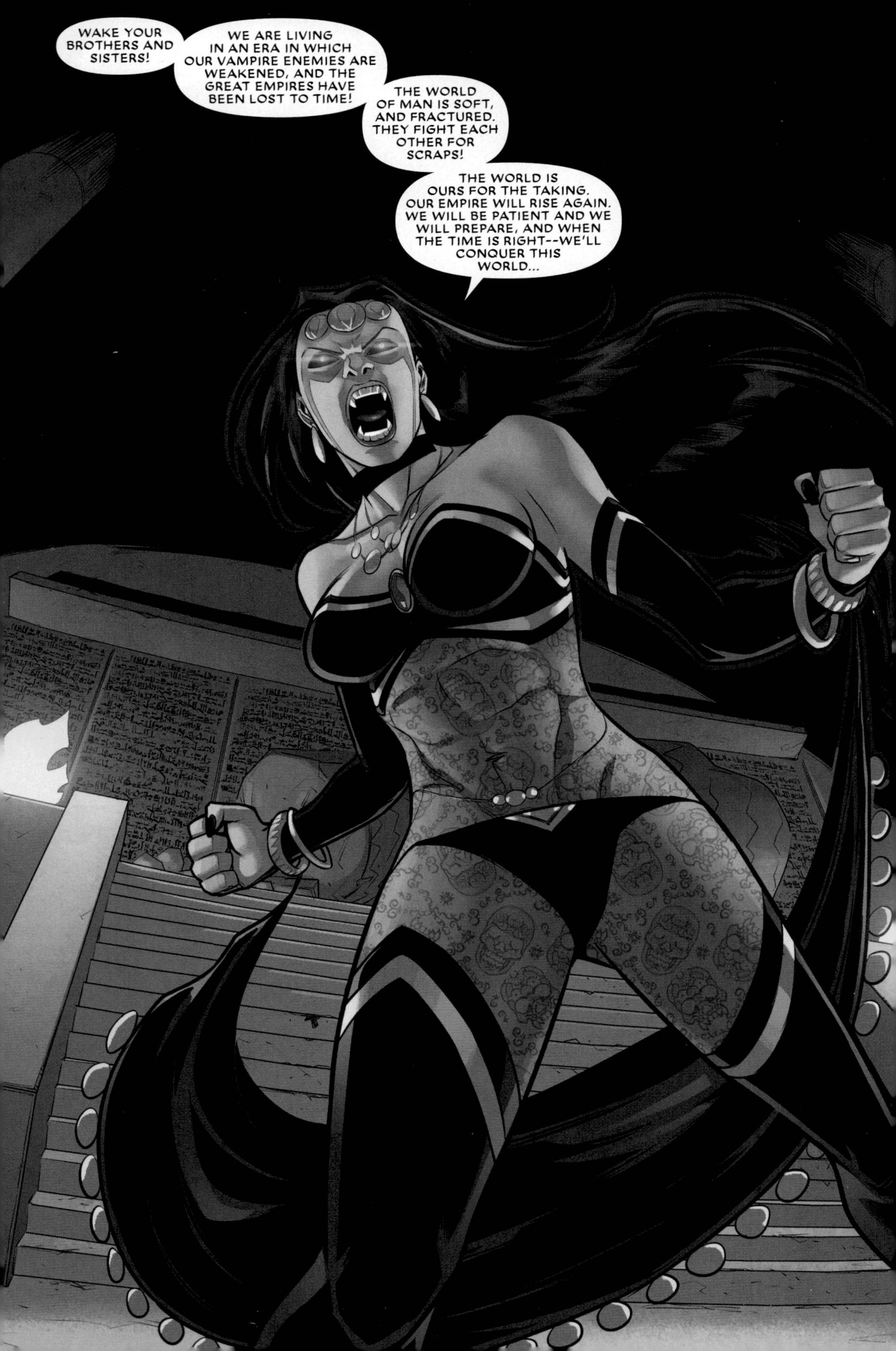
WAKE YOUR BROTHERS AND SISTERS!
WE ARE LIVING IN AN ERA IN WHICH OUR VAMPIRE ENEMIES ARE WEAKENED, AND THE GREAT EMPIRES HAVE BEEN LOST TO TIME!
THE WORLD OF MAN IS SOFT, AND FRACTURED. THEY FIGHT EACH OTHER FOR SCRAPS!
THE WORLD IS OURS FOR THE TAKING. OUR EMPIRE WILL RISE AGAIN. WE WILL BE PATIENT AND WE WILL PREPARE, AND WHEN THE TIME IS RIGHT--WE'LL CONQUER THIS WORLD...

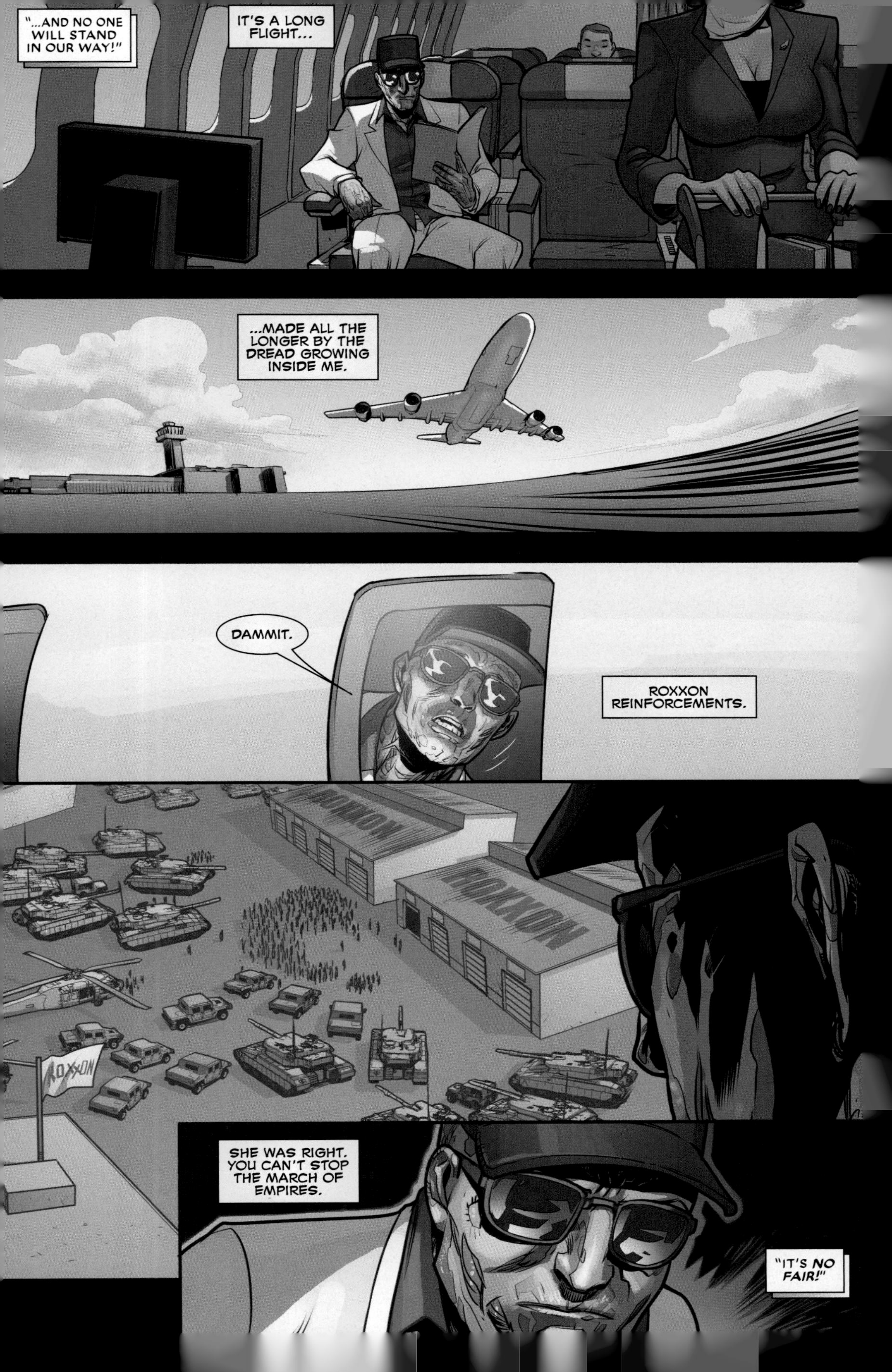
"...AND NO ONE WILL STAND IN OUR WAY!"
IT'S A LONG FLIGHT...
...MADE ALL THE LONGER BY THE DREAD GROWING INSIDE ME.
DAMMIT.
ROXXON REINFORCEMENTS.
ROXXON
ROXXON
ROXXON
SHE WAS RIGHT. YOU CAN'T STOP THE MARCH OF EMPIRES.
"IT'S NO FAIR!"

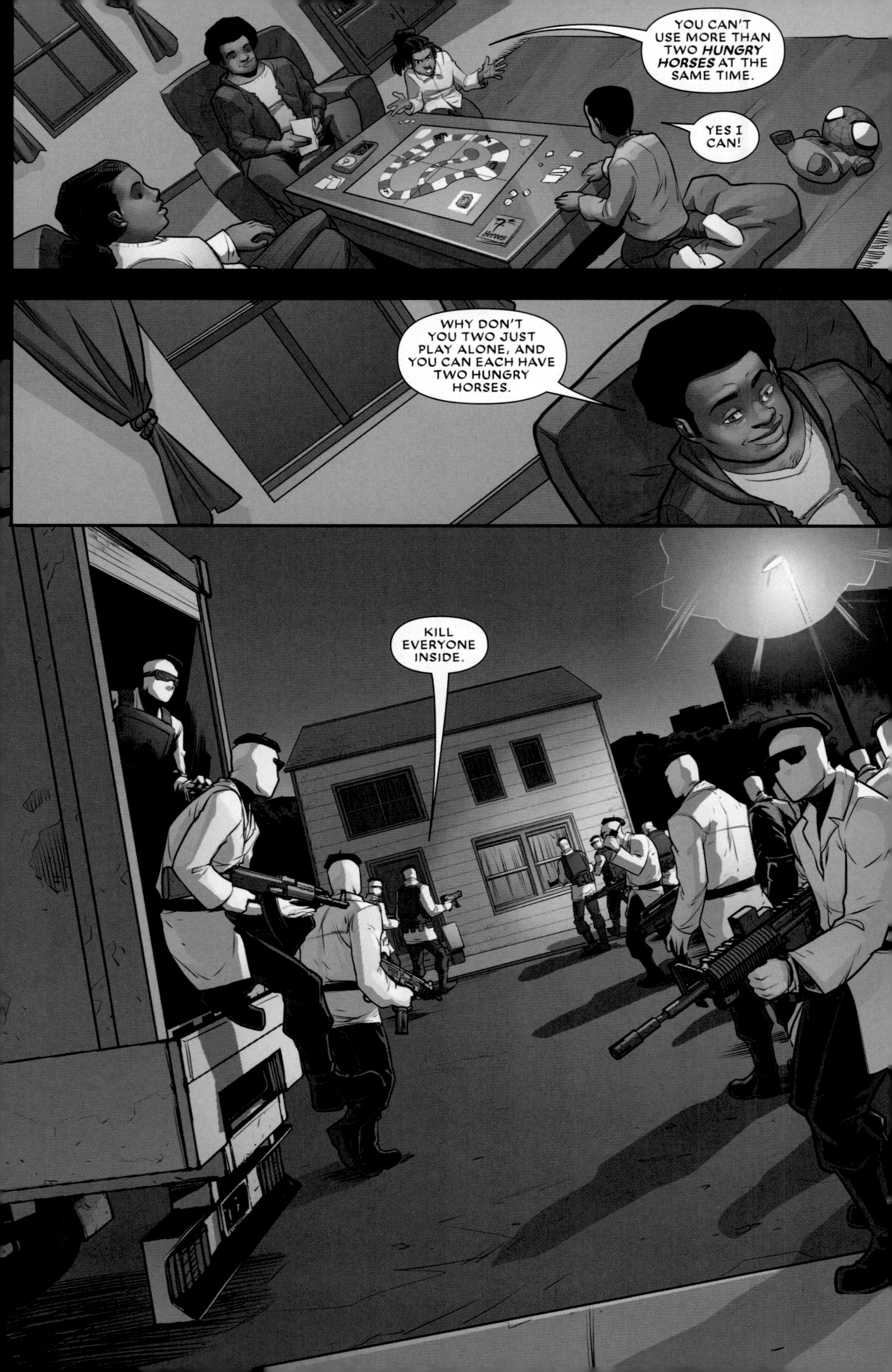
YOU CAN'T USE MORE THAN TWO *HUNGRY HORSES* AT THE SAME TIME.
YES I CAN!
WHY DON'T YOU TWO JUST PLAY ALONE, AND YOU CAN EACH HAVE TWO HUNGRY HORSES.
KILL EVERYONE INSIDE.

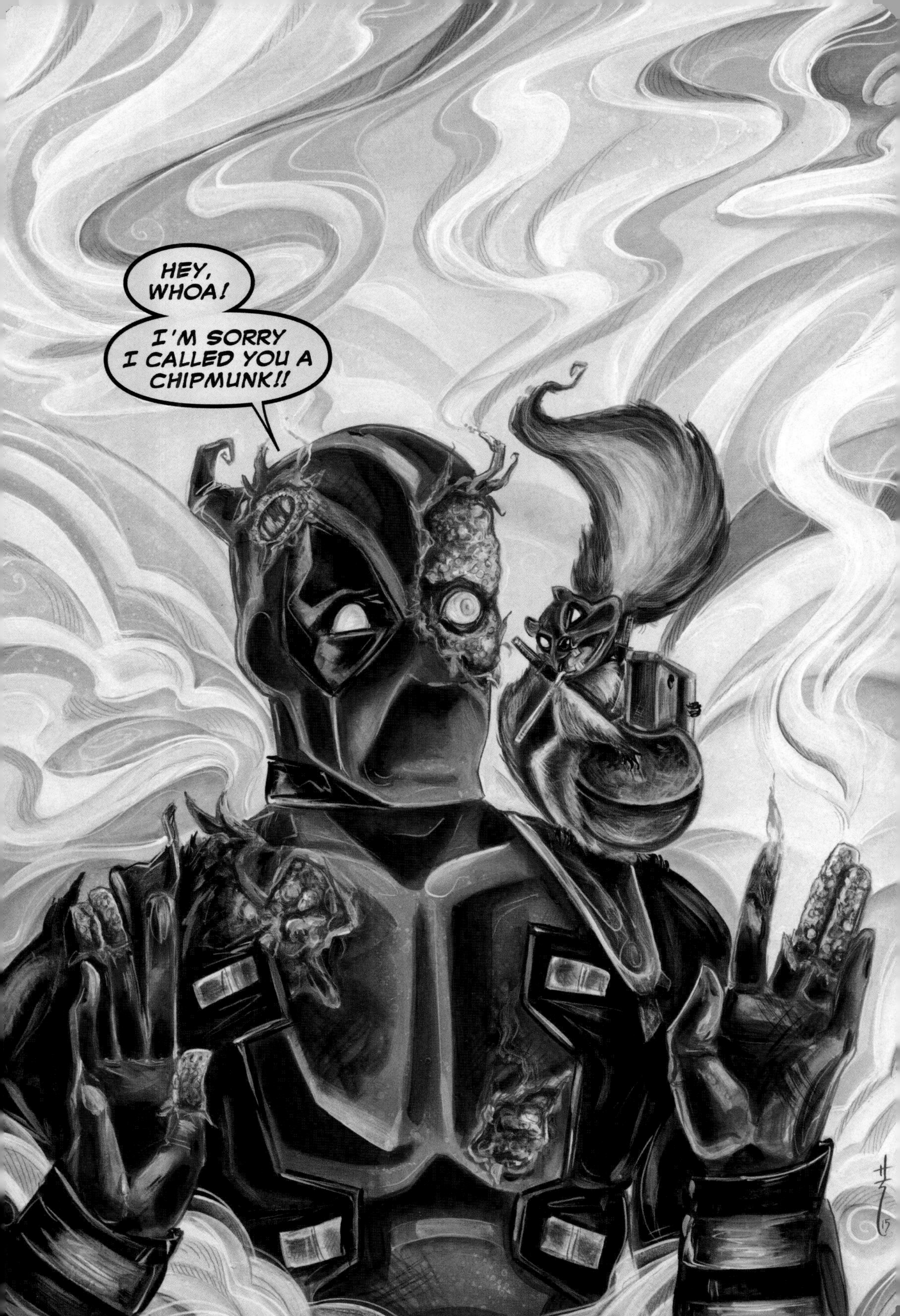
HEY, WHOA!
I'M SORRY I CALLED YOU A CHIPMUNK!!

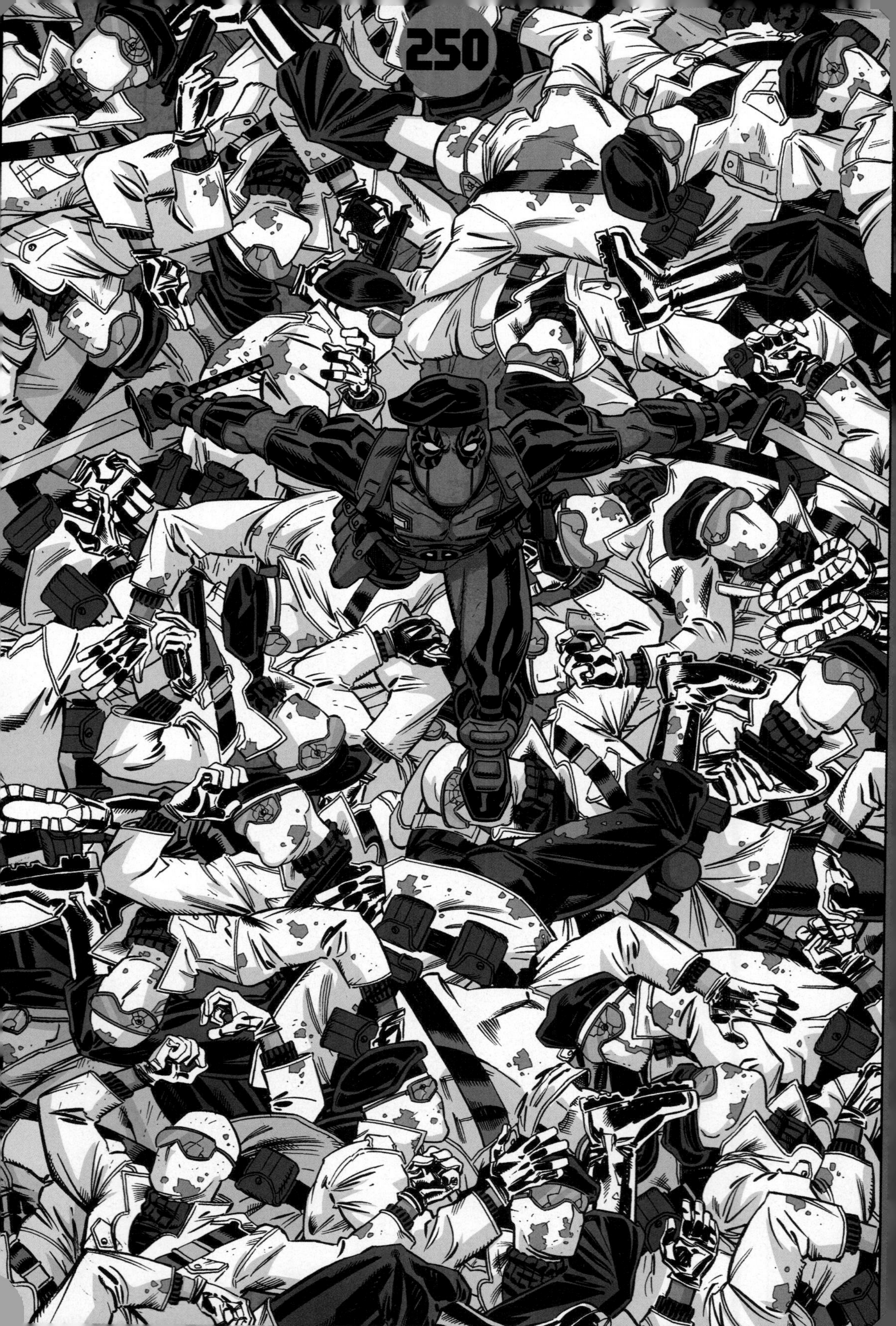
250

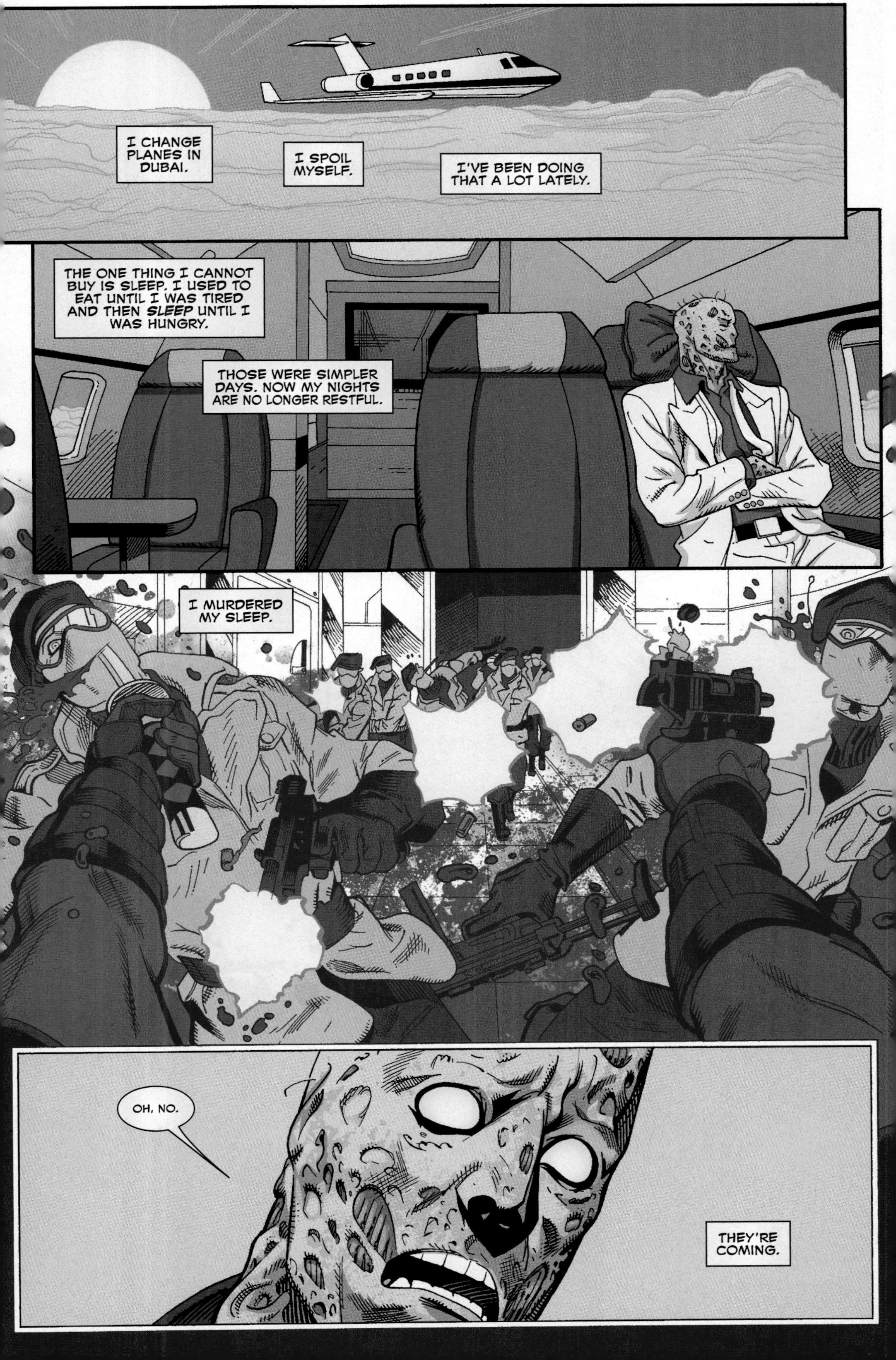
I CHANGE PLANES IN DUBAI.
I SPOIL MYSELF.
I'VE BEEN DOING THAT A LOT LATELY.
THE ONE THING I CANNOT BUY IS SLEEP. I USED TO EAT UNTIL I WAS TIRED AND THEN *SLEEP* UNTIL I WAS HUNGRY.
THOSE WERE SIMPLER DAYS. NOW MY NIGHTS ARE NO LONGER RESTFUL.
I MURDERED MY SLEEP.
OH, NO.
THEY'RE COMING.

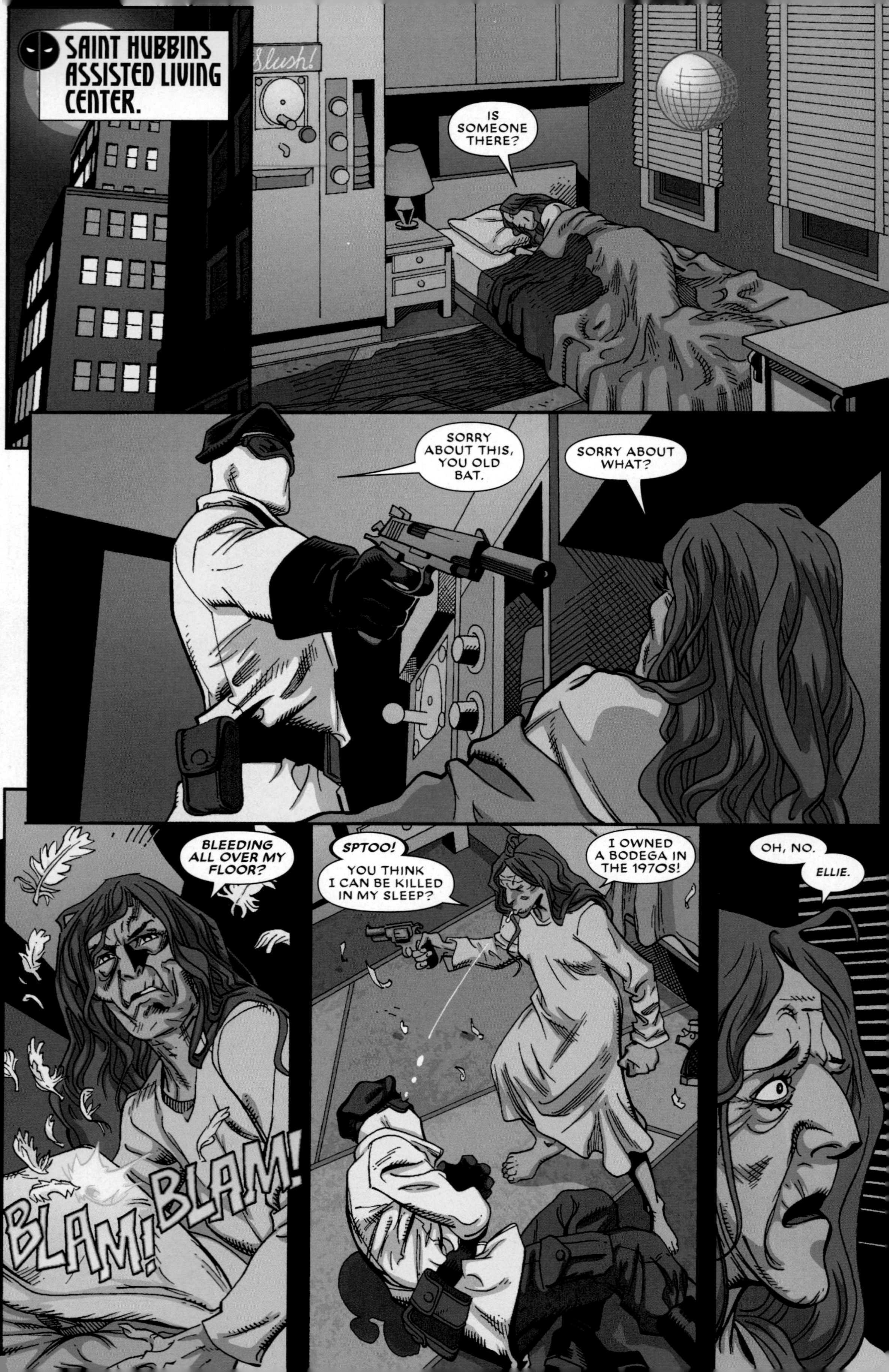
SAINT HUBBINS ASSISTED LIVING CENTER.
Slush!
IS SOMEONE THERE?
SORRY ABOUT THIS, YOU OLD BAT.
SORRY ABOUT WHAT?
BLEEDING ALL OVER MY FLOOR?
BLAM! BLAM!
SPTOO!
YOU THINK I CAN BE KILLED IN MY SLEEP?
I OWNED A BODEGA IN THE 1970S!
OH, NO.
ELLIE.

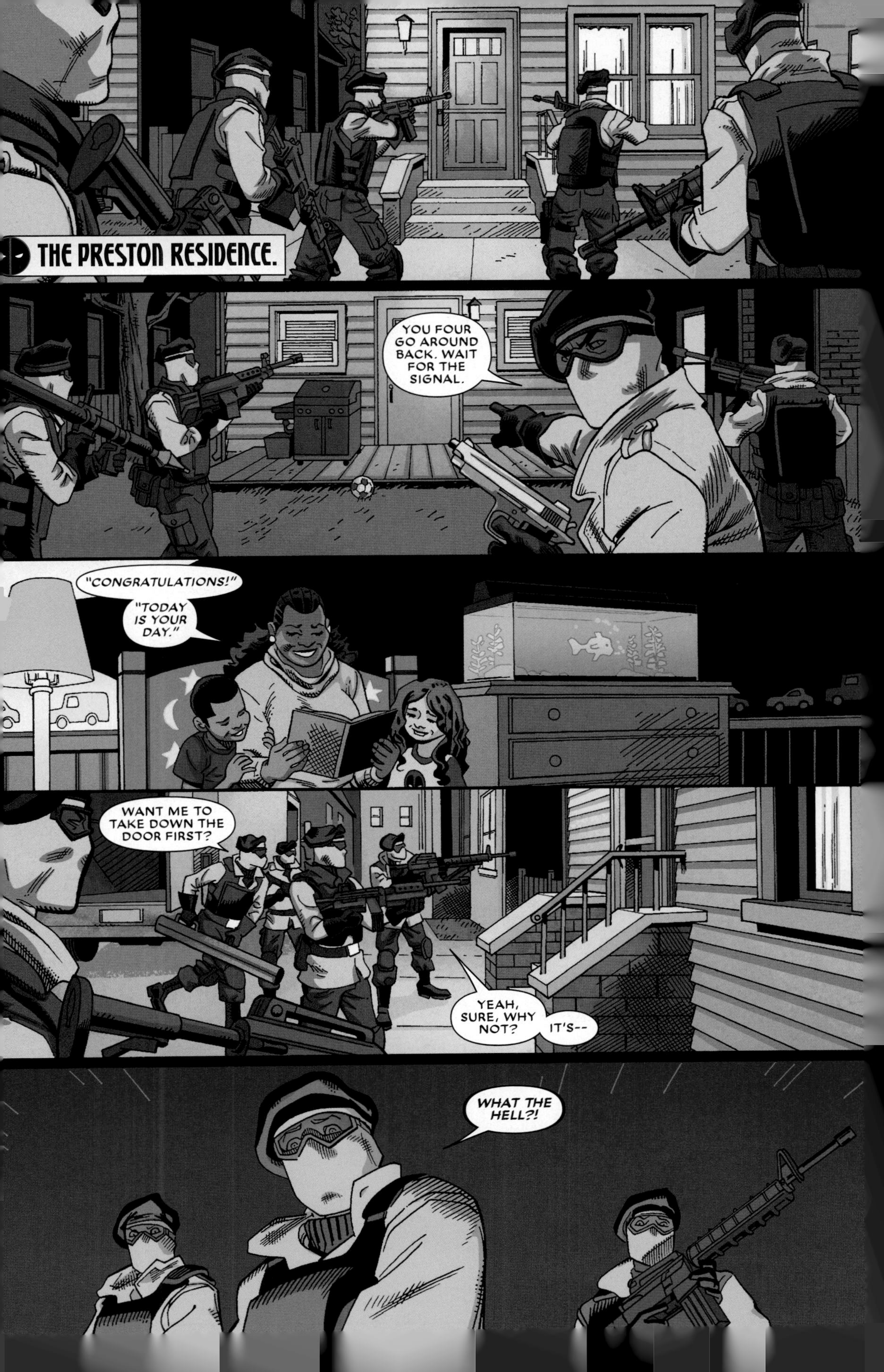
THE PRESTON RESIDENCE.
YOU FOUR GO AROUND BACK. WAIT FOR THE SIGNAL.
"CONGRATULATIONS!"
"TODAY IS YOUR DAY."
WANT ME TO TAKE DOWN THE DOOR FIRST?
YEAH, SURE, WHY NOT?
IT'S--
WHAT THE HELL?!

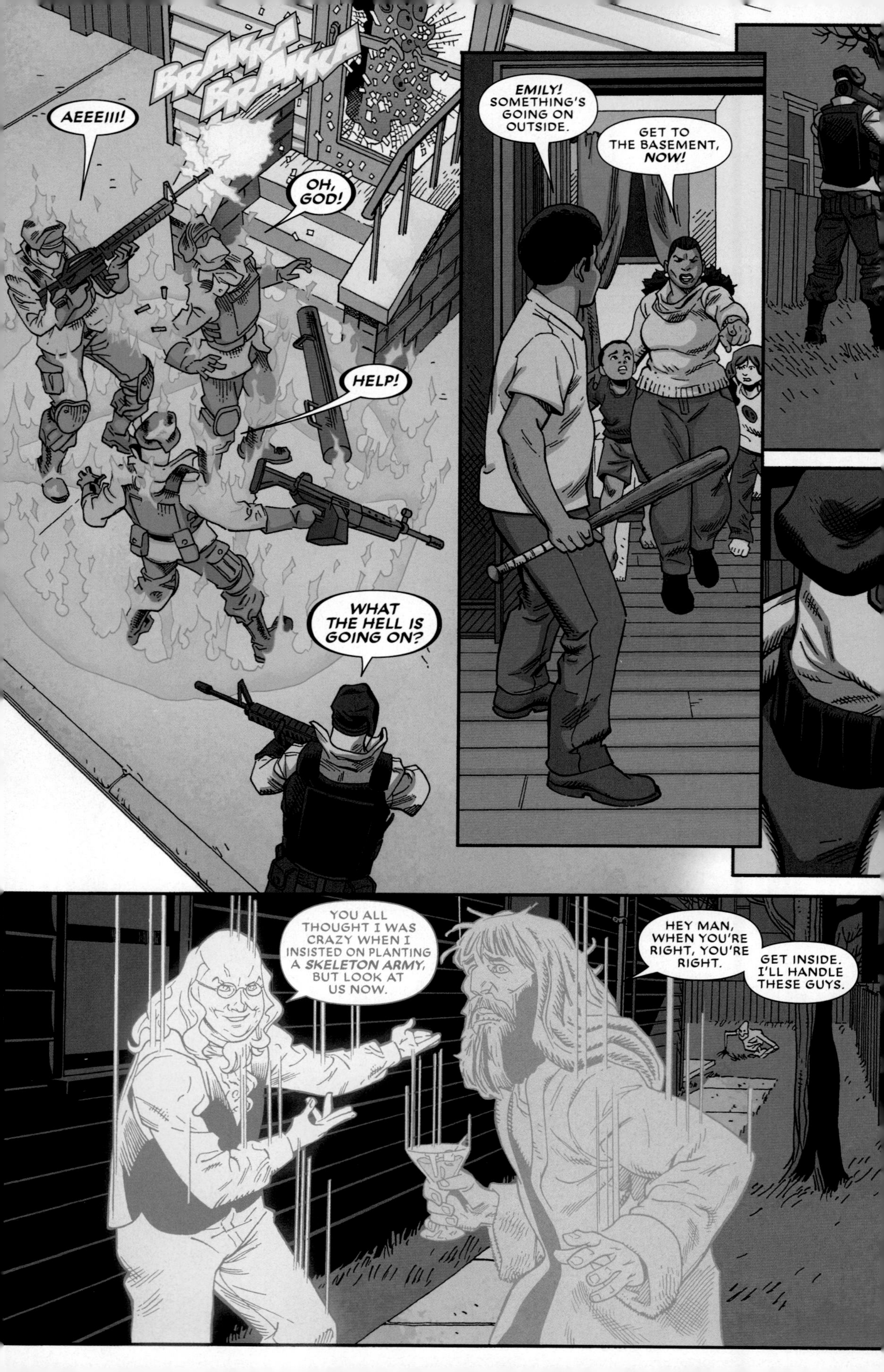
BRAKKA BRAKKA
AEEEIII!
OH, GOD!
HELP!
WHAT THE HELL IS GOING ON?
EMILY! SOMETHING'S GOING ON OUTSIDE.
GET TO THE BASEMENT, NOW!
YOU ALL THOUGHT I WAS CRAZY WHEN I INSISTED ON PLANTING A SKELETON ARMY, BUT LOOK AT US NOW.
HEY MAN, WHEN YOU'RE RIGHT, YOU'RE RIGHT.
GET INSIDE. I'LL HANDLE THESE GUYS.

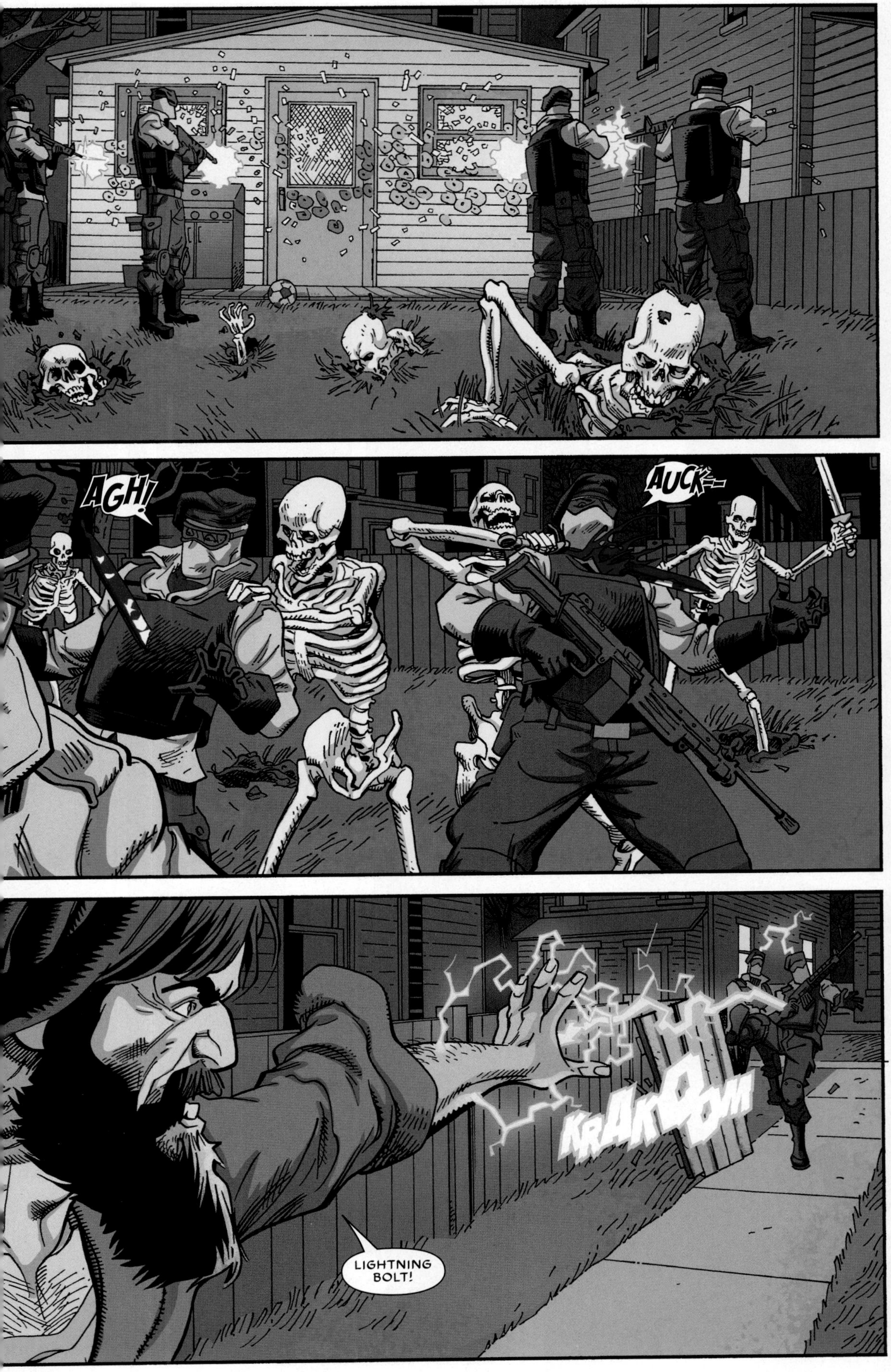
AGH!
AUCK--
LIGHTNING BOLT!
KRAKOOM

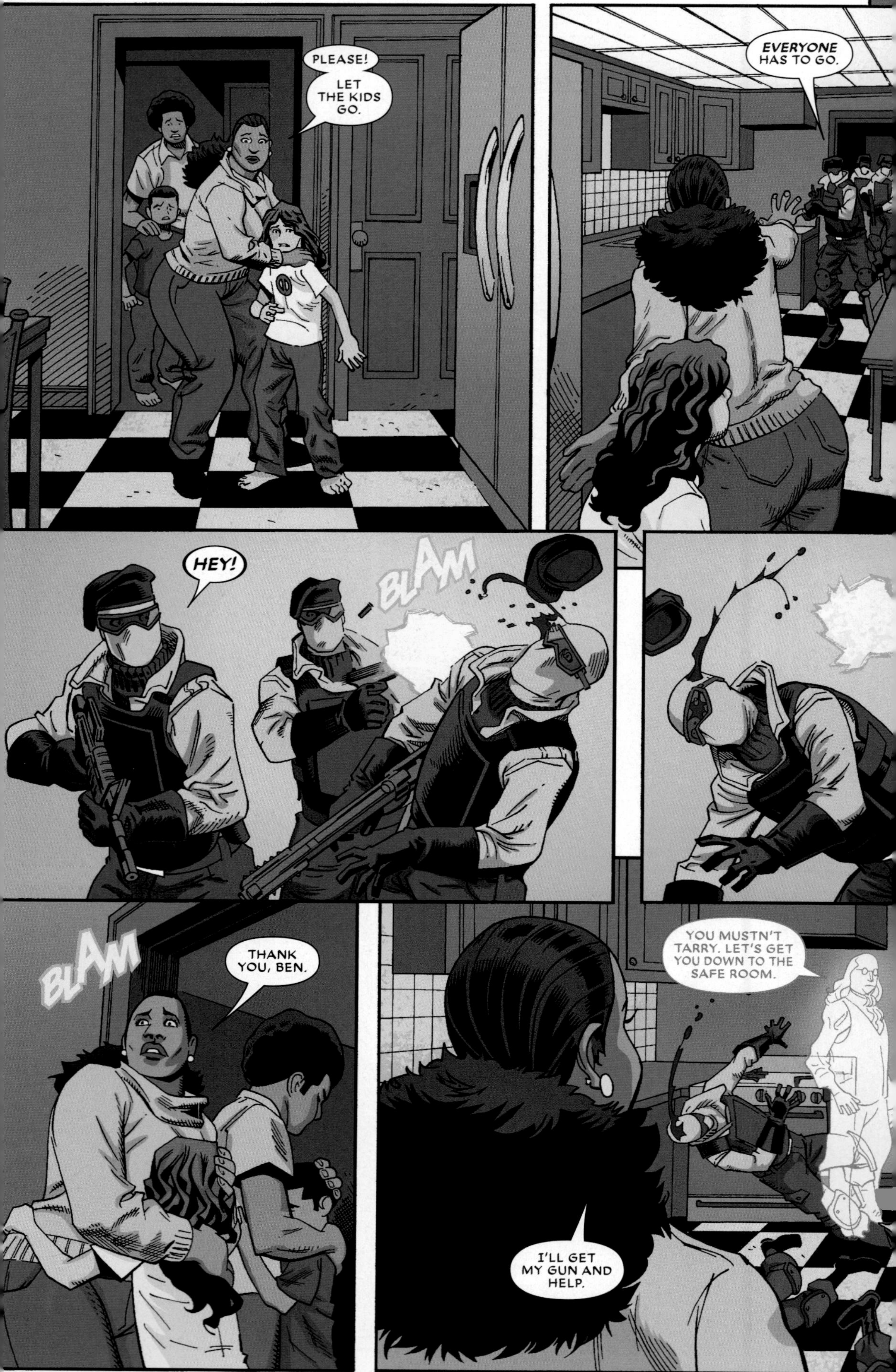
PLEASE!
LET THE KIDS GO.
EVERYONE HAS TO GO.
HEY!
BLAM
BLAM
THANK YOU, BEN.
YOU MUSTN'T TARRY. LET'S GET YOU DOWN TO THE SAFE ROOM.
I'LL GET MY GUN AND HELP.

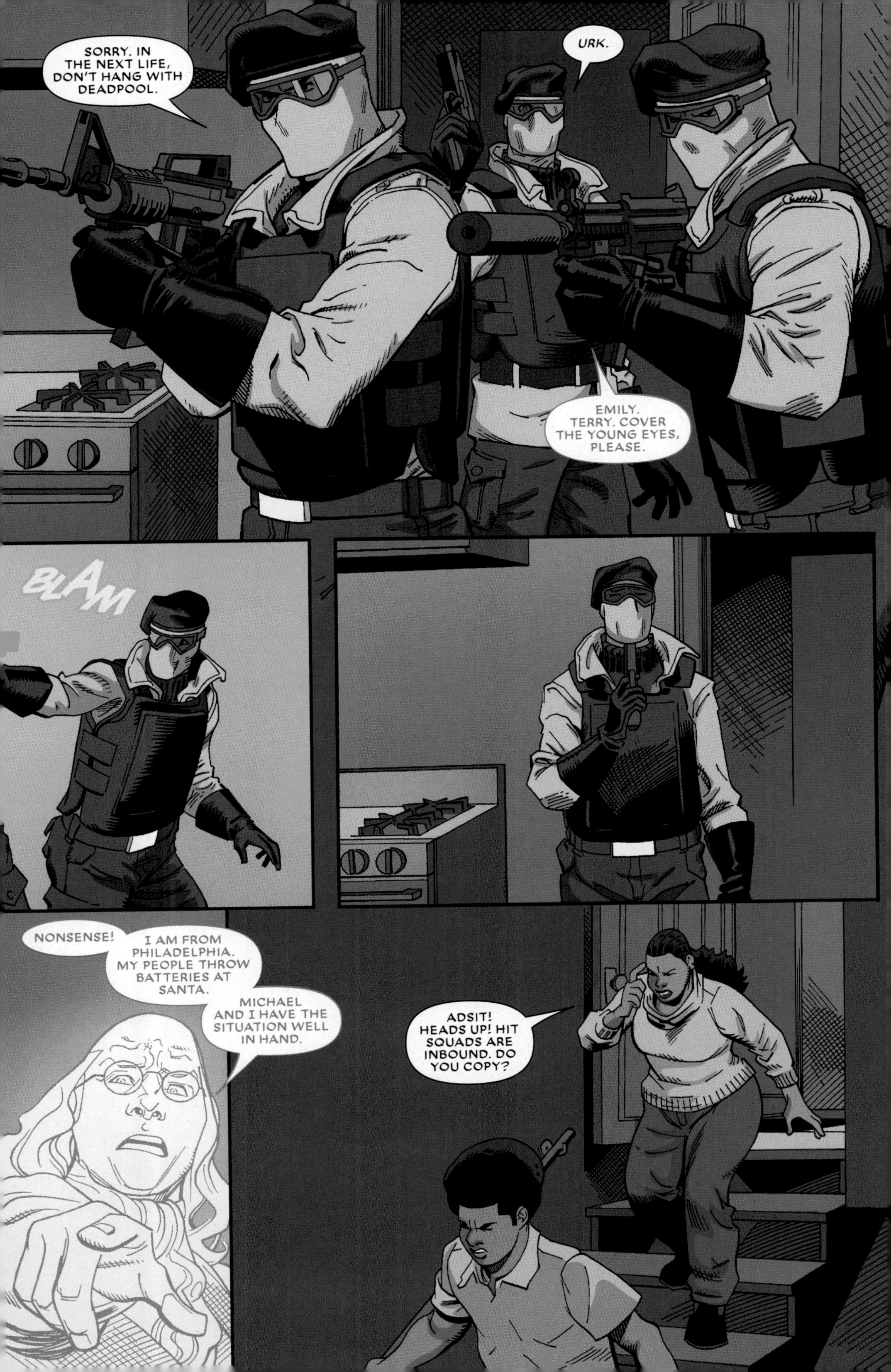

SORRY. IN THE NEXT LIFE, DON'T HANG WITH DEADPOOL.
URK.
EMILY. TERRY. COVER THE YOUNG EYES, PLEASE.
BLAM
NONSENSE!
I AM FROM PHILADELPHIA. MY PEOPLE THROW BATTERIES AT SANTA.
MICHAEL AND I HAVE THE SITUATION WELL IN HAND.
ADSIT! HEADS UP! HIT SQUADS ARE INBOUND. DO YOU COPY?

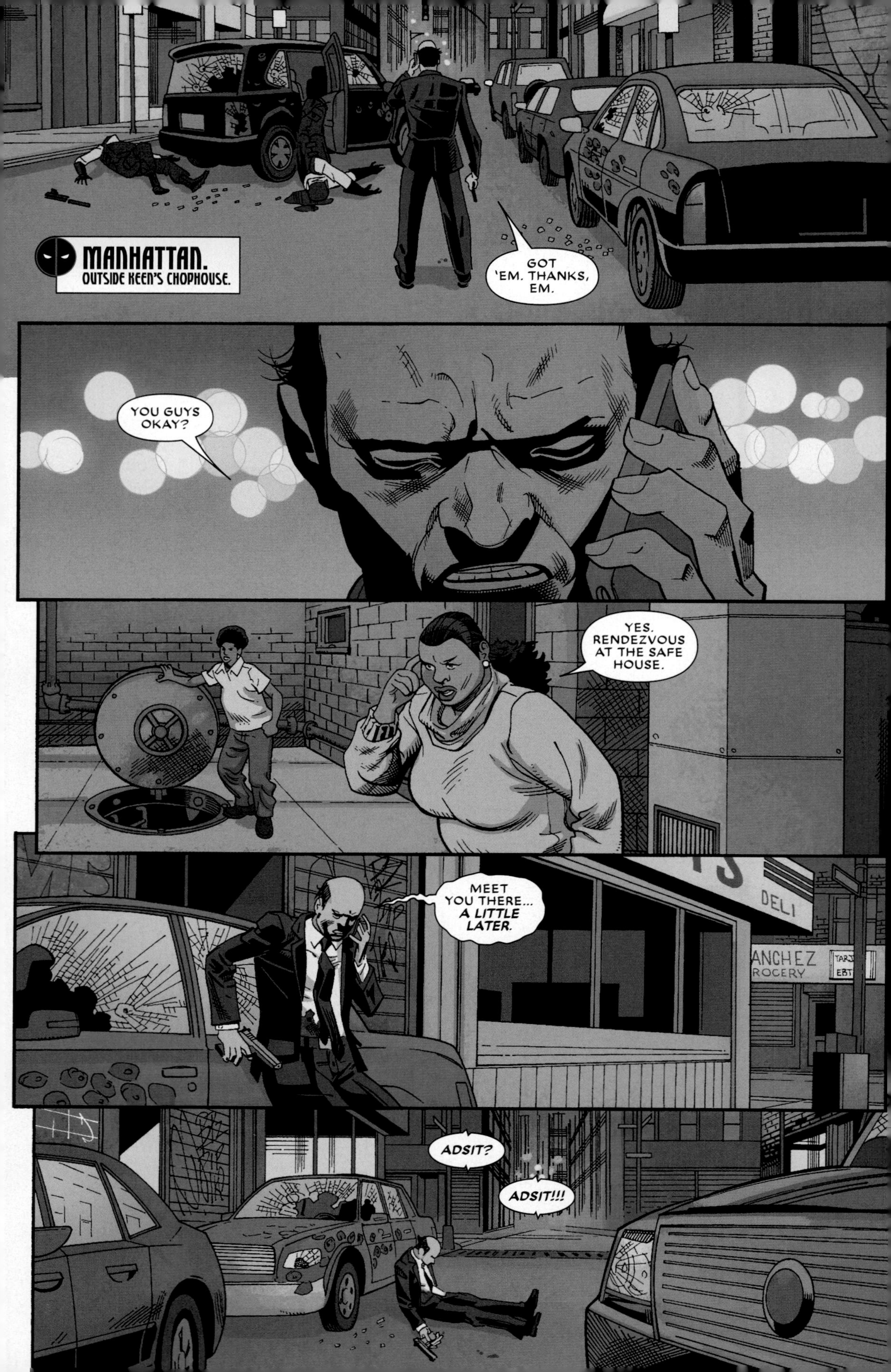
MANHATTAN.
OUTSIDE KEEN'S CHOPHOUSE.
GOT 'EM. THANKS, EM.
YOU GUYS OKAY?
YES. RENDEZVOUS AT THE SAFE HOUSE.
MEET YOU THERE... *A LITTLE LATER.*
DELI
ANCHEZ
ROCERY
TARJ
EBT
ADSIT?
ADSIT!!!

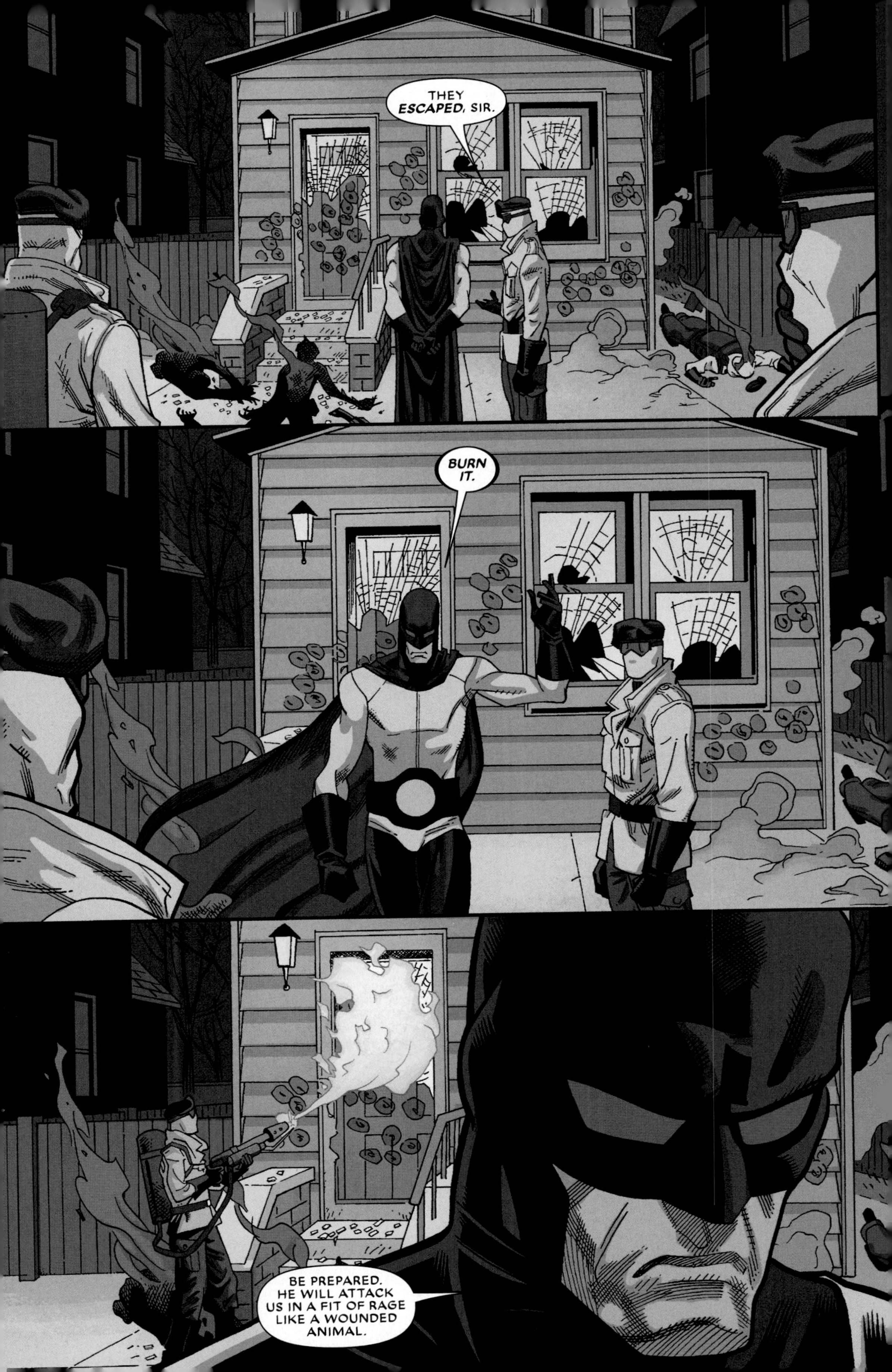
THEY ESCAPED, SIR.
BURN IT.
BE PREPARED. HE WILL ATTACK US IN A FIT OF RAGE LIKE A WOUNDED ANIMAL.

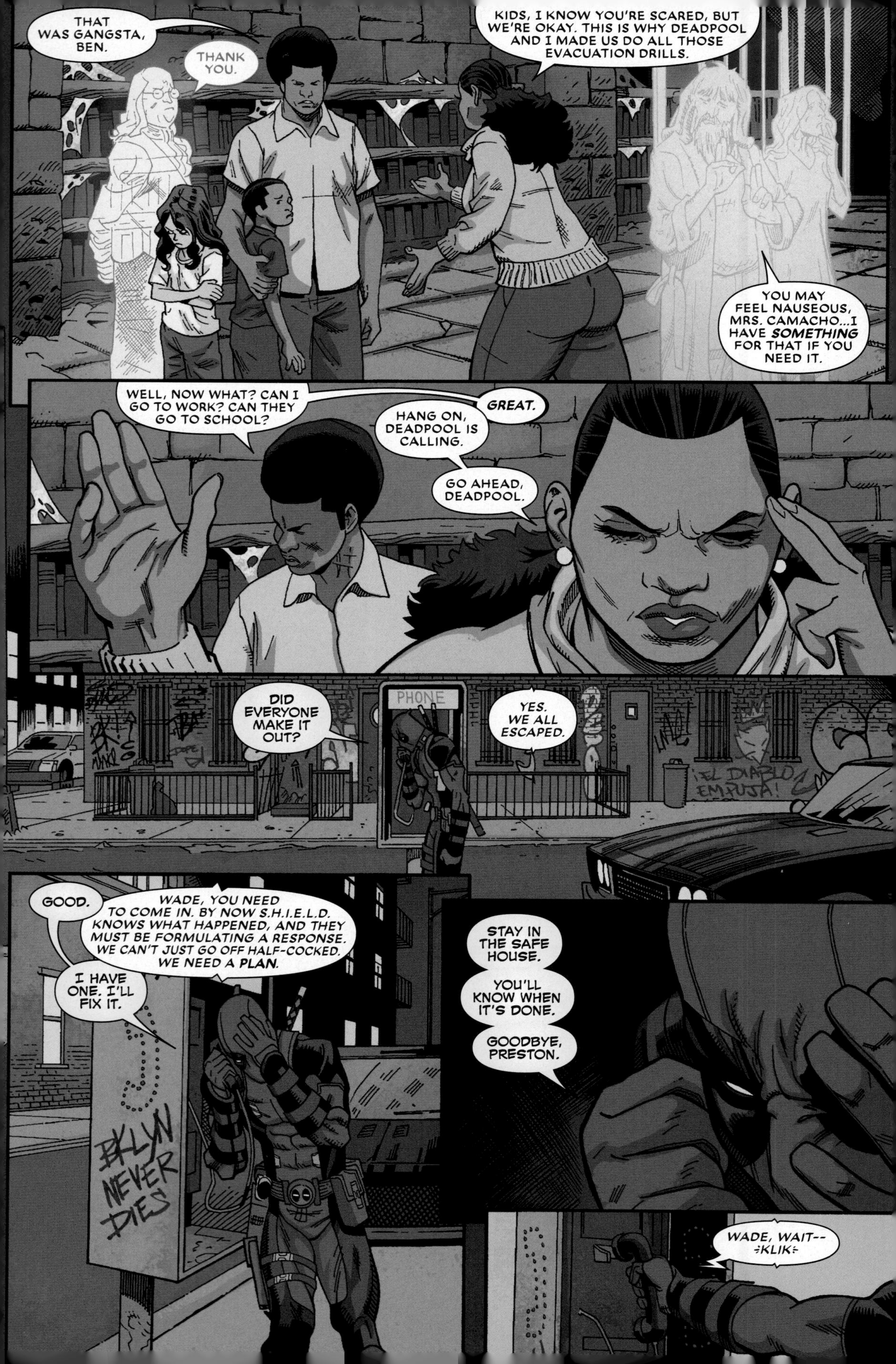

THAT WAS GANGSTA, BEN.
THANK YOU.
KIDS, I KNOW YOU'RE SCARED, BUT WE'RE OKAY. THIS IS WHY DEADPOOL AND I MADE US DO ALL THOSE EVACUATION DRILLS.
YOU MAY FEEL NAUSEOUS, MRS. CAMACHO...I HAVE *SOMETHING* FOR THAT IF YOU NEED IT.
WELL, NOW WHAT? CAN I GO TO WORK? CAN THEY GO TO SCHOOL?
GREAT.
HANG ON, DEADPOOL IS CALLING.
GO AHEAD, DEADPOOL.
PHONE
DID EVERYONE MAKE IT OUT?
YES. WE ALL ESCAPED.
¡EL DIABLO EMPUJA!
GOOD.
WADE, YOU NEED TO COME IN. BY NOW S.H.I.E.L.D. KNOWS WHAT HAPPENED, AND THEY MUST BE FORMULATING A RESPONSE. WE CAN'T JUST GO OFF HALF-COCKED. WE NEED A **PLAN**.
I HAVE ONE. I'LL FIX IT.
BKLYN NEVER DIES
STAY IN THE SAFE HOUSE.
YOU'LL KNOW WHEN IT'S DONE.
GOODBYE, PRESTON.
WADE, WAIT--
KLIK

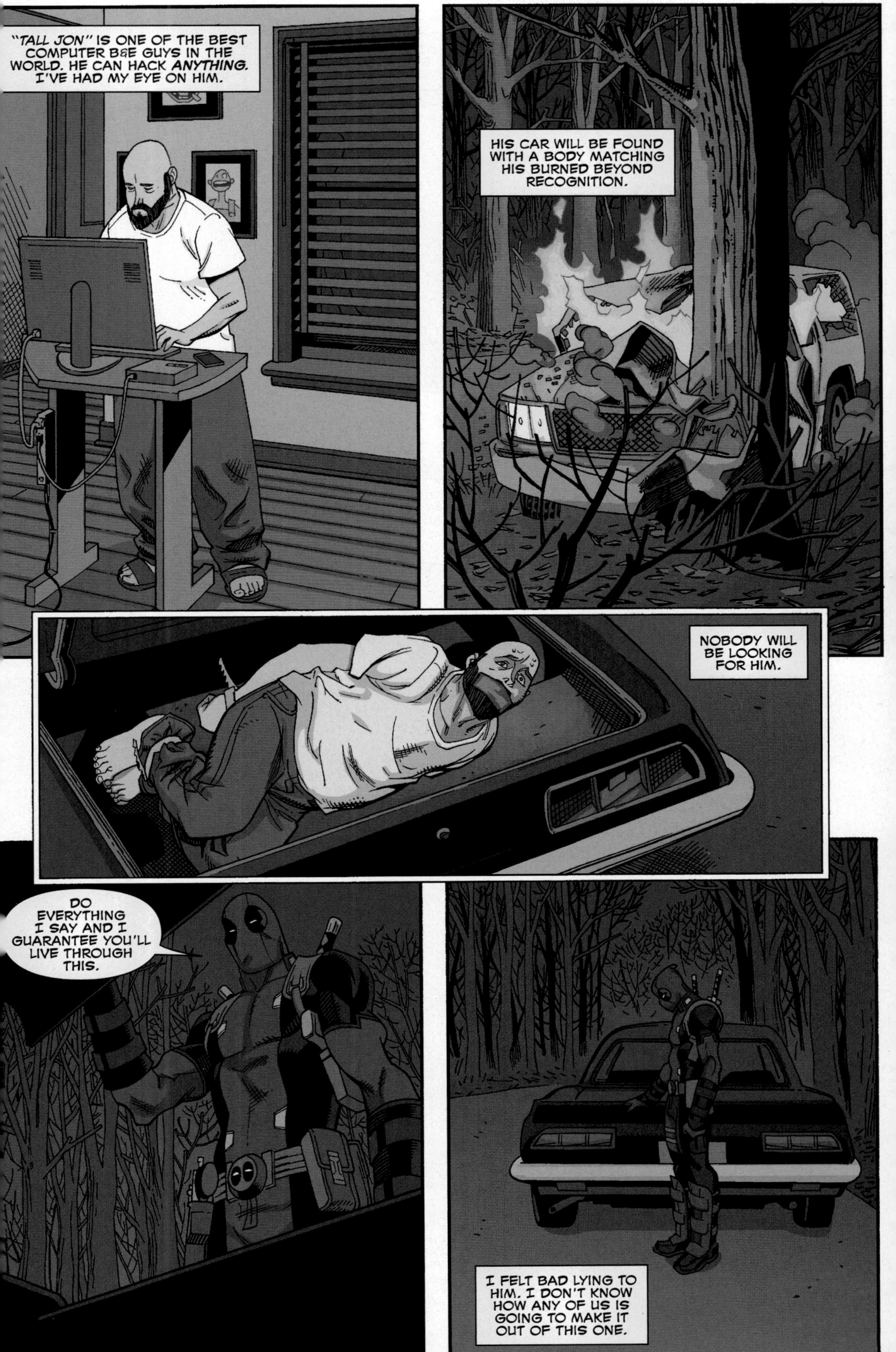
"TALL JON" IS ONE OF THE BEST COMPUTER B&E GUYS IN THE WORLD. HE CAN HACK ANYTHING. I'VE HAD MY EYE ON HIM.
HIS CAR WILL BE FOUND WITH A BODY MATCHING HIS BURNED BEYOND RECOGNITION.
NOBODY WILL BE LOOKING FOR HIM.
DO EVERYTHING I SAY AND I GUARANTEE YOU'LL LIVE THROUGH THIS.
I FELT BAD LYING TO HIM. I DON'T KNOW HOW ANY OF US IS GOING TO MAKE IT OUT OF THIS ONE.

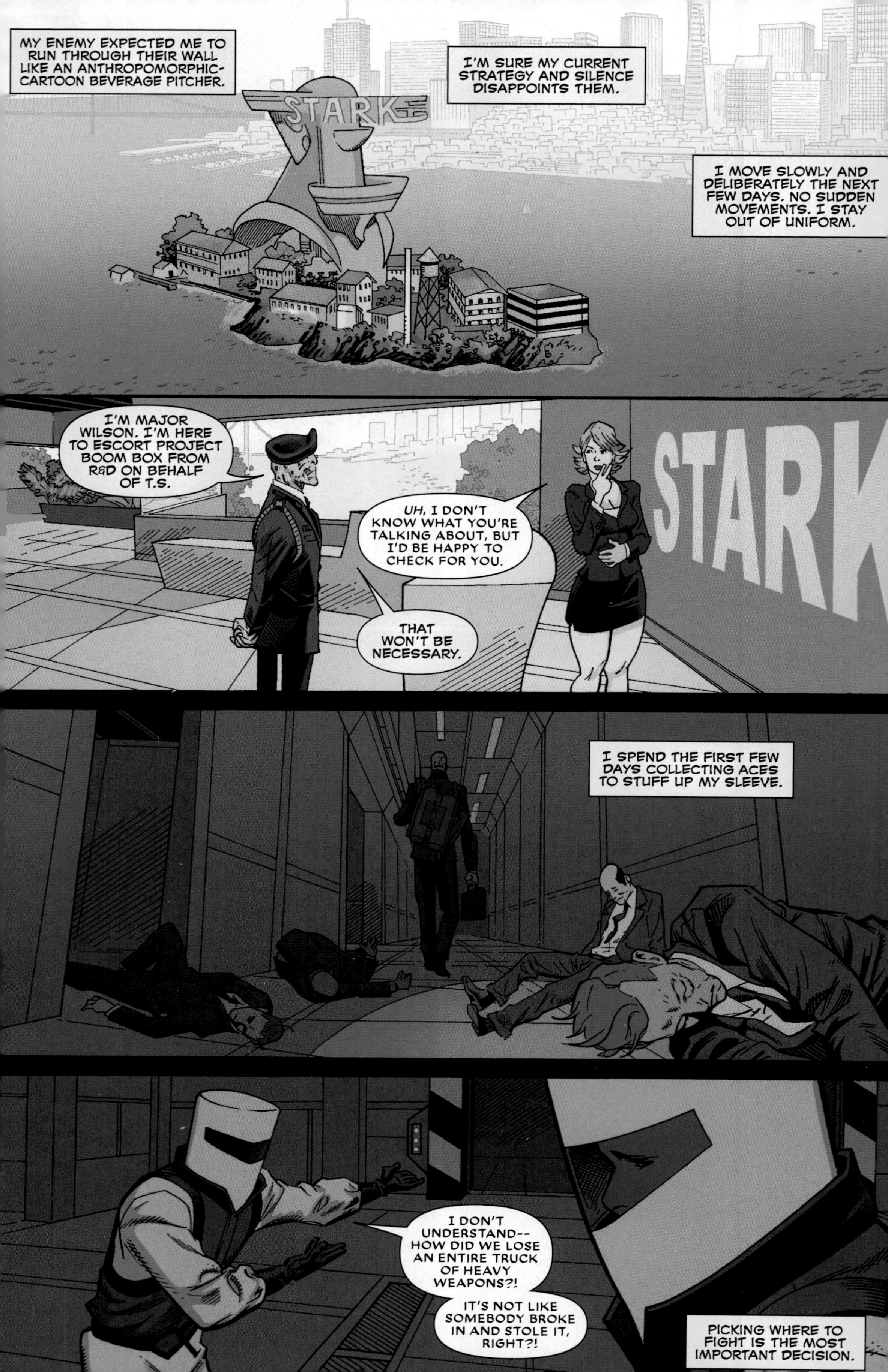
MY ENEMY EXPECTED ME TO RUN THROUGH THEIR WALL LIKE AN ANTHROPOMORPHIC-CARTOON BEVERAGE PITCHER.
STARK
I'M SURE MY CURRENT STRATEGY AND SILENCE DISAPPOINTS THEM.
I MOVE SLOWLY AND DELIBERATELY THE NEXT FEW DAYS. NO SUDDEN MOVEMENTS. I STAY OUT OF UNIFORM.
I'M MAJOR WILSON. I'M HERE TO ESCORT PROJECT BOOM BOX FROM R&D ON BEHALF OF T.S.
UH, I DON'T KNOW WHAT YOU'RE TALKING ABOUT, BUT I'D BE HAPPY TO CHECK FOR YOU.
STARK
THAT WON'T BE NECESSARY.
I SPEND THE FIRST FEW DAYS COLLECTING ACES TO STUFF UP MY SLEEVE.
I DON'T UNDERSTAND-- HOW DID WE LOSE AN ENTIRE TRUCK OF HEAVY WEAPONS?!
IT'S NOT LIKE SOMEBODY BROKE IN AND STOLE IT, RIGHT?!
PICKING WHERE TO FIGHT IS THE MOST IMPORTANT DECISION.

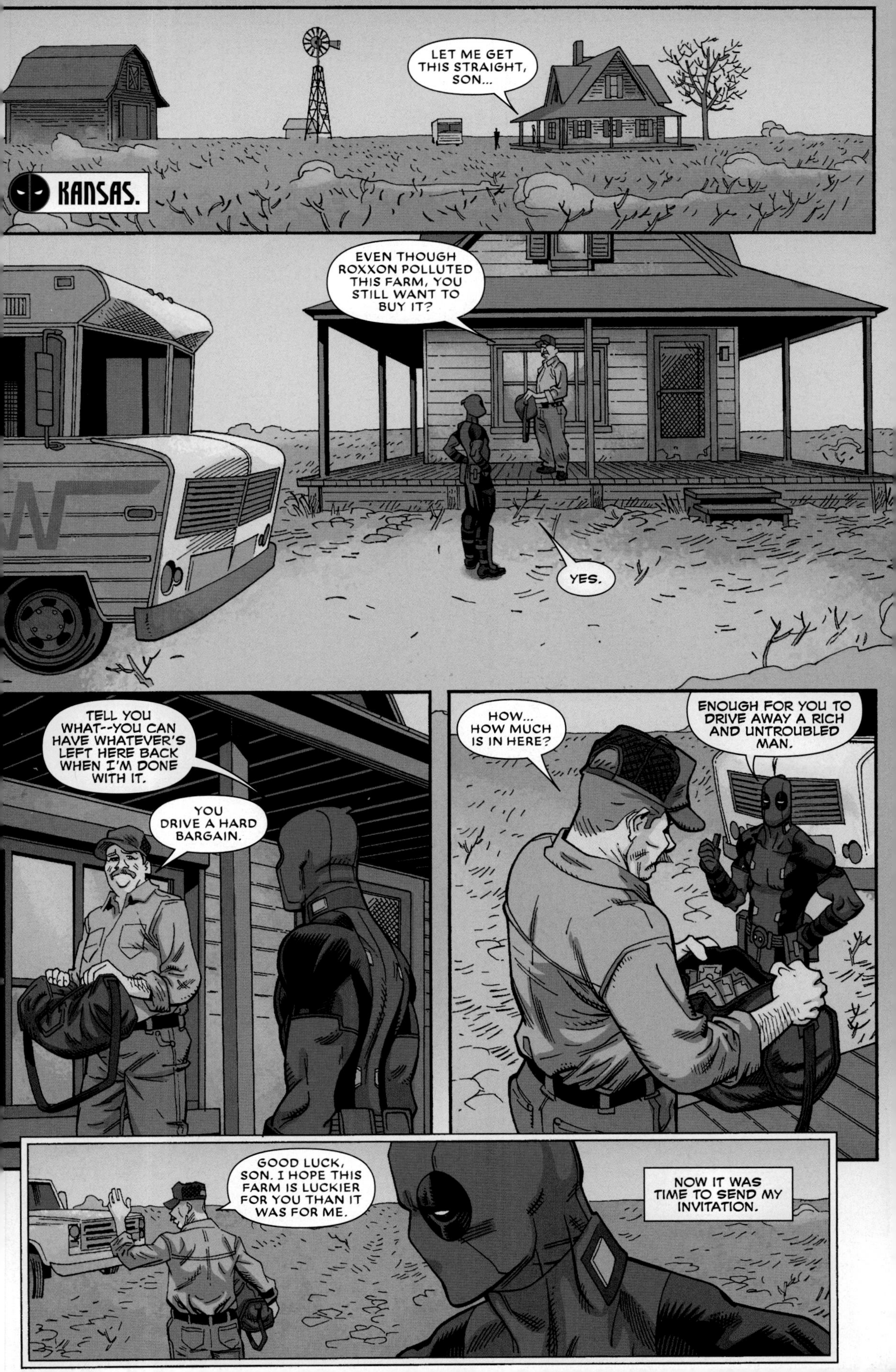
LET ME GET THIS STRAIGHT, SON...
KANSAS.
EVEN THOUGH ROXXON POLLUTED THIS FARM, YOU STILL WANT TO BUY IT?
YES.
TELL YOU WHAT--YOU CAN HAVE WHATEVER'S LEFT HERE BACK WHEN I'M DONE WITH IT.
YOU DRIVE A HARD BARGAIN.
HOW... HOW MUCH IS IN HERE?
ENOUGH FOR YOU TO DRIVE AWAY A RICH AND UNTROUBLED MAN.
GOOD LUCK, SON. I HOPE THIS FARM IS LUCKIER FOR YOU THAN IT WAS FOR ME.
NOW IT WAS TIME TO SEND MY INVITATION.

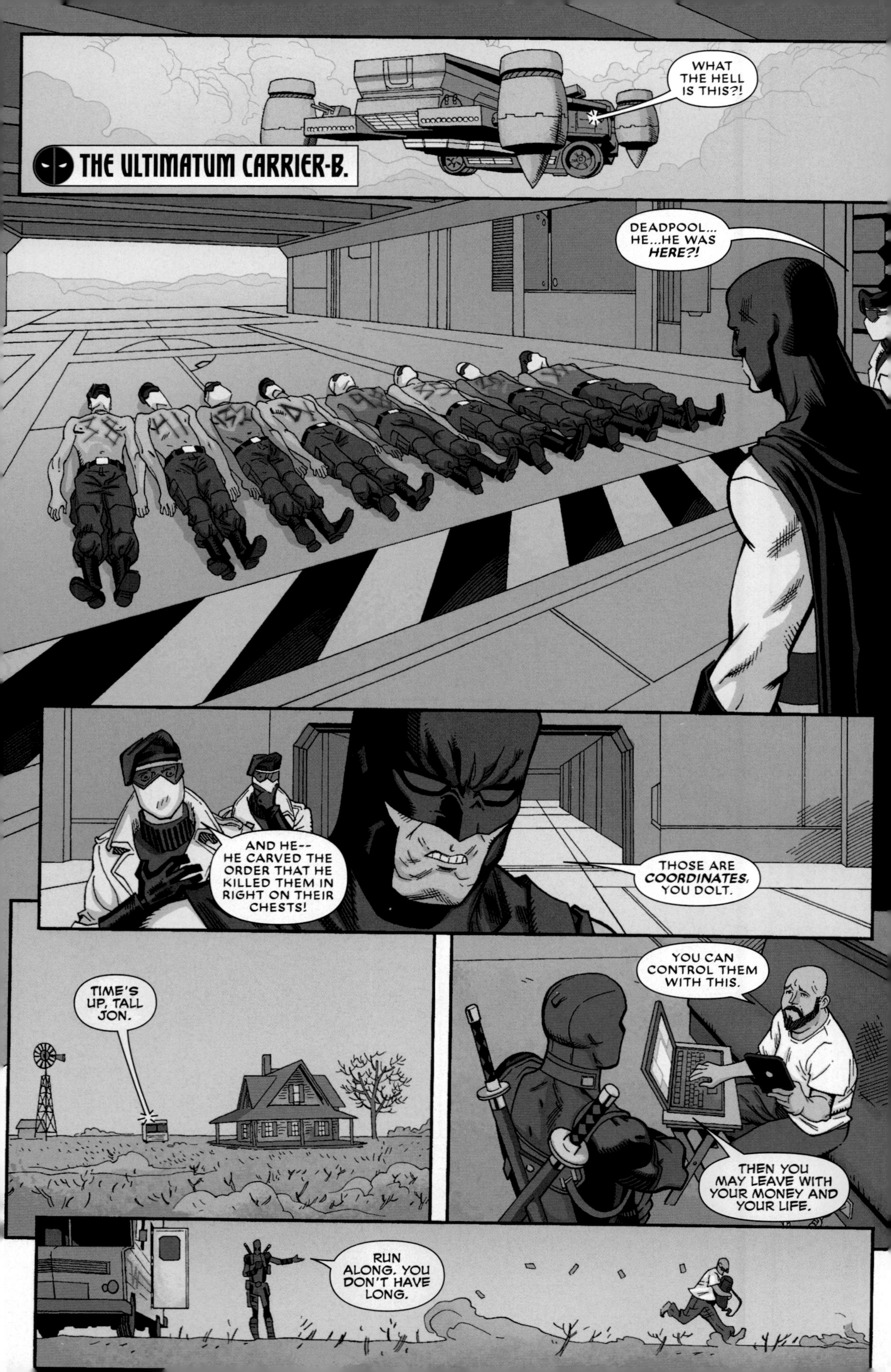
THE ULTIMATUM CARRIER-B.
WHAT THE HELL IS THIS?!
DEADPOOL... HE...HE WAS HERE?!
AND HE-- HE CARVED THE ORDER THAT HE KILLED THEM IN RIGHT ON THEIR CHESTS!
THOSE ARE COORDINATES, YOU DOLT.
TIME'S UP, TALL JON.
YOU CAN CONTROL THEM WITH THIS.
THEN YOU MAY LEAVE WITH YOUR MONEY AND YOUR LIFE.
RUN ALONG. YOU DON'T HAVE LONG.

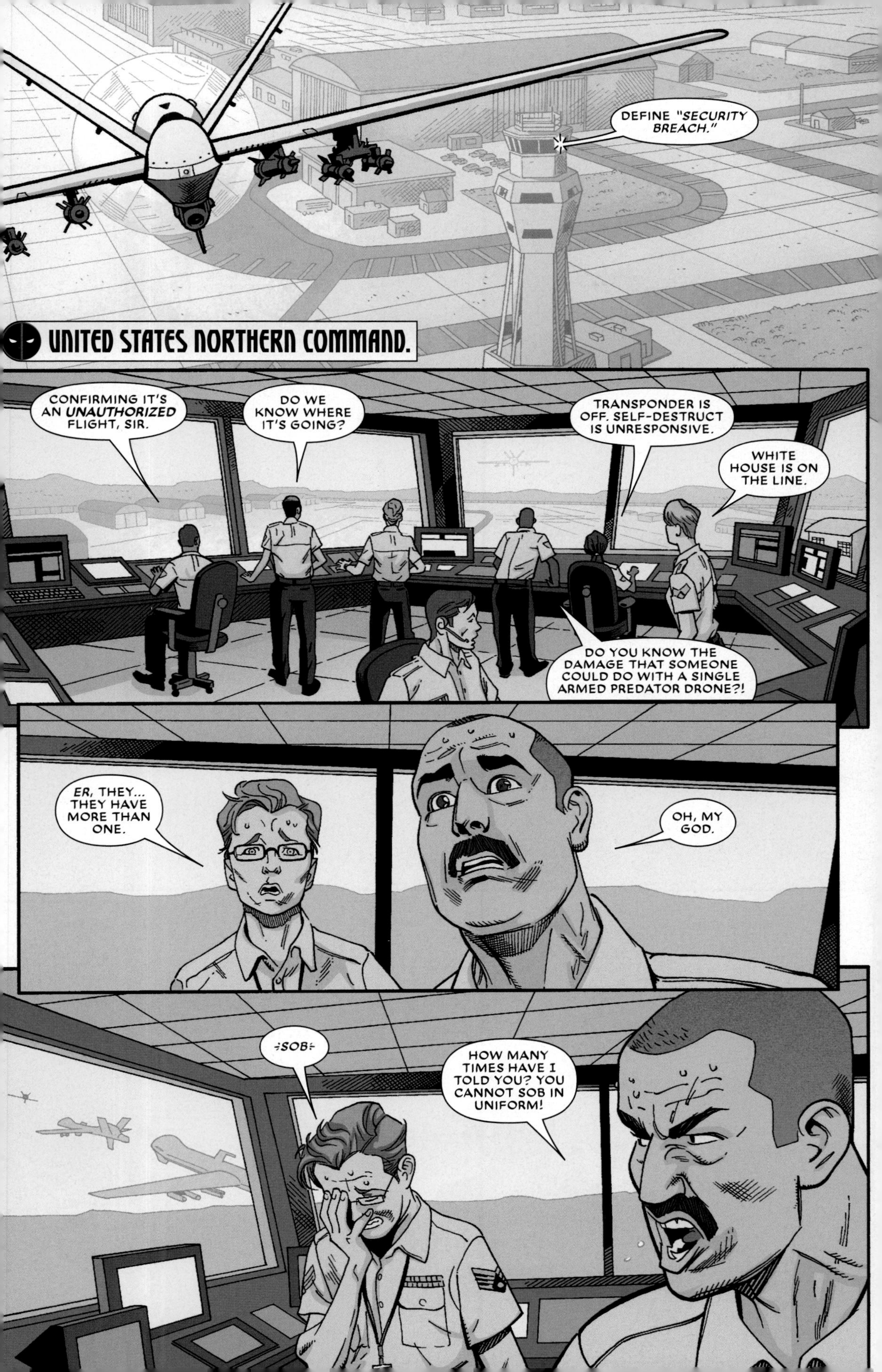
DEFINE "SECURITY BREACH."
UNITED STATES NORTHERN COMMAND.
CONFIRMING IT'S AN UNAUTHORIZED FLIGHT, SIR.
DO WE KNOW WHERE IT'S GOING?
TRANSPONDER IS OFF. SELF-DESTRUCT IS UNRESPONSIVE.
WHITE HOUSE IS ON THE LINE.
DO YOU KNOW THE DAMAGE THAT SOMEONE COULD DO WITH A SINGLE ARMED PREDATOR DRONE?!
ER, THEY... THEY HAVE MORE THAN ONE.
OH, MY GOD.
SOB
HOW MANY TIMES HAVE I TOLD YOU? YOU CANNOT SOB IN UNIFORM!

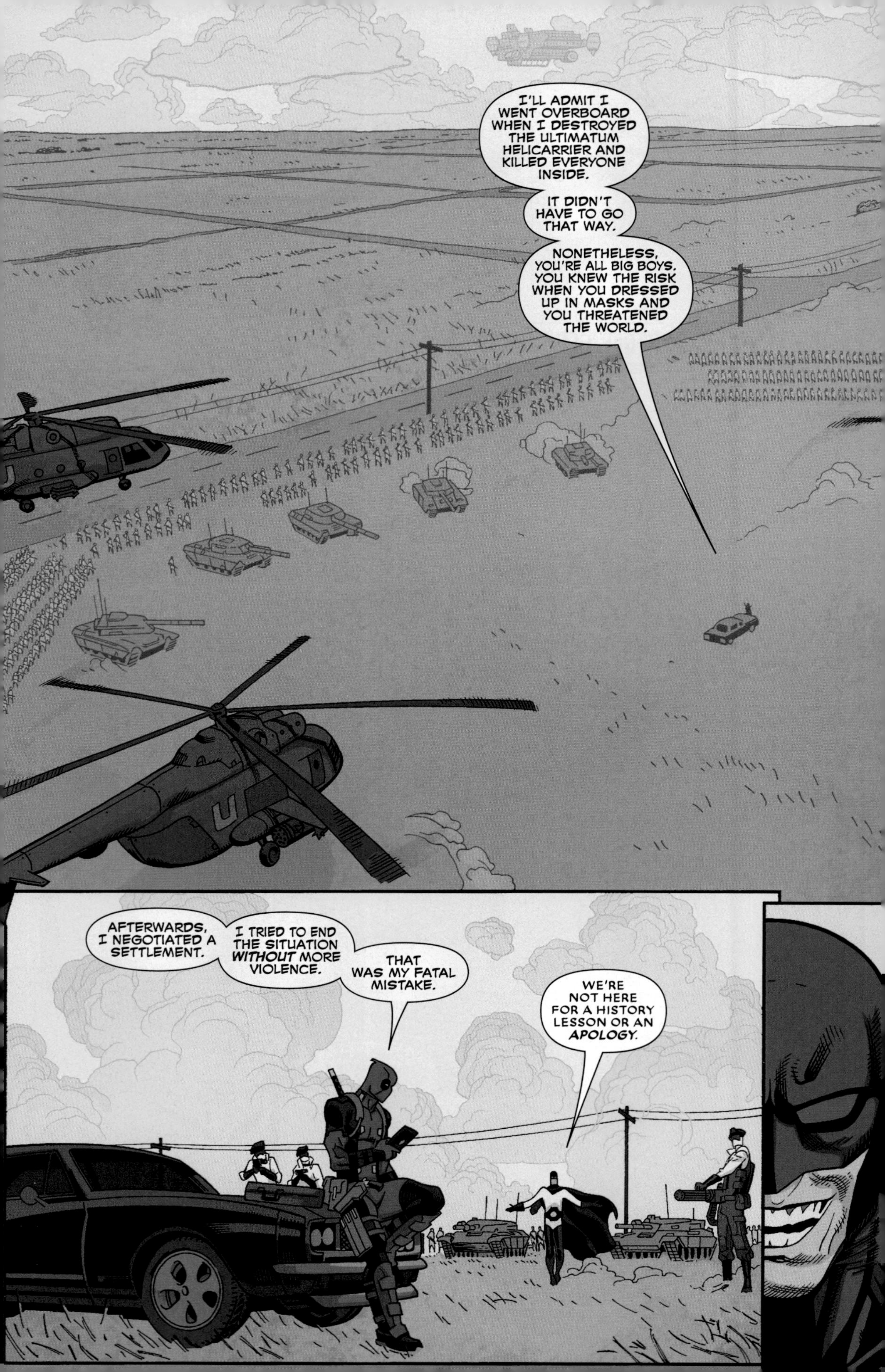
I'LL ADMIT I WENT OVERBOARD WHEN I DESTROYED THE ULTIMATUM HELICARRIER AND KILLED EVERYONE INSIDE.
IT DIDN'T HAVE TO GO THAT WAY.
NONETHELESS, YOU'RE ALL BIG BOYS. YOU KNEW THE RISK WHEN YOU DRESSED UP IN MASKS AND YOU THREATENED THE WORLD.
AFTERWARDS, I NEGOTIATED A SETTLEMENT.
I TRIED TO END THE SITUATION *WITHOUT* MORE VIOLENCE.
THAT WAS MY FATAL MISTAKE.
WE'RE NOT HERE FOR A HISTORY LESSON OR AN *APOLOGY*.

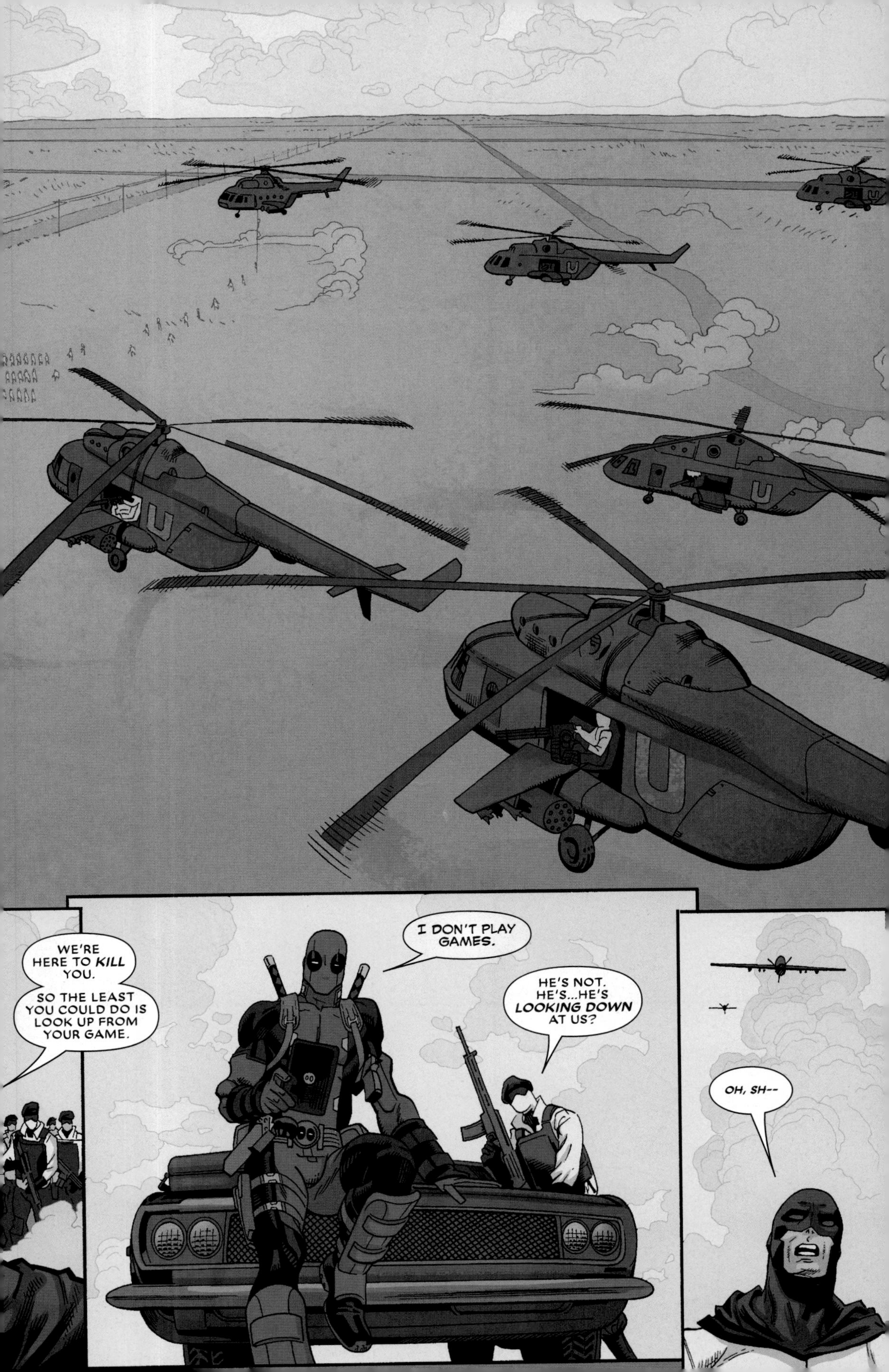

WE'RE HERE TO KILL YOU.
SO THE LEAST YOU COULD DO IS LOOK UP FROM YOUR GAME.
I DON'T PLAY GAMES.
HE'S NOT. HE'S...HE'S LOOKING DOWN AT US?
OH, SH--

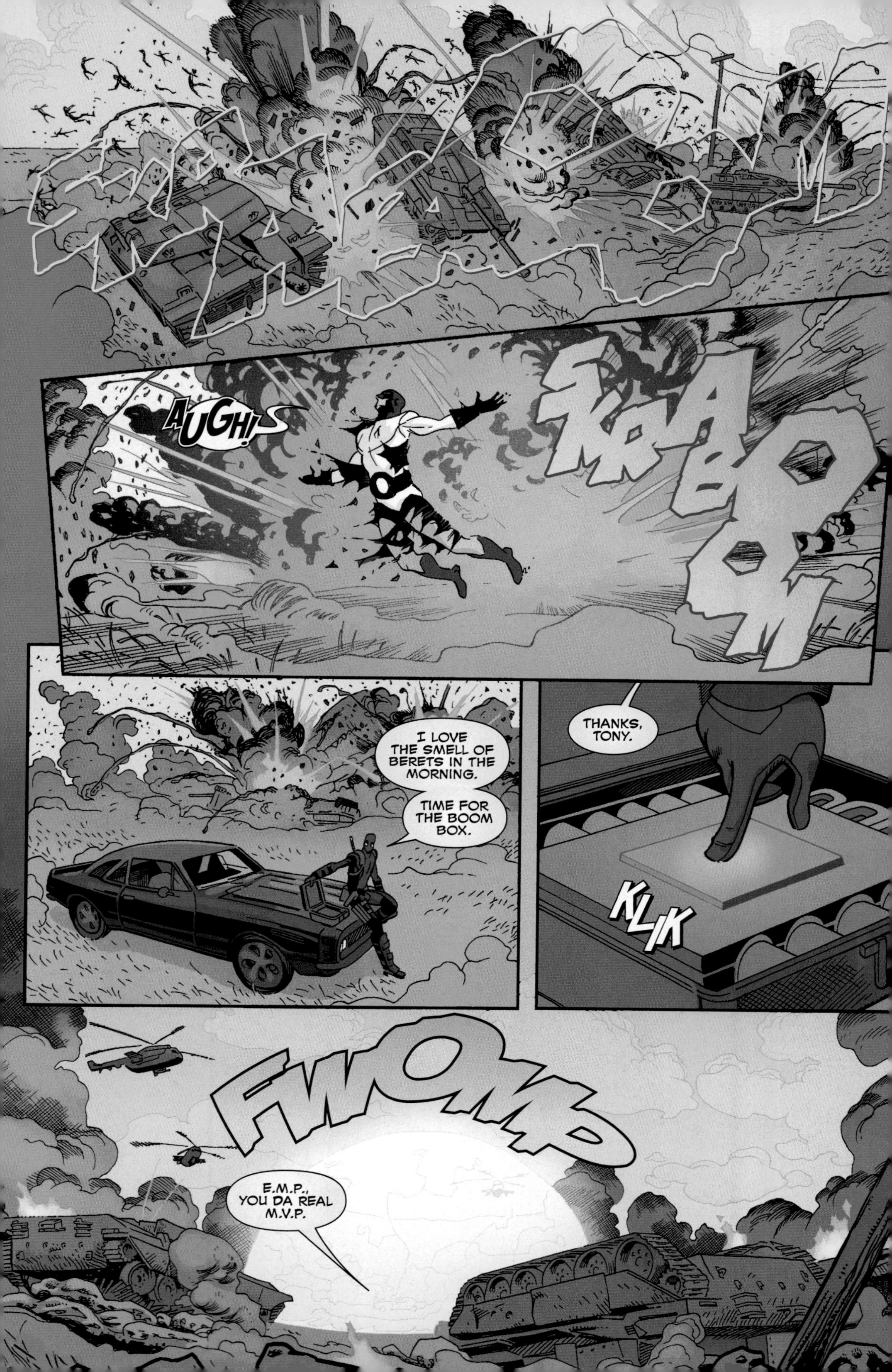
AUGH!
I LOVE THE SMELL OF BERETS IN THE MORNING.
TIME FOR THE BOOM BOX.
THANKS, TONY.
KLIK
FWOMP
E.M.P., YOU DA REAL M.V.P.

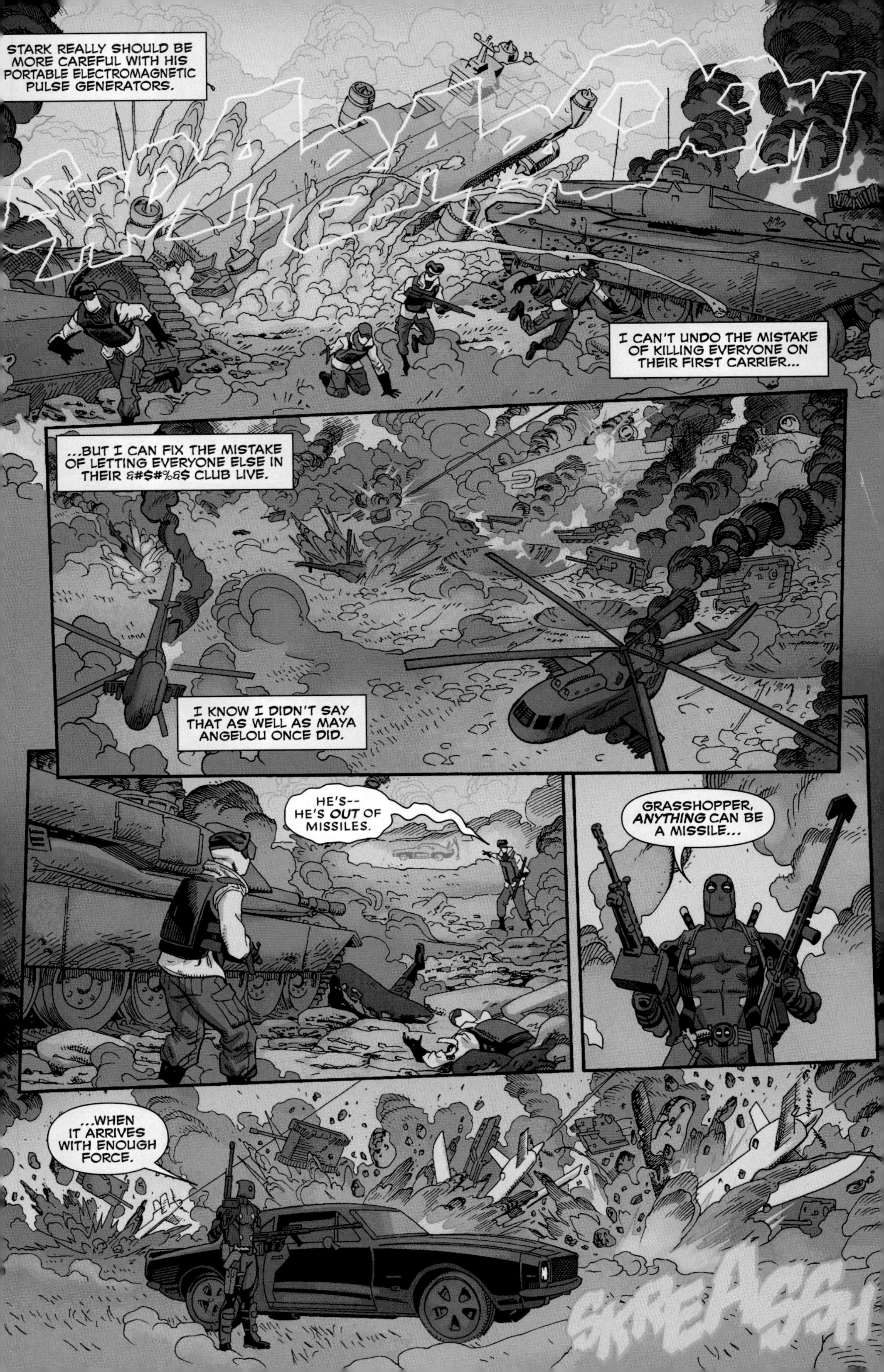
STARK REALLY SHOULD BE MORE CAREFUL WITH HIS PORTABLE ELECTROMAGNETIC PULSE GENERATORS.
I CAN'T UNDO THE MISTAKE OF KILLING EVERYONE ON THEIR FIRST CARRIER...
...BUT I CAN FIX THE MISTAKE OF LETTING EVERYONE ELSE IN THEIR &#$#%&$ CLUB LIVE.
I KNOW I DIDN'T SAY THAT AS WELL AS MAYA ANGELOU ONCE DID.
HE'S-- HE'S OUT OF MISSILES.
GRASSHOPPER, ANYTHING CAN BE A MISSILE...
...WHEN IT ARRIVES WITH ENOUGH FORCE.
SKREASSH

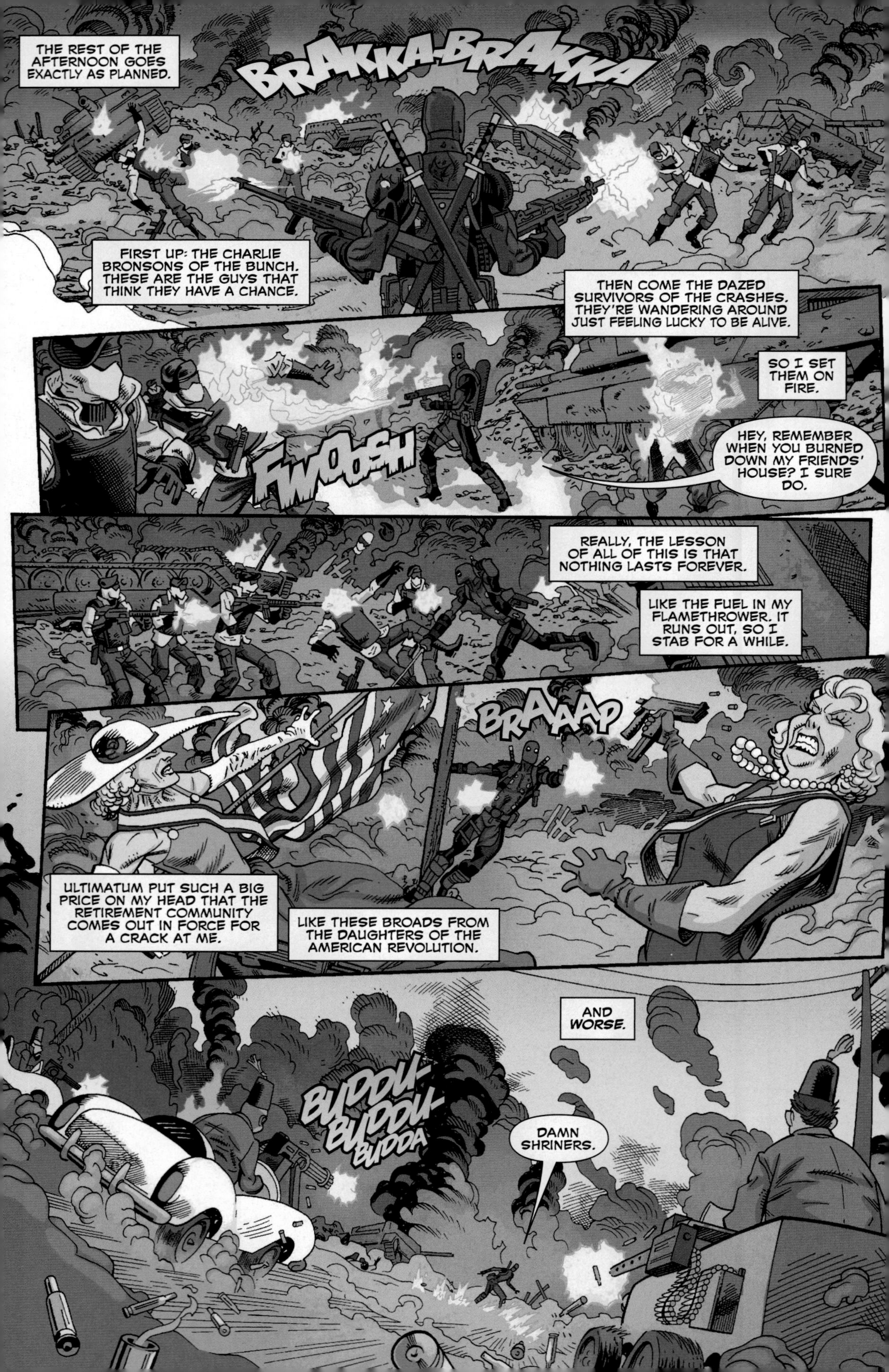
THE REST OF THE AFTERNOON GOES EXACTLY AS PLANNED.
BRAKKA-BRAKKA
FIRST UP: THE CHARLIE BRONSONS OF THE BUNCH. THESE ARE THE GUYS THAT THINK THEY HAVE A CHANCE.
THEN COME THE DAZED SURVIVORS OF THE CRASHES. THEY'RE WANDERING AROUND JUST FEELING LUCKY TO BE ALIVE.
SO I SET THEM ON FIRE.
FWOOSH
HEY, REMEMBER WHEN YOU BURNED DOWN MY FRIENDS' HOUSE? I SURE DO.
REALLY, THE LESSON OF ALL OF THIS IS THAT NOTHING LASTS FOREVER.
LIKE THE FUEL IN MY FLAMETHROWER. IT RUNS OUT, SO I STAB FOR A WHILE.
BRAAAP
ULTIMATUM PUT SUCH A BIG PRICE ON MY HEAD THAT THE RETIREMENT COMMUNITY COMES OUT IN FORCE FOR A CRACK AT ME.
LIKE THESE BROADS FROM THE DAUGHTERS OF THE AMERICAN REVOLUTION.
AND WORSE.
BUDDU-BUDDU-BUDDA
DAMN SHRINERS.

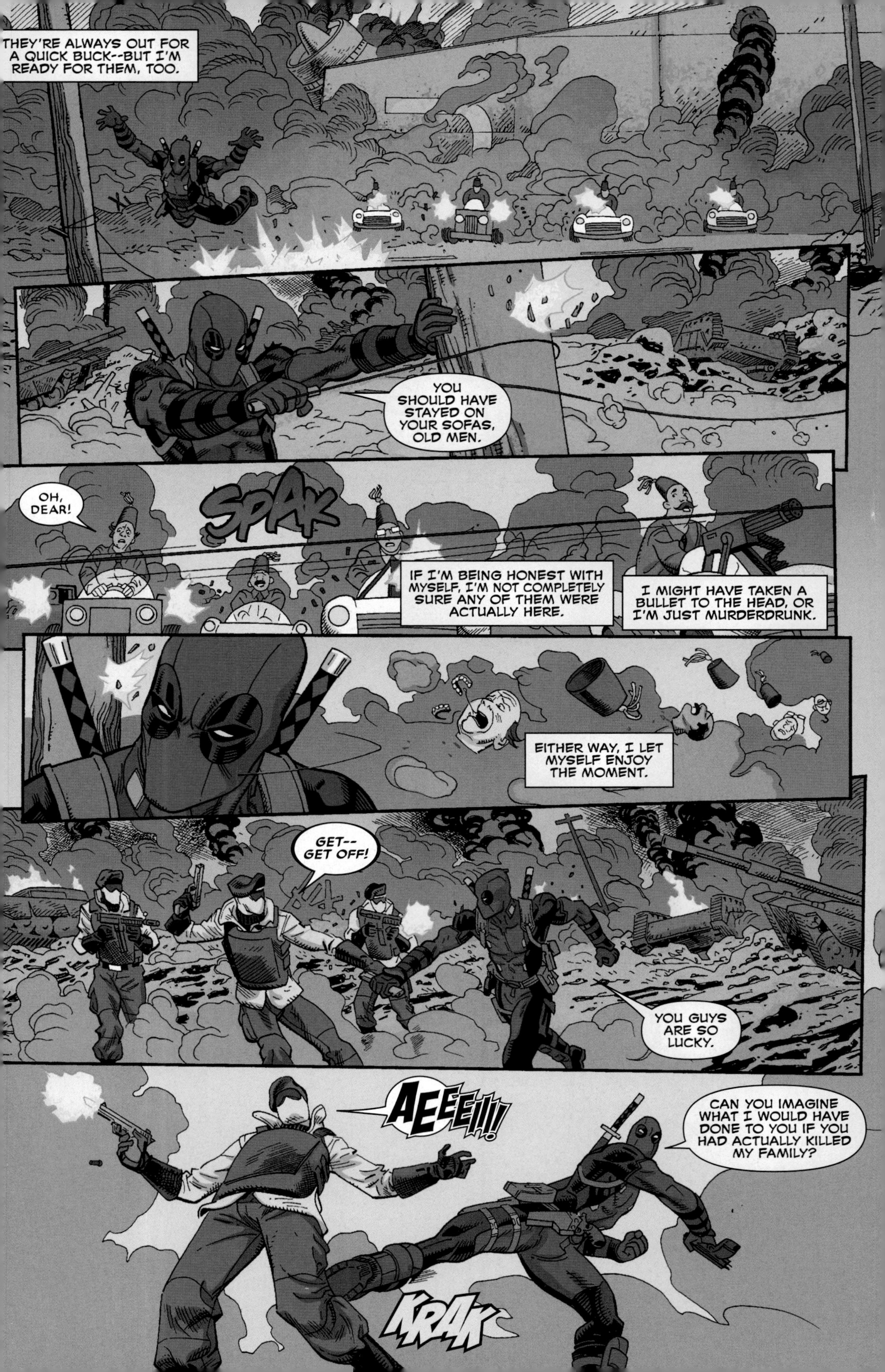
THEY'RE ALWAYS OUT FOR A QUICK BUCK--BUT I'M READY FOR THEM, TOO.
YOU SHOULD HAVE STAYED ON YOUR SOFAS, OLD MEN.
OH, DEAR!
SPAK
IF I'M BEING HONEST WITH MYSELF, I'M NOT COMPLETELY SURE ANY OF THEM WERE ACTUALLY HERE.
I MIGHT HAVE TAKEN A BULLET TO THE HEAD, OR I'M JUST MURDERDRUNK.
EITHER WAY, I LET MYSELF ENJOY THE MOMENT.
GET-- GET OFF!
YOU GUYS ARE SO LUCKY.
AEEEIII!
CAN YOU IMAGINE WHAT I WOULD HAVE DONE TO YOU IF YOU HAD ACTUALLY KILLED MY FAMILY?
KRAK

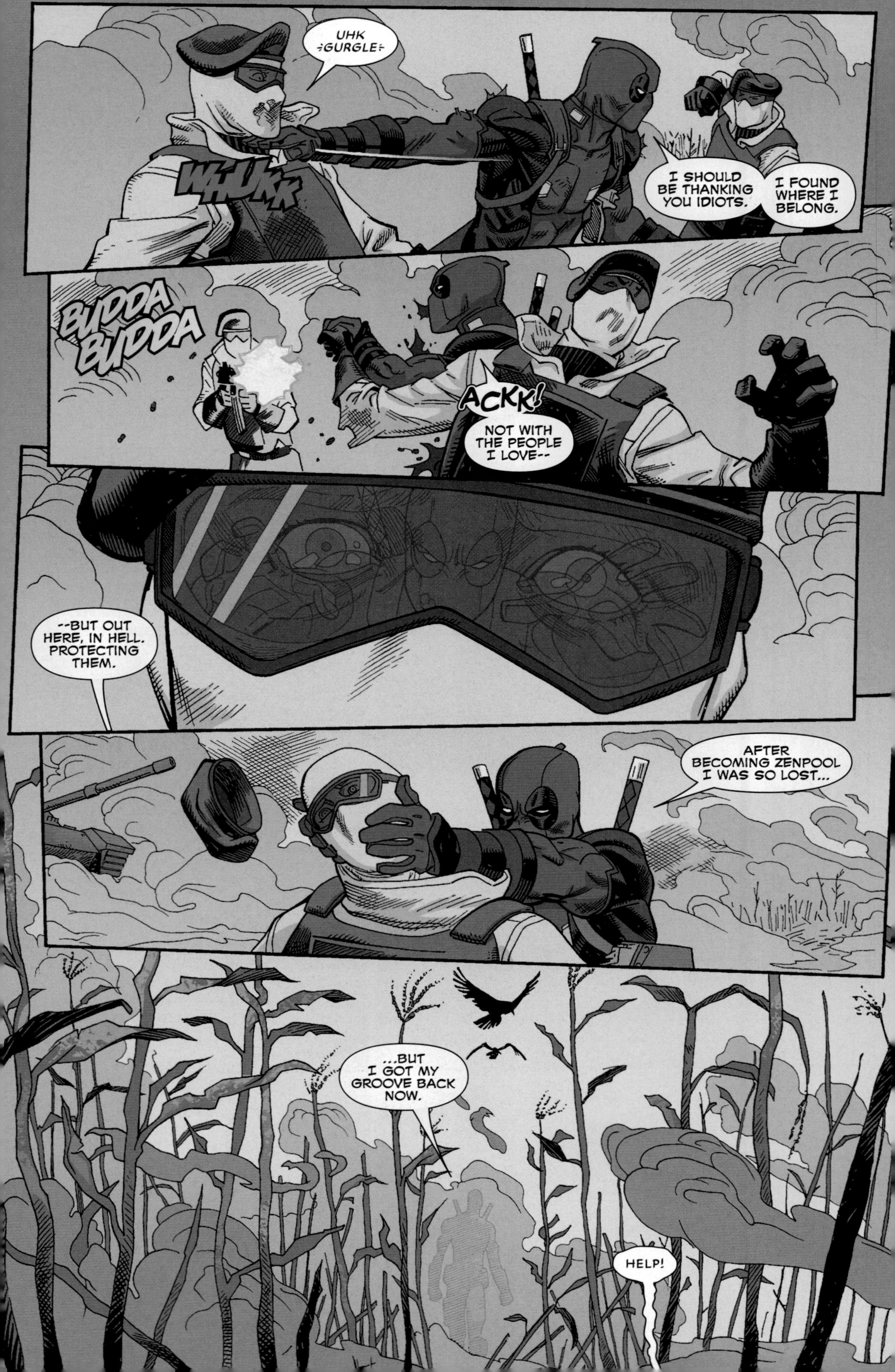
UHK ⚡GURGLE⚡
WHUKK
I SHOULD BE THANKING YOU IDIOTS.
I FOUND WHERE I BELONG.
BUDDA BUDDA
ACKK!
NOT WITH THE PEOPLE I LOVE--
--BUT OUT HERE, IN HELL. PROTECTING THEM.
AFTER BECOMING ZENPOOL I WAS SO LOST...
...BUT I GOT MY GROOVE BACK NOW.
HELP!

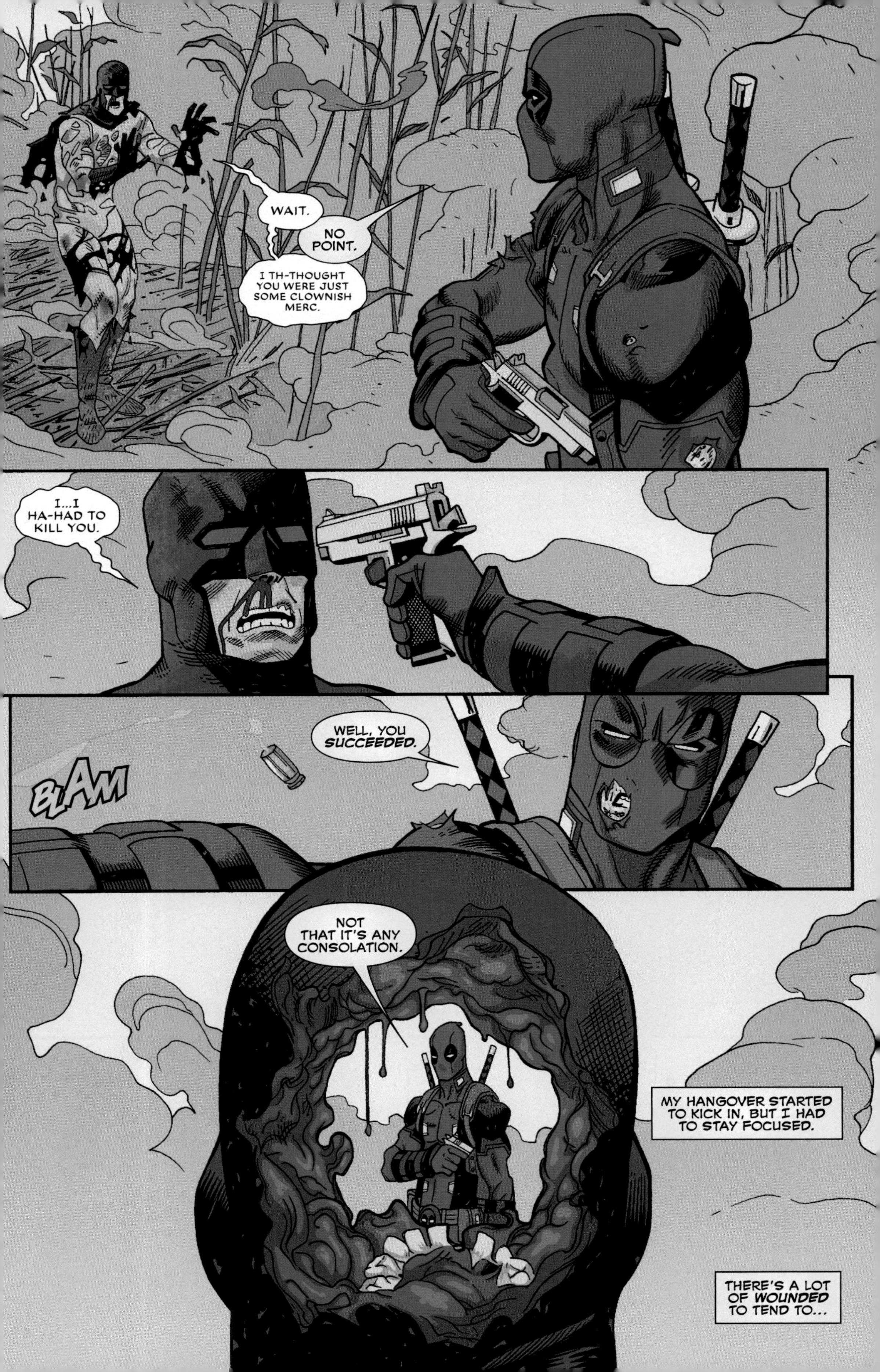
WAIT.
NO POINT.
I TH-THOUGHT YOU WERE JUST SOME CLOWNISH MERC.
I...I HA-HAD TO KILL YOU.
BLAM
WELL, YOU *SUCCEEDED.*
NOT THAT IT'S ANY CONSOLATION.
MY HANGOVER STARTED TO KICK IN, BUT I HAD TO STAY FOCUSED.
THERE'S A LOT OF *WOUNDED* TO TEND TO...

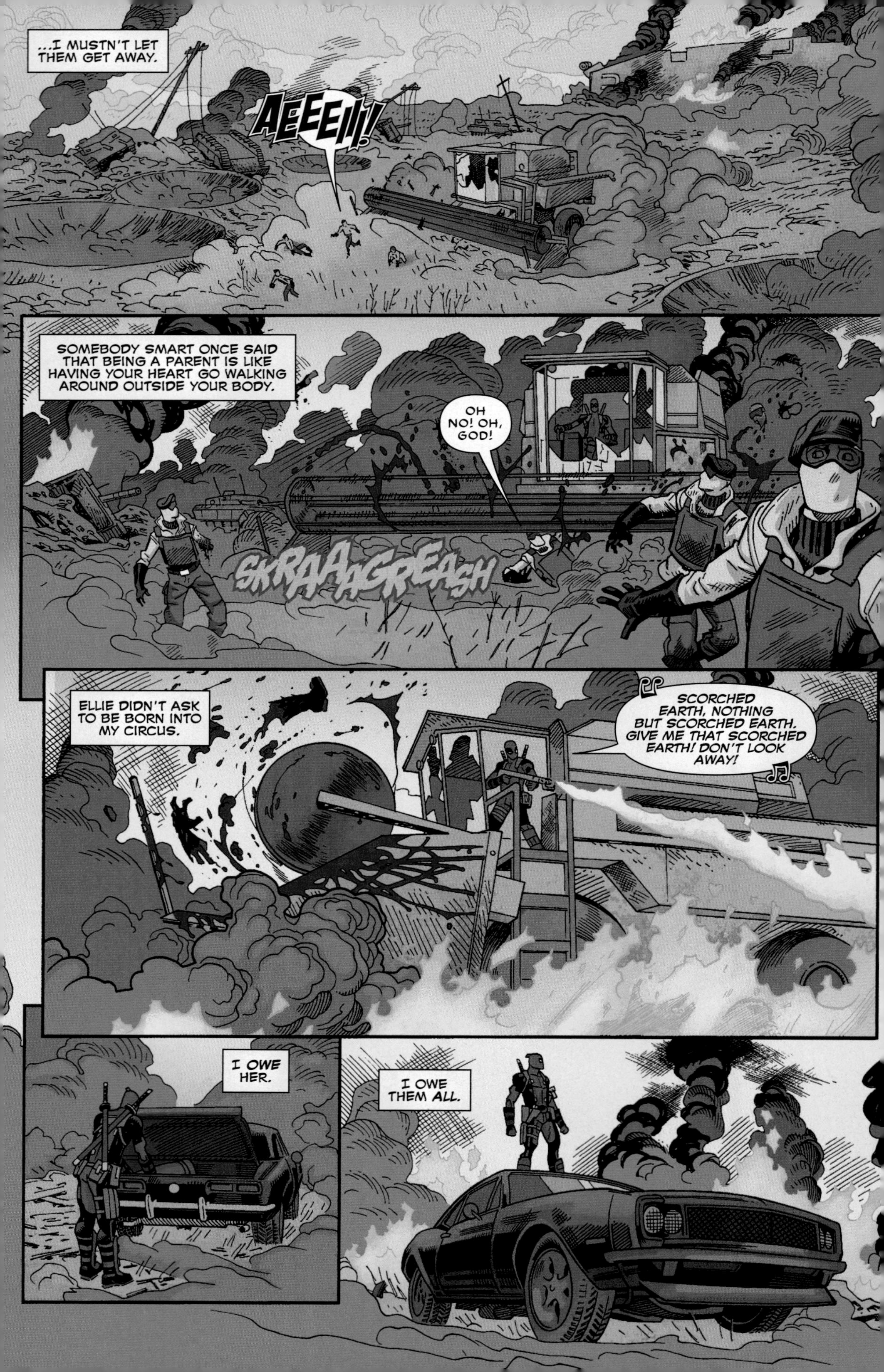
...I MUSTN'T LET THEM GET AWAY.
AEEEIII!
SOMEBODY SMART ONCE SAID THAT BEING A PARENT IS LIKE HAVING YOUR HEART GO WALKING AROUND OUTSIDE YOUR BODY.
OH NO! OH, GOD!
SKRAAAAGREASH
ELLIE DIDN'T ASK TO BE BORN INTO MY CIRCUS.
SCORCHED EARTH, NOTHING BUT SCORCHED EARTH. GIVE ME THAT SCORCHED EARTH! DON'T LOOK AWAY!
I OWE HER.
I OWE THEM ALL.

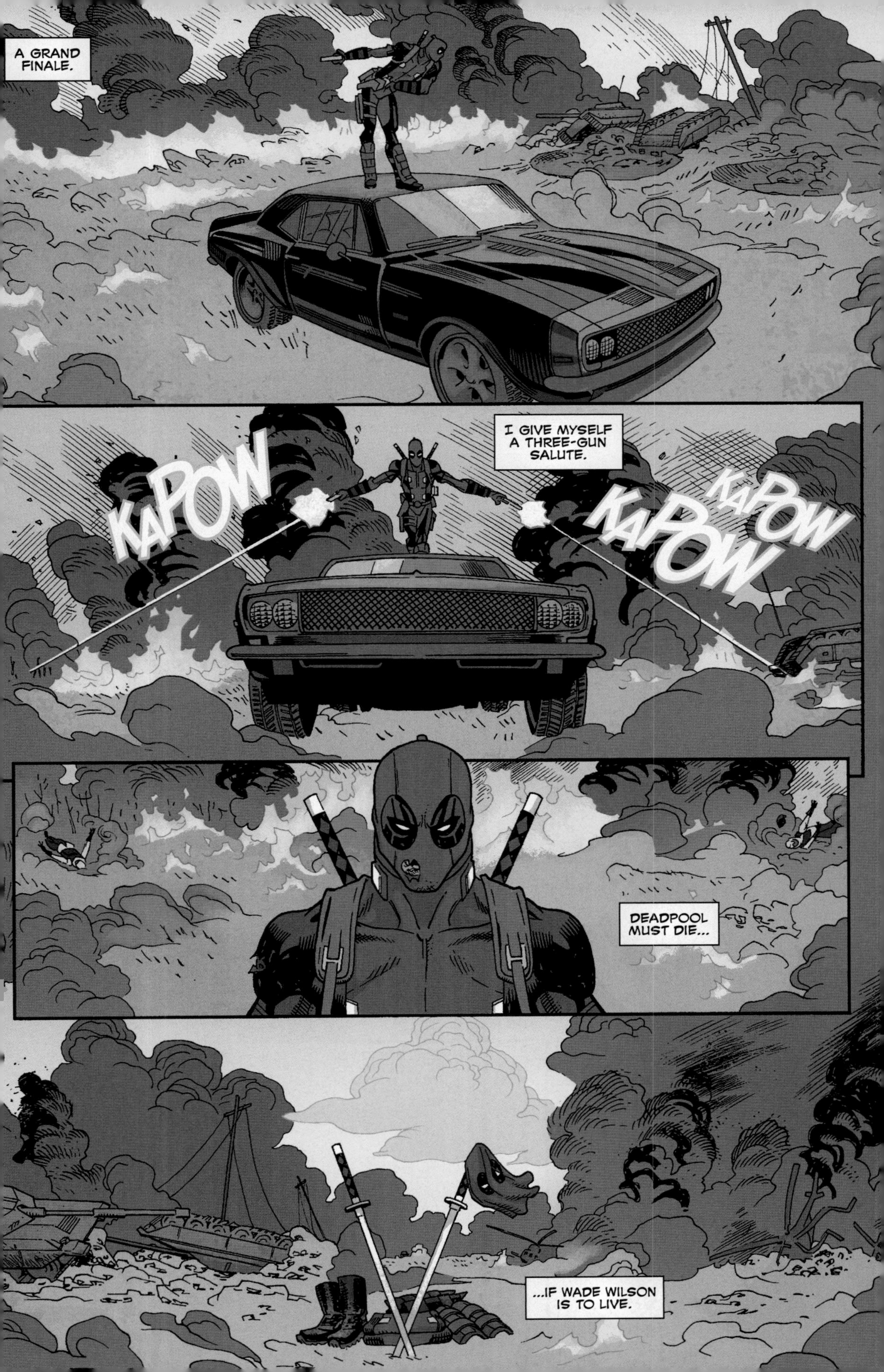

A GRAND FINALE.
I GIVE MYSELF A THREE-GUN SALUTE.
KAPOW
KAPOW
KAPOW
DEADPOOL MUST DIE...
...IF WADE WILSON IS TO LIVE.

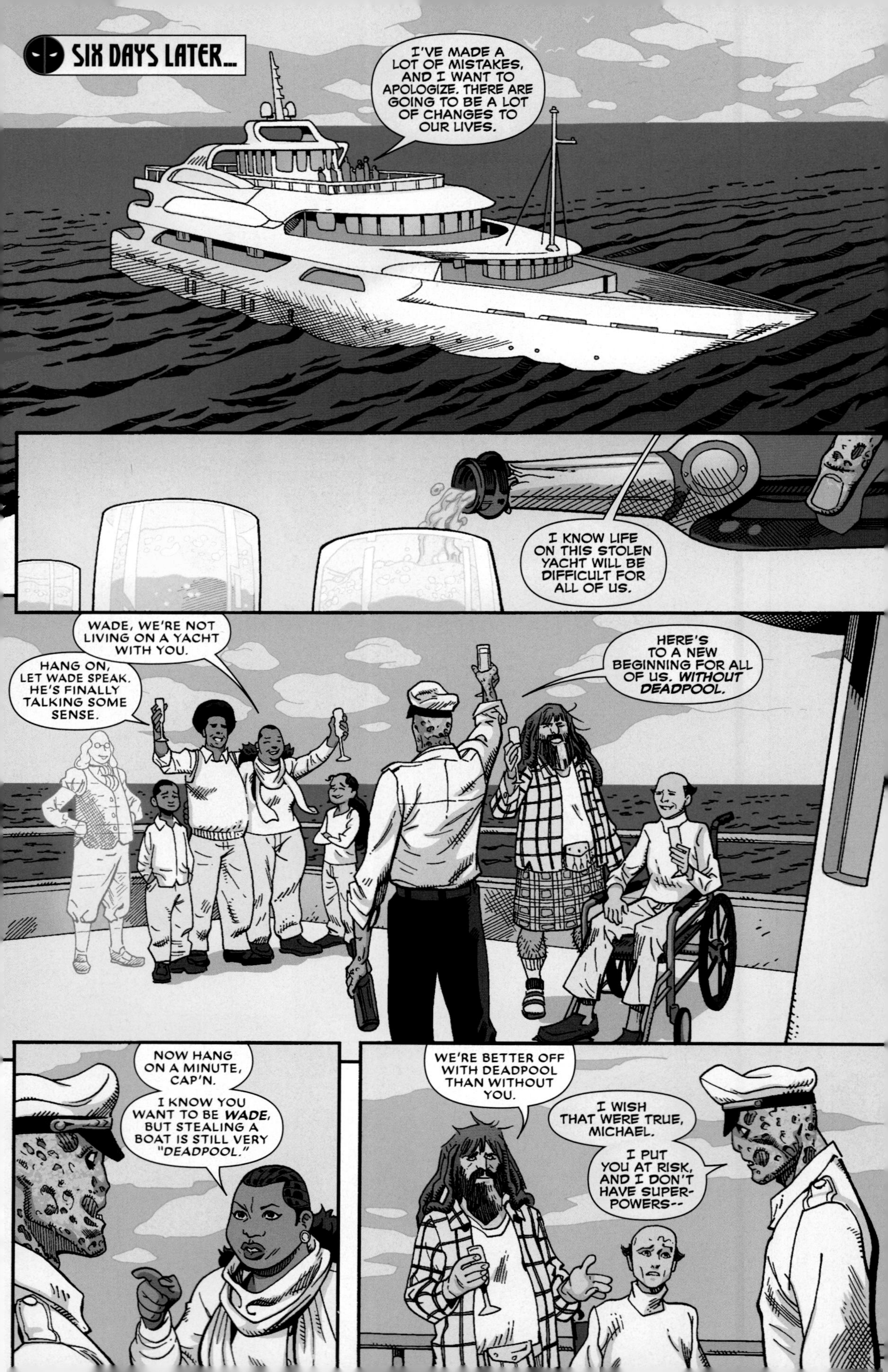
SIX DAYS LATER...
I'VE MADE A LOT OF MISTAKES, AND I WANT TO APOLOGIZE. THERE ARE GOING TO BE A LOT OF CHANGES TO OUR LIVES.
I KNOW LIFE ON THIS STOLEN YACHT WILL BE DIFFICULT FOR ALL OF US.
WADE, WE'RE NOT LIVING ON A YACHT WITH YOU.
HANG ON, LET WADE SPEAK. HE'S FINALLY TALKING SOME SENSE.
HERE'S TO A NEW BEGINNING FOR ALL OF US. *WITHOUT DEADPOOL.*
NOW HANG ON A MINUTE, CAP'N.
I KNOW YOU WANT TO BE *WADE*, BUT STEALING A BOAT IS STILL VERY "*DEADPOOL.*"
WE'RE BETTER OFF WITH DEADPOOL THAN WITHOUT YOU.
I WISH THAT WERE TRUE, MICHAEL.
I PUT YOU AT RISK, AND I DON'T HAVE SUPER-POWERS--

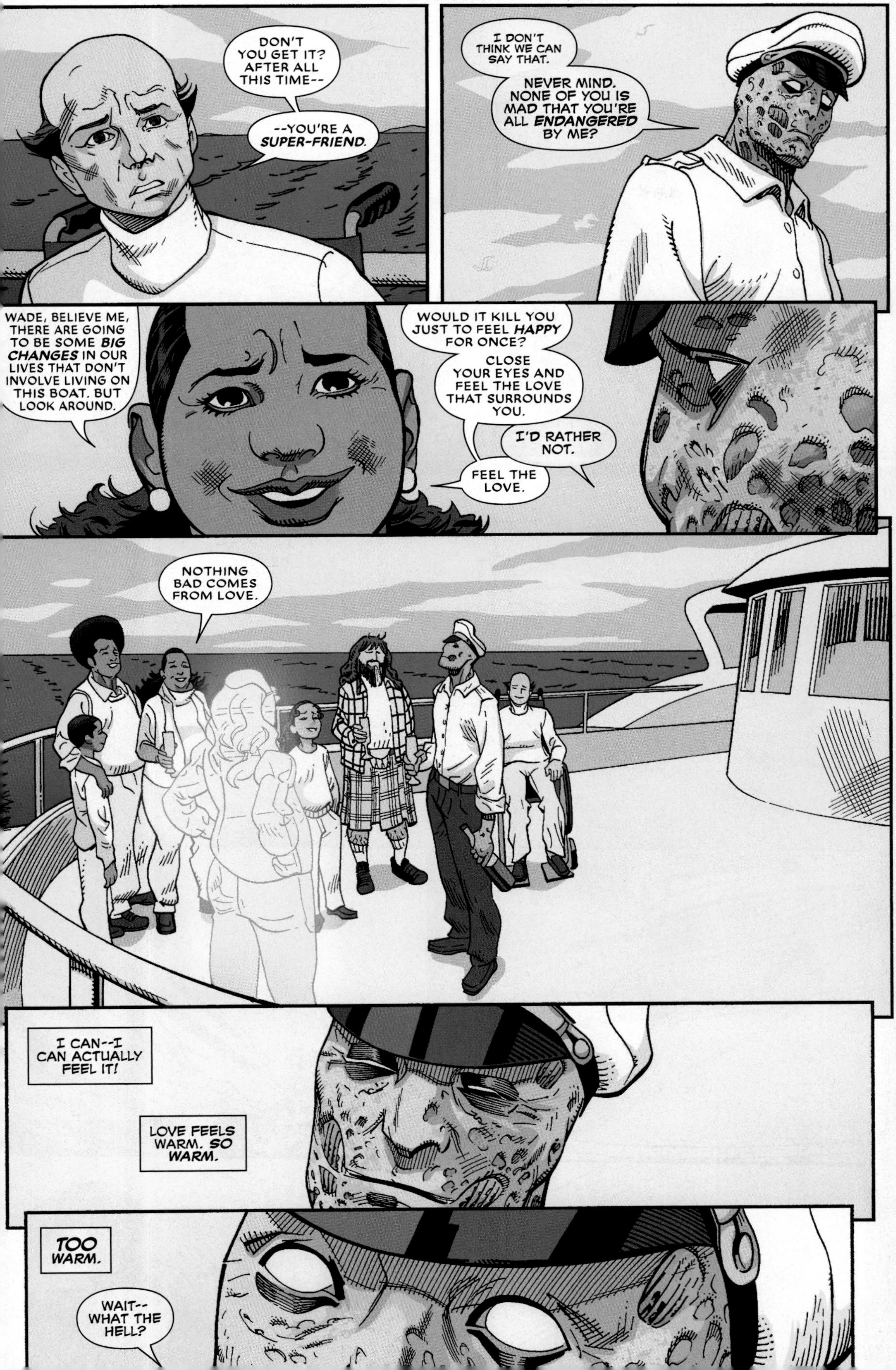
DON'T YOU GET IT? AFTER ALL THIS TIME--
--YOU'RE A SUPER-FRIEND.
I DON'T THINK WE CAN SAY THAT.
NEVER MIND. NONE OF YOU IS MAD THAT YOU'RE ALL ENDANGERED BY ME?
WADE, BELIEVE ME, THERE ARE GOING TO BE SOME BIG CHANGES IN OUR LIVES THAT DON'T INVOLVE LIVING ON THIS BOAT. BUT LOOK AROUND.
WOULD IT KILL YOU JUST TO FEEL HAPPY FOR ONCE?
CLOSE YOUR EYES AND FEEL THE LOVE THAT SURROUNDS YOU.
I'D RATHER NOT.
FEEL THE LOVE.
NOTHING BAD COMES FROM LOVE.
I CAN--I CAN ACTUALLY FEEL IT!
LOVE FEELS WARM. SO WARM.
TOO WARM.
WAIT-- WHAT THE HELL?

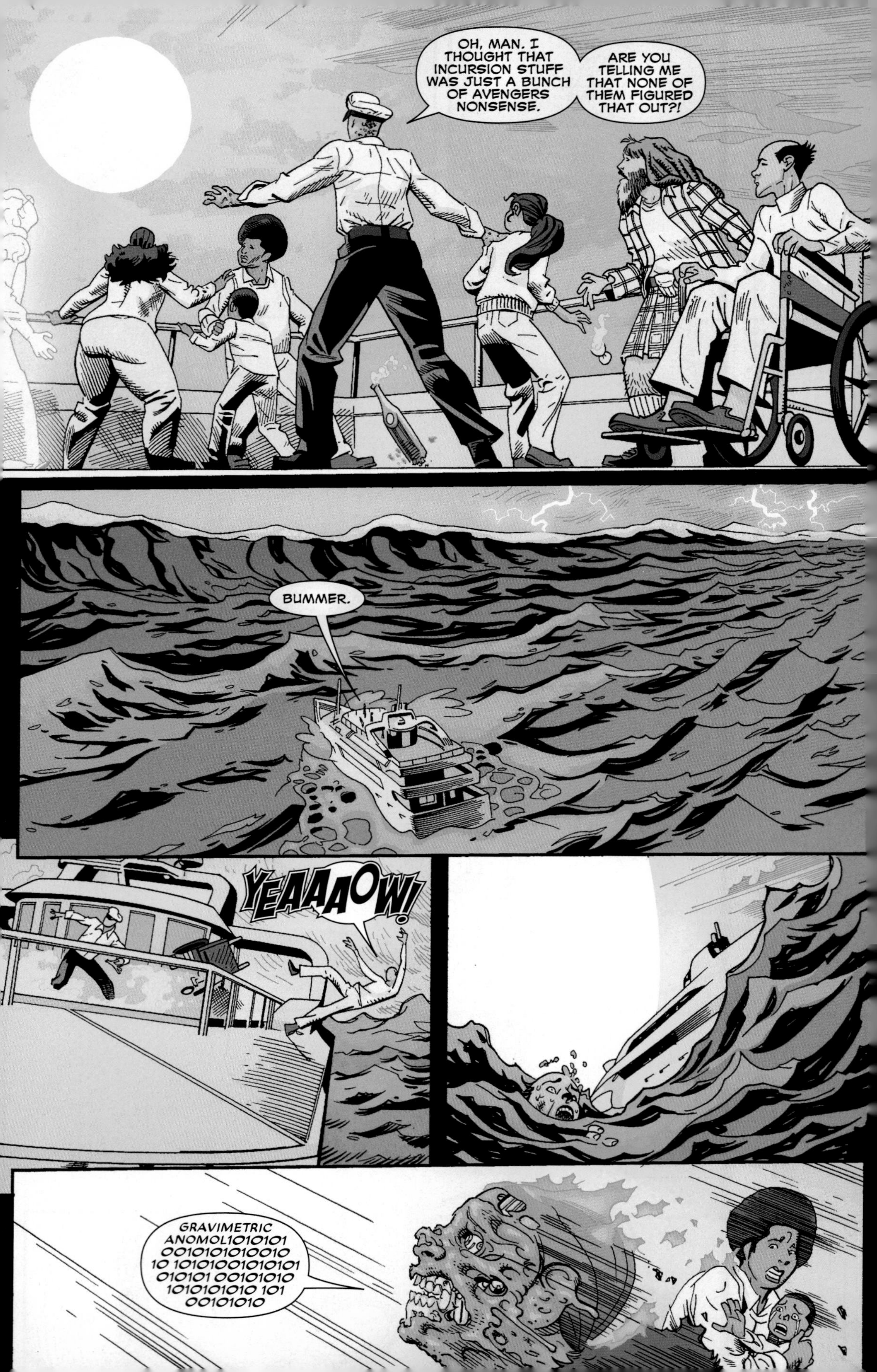
OH, MAN. I THOUGHT THAT INCURSION STUFF WAS JUST A BUNCH OF AVENGERS NONSENSE.
ARE YOU TELLING ME THAT NONE OF THEM FIGURED THAT OUT?!
BUMMER.
YEAAAAOW!
GRAVIMETRIC ANOMOL1010101 0010101010010 10 1010100101010101 010101 00101010 1010101010 101 00101010

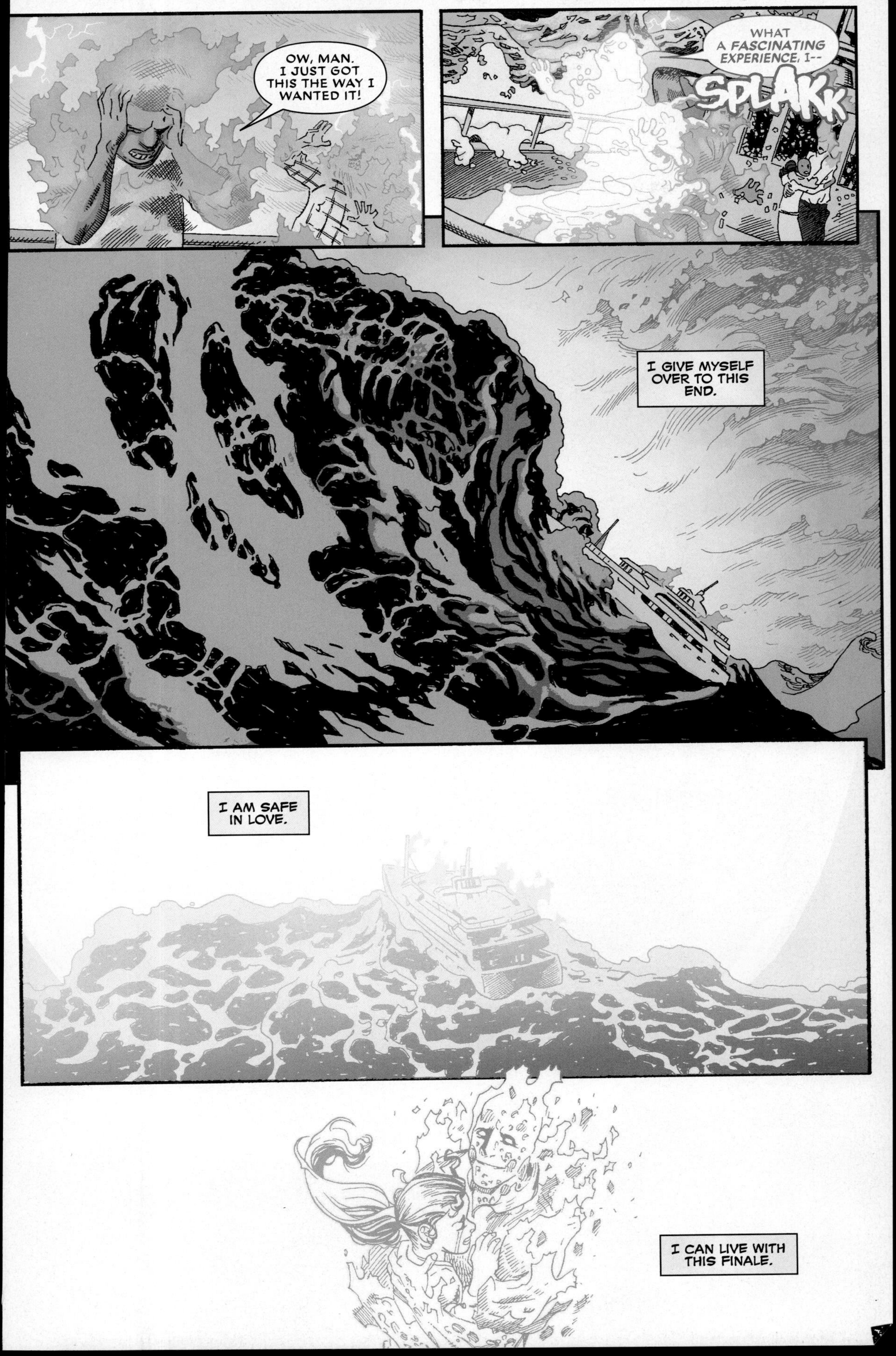
OW, MAN. I JUST GOT THIS THE WAY I WANTED IT!
WHAT A FASCINATING EXPERIENCE. I--
SPLAKK
I GIVE MYSELF OVER TO THIS END.
I AM SAFE IN LOVE.
I CAN LIVE WITH THIS FINALE.

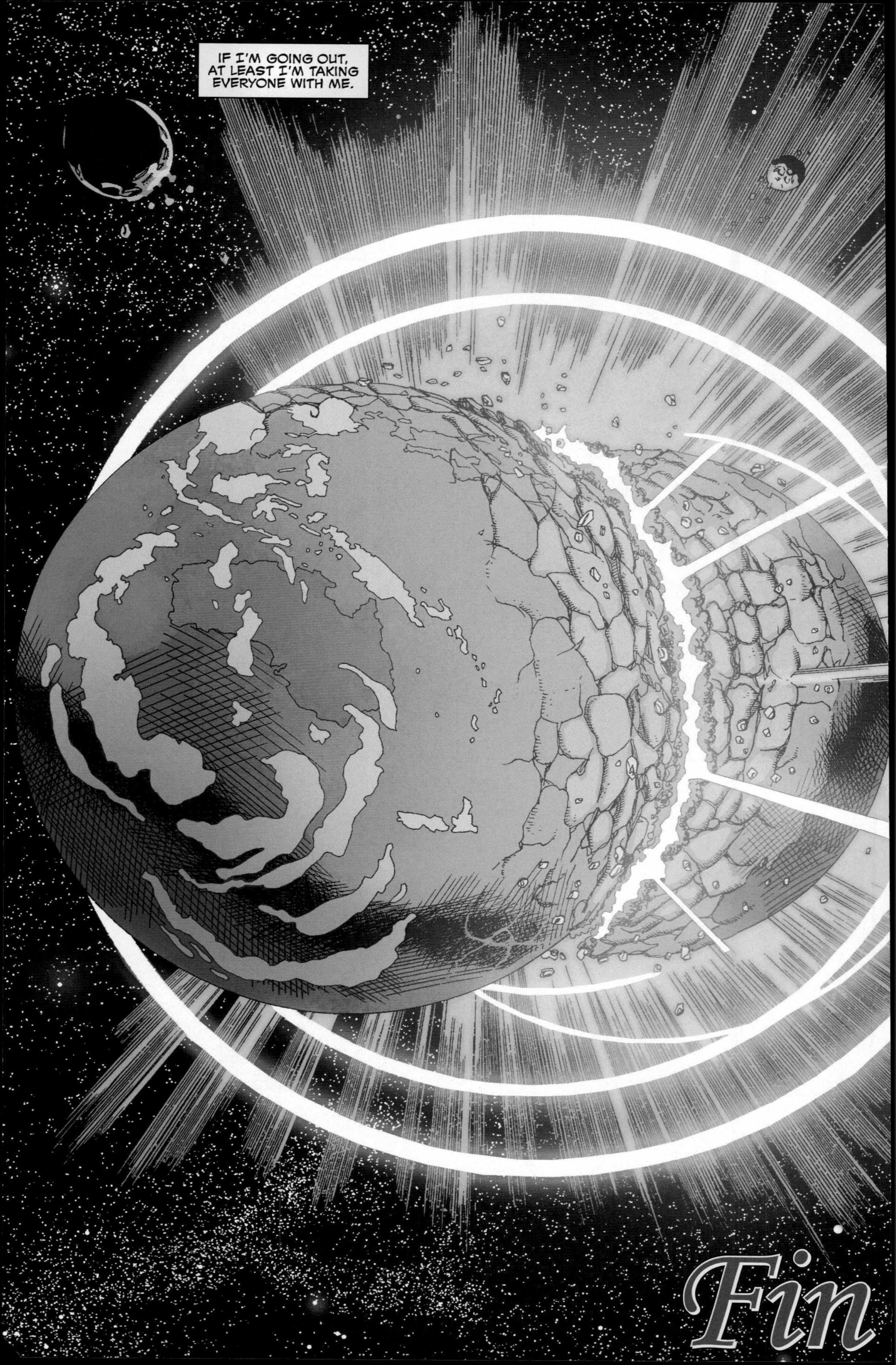
IF I'M GOING OUT, AT LEAST I'M TAKING EVERYONE WITH ME.
Fin

OH, DAMN--I'M DEAD.

AND SO IS EVERYONE ELSE. DAG, THAT'S A REAL BUMMER.

SO, ANYWAYS, BEFORE WE ALL SLIP AWAY INTO THE NOTHINGNESS OF THE ABYSS, WE THOUGHT IT MIGHT BE NICE TO PUT A SPOTLIGHT ON SOME OF THE GREAT FRIENDS I'VE MADE IN THIS RUN.

WE CALLED UP SOME AWESOME SPECIAL GUEST WRITERS TO SHINE A SPOTLIGHT/HANG A LAMPSHADE ON OUR SUPPORTING CAST.

GEEZ, WHEN WE PLANNED THIS I DIDN'T REALIZE THESE STORIES WOULD BE MEMORIALS, TOO!

OH, WELL, ENJOY!

R.I.P.
WADE WILSON
A.K.A. DEADPOOL

LI'L DEADPOOL'S TOMBSTONE ART BY
IRENE Y. LEE

DEADPOOL'S PALS 'N' GALS

Shiklah in
SHIKLAH'S CATCHING UP

Mike Drucker
writer

J.J. Kirby
artist

Veronica Gandini
colorist

Agent Preston in
THE FAMILY S.H.I.E.L.D.

Paul Scheer & Nick Giovannetti
writers

Ty Templeton
artist

Evan Sabahnur in
WHAT DO WE WANT? APOCALYPSE! WHEN DO WE WANT IT? NOW!

Ben Acker & Ben Blacker
writers

Natalie Nourigat
artist

Agent Scott Adsit in
THE THWIPSTER AND THE QUIPSTER BATTLE THE HIPSTERS!

Scott Aukerman
writer

Mirko Colak
artist

Ruth Redmond
colorist

Benjamin Franklin in
ALL ABOUT THE BENJAMINS

Jason Mantzoukas
writer

Todd Nauck
artist

Veronica Gandini
colorist

Michael the Necromancer in
PARENTS: THE MEETING

Matt Selman
writer

Jacob Chabot
artist

all lettered by VC'S Joe Sabino

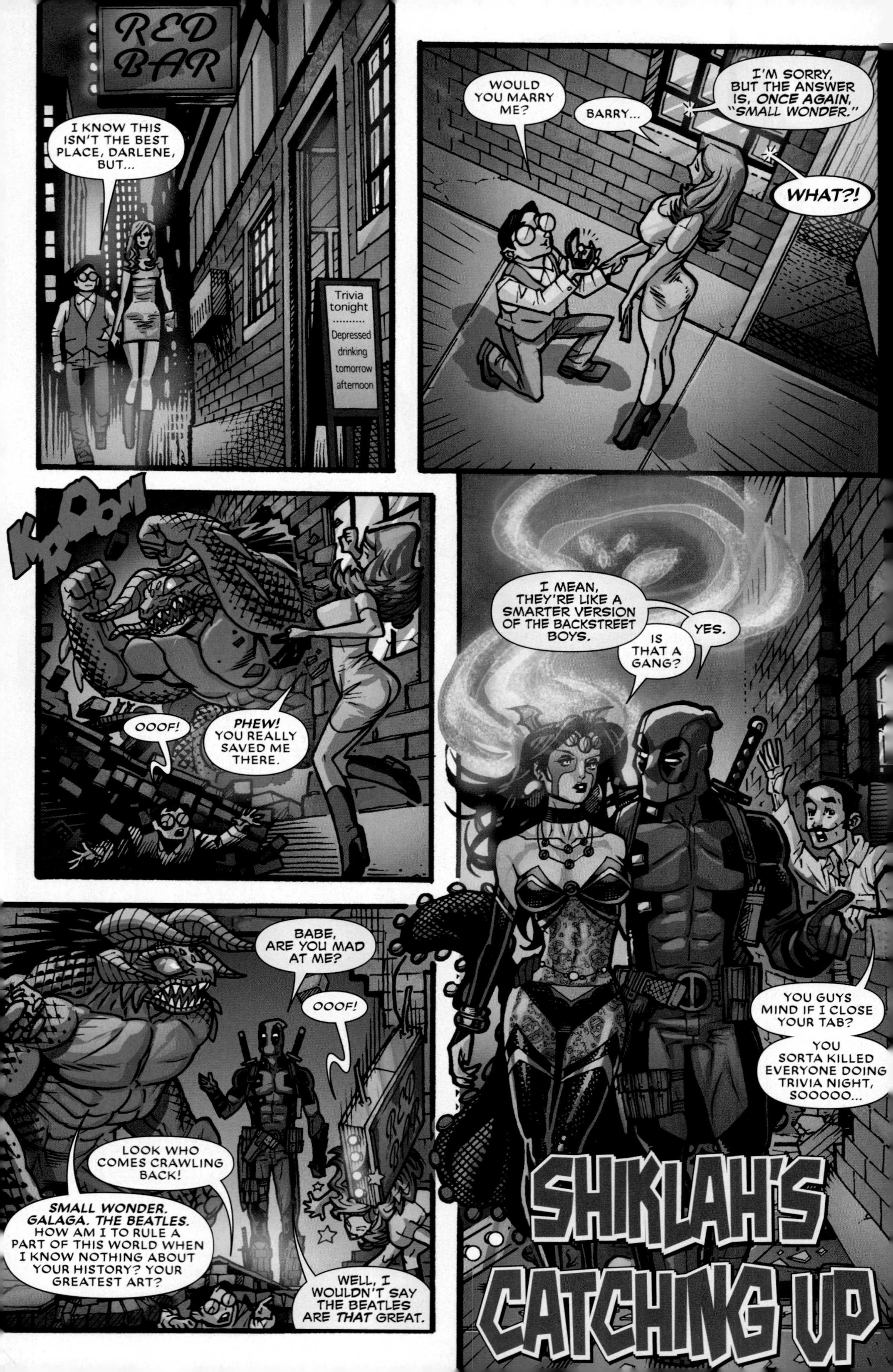
RED BAR
I KNOW THIS ISN'T THE BEST PLACE, DARLENE, BUT...
Trivia tonight
Depressed drinking tomorrow afternoon
WOULD YOU MARRY ME?
BARRY...
I'M SORRY, BUT THE ANSWER IS, ONCE AGAIN, "SMALL WONDER."
WHAT?!
KRAKOOM
OOOF!
PHEW! YOU REALLY SAVED ME THERE.
BABE, ARE YOU MAD AT ME?
OOOF!
LOOK WHO COMES CRAWLING BACK!
SMALL WONDER. GALAGA. THE BEATLES. HOW AM I TO RULE A PART OF THIS WORLD WHEN I KNOW NOTHING ABOUT YOUR HISTORY? YOUR GREATEST ART?
WELL, I WOULDN'T SAY THE BEATLES ARE THAT GREAT.
I MEAN, THEY'RE LIKE A SMARTER VERSION OF THE BACKSTREET BOYS.
IS THAT A GANG?
YES.
YOU GUYS MIND IF I CLOSE YOUR TAB?
YOU SORTA KILLED EVERYONE DOING TRIVIA NIGHT, SOOOOO...
SHIKLAH'S CATCHING UP

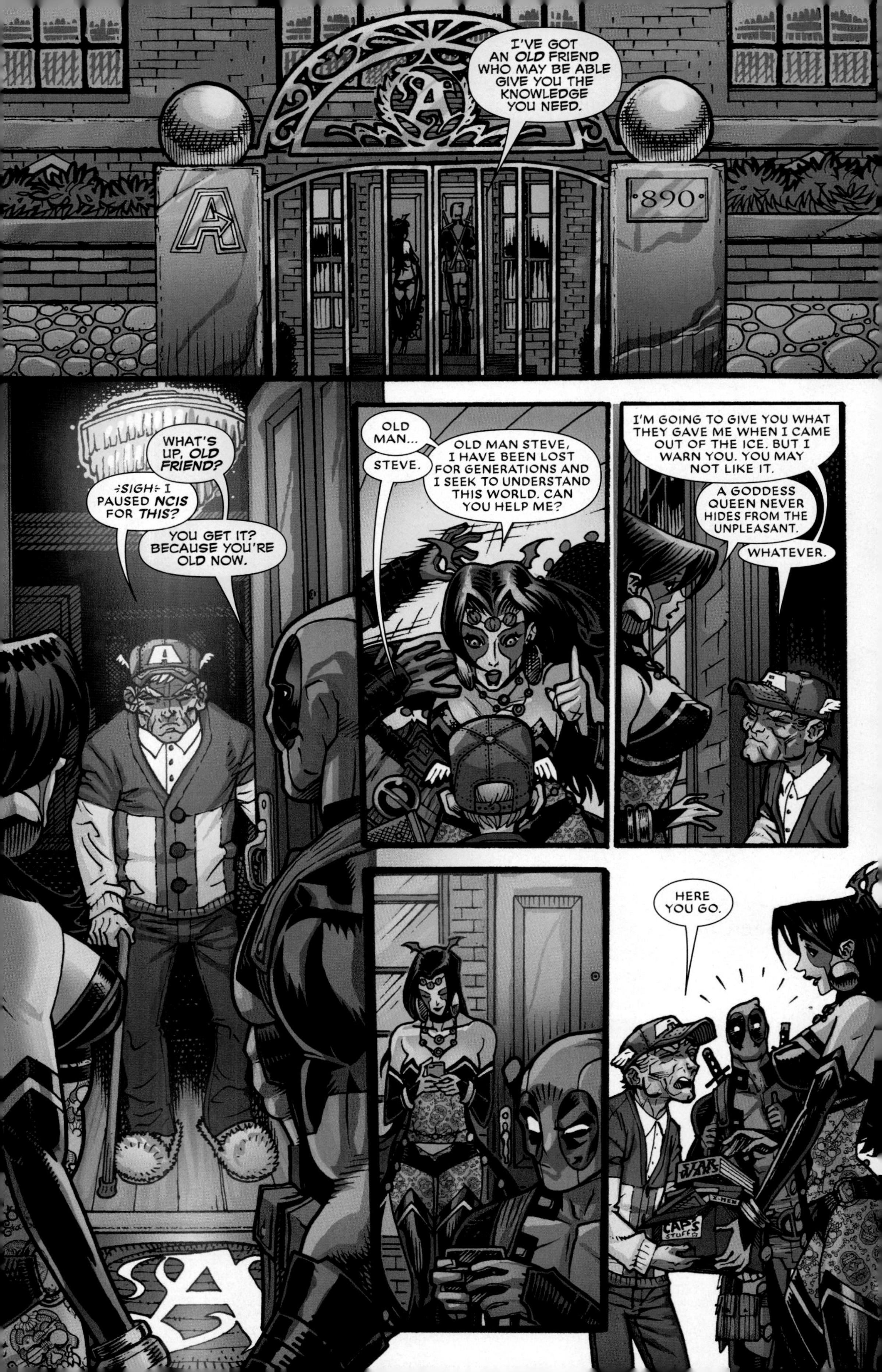
I'VE GOT AN OLD FRIEND WHO MAY BE ABLE GIVE YOU THE KNOWLEDGE YOU NEED.
890
WHAT'S UP, OLD FRIEND?
÷SIGH÷ I PAUSED NCIS FOR THIS?
YOU GET IT? BECAUSE YOU'RE OLD NOW.
OLD MAN...
STEVE.
OLD MAN STEVE, I HAVE BEEN LOST FOR GENERATIONS AND I SEEK TO UNDERSTAND THIS WORLD. CAN YOU HELP ME?
I'M GOING TO GIVE YOU WHAT THEY GAVE ME WHEN I CAME OUT OF THE ICE. BUT I WARN YOU. YOU MAY NOT LIKE IT.
A GODDESS QUEEN NEVER HIDES FROM THE UNPLEASANT.
WHATEVER.
HERE YOU GO.
STAR WARS
X-MEN
CAP'S STUFF

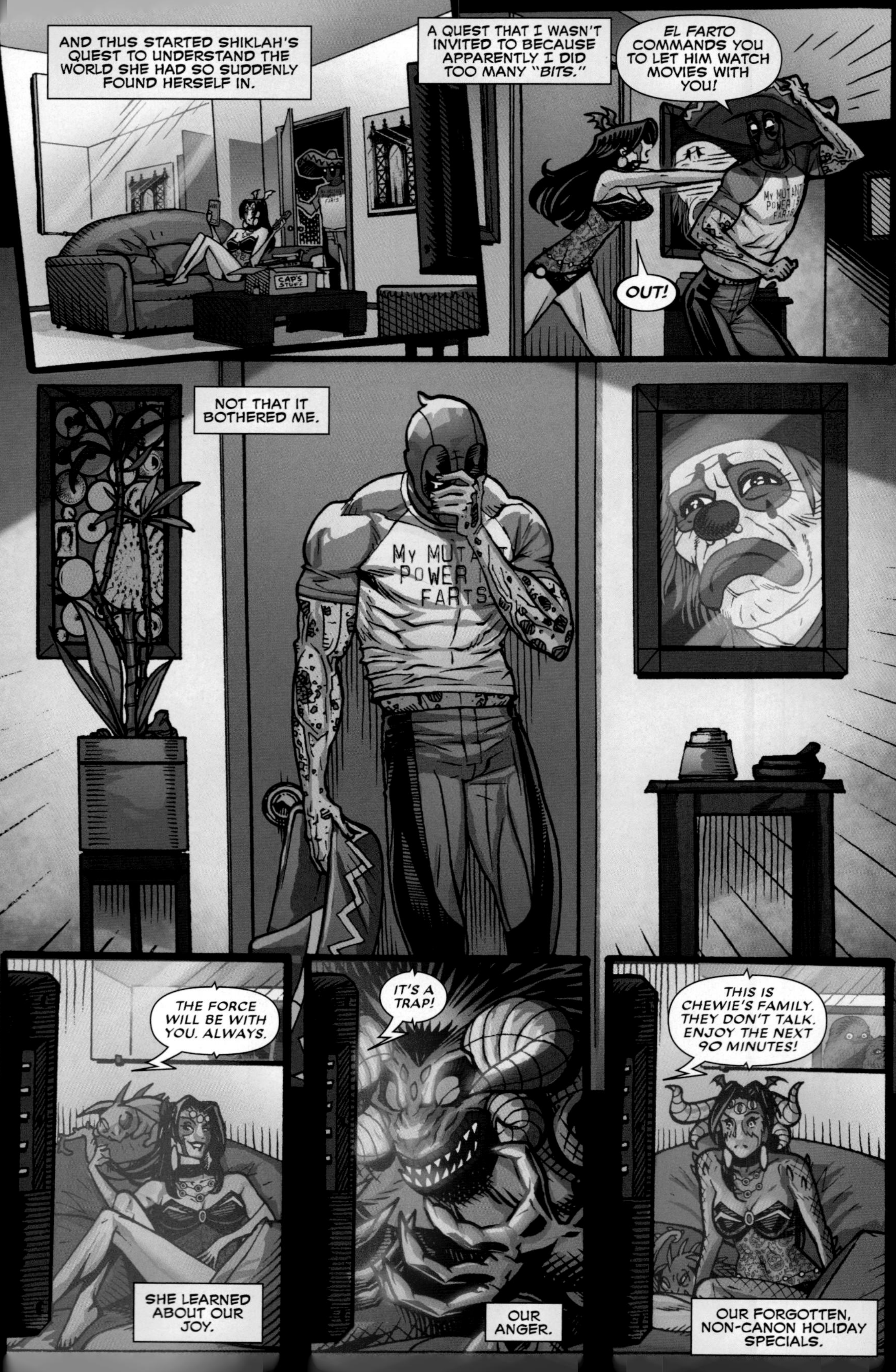
AND THUS STARTED SHIKLAH'S QUEST TO UNDERSTAND THE WORLD SHE HAD SO SUDDENLY FOUND HERSELF IN.
CAP'S STUFF
A QUEST THAT I WASN'T INVITED TO BECAUSE APPARENTLY I DID TOO MANY "BITS."
EL FARTO COMMANDS YOU TO LET HIM WATCH MOVIES WITH YOU!
OUT!
NOT THAT IT BOTHERED ME.
MY MUTANT POWER IS FARTS
THE FORCE WILL BE WITH YOU. ALWAYS.
SHE LEARNED ABOUT OUR JOY.
IT'S A TRAP!
OUR ANGER.
THIS IS CHEWIE'S FAMILY. THEY DON'T TALK. ENJOY THE NEXT 90 MINUTES!
OUR FORGOTTEN, NON-CANON HOLIDAY SPECIALS.

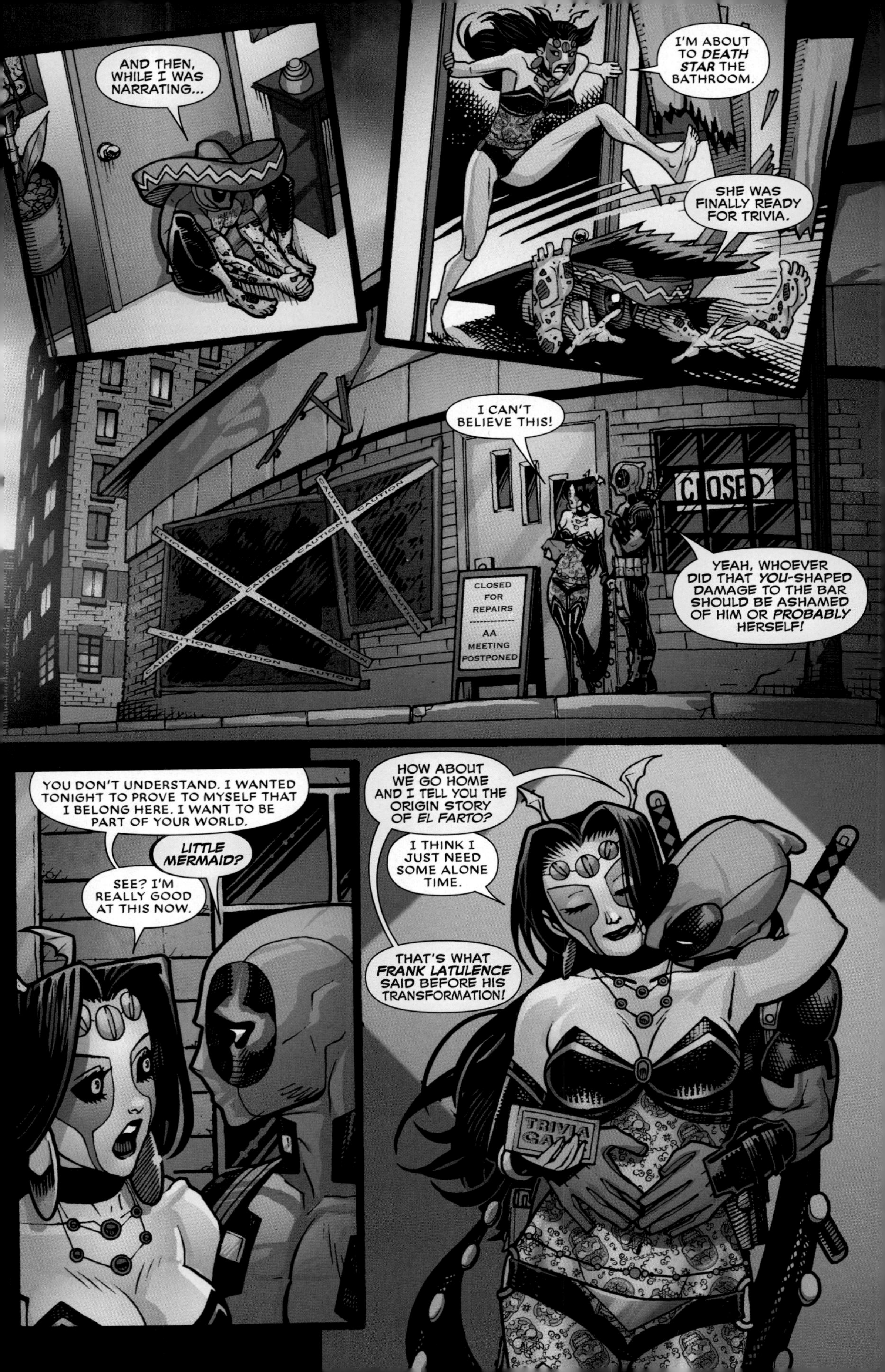
AND THEN, WHILE I WAS NARRATING...
I'M ABOUT TO *DEATH STAR* THE BATHROOM.
SHE WAS FINALLY READY FOR TRIVIA.
I CAN'T BELIEVE THIS!
CLOSED
CAUTION
CLOSED FOR REPAIRS
AA MEETING POSTPONED
YEAH, WHOEVER DID THAT *YOU*-SHAPED DAMAGE TO THE BAR SHOULD BE ASHAMED OF HIM OR *PROBABLY* HERSELF!
YOU DON'T UNDERSTAND. I WANTED TONIGHT TO PROVE TO MYSELF THAT I BELONG HERE. I WANT TO BE PART OF YOUR WORLD.
LITTLE MERMAID?
SEE? I'M REALLY GOOD AT THIS NOW.
HOW ABOUT WE GO HOME AND I TELL YOU THE ORIGIN STORY OF *EL FARTO?*
I THINK I JUST NEED SOME ALONE TIME.
THAT'S WHAT *FRANK LATULENCE* SAID BEFORE HIS TRANSFORMATION!
TRIVIA GAME

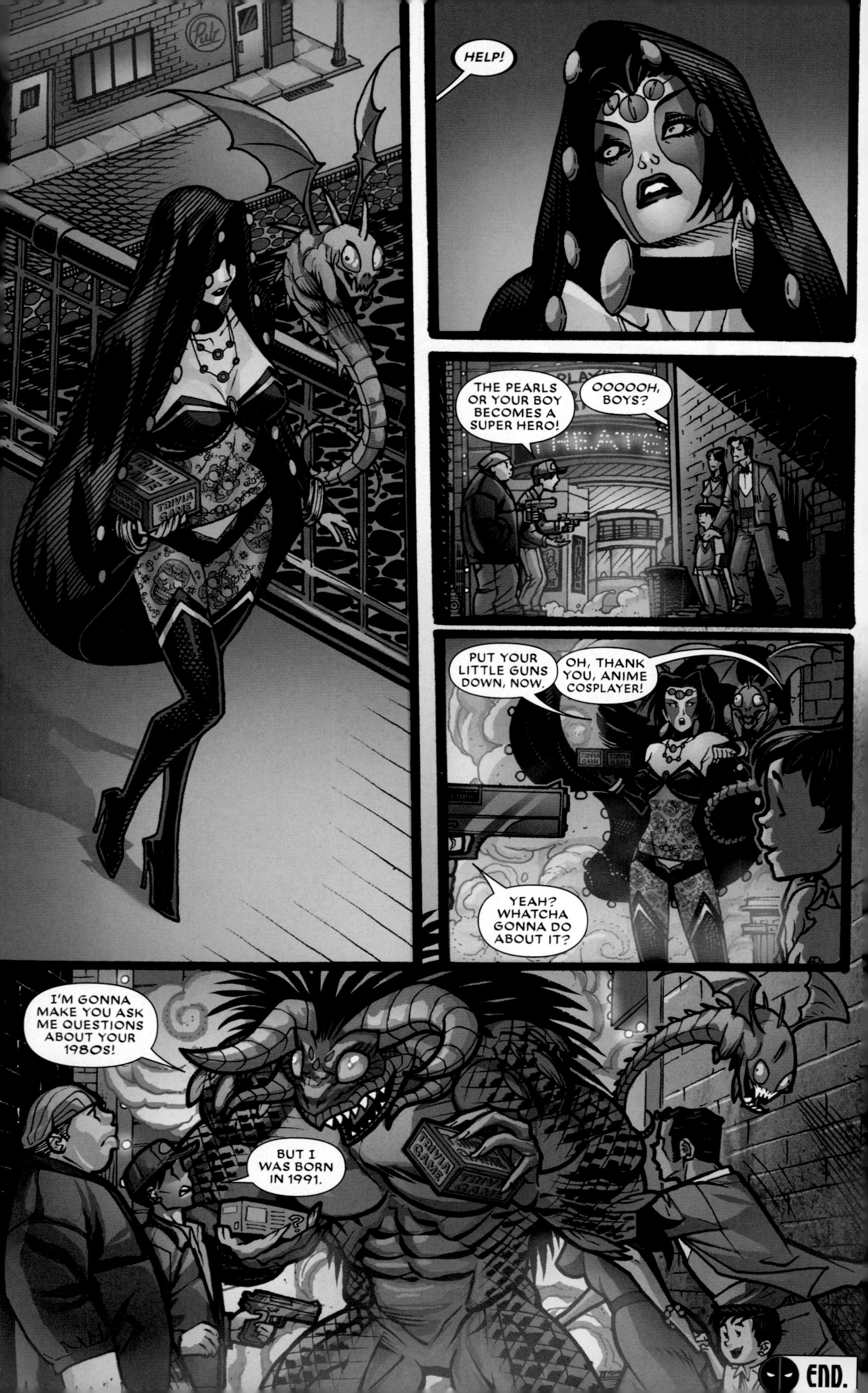
HELP!
THE PEARLS OR YOUR BOY BECOMES A SUPER HERO!
OOOOOH, BOYS?
PUT YOUR LITTLE GUNS DOWN, NOW.
OH, THANK YOU, ANIME COSPLAYER!
YEAH? WHATCHA GONNA DO ABOUT IT?
I'M GONNA MAKE YOU ASK ME QUESTIONS ABOUT YOUR 1980S!
BUT I WAS BORN IN 1991.
TRIVIA GAME
END.

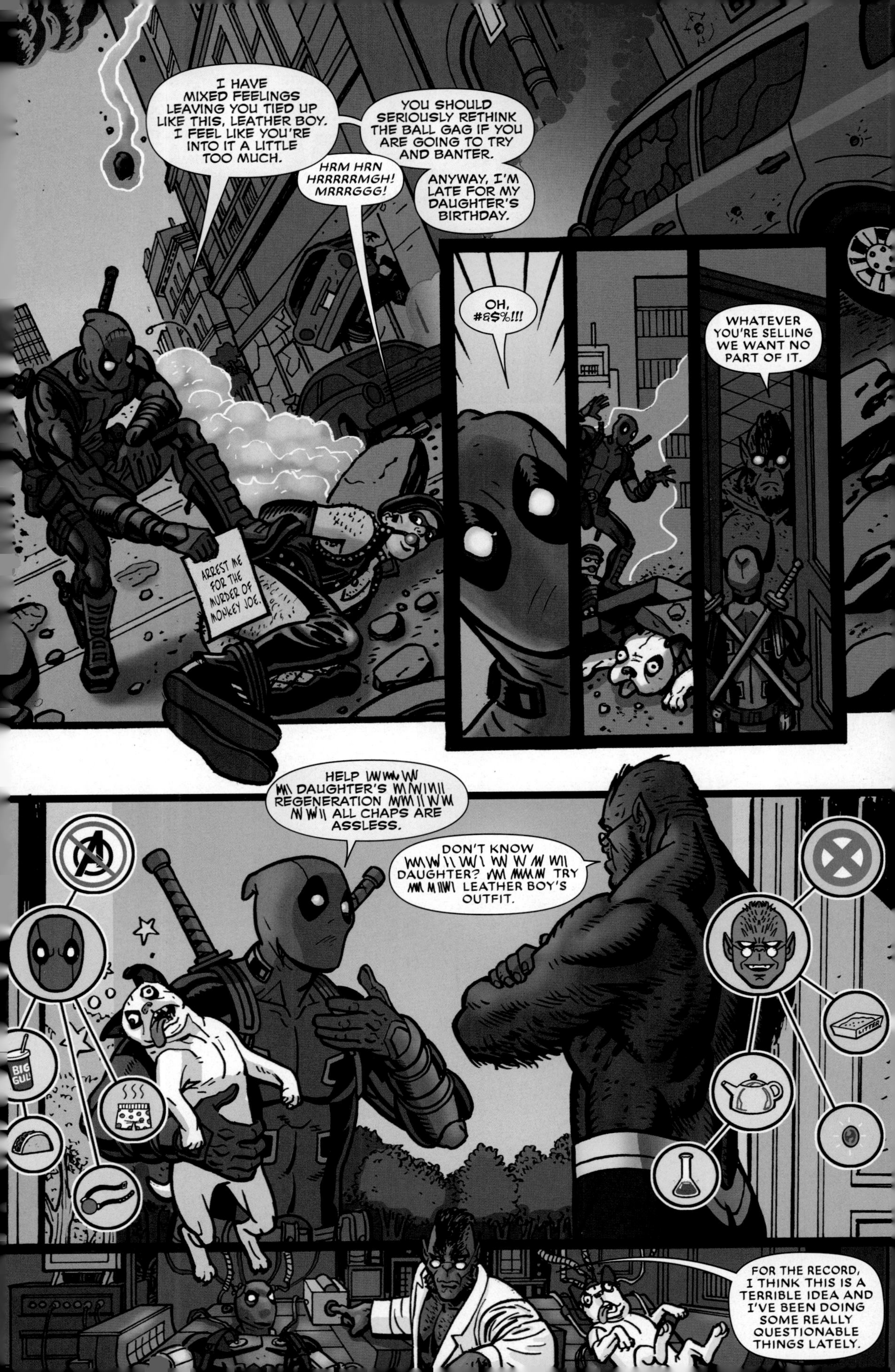
I HAVE MIXED FEELINGS LEAVING YOU TIED UP LIKE THIS, LEATHER BOY. I FEEL LIKE YOU'RE INTO IT A LITTLE TOO MUCH.
YOU SHOULD SERIOUSLY RETHINK THE BALL GAG IF YOU ARE GOING TO TRY AND BANTER.
HRM HRN HRRRRRMGH! MRRRGGG!
ANYWAY, I'M LATE FOR MY DAUGHTER'S BIRTHDAY.
ARREST ME FOR THE MURDER OF MONKEY JOE.
OH, #a$%!!!
WHATEVER YOU'RE SELLING WE WANT NO PART OF IT.
HELP DAUGHTER'S REGENERATION ALL CHAPS ARE ASSLESS.
DON'T KNOW DAUGHTER? TRY LEATHER BOY'S OUTFIT.
BIG GUL
LITTER
FOR THE RECORD, I THINK THIS IS A TERRIBLE IDEA AND I'VE BEEN DOING SOME REALLY QUESTIONABLE THINGS LATELY.

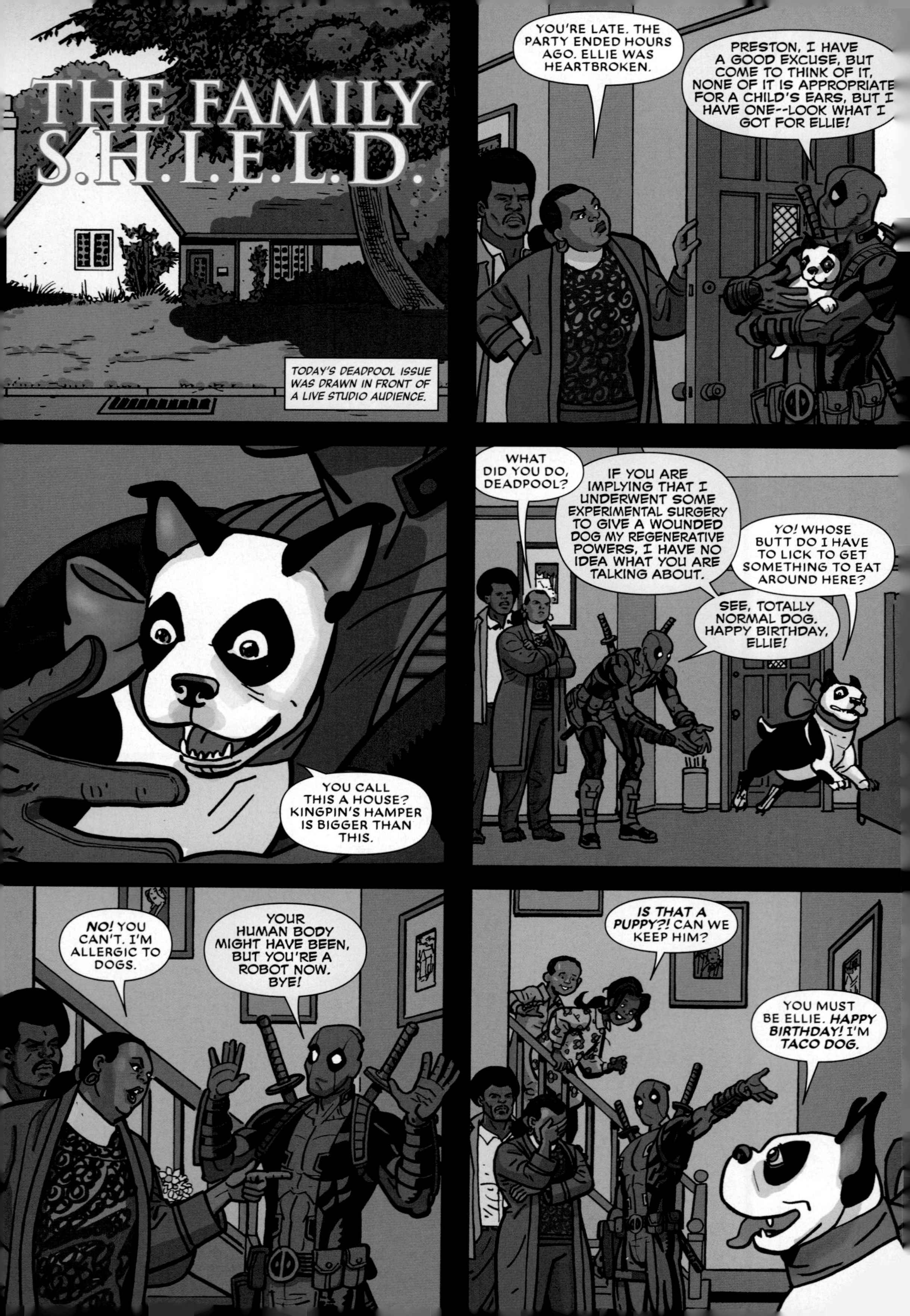
THE FAMILY S.H.I.E.L.D.
TODAY'S DEADPOOL ISSUE WAS DRAWN IN FRONT OF A LIVE STUDIO AUDIENCE.
YOU'RE LATE. THE PARTY ENDED HOURS AGO. ELLIE WAS HEARTBROKEN.
PRESTON, I HAVE A GOOD EXCUSE, BUT COME TO THINK OF IT, NONE OF IT IS APPROPRIATE FOR A CHILD'S EARS, BUT I HAVE ONE--LOOK WHAT I GOT FOR ELLIE!
YOU CALL THIS A HOUSE? KINGPIN'S HAMPER IS BIGGER THAN THIS.
WHAT DID YOU DO, DEADPOOL?
IF YOU ARE IMPLYING THAT I UNDERWENT SOME EXPERIMENTAL SURGERY TO GIVE A WOUNDED DOG MY REGENERATIVE POWERS, I HAVE NO IDEA WHAT YOU ARE TALKING ABOUT.
YO! WHOSE BUTT DO I HAVE TO LICK TO GET SOMETHING TO EAT AROUND HERE?
SEE, TOTALLY NORMAL DOG. HAPPY BIRTHDAY, ELLIE!
NO! YOU CAN'T. I'M ALLERGIC TO DOGS.
YOUR HUMAN BODY MIGHT HAVE BEEN, BUT YOU'RE A ROBOT NOW. BYE!
IS THAT A PUPPY?! CAN WE KEEP HIM?
YOU MUST BE ELLIE. HAPPY BIRTHDAY! I'M TACO DOG.

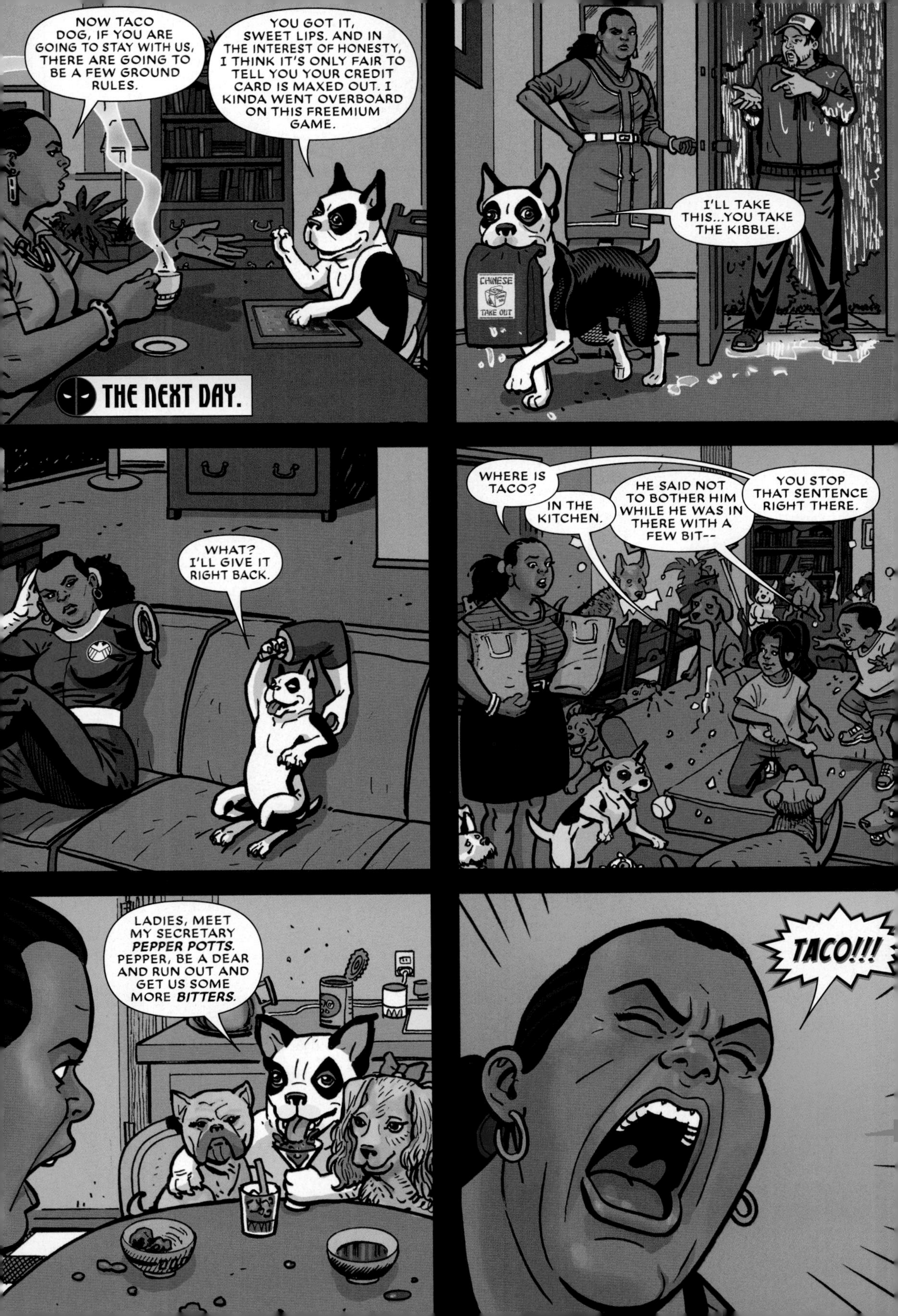

NOW TACO DOG, IF YOU ARE GOING TO STAY WITH US, THERE ARE GOING TO BE A FEW GROUND RULES.
YOU GOT IT, SWEET LIPS. AND IN THE INTEREST OF HONESTY, I THINK IT'S ONLY FAIR TO TELL YOU YOUR CREDIT CARD IS MAXED OUT. I KINDA WENT OVERBOARD ON THIS FREEMIUM GAME.
THE NEXT DAY.
CHINESE TAKE OUT
I'LL TAKE THIS...YOU TAKE THE KIBBLE.
WHAT? I'LL GIVE IT RIGHT BACK.
WHERE IS TACO?
IN THE KITCHEN.
HE SAID NOT TO BOTHER HIM WHILE HE WAS IN THERE WITH A FEW BIT--
YOU STOP THAT SENTENCE RIGHT THERE.
LADIES, MEET MY SECRETARY *PEPPER POTTS*. PEPPER, BE A DEAR AND RUN OUT AND GET US SOME MORE *BITTERS*.
TACO!!!

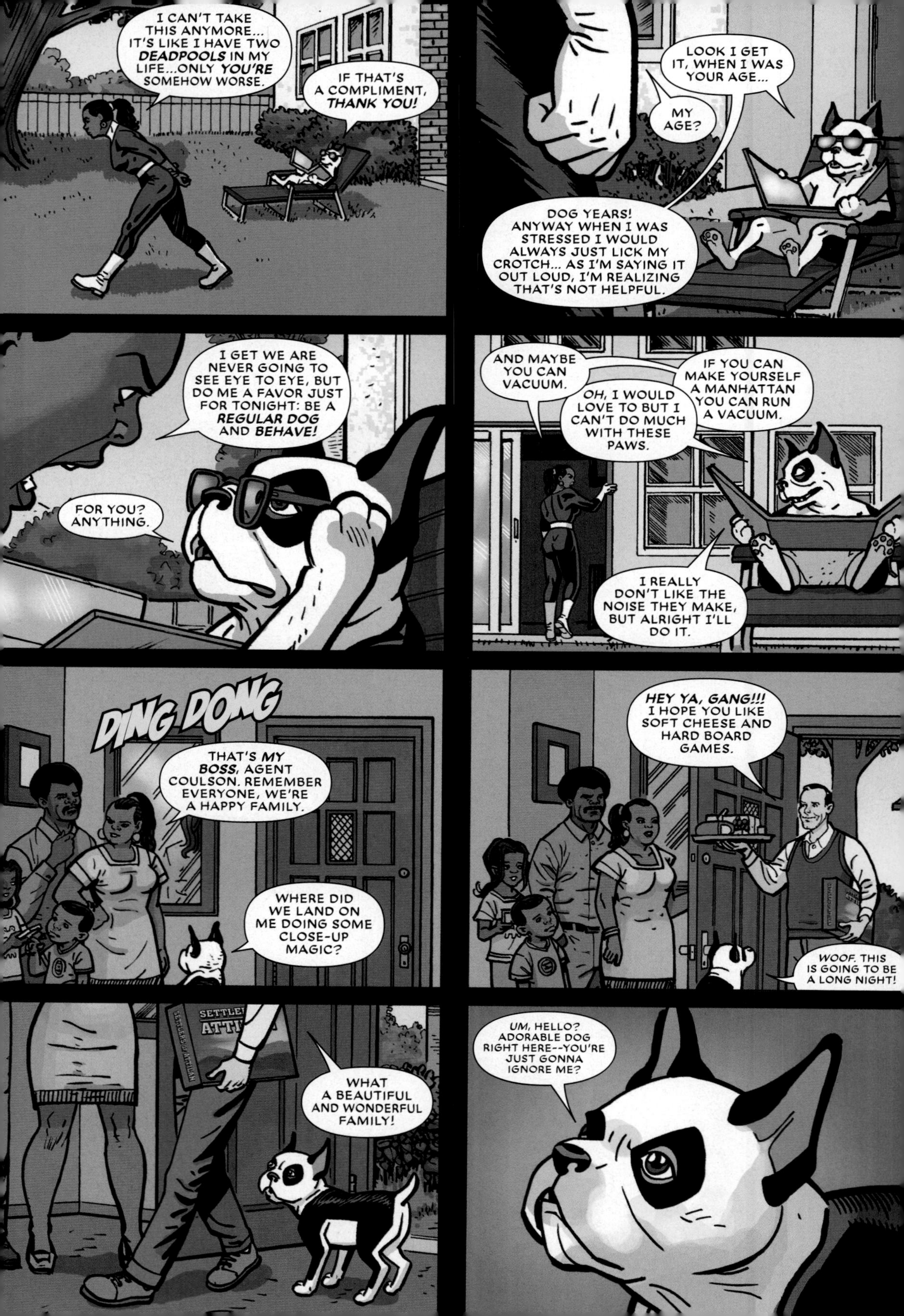
I CAN'T TAKE THIS ANYMORE... IT'S LIKE I HAVE TWO *DEADPOOLS* IN MY LIFE...ONLY *YOU'RE* SOMEHOW WORSE.
IF THAT'S A COMPLIMENT, *THANK YOU!*
LOOK I GET IT, WHEN I WAS YOUR AGE...
MY AGE?
DOG YEARS! ANYWAY WHEN I WAS STRESSED I WOULD ALWAYS JUST LICK MY CROTCH... AS I'M SAYING IT OUT LOUD, I'M REALIZING THAT'S NOT HELPFUL.
I GET WE ARE NEVER GOING TO SEE EYE TO EYE, BUT DO ME A FAVOR JUST FOR TONIGHT: BE A *REGULAR DOG* AND *BEHAVE!*
FOR YOU? ANYTHING.
AND MAYBE YOU CAN VACUUM.
OH, I WOULD LOVE TO BUT I CAN'T DO MUCH WITH THESE PAWS.
IF YOU CAN MAKE YOURSELF A MANHATTAN YOU CAN RUN A VACUUM.
I REALLY DON'T LIKE THE NOISE THEY MAKE, BUT ALRIGHT I'LL DO IT.
DING DONG
THAT'S *MY BOSS*, AGENT COULSON. REMEMBER EVERYONE, WE'RE A HAPPY FAMILY.
WHERE DID WE LAND ON ME DOING SOME CLOSE-UP MAGIC?
HEY YA, GANG!!! I HOPE YOU LIKE SOFT CHEESE AND HARD BOARD GAMES.
WOOF. THIS IS GOING TO BE A LONG NIGHT!
SETTLERS OF ATTILAN
WHAT A BEAUTIFUL AND WONDERFUL FAMILY!
UM, HELLO? ADORABLE DOG RIGHT HERE--YOU'RE JUST GONNA IGNORE ME?

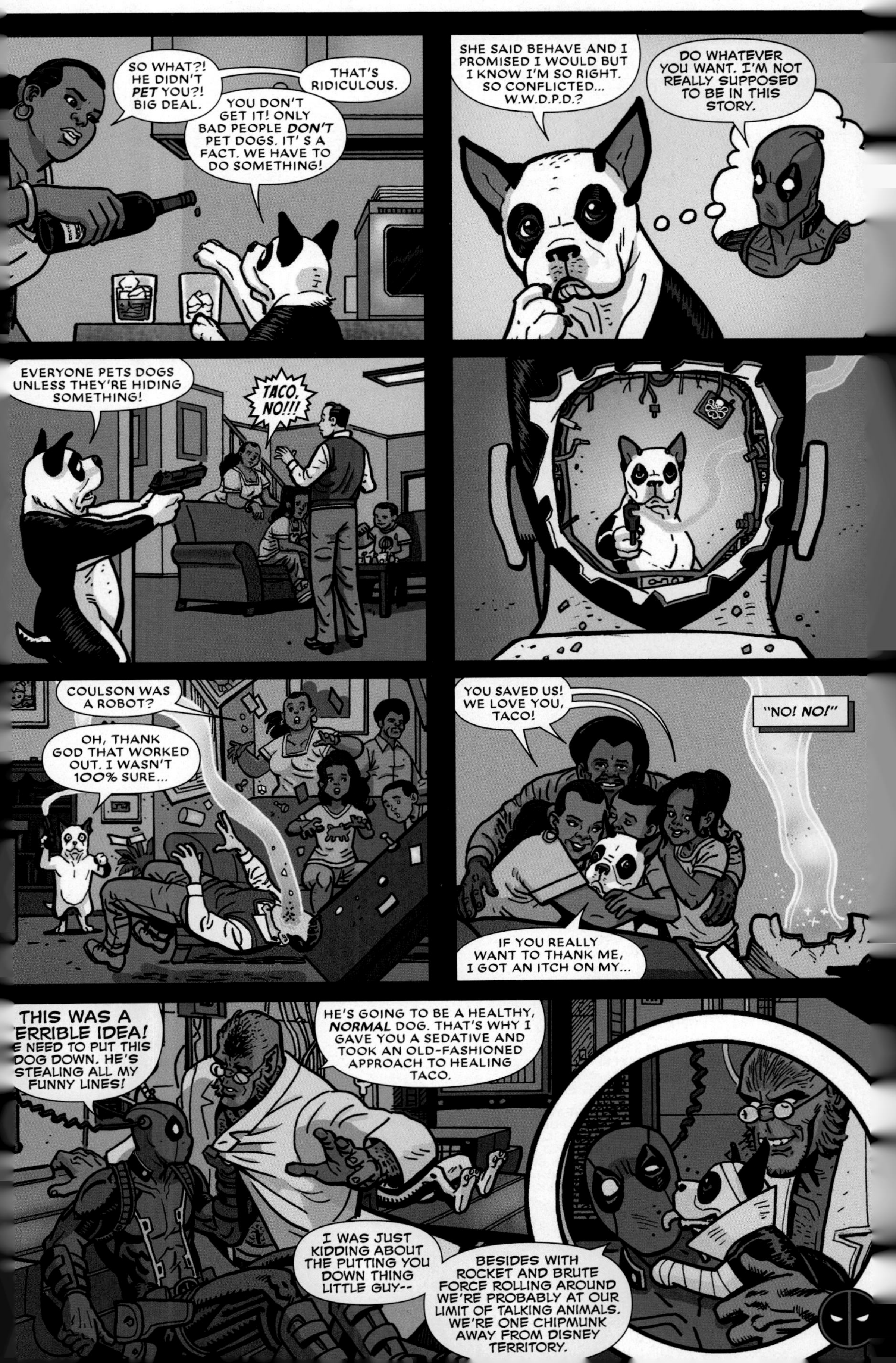
SO WHAT?! HE DIDN'T PET YOU?! BIG DEAL.
THAT'S RIDICULOUS.
YOU DON'T GET IT! ONLY BAD PEOPLE DON'T PET DOGS. IT'S A FACT. WE HAVE TO DO SOMETHING!
SHE SAID BEHAVE AND I PROMISED I WOULD BUT I KNOW I'M SO RIGHT. SO CONFLICTED... W.W.D.P.D.?
DO WHATEVER YOU WANT. I'M NOT REALLY SUPPOSED TO BE IN THIS STORY.
EVERYONE PETS DOGS UNLESS THEY'RE HIDING SOMETHING!
TACO, NO!!!
COULSON WAS A ROBOT?
OH, THANK GOD THAT WORKED OUT. I WASN'T 100% SURE...
YOU SAVED US! WE LOVE YOU, TACO!
"NO! NO!"
IF YOU REALLY WANT TO THANK ME, I GOT AN ITCH ON MY...
THIS WAS A TERRIBLE IDEA! E NEED TO PUT THIS DOG DOWN. HE'S STEALING ALL MY FUNNY LINES!
HE'S GOING TO BE A HEALTHY, NORMAL DOG. THAT'S WHY I GAVE YOU A SEDATIVE AND TOOK AN OLD-FASHIONED APPROACH TO HEALING TACO.
I WAS JUST KIDDING ABOUT THE PUTTING YOU DOWN THING LITTLE GUY--
BESIDES WITH ROCKET AND BRUTE FORCE ROLLING AROUND WE'RE PROBABLY AT OUR LIMIT OF TALKING ANIMALS. WE'RE ONE CHIPMUNK AWAY FROM DISNEY TERRITORY.

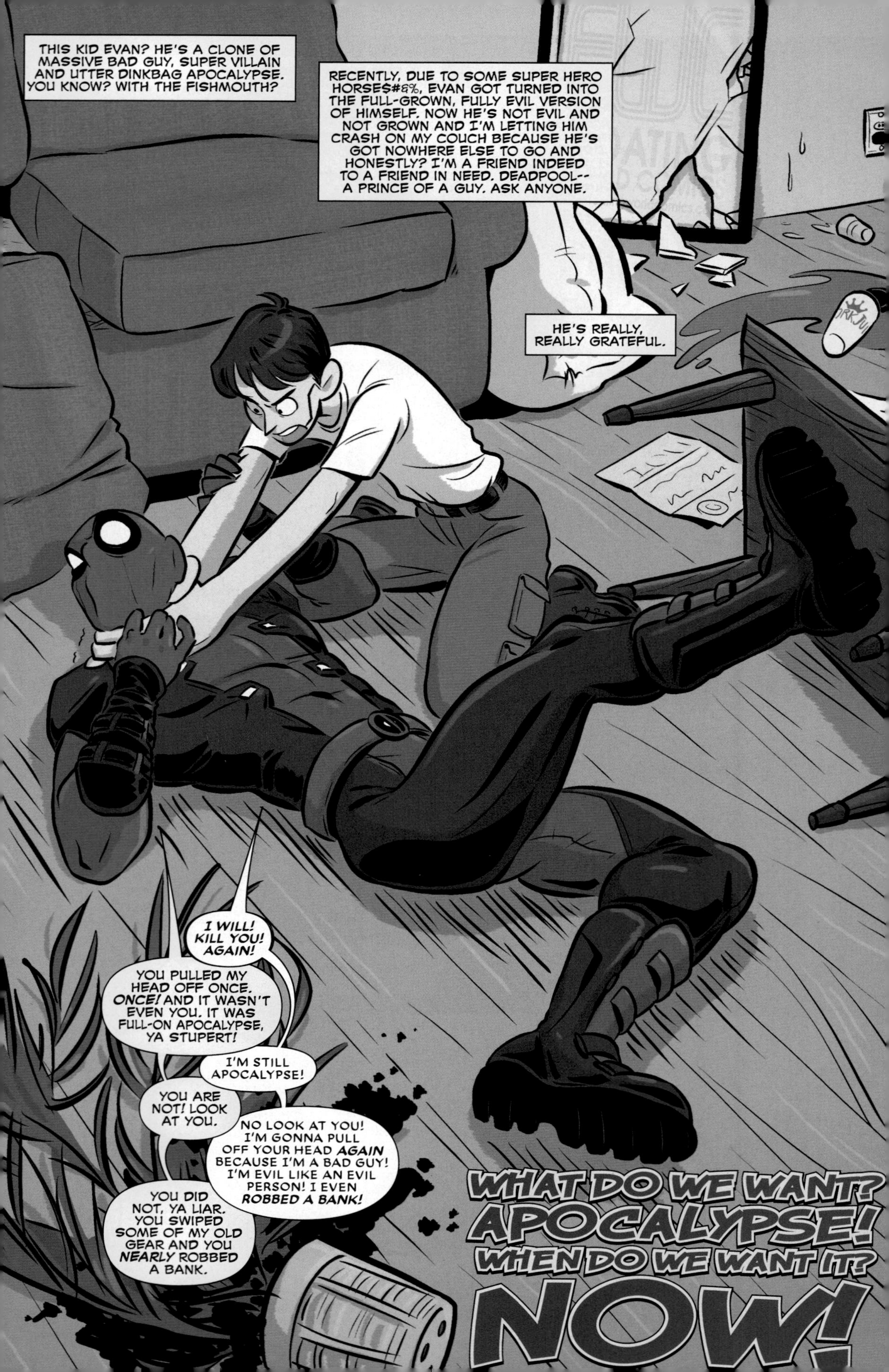
THIS KID EVAN? HE'S A CLONE OF MASSIVE BAD GUY, SUPER VILLAIN AND UTTER DINKBAG APOCALYPSE. YOU KNOW? WITH THE FISHMOUTH?
RECENTLY, DUE TO SOME SUPER HERO HORSE$#&%, EVAN GOT TURNED INTO THE FULL-GROWN, FULLY EVIL VERSION OF HIMSELF. NOW HE'S NOT EVIL AND NOT GROWN AND I'M LETTING HIM CRASH ON MY COUCH BECAUSE HE'S GOT NOWHERE ELSE TO GO AND HONESTLY? I'M A FRIEND INDEED TO A FRIEND IN NEED. DEADPOOL-- A PRINCE OF A GUY. ASK ANYONE.
HE'S REALLY, REALLY GRATEFUL.
I WILL! KILL YOU! AGAIN!
YOU PULLED MY HEAD OFF ONCE. ONCE! AND IT WASN'T EVEN YOU. IT WAS FULL-ON APOCALYPSE, YA STUPERT!
I'M STILL APOCALYPSE!
YOU ARE NOT! LOOK AT YOU.
NO LOOK AT YOU! I'M GONNA PULL OFF YOUR HEAD AGAIN BECAUSE I'M A BAD GUY! I'M EVIL LIKE AN EVIL PERSON! I EVEN ROBBED A BANK!
YOU DID NOT, YA LIAR. YOU SWIPED SOME OF MY OLD GEAR AND YOU NEARLY ROBBED A BANK.
WHAT DO WE WANT? APOCALYPSE! WHEN DO WE WANT IT? NOW!

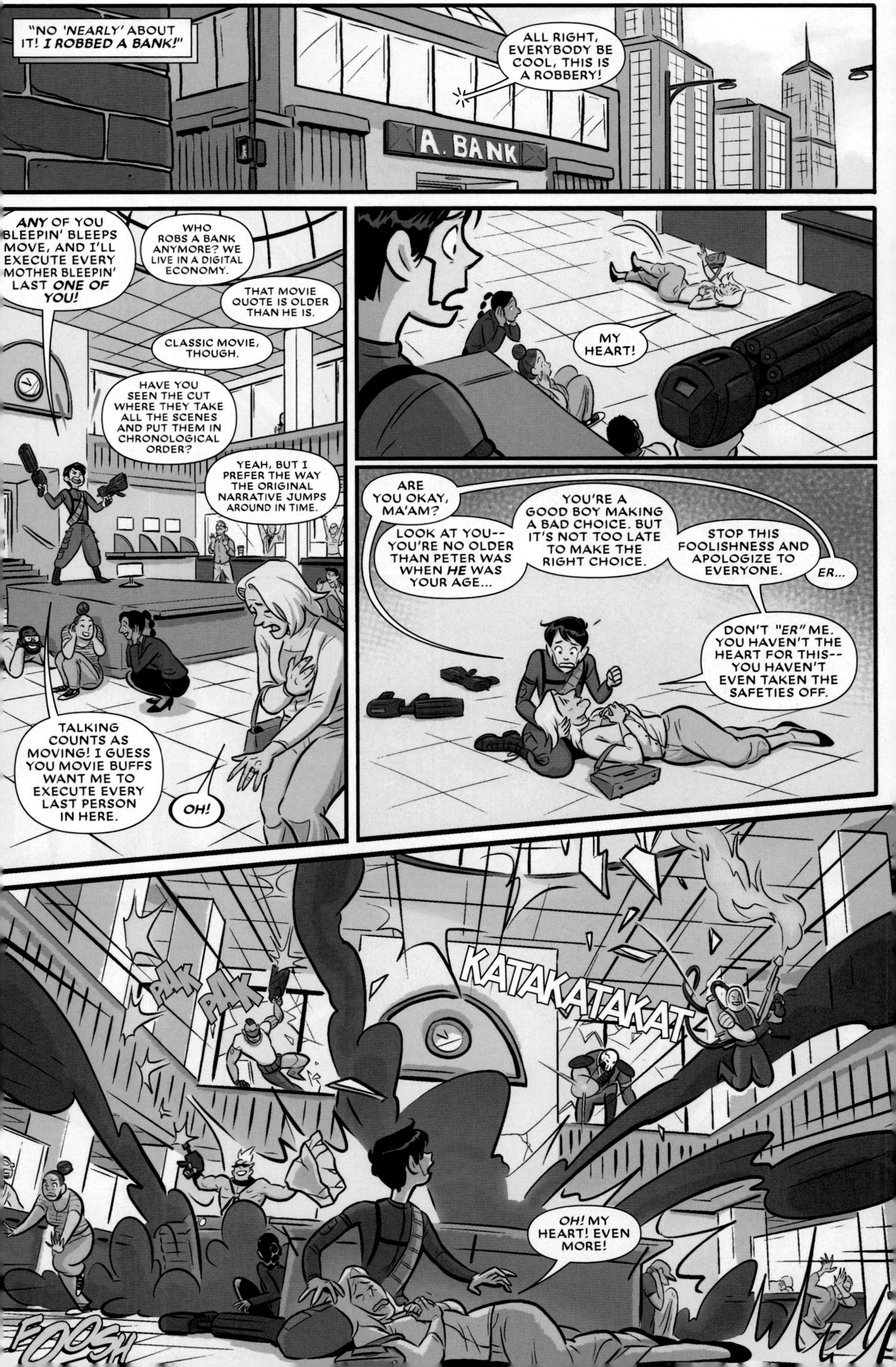

"NO 'NEARLY' ABOUT IT! I ROBBED A BANK!"
ALL RIGHT, EVERYBODY BE COOL, THIS IS A ROBBERY!
A. BANK
ANY OF YOU BLEEPIN' BLEEPS MOVE, AND I'LL EXECUTE EVERY MOTHER BLEEPIN' LAST ONE OF YOU!
WHO ROBS A BANK ANYMORE? WE LIVE IN A DIGITAL ECONOMY.
THAT MOVIE QUOTE IS OLDER THAN HE IS.
CLASSIC MOVIE, THOUGH.
HAVE YOU SEEN THE CUT WHERE THEY TAKE ALL THE SCENES AND PUT THEM IN CHRONOLOGICAL ORDER?
YEAH, BUT I PREFER THE WAY THE ORIGINAL NARRATIVE JUMPS AROUND IN TIME.
TALKING COUNTS AS MOVING! I GUESS YOU MOVIE BUFFS WANT ME TO EXECUTE EVERY LAST PERSON IN HERE.
OH!
MY HEART!
ARE YOU OKAY, MA'AM?
LOOK AT YOU-- YOU'RE NO OLDER THAN PETER WAS WHEN HE WAS YOUR AGE...
YOU'RE A GOOD BOY MAKING A BAD CHOICE. BUT IT'S NOT TOO LATE TO MAKE THE RIGHT CHOICE.
STOP THIS FOOLISHNESS AND APOLOGIZE TO EVERYONE.
ER...
DON'T "ER" ME. YOU HAVEN'T THE HEART FOR THIS-- YOU HAVEN'T EVEN TAKEN THE SAFETIES OFF.
PAK PAK
KATAKATAKAT
OH! MY HEART! EVEN MORE!
FOOSH

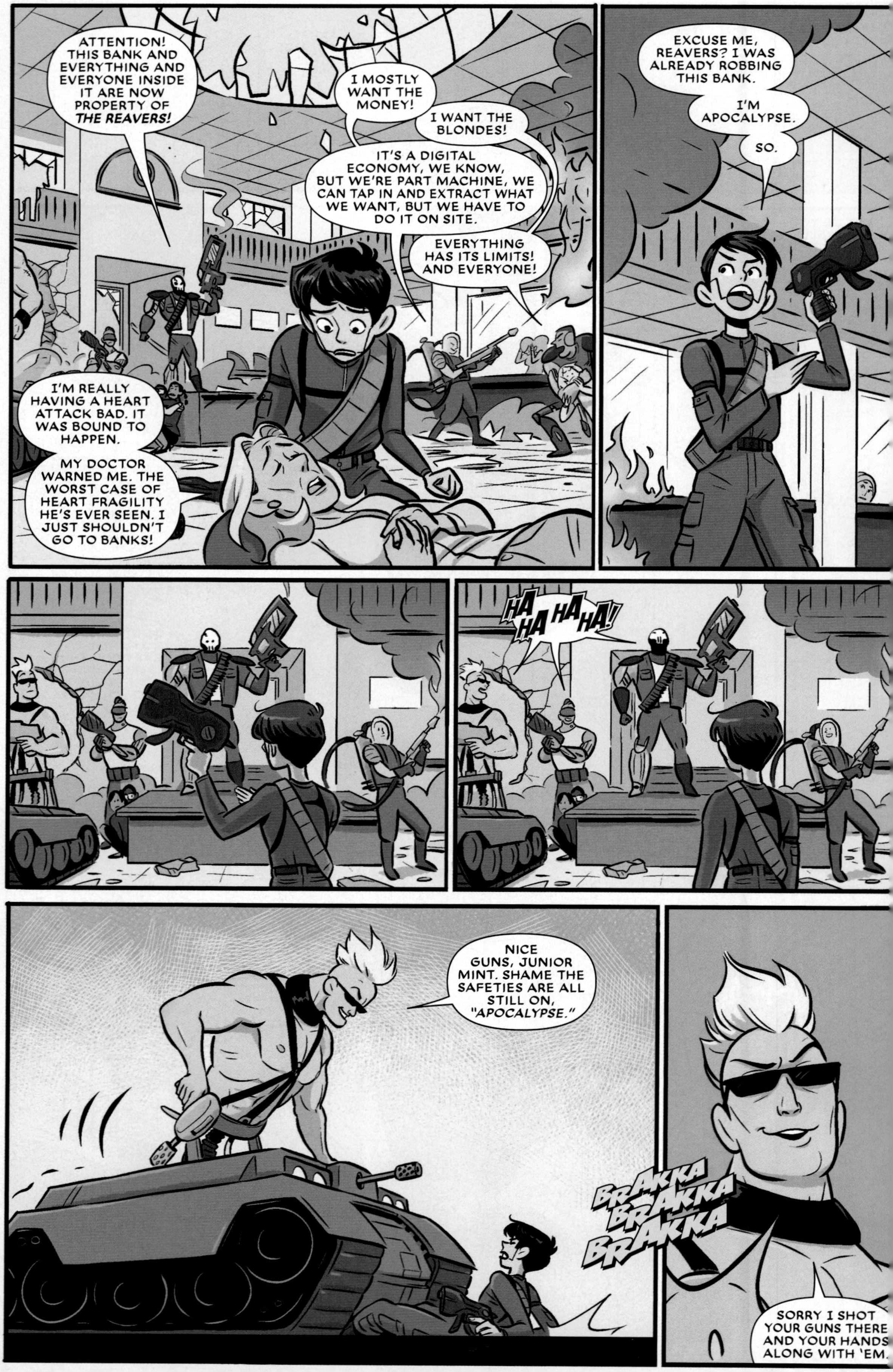
ATTENTION! THIS BANK AND EVERYTHING AND EVERYONE INSIDE IT ARE NOW PROPERTY OF *THE REAVERS!*
I MOSTLY WANT THE MONEY!
I WANT THE BLONDES!
IT'S A DIGITAL ECONOMY, WE KNOW, BUT WE'RE PART MACHINE, WE CAN TAP IN AND EXTRACT WHAT WE WANT, BUT WE HAVE TO DO IT ON SITE.
EVERYTHING HAS ITS LIMITS! AND EVERYONE!
I'M REALLY HAVING A HEART ATTACK BAD. IT WAS BOUND TO HAPPEN.
MY DOCTOR WARNED ME. THE WORST CASE OF HEART FRAGILITY HE'S EVER SEEN. I JUST SHOULDN'T GO TO BANKS!
EXCUSE ME, REAVERS? I WAS ALREADY ROBBING THIS BANK.
I'M APOCALYPSE.
SO.
HA HA HA HA!
NICE GUNS, JUNIOR MINT. SHAME THE SAFETIES ARE ALL STILL ON, *"APOCALYPSE."*
BRAKKA BRAKKA BRAKKA
SORRY I SHOT YOUR GUNS THERE AND YOUR HANDS ALONG WITH 'EM.

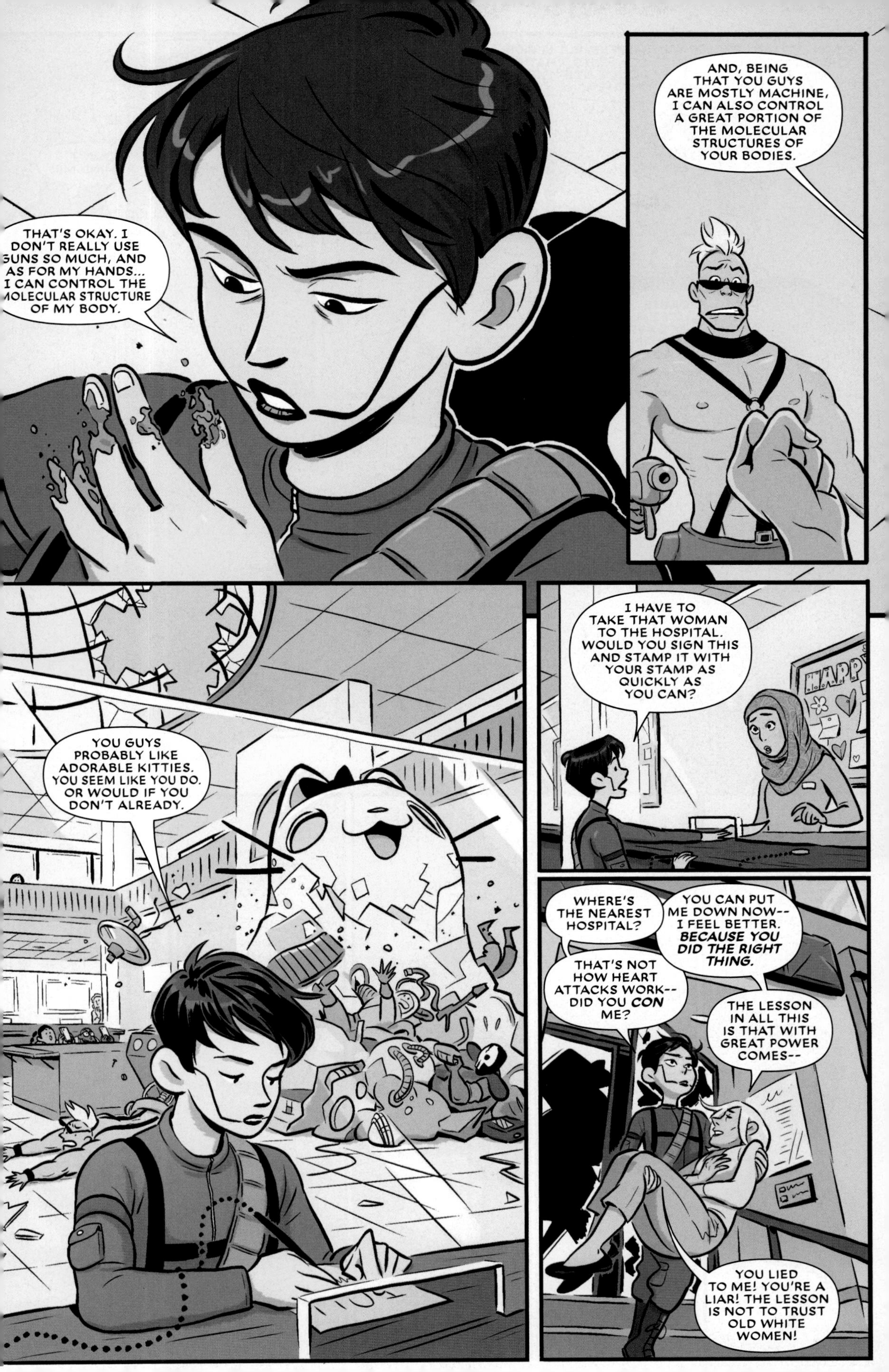
THAT'S OKAY. I DON'T REALLY USE GUNS SO MUCH, AND AS FOR MY HANDS... I CAN CONTROL THE MOLECULAR STRUCTURE OF MY BODY.
AND, BEING THAT YOU GUYS ARE MOSTLY MACHINE, I CAN ALSO CONTROL A GREAT PORTION OF THE MOLECULAR STRUCTURES OF YOUR BODIES.
YOU GUYS PROBABLY LIKE ADORABLE KITTIES. YOU SEEM LIKE YOU DO. OR WOULD IF YOU DON'T ALREADY.
I HAVE TO TAKE THAT WOMAN TO THE HOSPITAL. WOULD YOU SIGN THIS AND STAMP IT WITH YOUR STAMP AS QUICKLY AS YOU CAN?
WHERE'S THE NEAREST HOSPITAL?
YOU CAN PUT ME DOWN NOW-- I FEEL BETTER. *BECAUSE YOU DID THE RIGHT THING.*
THAT'S NOT HOW HEART ATTACKS WORK-- DID YOU *CON* ME?
THE LESSON IN ALL THIS IS THAT WITH GREAT POWER COMES--
YOU LIED TO ME! YOU'RE A LIAR! THE LESSON IS NOT TO TRUST OLD WHITE WOMEN!

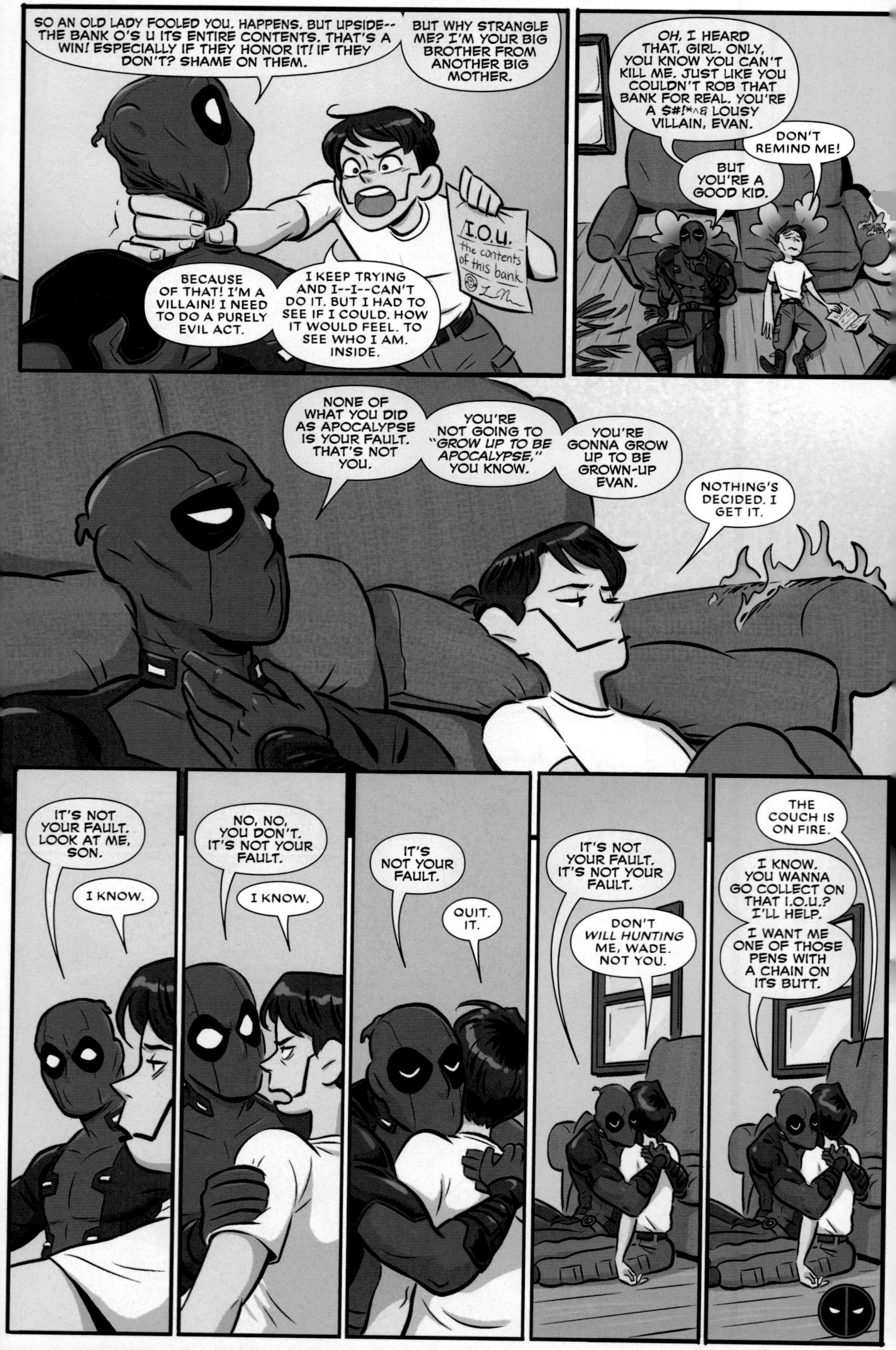

SO AN OLD LADY FOOLED YOU. HAPPENS. BUT UPSIDE-- THE BANK O'S U ITS ENTIRE CONTENTS. THAT'S A WIN! ESPECIALLY IF THEY HONOR IT! IF THEY DON'T? SHAME ON THEM.
BUT WHY STRANGLE ME? I'M YOUR BIG BROTHER FROM ANOTHER BIG MOTHER.
I.O.U. the contents of this bank.
BECAUSE OF THAT! I'M A VILLAIN! I NEED TO DO A PURELY EVIL ACT.
I KEEP TRYING AND I--I--CAN'T DO IT. BUT I HAD TO SEE IF I COULD. HOW IT WOULD FEEL. TO SEE WHO I AM. INSIDE.
OH, I HEARD THAT, GIRL. ONLY, YOU KNOW YOU CAN'T KILL ME. JUST LIKE YOU COULDN'T ROB THAT BANK FOR REAL. YOU'RE A $#!*^& LOUSY VILLAIN, EVAN.
DON'T REMIND ME!
BUT YOU'RE A GOOD KID.
NONE OF WHAT YOU DID AS APOCALYPSE IS YOUR FAULT. THAT'S NOT YOU.
YOU'RE NOT GOING TO "GROW UP TO BE APOCALYPSE," YOU KNOW.
YOU'RE GONNA GROW UP TO BE GROWN-UP EVAN.
NOTHING'S DECIDED. I GET IT.
IT'S NOT YOUR FAULT. LOOK AT ME, SON.
I KNOW.
NO, NO, YOU DON'T. IT'S NOT YOUR FAULT.
I KNOW.
IT'S NOT YOUR FAULT.
QUIT. IT.
IT'S NOT YOUR FAULT. IT'S NOT YOUR FAULT.
DON'T WILL HUNTING ME, WADE. NOT YOU.
THE COUCH IS ON FIRE.
I KNOW. YOU WANNA GO COLLECT ON THAT I.O.U.? I'LL HELP.
I WANT ME ONE OF THOSE PENS WITH A CHAIN ON ITS BUTT.

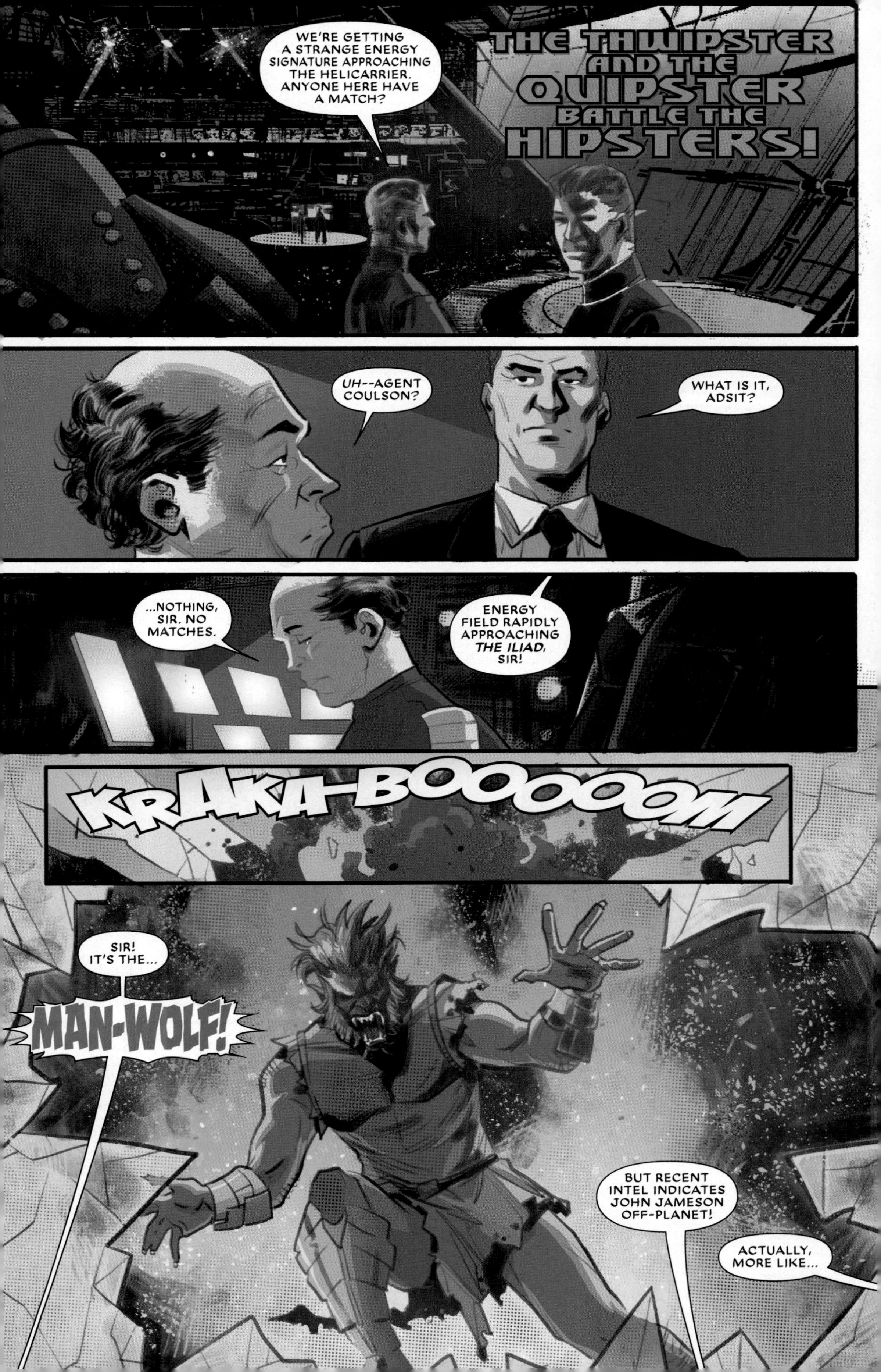
WE'RE GETTING A STRANGE ENERGY SIGNATURE APPROACHING THE HELICARRIER. ANYONE HERE HAVE A MATCH?
THE THWIPSTER AND THE QUIPSTER BATTLE THE HIPSTERS!
UH--AGENT COULSON?
WHAT IS IT, ADSIT?
...NOTHING, SIR. NO MATCHES.
ENERGY FIELD RAPIDLY APPROACHING THE ILIAD, SIR!
KRAKA-BOOOOOOM
SIR! IT'S THE...
MAN-WOLF!
BUT RECENT INTEL INDICATES JOHN JAMESON OFF-PLANET!
ACTUALLY, MORE LIKE...

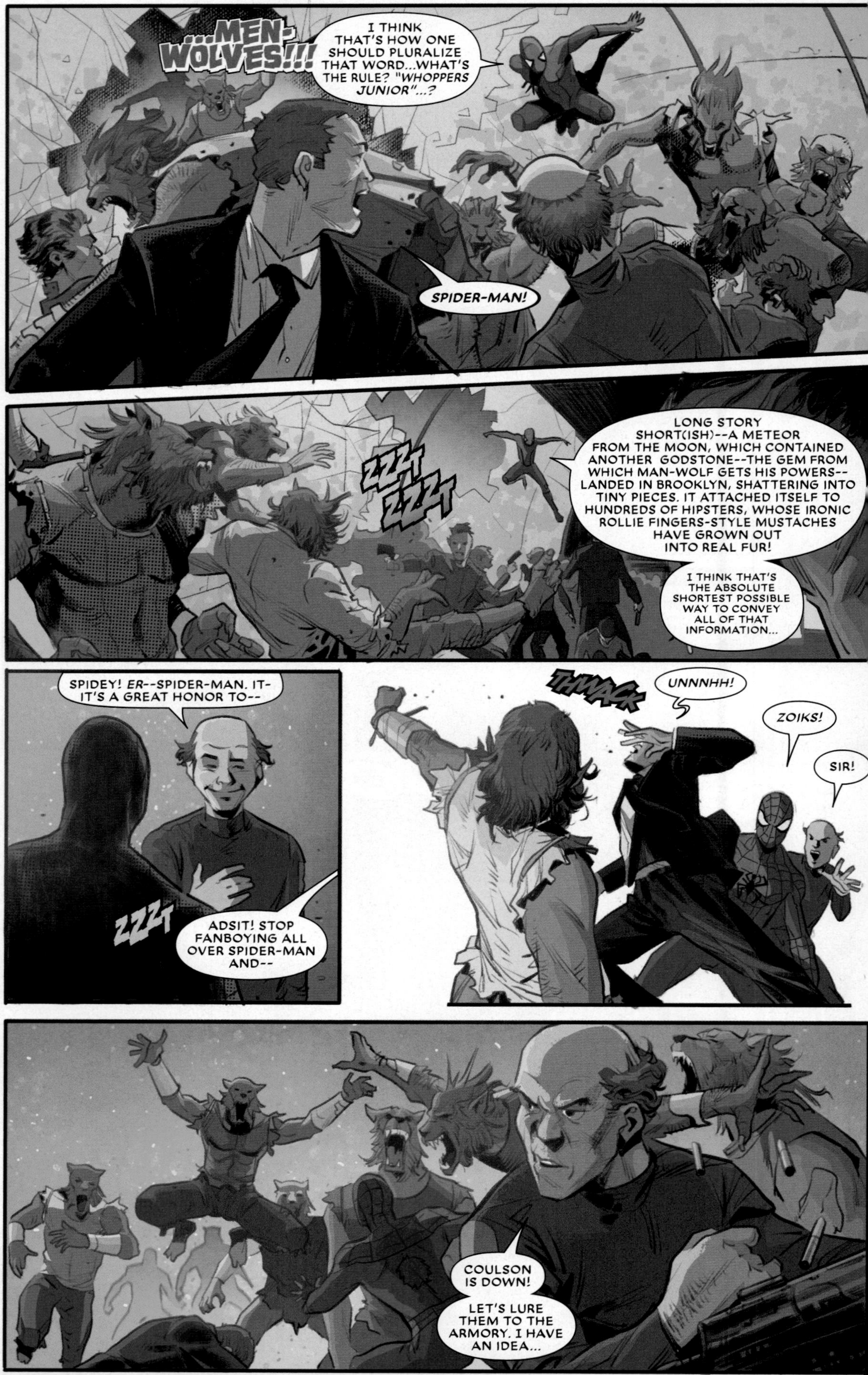
...MEN-WOLVES!!!
I THINK THAT'S HOW ONE SHOULD PLURALIZE THAT WORD...WHAT'S THE RULE? "WHOPPERS JUNIOR"...?
SPIDER-MAN!
ZZZT ZZZT
LONG STORY SHORT(ISH)--A METEOR FROM THE MOON, WHICH CONTAINED ANOTHER GODSTONE--THE GEM FROM WHICH MAN-WOLF GETS HIS POWERS--LANDED IN BROOKLYN, SHATTERING INTO TINY PIECES. IT ATTACHED ITSELF TO HUNDREDS OF HIPSTERS, WHOSE IRONIC ROLLIE FINGERS-STYLE MUSTACHES HAVE GROWN OUT INTO REAL FUR!
I THINK THAT'S THE ABSOLUTE SHORTEST POSSIBLE WAY TO CONVEY ALL OF THAT INFORMATION...
SPIDEY! ER--SPIDER-MAN. IT-IT'S A GREAT HONOR TO--
ZZZT
ADSIT! STOP FANBOYING ALL OVER SPIDER-MAN AND--
THWACK
UNNNHH!
ZOIKS!
SIR!
COULSON IS DOWN!
LET'S LURE THEM TO THE ARMORY. I HAVE AN IDEA...

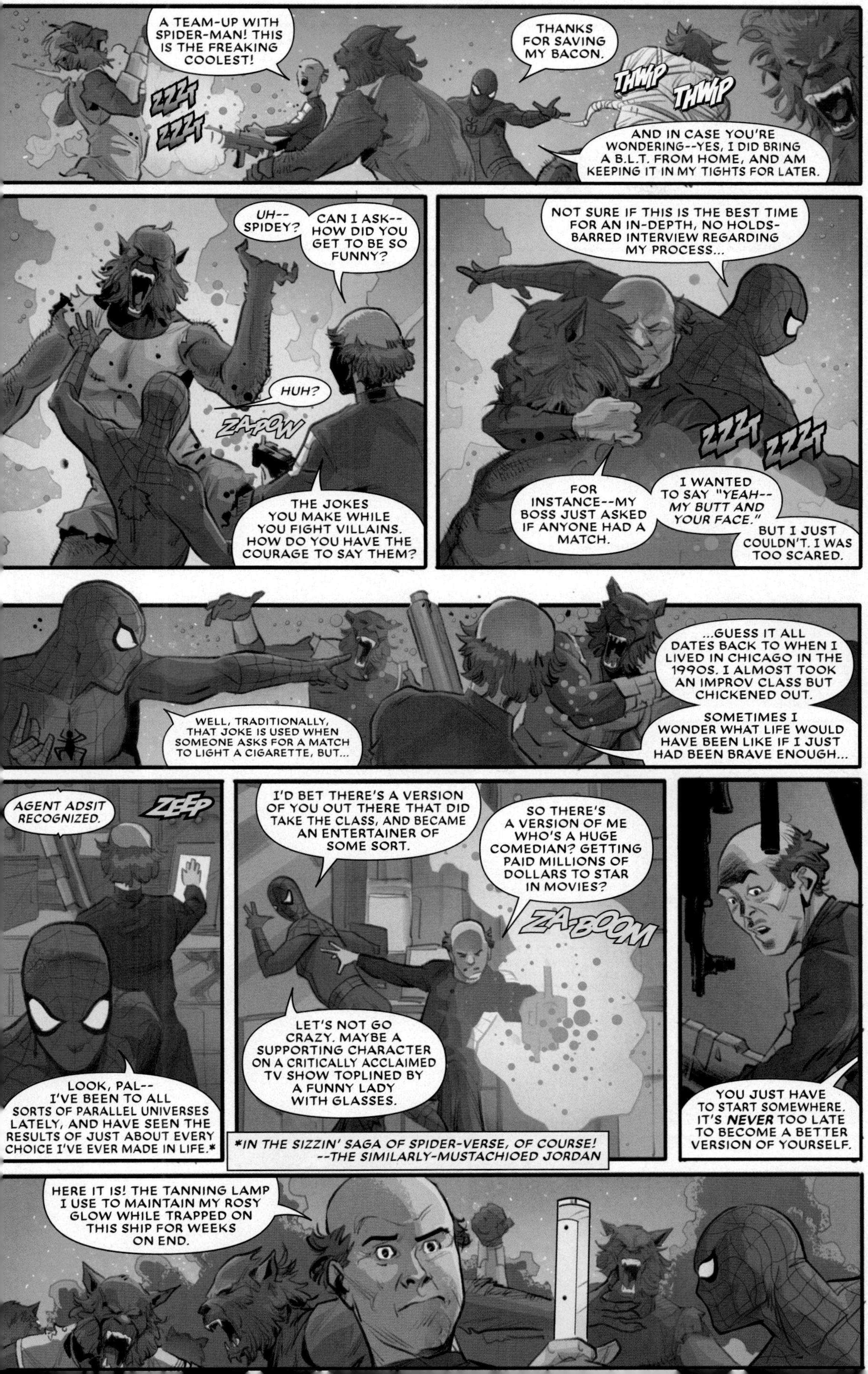
A TEAM-UP WITH SPIDER-MAN! THIS IS THE FREAKING COOLEST!
ZZZT
ZZZT
THANKS FOR SAVING MY BACON.
THWIP
THWIP
AND IN CASE YOU'RE WONDERING--YES, I DID BRING A B.L.T. FROM HOME, AND AM KEEPING IT IN MY TIGHTS FOR LATER.
UH-- SPIDEY?
CAN I ASK-- HOW DID YOU GET TO BE SO FUNNY?
HUH?
ZAPOW
THE JOKES YOU MAKE WHILE YOU FIGHT VILLAINS. HOW DO YOU HAVE THE COURAGE TO SAY THEM?
NOT SURE IF THIS IS THE BEST TIME FOR AN IN-DEPTH, NO HOLDS-BARRED INTERVIEW REGARDING MY PROCESS...
ZZZT
ZZZT
FOR INSTANCE--MY BOSS JUST ASKED IF ANYONE HAD A MATCH.
I WANTED TO SAY "YEAH-- MY BUTT AND YOUR FACE."
BUT I JUST COULDN'T. I WAS TOO SCARED.
WELL, TRADITIONALLY, THAT JOKE IS USED WHEN SOMEONE ASKS FOR A MATCH TO LIGHT A CIGARETTE, BUT...
...GUESS IT ALL DATES BACK TO WHEN I LIVED IN CHICAGO IN THE 1990S. I ALMOST TOOK AN IMPROV CLASS BUT CHICKENED OUT.
SOMETIMES I WONDER WHAT LIFE WOULD HAVE BEEN LIKE IF I JUST HAD BEEN BRAVE ENOUGH...
AGENT ADSIT RECOGNIZED.
ZEEP
LOOK, PAL-- I'VE BEEN TO ALL SORTS OF PARALLEL UNIVERSES LATELY, AND HAVE SEEN THE RESULTS OF JUST ABOUT EVERY CHOICE I'VE EVER MADE IN LIFE.*
I'D BET THERE'S A VERSION OF YOU OUT THERE THAT DID TAKE THE CLASS, AND BECAME AN ENTERTAINER OF SOME SORT.
SO THERE'S A VERSION OF ME WHO'S A HUGE COMEDIAN? GETTING PAID MILLIONS OF DOLLARS TO STAR IN MOVIES?
ZA-BOOM
LET'S NOT GO CRAZY. MAYBE A SUPPORTING CHARACTER ON A CRITICALLY ACCLAIMED TV SHOW TOPLINED BY A FUNNY LADY WITH GLASSES.
*IN THE SIZZIN' SAGA OF SPIDER-VERSE, OF COURSE! --THE SIMILARLY-MUSTACHIOED JORDAN
YOU JUST HAVE TO START SOMEWHERE. IT'S NEVER TOO LATE TO BECOME A BETTER VERSION OF YOURSELF.
HERE IT IS! THE TANNING LAMP I USE TO MAINTAIN MY ROSY GLOW WHILE TRAPPED ON THIS SHIP FOR WEEKS ON END.

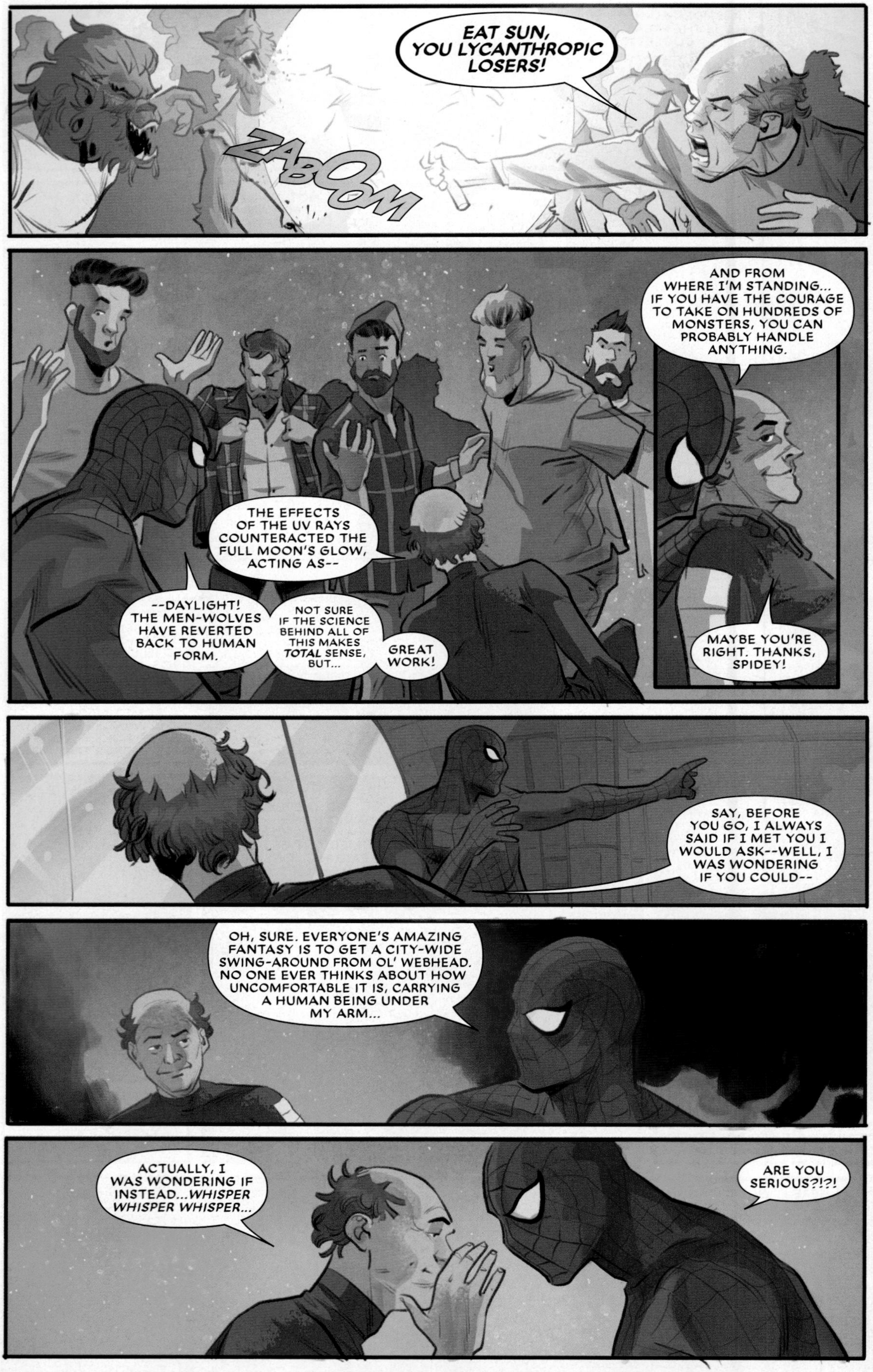
EAT SUN, YOU LYCANTHROPIC LOSERS!
ZABOOOM
THE EFFECTS OF THE UV RAYS COUNTERACTED THE FULL MOON'S GLOW, ACTING AS--
--DAYLIGHT! THE MEN-WOLVES HAVE REVERTED BACK TO HUMAN FORM.
NOT SURE IF THE SCIENCE BEHIND ALL OF THIS MAKES TOTAL SENSE, BUT...
GREAT WORK!
AND FROM WHERE I'M STANDING... IF YOU HAVE THE COURAGE TO TAKE ON HUNDREDS OF MONSTERS, YOU CAN PROBABLY HANDLE ANYTHING.
MAYBE YOU'RE RIGHT. THANKS, SPIDEY!
SAY, BEFORE YOU GO, I ALWAYS SAID IF I MET YOU I WOULD ASK--WELL, I WAS WONDERING IF YOU COULD--
OH, SURE. EVERYONE'S AMAZING FANTASY IS TO GET A CITY-WIDE SWING-AROUND FROM OL' WEBHEAD. NO ONE EVER THINKS ABOUT HOW UNCOMFORTABLE IT IS, CARRYING A HUMAN BEING UNDER MY ARM...
ACTUALLY, I WAS WONDERING IF INSTEAD...WHISPER WHISPER WHISPER...
ARE YOU SERIOUS?!?!

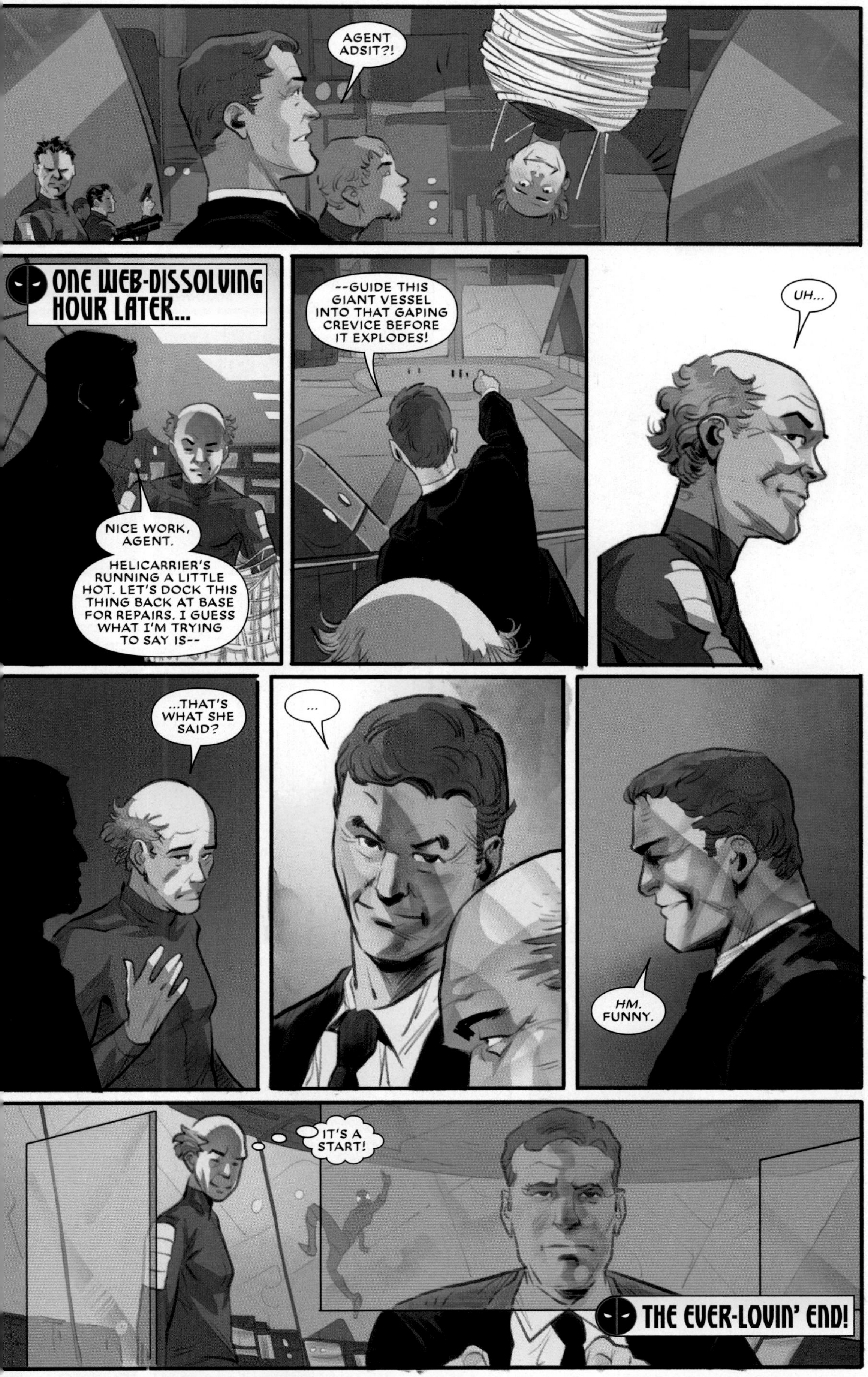

AGENT ADSIT?!
ONE WEB-DISSOLVING HOUR LATER...
NICE WORK, AGENT.
HELICARRIER'S RUNNING A LITTLE HOT. LET'S DOCK THIS THING BACK AT BASE FOR REPAIRS. I GUESS WHAT I'M TRYING TO SAY IS--
--GUIDE THIS GIANT VESSEL INTO THAT GAPING CREVICE BEFORE IT EXPLODES!
UH...
...THAT'S WHAT SHE SAID?
...
HM. FUNNY.
IT'S A START!
THE EVER-LOVIN' END!

MANN

SAL! ORDER UP FOR... UH-OH.

HEY RAMON, CLEAR THE DECKS, WE HAVE A GUEST!

GOOD AFTERNOON, MR. GRIMM. YOU HUNGRY?

MANNY'S

ALL ABOUT THE BENJAMINS

UGH! I SPENT THE WHOLE MORNING IN THE NEGATIVE ZONE HELPING 25 OF THOSE DAMN REED RICHARDS BUILD SOME COCKAMAMIE MACHINE.

"LIFT THAT, BEND THIS," I'LL BEND IT RIGHT AROUND YOUR STRETCHY NECK, YOU WEIRD, ONE-ARMED REED, SON OF A--

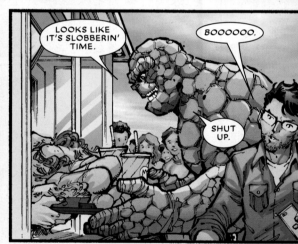

LOOKS LIKE IT'S SLOBBERIN' TIME.

BOOOOOO.

SHUT UP.

NOTHING AND NOBODY'S GONNA INTERRUPT MY--UH-OH.

HEY FELLA, QUICK QUESTION, IS THERE A BIG GIANT ROBOT OR SOMETHING BEHIND ME?

NO, SIR.

PHEW. I'M TOO HUNGRY TO DEAL WITH ANY OF THAT CRAP!

IT LOOKS LIKE MORE OF A MONSTER THAN A ROBOT...

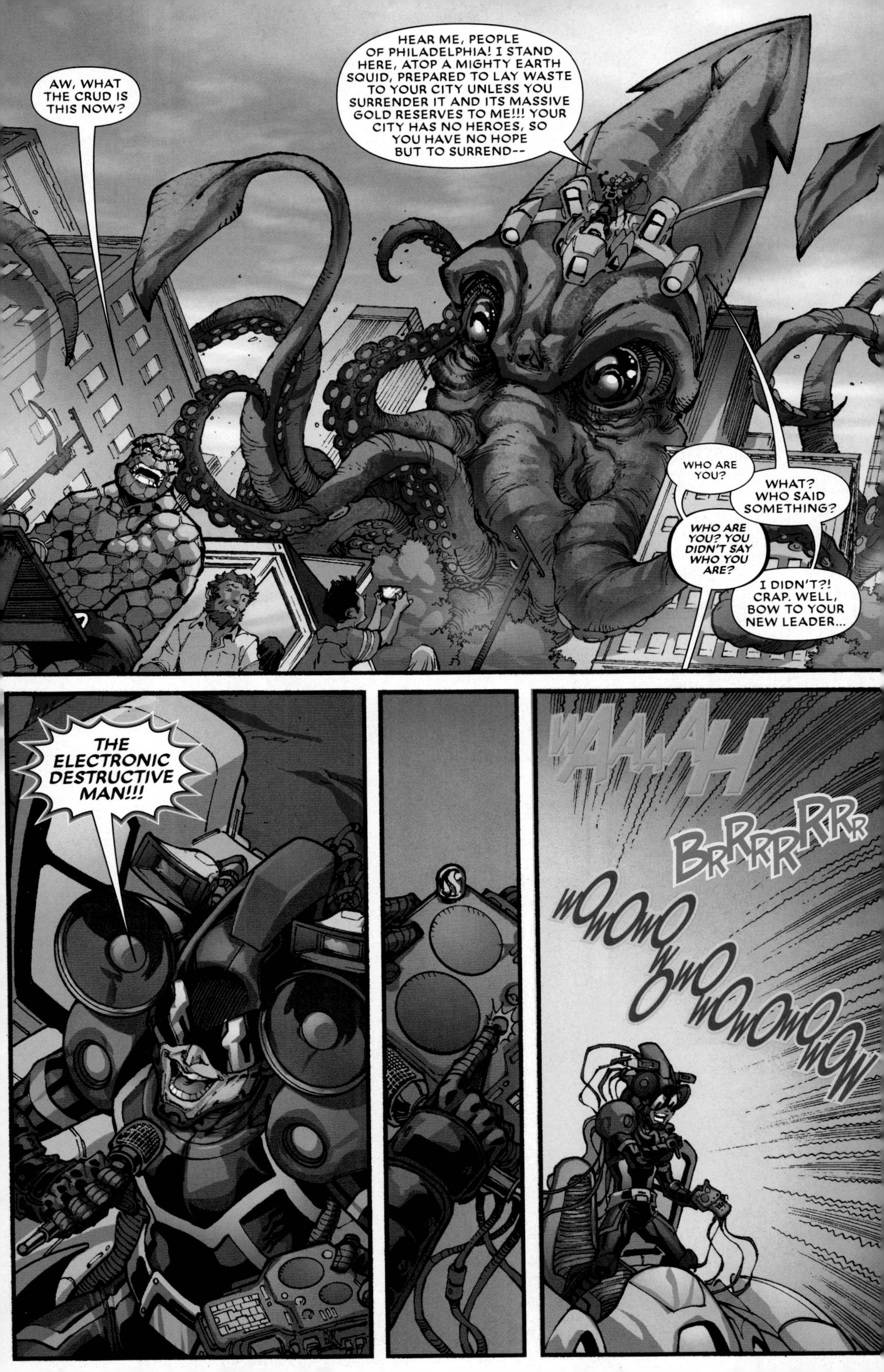
AW, WHAT THE CRUD IS THIS NOW?
HEAR ME, PEOPLE OF PHILADELPHIA! I STAND HERE, ATOP A MIGHTY EARTH SQUID, PREPARED TO LAY WASTE TO YOUR CITY UNLESS YOU SURRENDER IT AND ITS MASSIVE GOLD RESERVES TO ME!!! YOUR CITY HAS NO HEROES, SO YOU HAVE NO HOPE BUT TO SURREND--
WHO ARE YOU?
WHAT? WHO SAID SOMETHING?
WHO ARE YOU? YOU DIDN'T SAY WHO YOU ARE?
I DIDN'T?! CRAP. WELL, BOW TO YOUR NEW LEADER...
THE ELECTRONIC DESTRUCTIVE MAN!!!
WAAAAH
BRRRRRRR
WOWOWOWOWOWOWOWOWOWOW

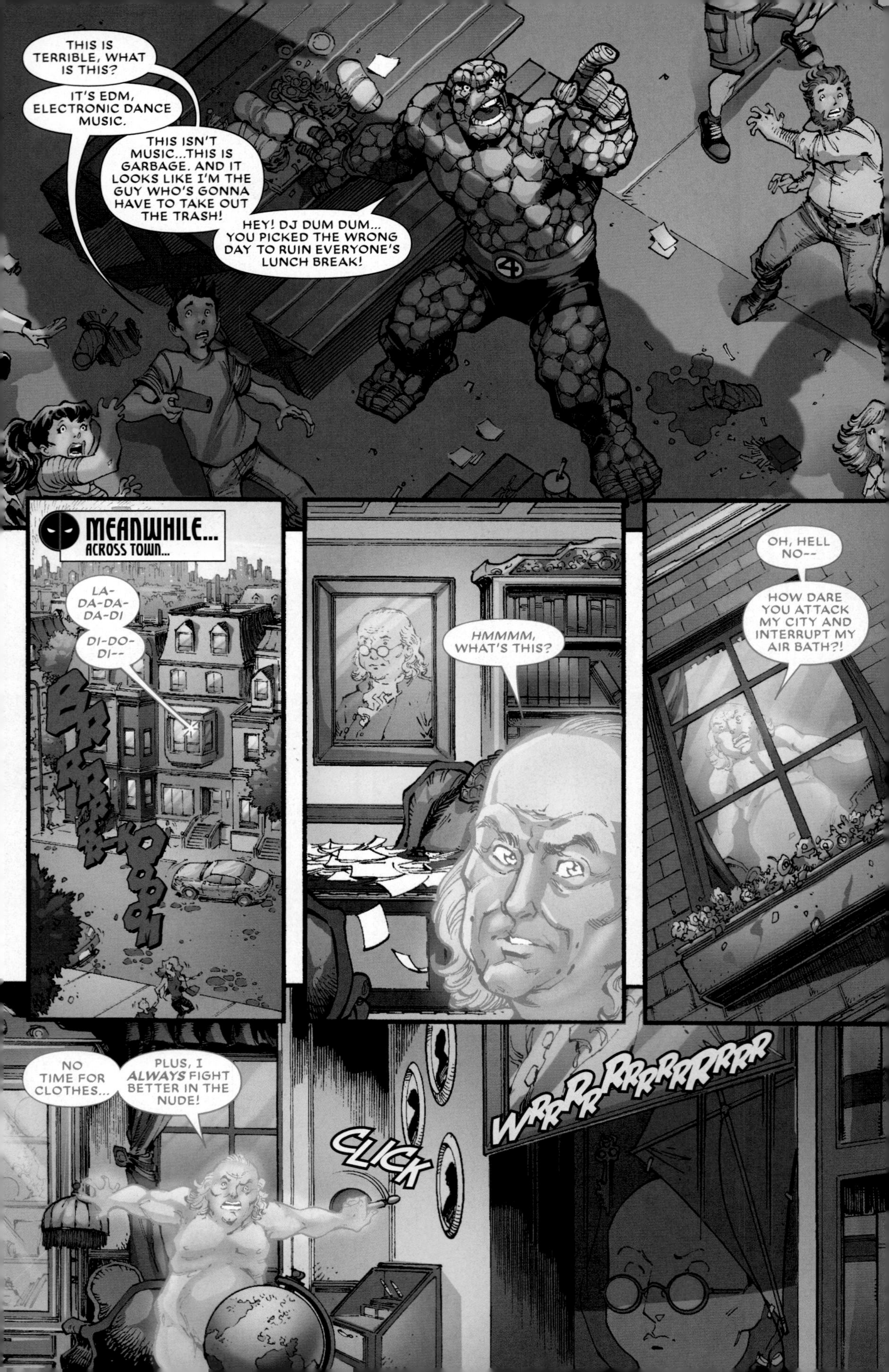
THIS IS TERRIBLE, WHAT IS THIS?
IT'S EDM, ELECTRONIC DANCE MUSIC.
THIS ISN'T MUSIC...THIS IS GARBAGE. AND IT LOOKS LIKE I'M THE GUY WHO'S GONNA HAVE TO TAKE OUT THE TRASH!
HEY! DJ DUM DUM... YOU PICKED THE WRONG DAY TO RUIN EVERYONE'S LUNCH BREAK!
MEANWHILE... ACROSS TOWN...
LA-DA-DA-DA-DI
DI-DO-DI--
HMMMM, WHAT'S THIS?
OH, HELL NO--
HOW DARE YOU ATTACK MY CITY AND INTERRUPT MY AIR BATH?!
NO TIME FOR CLOTHES...
PLUS, I ALWAYS FIGHT BETTER IN THE NUDE!
CLICK
WRRRRRRRRRRRRRRRR

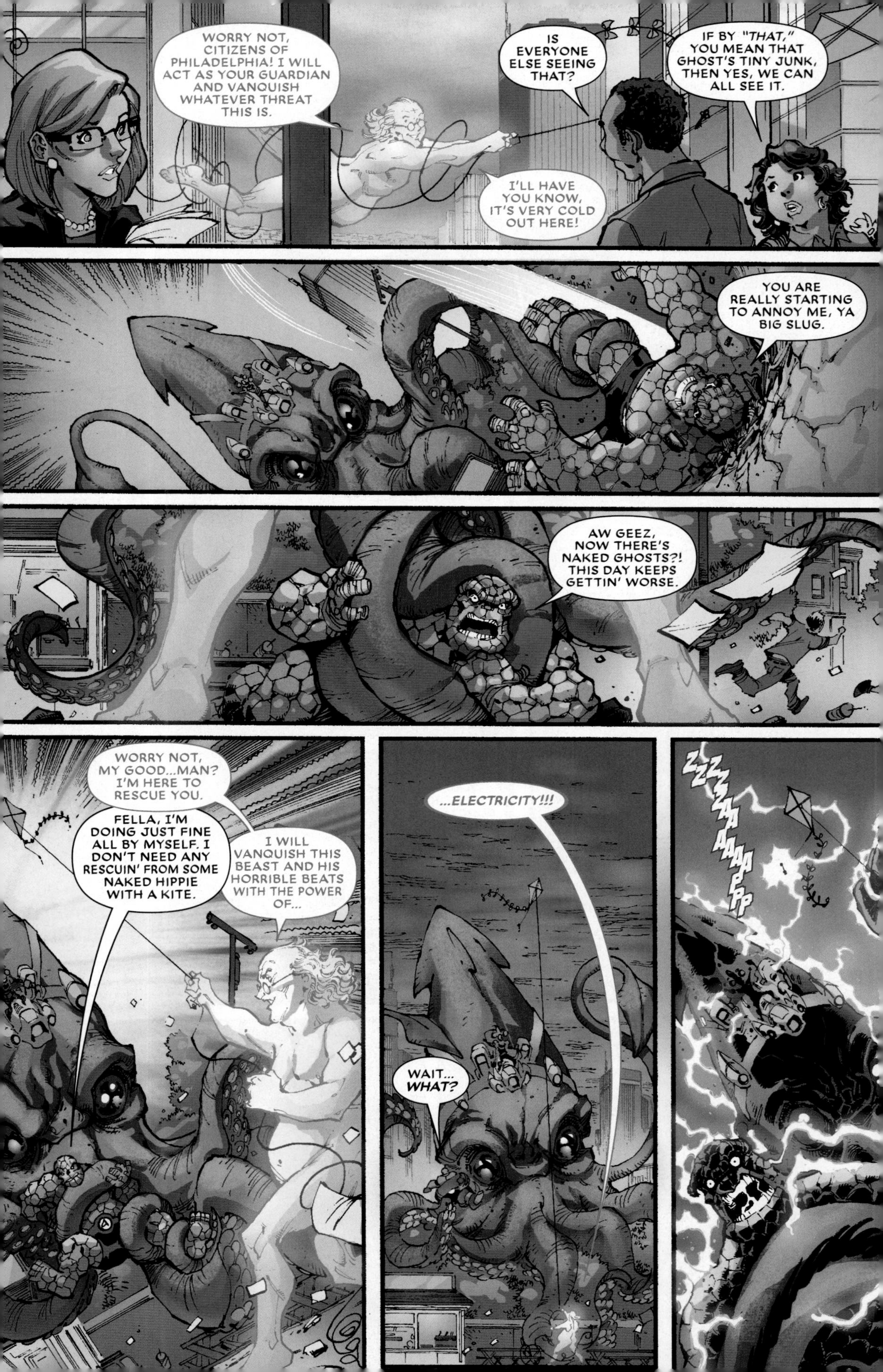

WORRY NOT, CITIZENS OF PHILADELPHIA! I WILL ACT AS YOUR GUARDIAN AND VANQUISH WHATEVER THREAT THIS IS.
IS EVERYONE ELSE SEEING THAT?
IF BY "THAT," YOU MEAN THAT GHOST'S TINY JUNK, THEN YES, WE CAN ALL SEE IT.
I'LL HAVE YOU KNOW, IT'S VERY COLD OUT HERE!
YOU ARE REALLY STARTING TO ANNOY ME, YA BIG SLUG.
AW GEEZ, NOW THERE'S NAKED GHOSTS?! THIS DAY KEEPS GETTIN' WORSE.
WORRY NOT, MY GOOD...MAN? I'M HERE TO RESCUE YOU.
FELLA, I'M DOING JUST FINE ALL BY MYSELF. I DON'T NEED ANY RESCUIN' FROM SOME NAKED HIPPIE WITH A KITE.
I WILL VANQUISH THIS BEAST AND HIS HORRIBLE BEATS WITH THE POWER OF...
...ELECTRICITY!!!
WAIT... WHAT?
ZZZZAAAAAPPPP

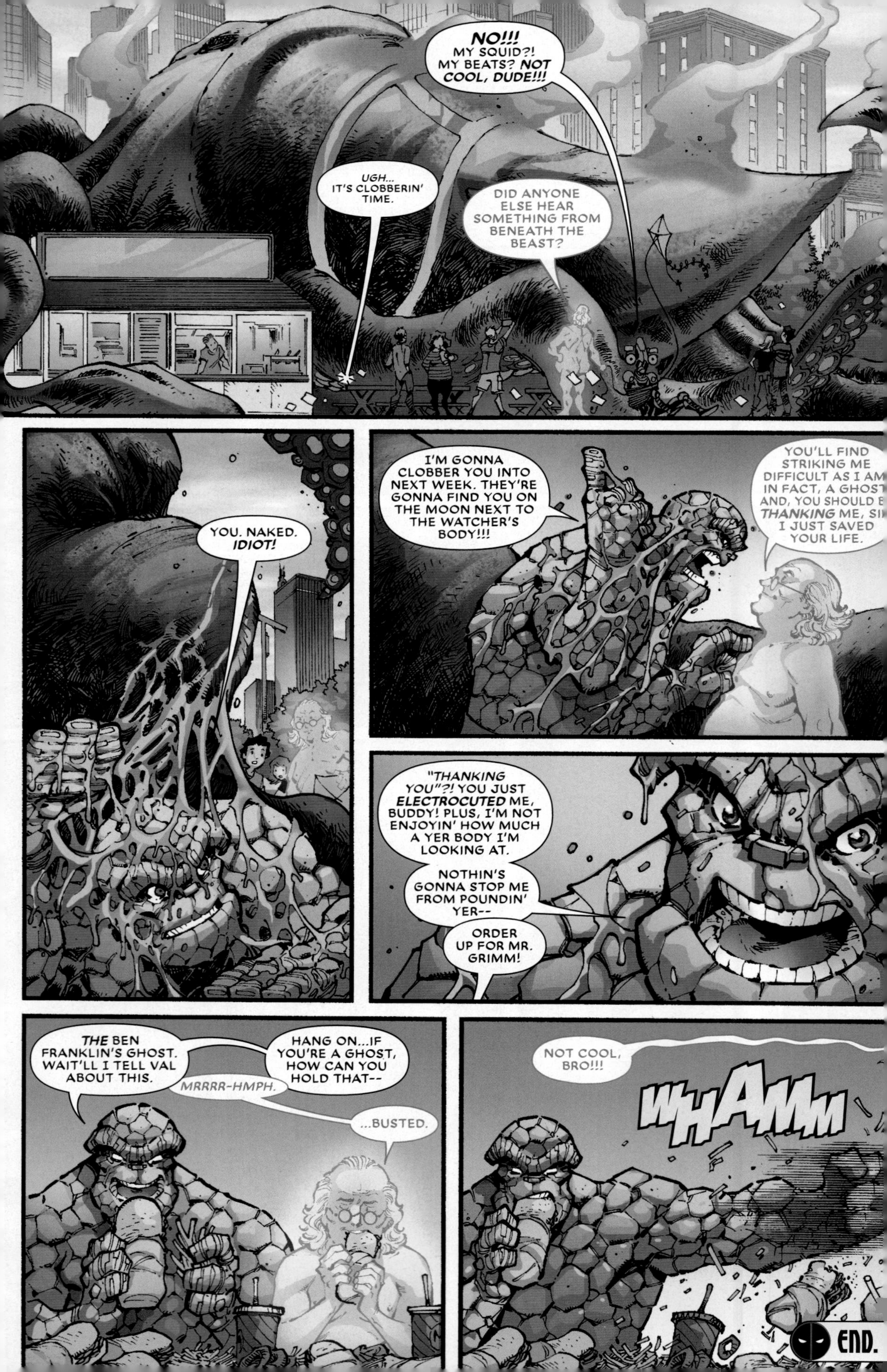
NO!!! MY SQUID?! MY BEATS? NOT COOL, DUDE!!!
UGH... IT'S CLOBBERIN' TIME.
DID ANYONE ELSE HEAR SOMETHING FROM BENEATH THE BEAST?
YOU. NAKED. IDIOT!
I'M GONNA CLOBBER YOU INTO NEXT WEEK. THEY'RE GONNA FIND YOU ON THE MOON NEXT TO THE WATCHER'S BODY!!!
YOU'LL FIND STRIKING ME DIFFICULT AS I AM IN FACT, A GHOST. AND, YOU SHOULD BE THANKING ME, SINCE I JUST SAVED YOUR LIFE.
"THANKING YOU"?! YOU JUST ELECTROCUTED ME, BUDDY! PLUS, I'M NOT ENJOYIN' HOW MUCH A YER BODY I'M LOOKING AT.
NOTHIN'S GONNA STOP ME FROM POUNDIN' YER--
ORDER UP FOR MR. GRIMM!
THE BEN FRANKLIN'S GHOST. WAIT'LL I TELL VAL ABOUT THIS.
HANG ON...IF YOU'RE A GHOST, HOW CAN YOU HOLD THAT--
MRRRR-HMPH.
...BUSTED.
NOT COOL, BRO!!!
WHAMM
END.

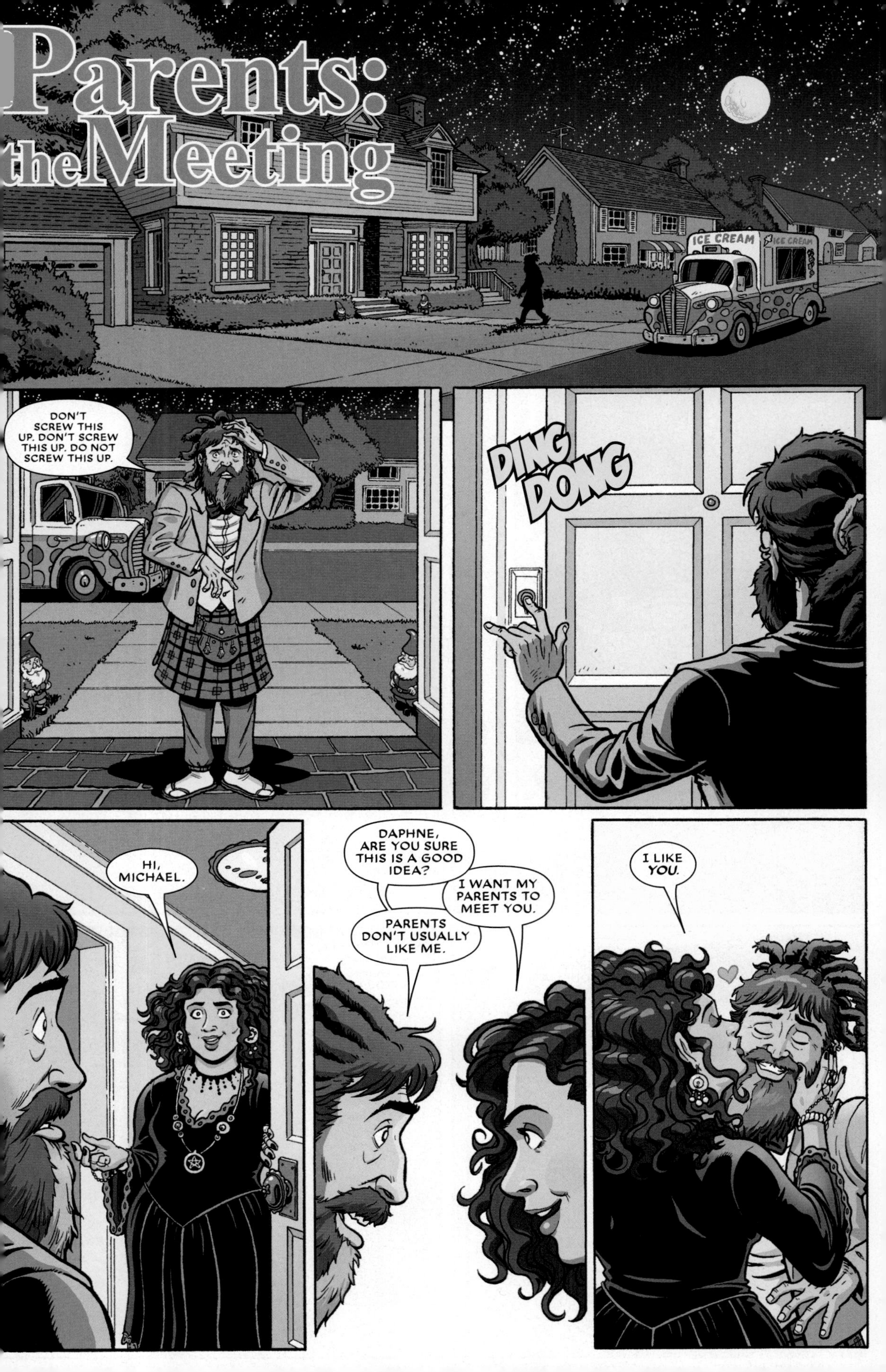
Parents: the Meeting
ICE CREAM
ICE CREAM
DON'T SCREW THIS UP. DON'T SCREW THIS UP. DO NOT SCREW THIS UP.
DING DONG
HI, MICHAEL.
DAPHNE, ARE YOU SURE THIS IS A GOOD IDEA?
PARENTS DON'T USUALLY LIKE ME.
I WANT MY PARENTS TO MEET YOU.
I LIKE *YOU*.

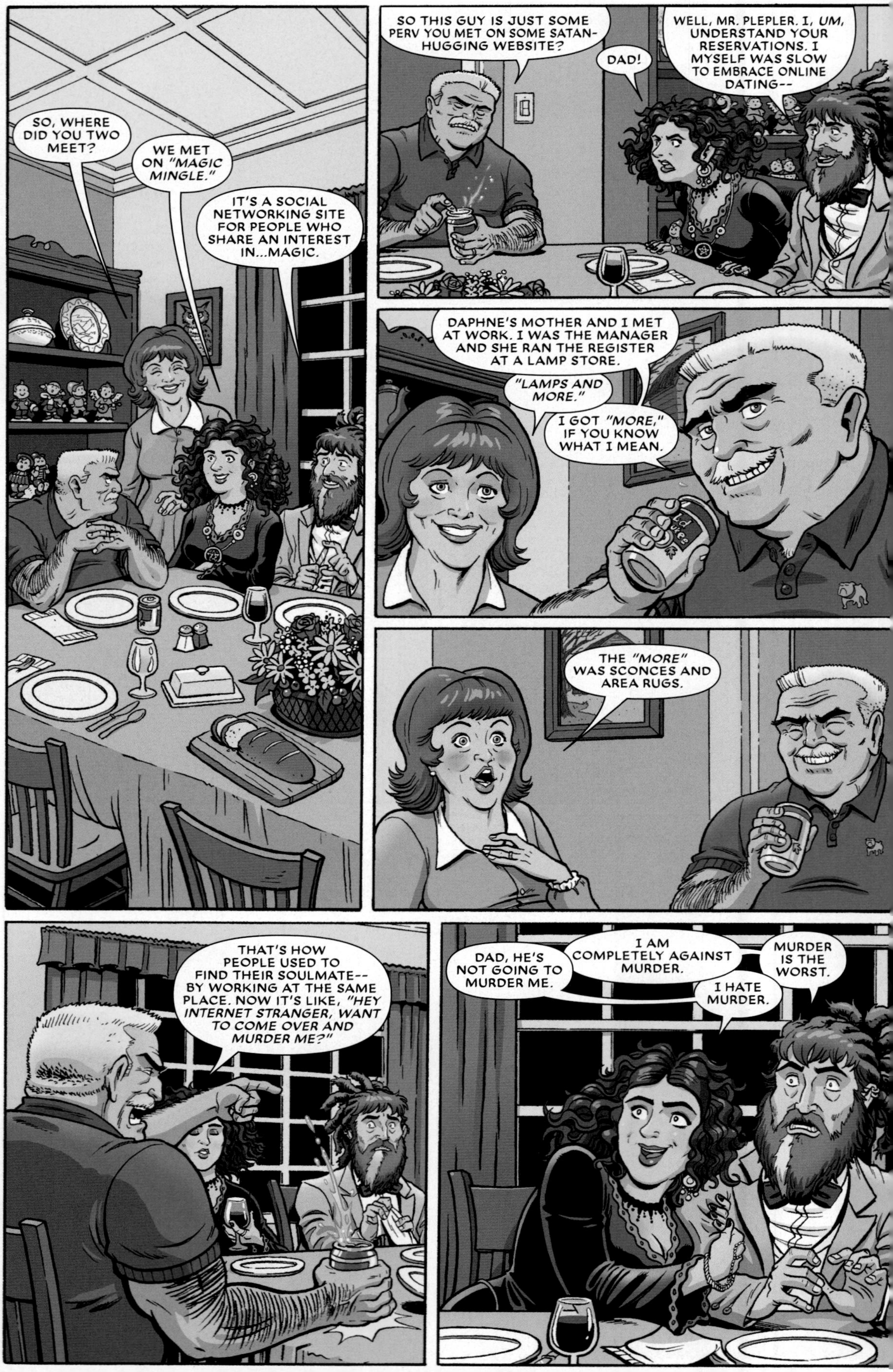

SO, WHERE DID YOU TWO MEET?
WE MET ON "MAGIC MINGLE."
IT'S A SOCIAL NETWORKING SITE FOR PEOPLE WHO SHARE AN INTEREST IN...MAGIC.
SO THIS GUY IS JUST SOME PERV YOU MET ON SOME SATAN-HUGGING WEBSITE?
DAD!
WELL, MR. PLEPLER. I, UM, UNDERSTAND YOUR RESERVATIONS. I MYSELF WAS SLOW TO EMBRACE ONLINE DATING--
DAPHNE'S MOTHER AND I MET AT WORK. I WAS THE MANAGER AND SHE RAN THE REGISTER AT A LAMP STORE.
"LAMPS AND MORE."
I GOT "MORE," IF YOU KNOW WHAT I MEAN.
THE "MORE" WAS SCONCES AND AREA RUGS.
THAT'S HOW PEOPLE USED TO FIND THEIR SOULMATE-- BY WORKING AT THE SAME PLACE. NOW IT'S LIKE, "HEY INTERNET STRANGER, WANT TO COME OVER AND MURDER ME?"
DAD, HE'S NOT GOING TO MURDER ME.
I AM COMPLETELY AGAINST MURDER.
MURDER IS THE WORST.
I HATE MURDER.

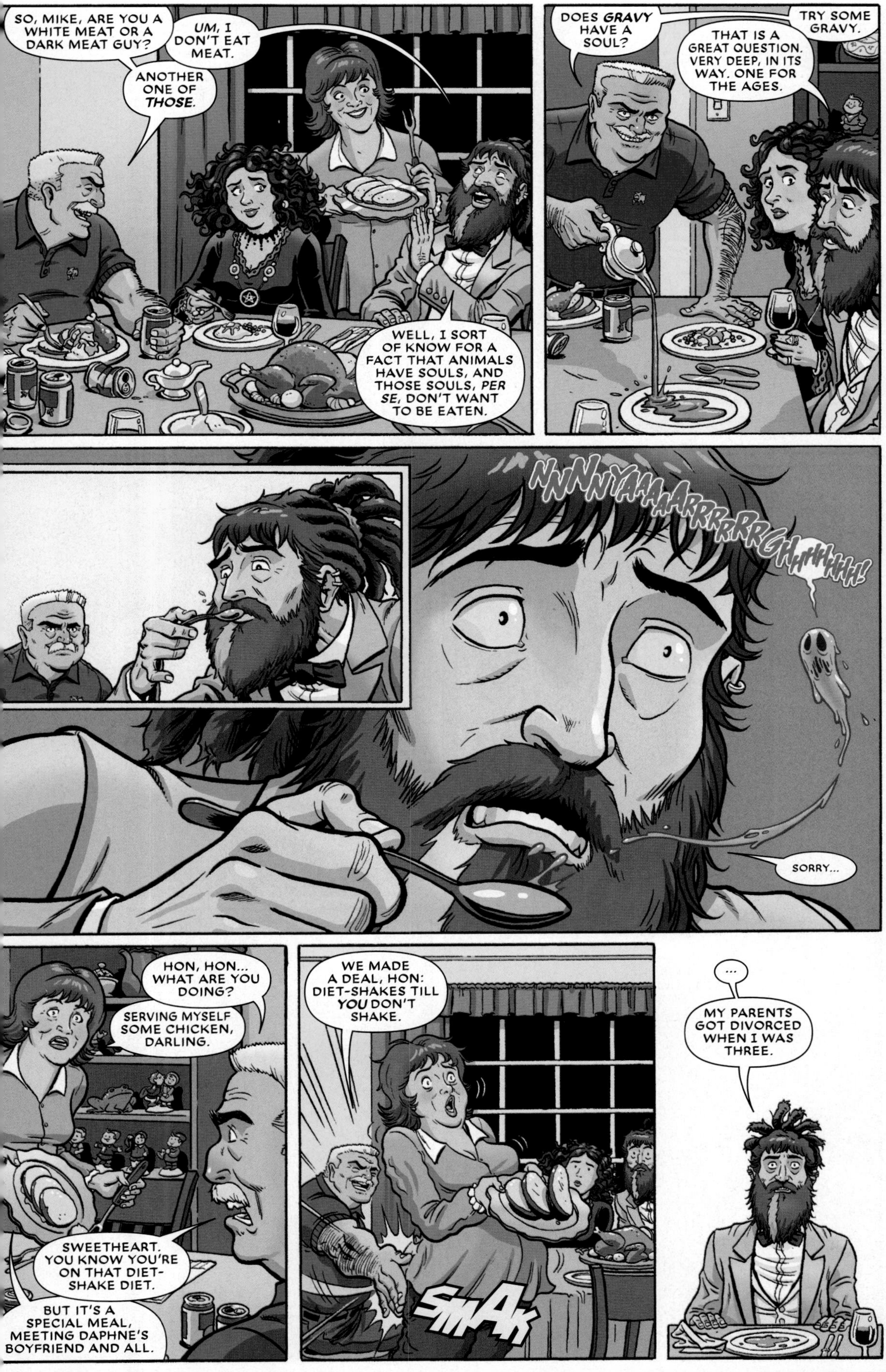
SO, MIKE, ARE YOU A WHITE MEAT OR A DARK MEAT GUY?
UM, I DON'T EAT MEAT.
ANOTHER ONE OF THOSE.
WELL, I SORT OF KNOW FOR A FACT THAT ANIMALS HAVE SOULS, AND THOSE SOULS, PER SE, DON'T WANT TO BE EATEN.
DOES GRAVY HAVE A SOUL?
TRY SOME GRAVY.
THAT IS A GREAT QUESTION. VERY DEEP, IN ITS WAY. ONE FOR THE AGES.
NNNNYAAAAARRRRRRGHHHHHH!
SORRY...
HON, HON... WHAT ARE YOU DOING?
SERVING MYSELF SOME CHICKEN, DARLING.
SWEETHEART. YOU KNOW YOU'RE ON THAT DIET-SHAKE DIET.
BUT IT'S A SPECIAL MEAL, MEETING DAPHNE'S BOYFRIEND AND ALL.
WE MADE A DEAL, HON: DIET-SHAKES TILL YOU DON'T SHAKE.
SMAK
...
MY PARENTS GOT DIVORCED WHEN I WAS THREE.

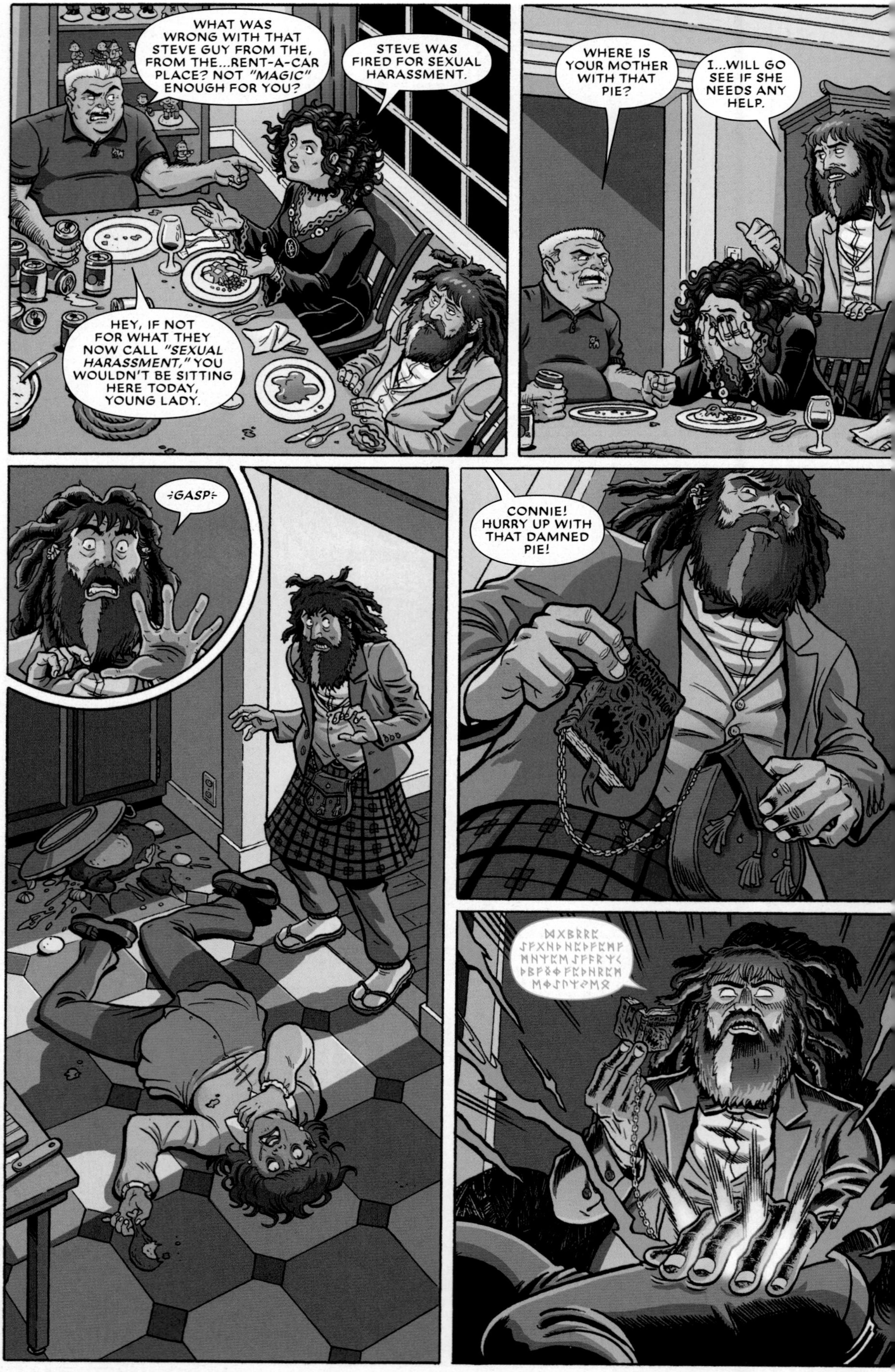
WHAT WAS WRONG WITH THAT STEVE GUY FROM THE, FROM THE...RENT-A-CAR PLACE? NOT "MAGIC" ENOUGH FOR YOU?
STEVE WAS FIRED FOR SEXUAL HARASSMENT.
HEY, IF NOT FOR WHAT THEY NOW CALL "SEXUAL HARASSMENT," YOU WOULDN'T BE SITTING HERE TODAY, YOUNG LADY.
WHERE IS YOUR MOTHER WITH THAT PIE?
I...WILL GO SEE IF SHE NEEDS ANY HELP.
GASP
CONNIE! HURRY UP WITH THAT DAMNED PIE!

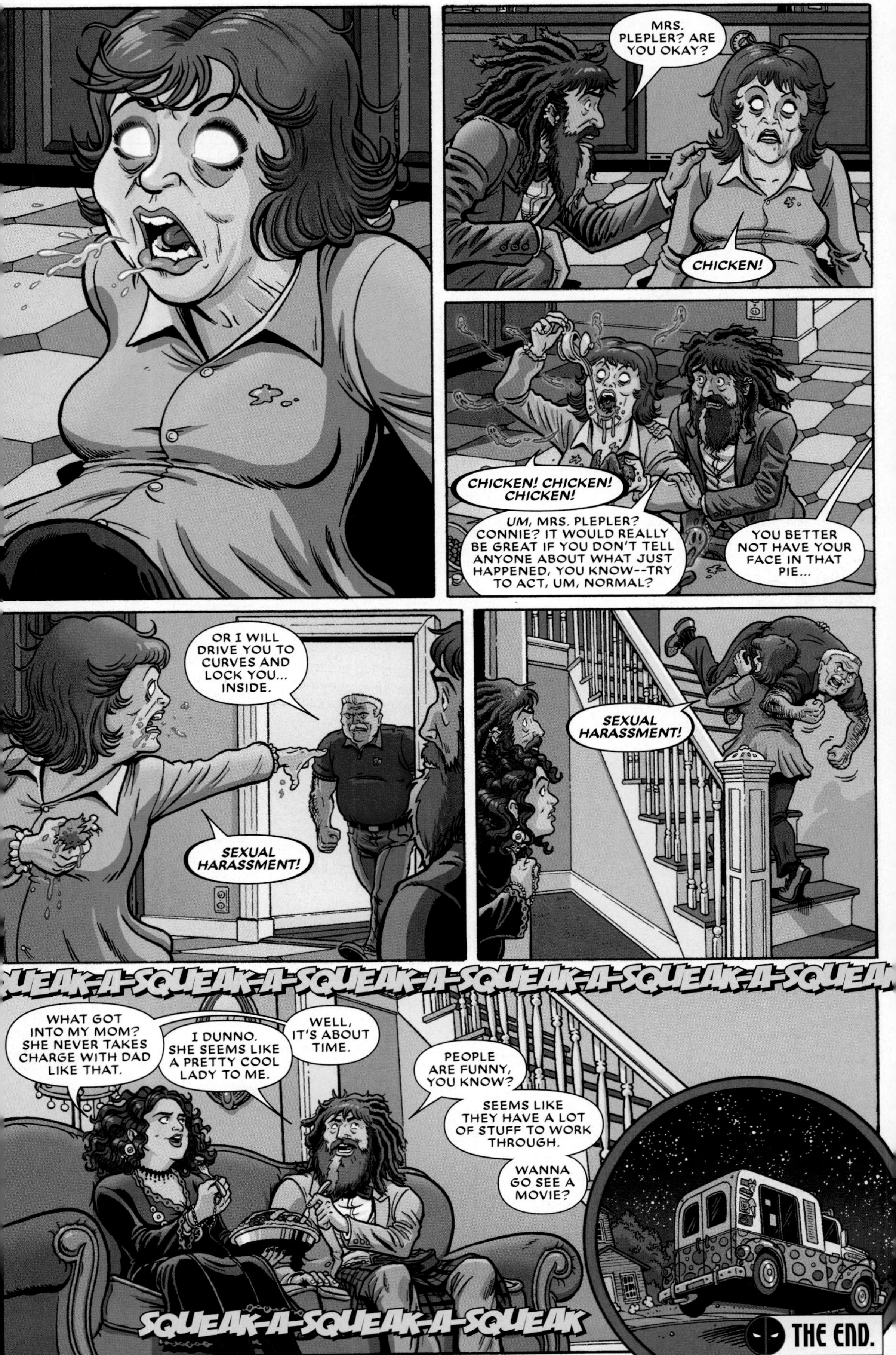

MRS. PLEPLER? ARE YOU OKAY?
CHICKEN!
CHICKEN! CHICKEN! CHICKEN!
UM, MRS. PLEPLER? CONNIE? IT WOULD REALLY BE GREAT IF YOU DON'T TELL ANYONE ABOUT WHAT JUST HAPPENED, YOU KNOW--TRY TO ACT, UM, NORMAL?
YOU BETTER NOT HAVE YOUR FACE IN THAT PIE...
OR I WILL DRIVE YOU TO CURVES AND LOCK YOU... INSIDE.
SEXUAL HARASSMENT!
SEXUAL HARASSMENT!
SQUEAK-A-SQUEAK-A-SQUEAK-A-SQUEAK-A-SQUEAK-A-SQUEAK
WHAT GOT INTO MY MOM? SHE NEVER TAKES CHARGE WITH DAD LIKE THAT.
I DUNNO. SHE SEEMS LIKE A PRETTY COOL LADY TO ME.
WELL, IT'S ABOUT TIME.
PEOPLE ARE FUNNY, YOU KNOW?
SEEMS LIKE THEY HAVE A LOT OF STUFF TO WORK THROUGH.
WANNA GO SEE A MOVIE?
SQUEAK-A-SQUEAK-A-SQUEAK
THE END.

Possibly the world's most skilled mercenary, definitely the world's most annoying, Wade Wilson was chosen for a top-secret government program that gave him a healing factor allowing him to heal from any wound. Now, Wade makes his way as a gun for hire, shooting his prey's faces off while talking his friends' ears off. Call him the Merc with the Mouth...call him the Regeneratin' Degenerate...call him...**DEADPOOL**.

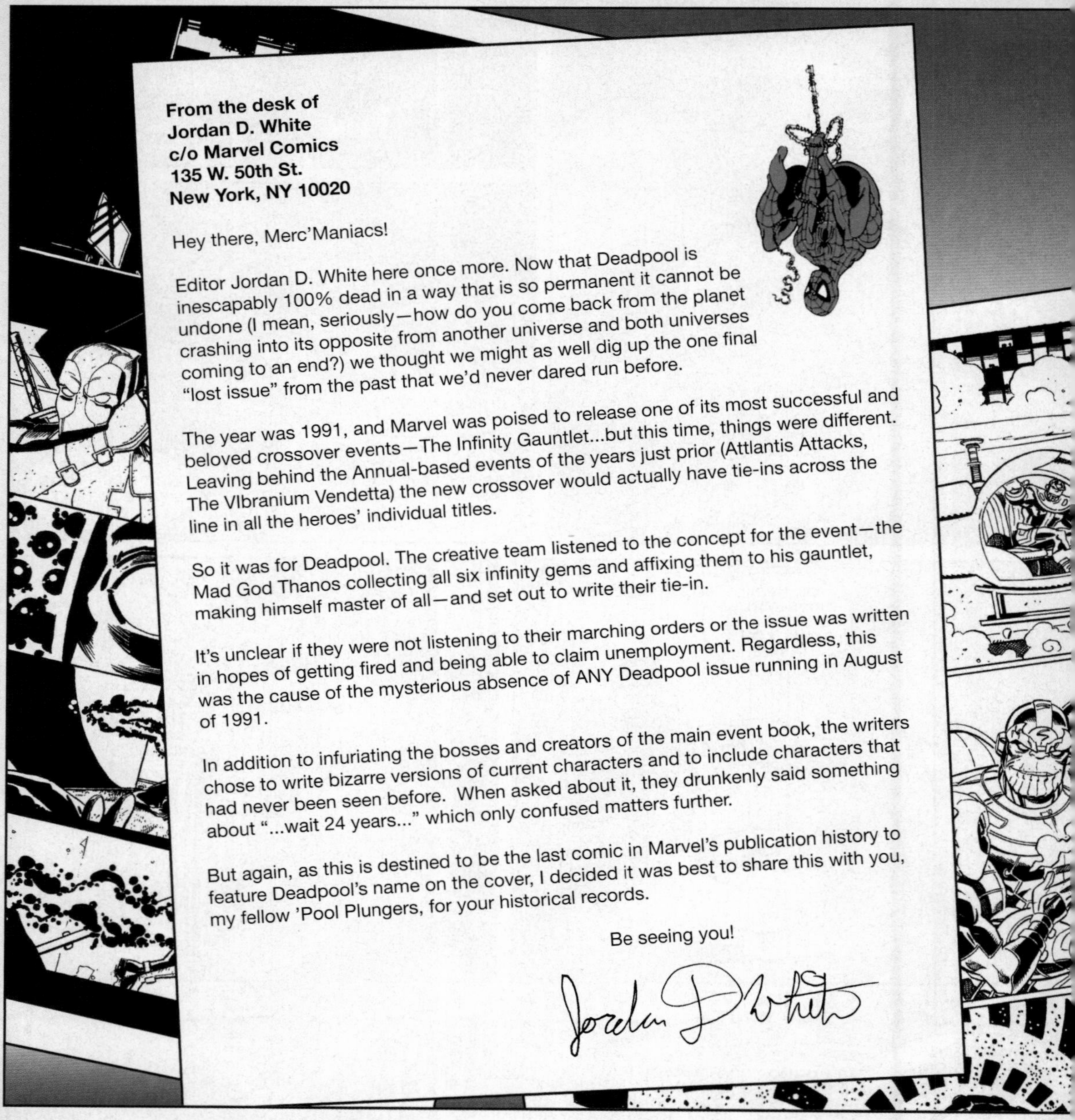

From the desk of
Jordan D. White
c/o Marvel Comics
135 W. 50th St.
New York, NY 10020

Hey there, Merc'Maniacs!

Editor Jordan D. White here once more. Now that Deadpool is inescapably 100% dead in a way that is so permanent it cannot be undone (I mean, seriously—how do you come back from the planet crashing into its opposite from another universe and both universes coming to an end?) we thought we might as well dig up the one final "lost issue" from the past that we'd never dared run before.

The year was 1991, and Marvel was poised to release one of its most successful and beloved crossover events—The Infinity Gauntlet...but this time, things were different. Leaving behind the Annual-based events of the years just prior (Atlantis Attacks, The VIbranium Vendetta) the new crossover would actually have tie-ins across the line in all the heroes' individual titles.

So it was for Deadpool. The creative team listened to the concept for the event—the Mad God Thanos collecting all six infinity gems and affixing them to his gauntlet, making himself master of all—and set out to write their tie-in.

It's unclear if they were not listening to their marching orders or the issue was written in hopes of getting fired and being able to claim unemployment. Regardless, this was the cause of the mysterious absence of ANY Deadpool issue running in August of 1991.

In addition to infuriating the bosses and creators of the main event book, the writers chose to write bizarre versions of current characters and to include characters that had never been seen before. When asked about it, they drunkenly said something about "...wait 24 years..." which only confused matters further.

But again, as this is destined to be the last comic in Marvel's publication history to feature Deadpool's name on the cover, I decided it was best to share this with you, my fellow 'Pool Plungers, for your historical records.

Be seeing you!

Jordan D White

DEADPOOL ROASTS THE MARVEL UNIVERSE

AN INFINITY GAUNTLET TIE-IN

GERRY DUGGAN & BRIAN POSEHN
WORDS

SCOTT KOBLISH
LINES

VAL STAPLES
HUES

VC'S JOE SABINO
BALLOONS

HEATHER ANTOS & CHARLES BEACHAM
ASSISTANT EDITS

JORDAN D. WHITE
EDITS

MIKE MARTS
X-MEN EDITOR

SPECIAL THANKS TO DAVID MANDELL

PASTE INDICIA HERE

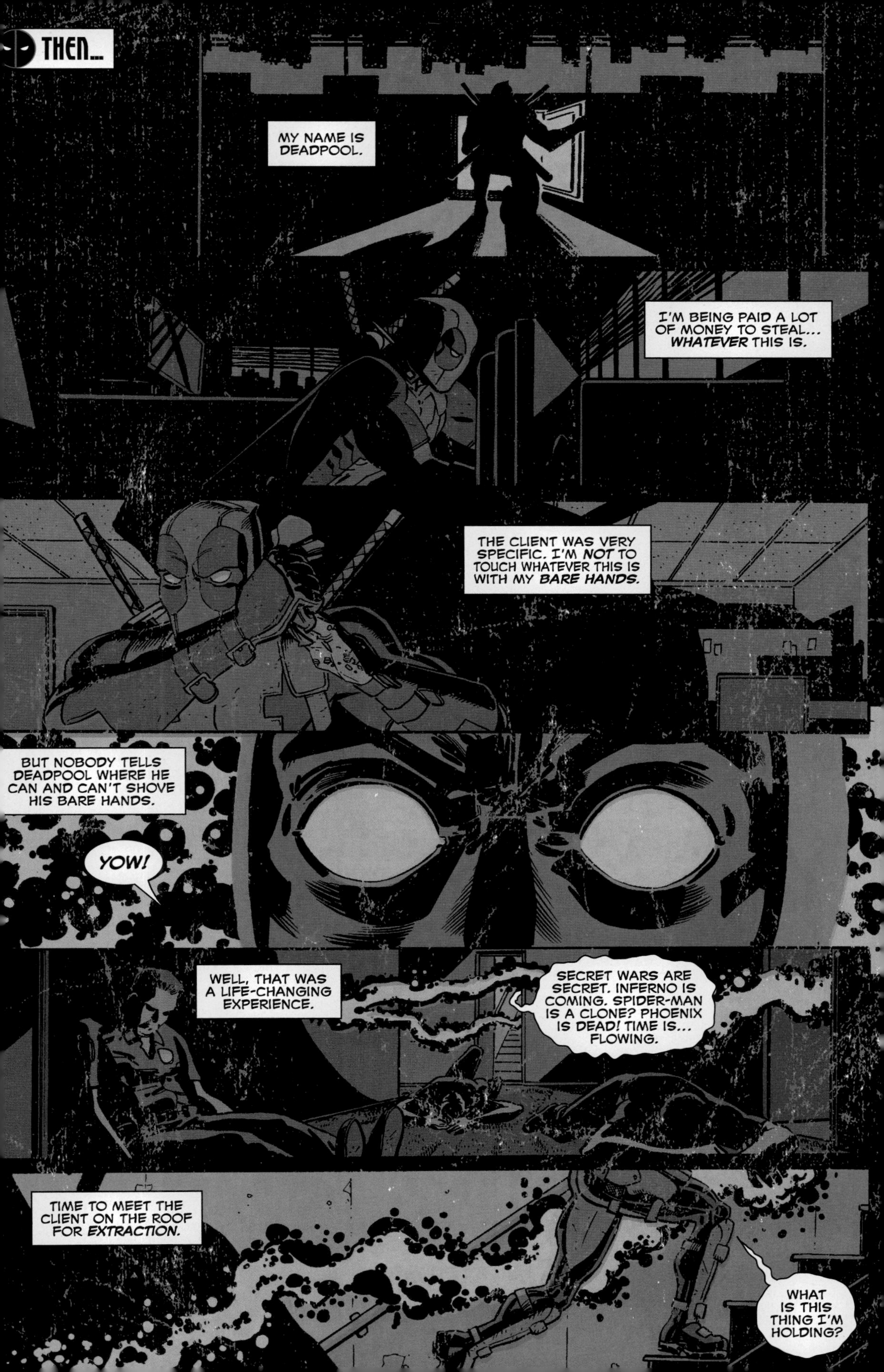
THEN...
MY NAME IS DEADPOOL.
I'M BEING PAID A LOT OF MONEY TO STEAL... WHATEVER THIS IS.
THE CLIENT WAS VERY SPECIFIC. I'M NOT TO TOUCH WHATEVER THIS IS WITH MY BARE HANDS.
BUT NOBODY TELLS DEADPOOL WHERE HE CAN AND CAN'T SHOVE HIS BARE HANDS.
YOW!
WELL, THAT WAS A LIFE-CHANGING EXPERIENCE.
SECRET WARS ARE SECRET. INFERNO IS COMING. SPIDER-MAN IS A CLONE? PHOENIX IS DEAD! TIME IS... FLOWING.
TIME TO MEET THE CLIENT ON THE ROOF FOR EXTRACTION.
WHAT IS THIS THING I'M HOLDING?

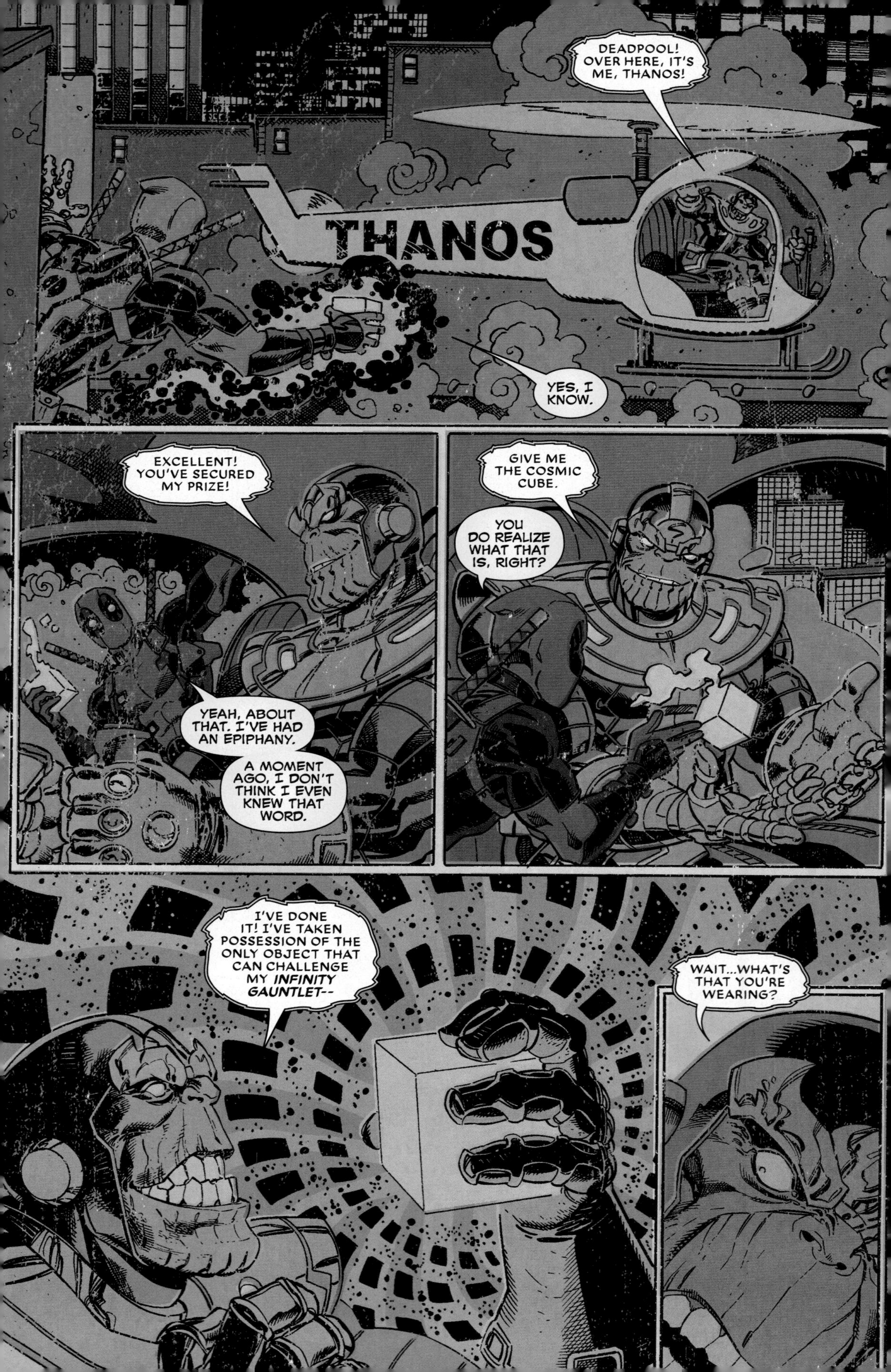
DEADPOOL! OVER HERE, IT'S ME, THANOS!
THANOS
YES, I KNOW.
EXCELLENT! YOU'VE SECURED MY PRIZE!
YEAH, ABOUT THAT. I'VE HAD AN EPIPHANY.
A MOMENT AGO, I DON'T THINK I EVEN KNEW THAT WORD.
GIVE ME THE COSMIC CUBE.
YOU DO REALIZE WHAT THAT IS, RIGHT?
I'VE DONE IT! I'VE TAKEN POSSESSION OF THE ONLY OBJECT THAT CAN CHALLENGE MY *INFINITY GAUNTLET*--
WAIT...WHAT'S THAT YOU'RE WEARING?

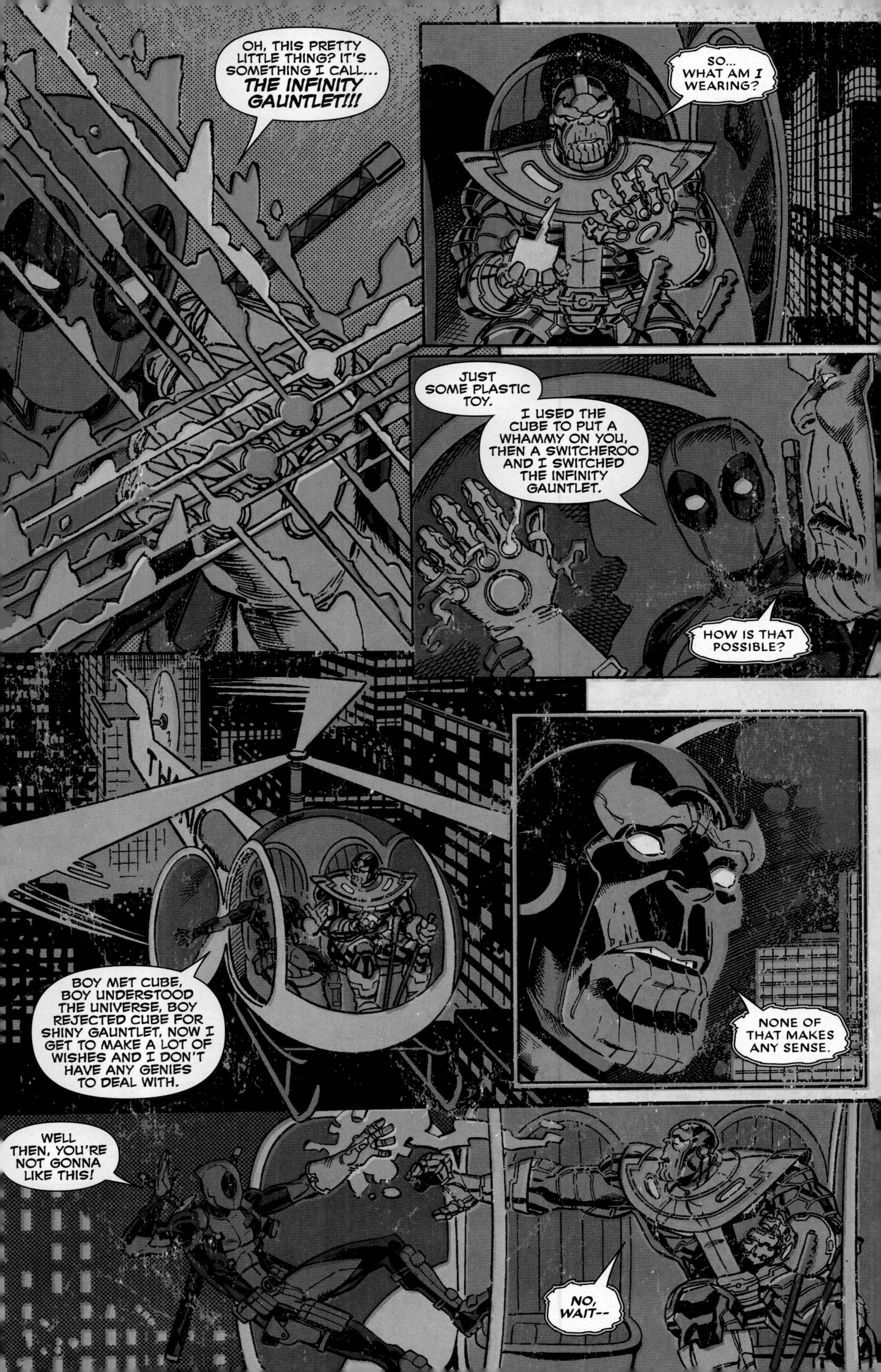
OH, THIS PRETTY LITTLE THING? IT'S SOMETHING I CALL... THE INFINITY GAUNTLET!!!
SO... WHAT AM I WEARING?
JUST SOME PLASTIC TOY.
I USED THE CUBE TO PUT A WHAMMY ON YOU, THEN A SWITCHEROO AND I SWITCHED THE INFINITY GAUNTLET.
HOW IS THAT POSSIBLE?
BOY MET CUBE, BOY UNDERSTOOD THE UNIVERSE, BOY REJECTED CUBE FOR SHINY GAUNTLET, NOW I GET TO MAKE A LOT OF WISHES AND I DON'T HAVE ANY GENIES TO DEAL WITH.
NONE OF THAT MAKES ANY SENSE.
WELL THEN, YOU'RE NOT GONNA LIKE THIS!
NO, WAIT--

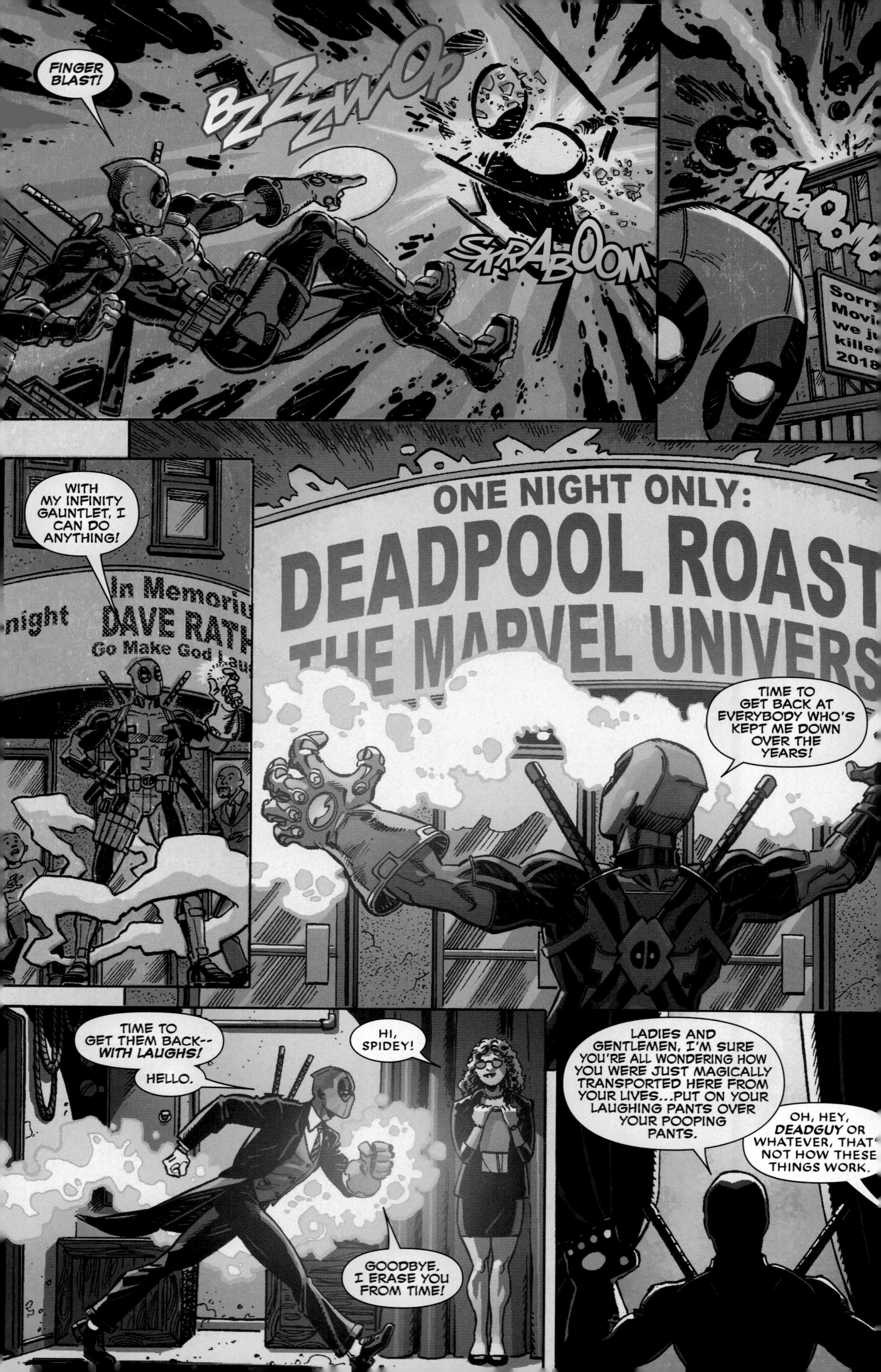
FINGER BLAST!
BZZZWOP
SKRABOOM
KABOOM
ONE NIGHT ONLY:
DEADPOOL ROAST
THE MARVEL UNIVERS
WITH MY INFINITY GAUNTLET, I CAN DO ANYTHING!
In Memoriu
DAVE RATH
Go Make God
TIME TO GET BACK AT EVERYBODY WHO'S KEPT ME DOWN OVER THE YEARS!
TIME TO GET THEM BACK-- WITH LAUGHS!
HELLO.
HI, SPIDEY!
GOODBYE. I ERASE YOU FROM TIME!
LADIES AND GENTLEMEN, I'M SURE YOU'RE ALL WONDERING HOW YOU WERE JUST MAGICALLY TRANSPORTED HERE FROM YOUR LIVES...PUT ON YOUR LAUGHING PANTS OVER YOUR POOPING PANTS.
OH, HEY, DEADGUY OR WHATEVER, THAT NOT HOW THESE THINGS WORK.

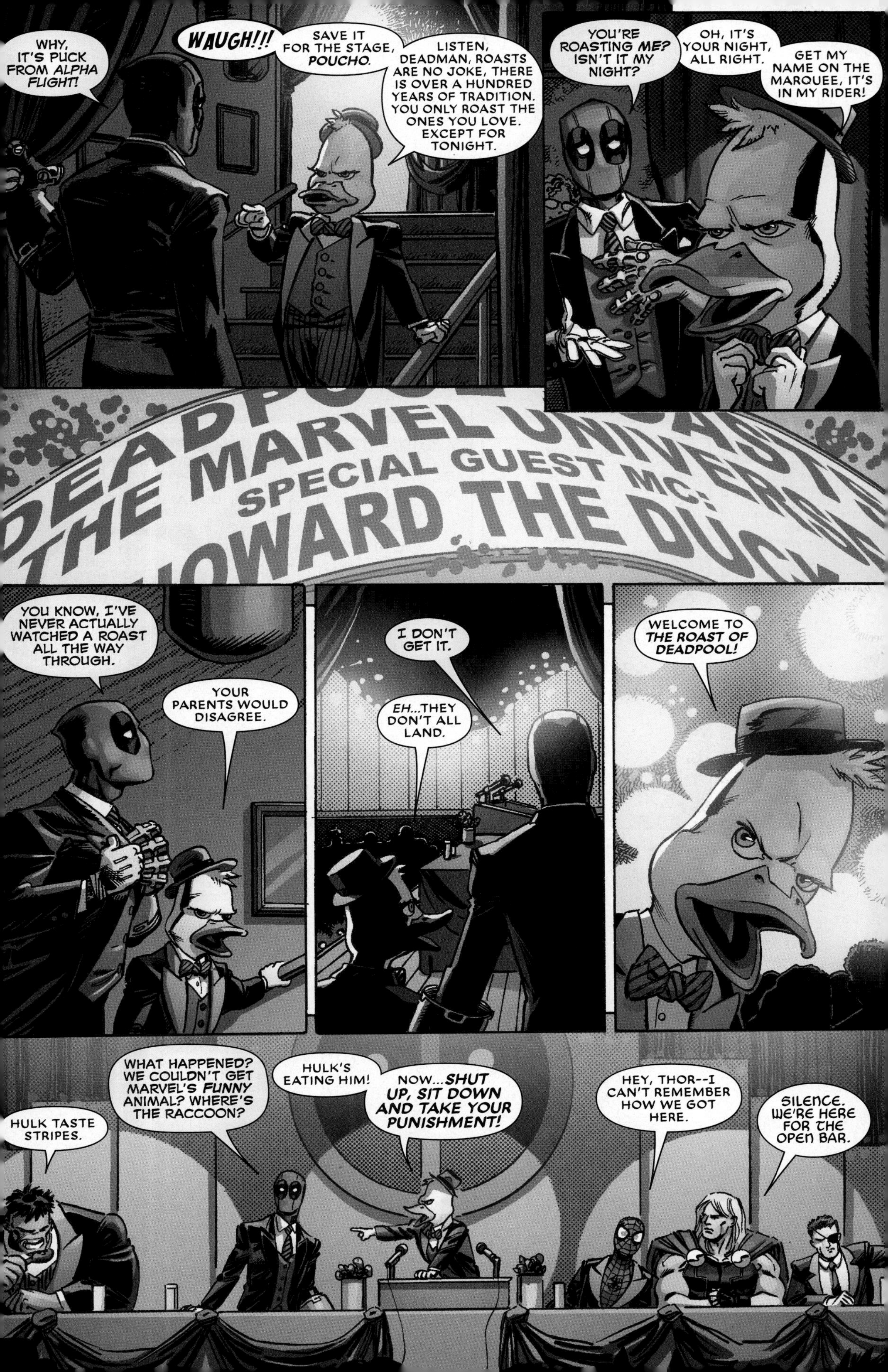
WHY, IT'S PUCK FROM ALPHA FLIGHT!
WAUGH!!!
SAVE IT FOR THE STAGE, POUCHO.
LISTEN, DEADMAN, ROASTS ARE NO JOKE, THERE IS OVER A HUNDRED YEARS OF TRADITION. YOU ONLY ROAST THE ONES YOU LOVE. EXCEPT FOR TONIGHT.
YOU'RE ROASTING ME? ISN'T IT MY NIGHT?
OH, IT'S YOUR NIGHT, ALL RIGHT.
GET MY NAME ON THE MARQUEE, IT'S IN MY RIDER!
THE MARVEL
SPECIAL GUEST MC:
HOWARD THE
YOU KNOW, I'VE NEVER ACTUALLY WATCHED A ROAST ALL THE WAY THROUGH.
YOUR PARENTS WOULD DISAGREE.
I DON'T GET IT.
EH...THEY DON'T ALL LAND.
WELCOME TO THE ROAST OF DEADPOOL!
HULK TASTE STRIPES.
WHAT HAPPENED? WE COULDN'T GET MARVEL'S FUNNY ANIMAL? WHERE'S THE RACCOON?
HULK'S EATING HIM!
NOW...SHUT UP, SIT DOWN AND TAKE YOUR PUNISHMENT!
HEY, THOR--I CAN'T REMEMBER HOW WE GOT HERE.
SILENCE. WE'RE HERE FOR THE OPEN BAR.

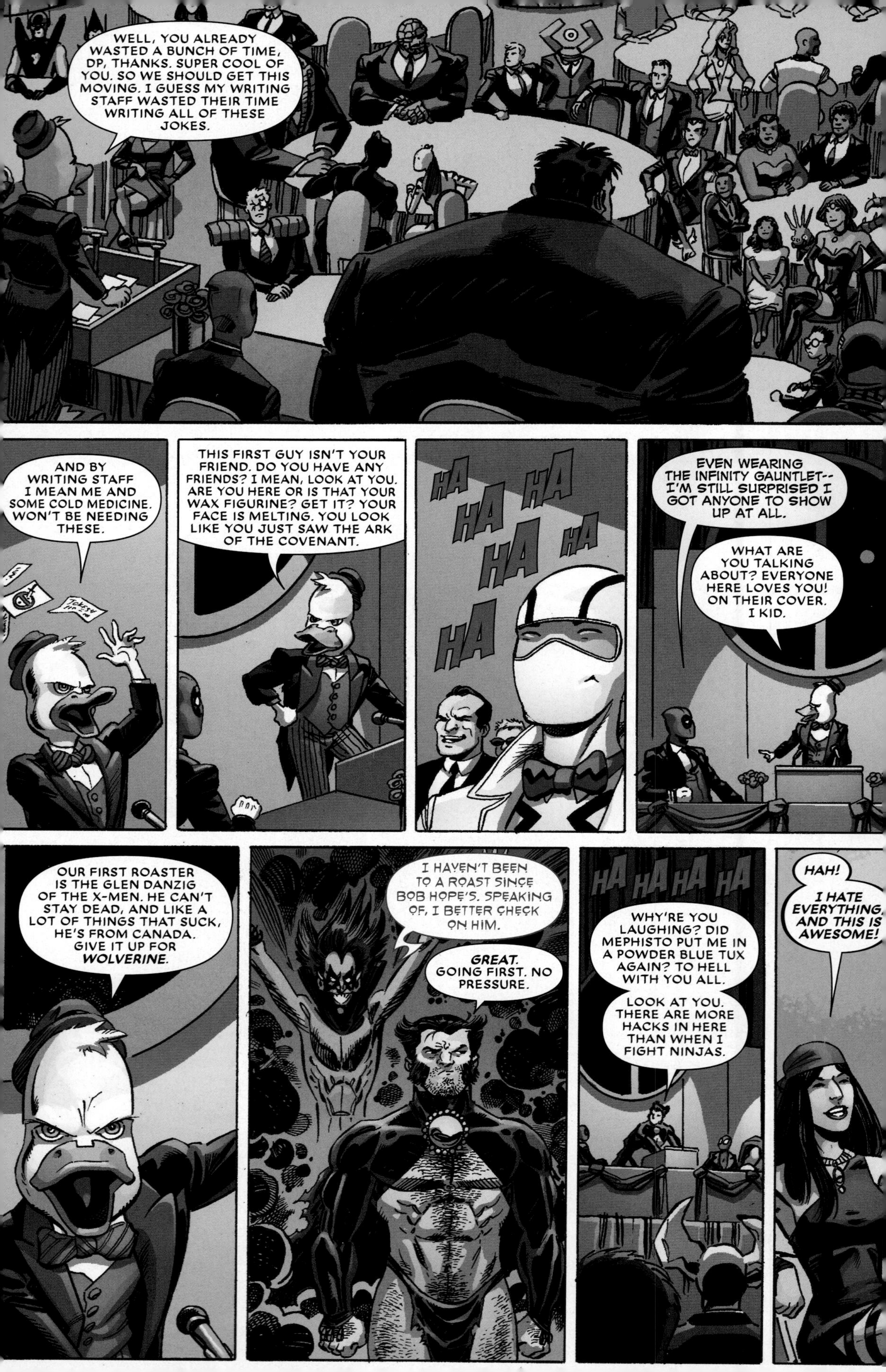

WELL, YOU ALREADY WASTED A BUNCH OF TIME, DP, THANKS. SUPER COOL OF YOU. SO WE SHOULD GET THIS MOVING. I GUESS MY WRITING STAFF WASTED THEIR TIME WRITING ALL OF THESE JOKES.
AND BY WRITING STAFF I MEAN ME AND SOME COLD MEDICINE. WON'T BE NEEDING THESE.
JOKES
THIS FIRST GUY ISN'T YOUR FRIEND. DO YOU HAVE ANY FRIENDS? I MEAN, LOOK AT YOU. ARE YOU HERE OR IS THAT YOUR WAX FIGURINE? GET IT? YOUR FACE IS MELTING. YOU LOOK LIKE YOU JUST SAW THE ARK OF THE COVENANT.
HA HA HA HA HA HA
EVEN WEARING THE INFINITY GAUNTLET-- I'M STILL SURPRISED I GOT ANYONE TO SHOW UP AT ALL.
WHAT ARE YOU TALKING ABOUT? EVERYONE HERE LOVES YOU! ON THEIR COVER. I KID.
OUR FIRST ROASTER IS THE GLEN DANZIG OF THE X-MEN. HE CAN'T STAY DEAD, AND LIKE A LOT OF THINGS THAT SUCK, HE'S FROM CANADA. GIVE IT UP FOR *WOLVERINE*.
I HAVEN'T BEEN TO A ROAST SINCE BOB HOPE'S. SPEAKING OF, I BETTER CHECK ON HIM.
GREAT. GOING FIRST. NO PRESSURE.
HA HA HA HA HA
WHY'RE YOU LAUGHING? DID MEPHISTO PUT ME IN A POWDER BLUE TUX AGAIN? TO HELL WITH YOU ALL.
LOOK AT YOU. THERE ARE MORE HACKS IN HERE THAN WHEN I FIGHT NINJAS.
HAH!
I HATE EVERYTHING, AND THIS IS AWESOME!

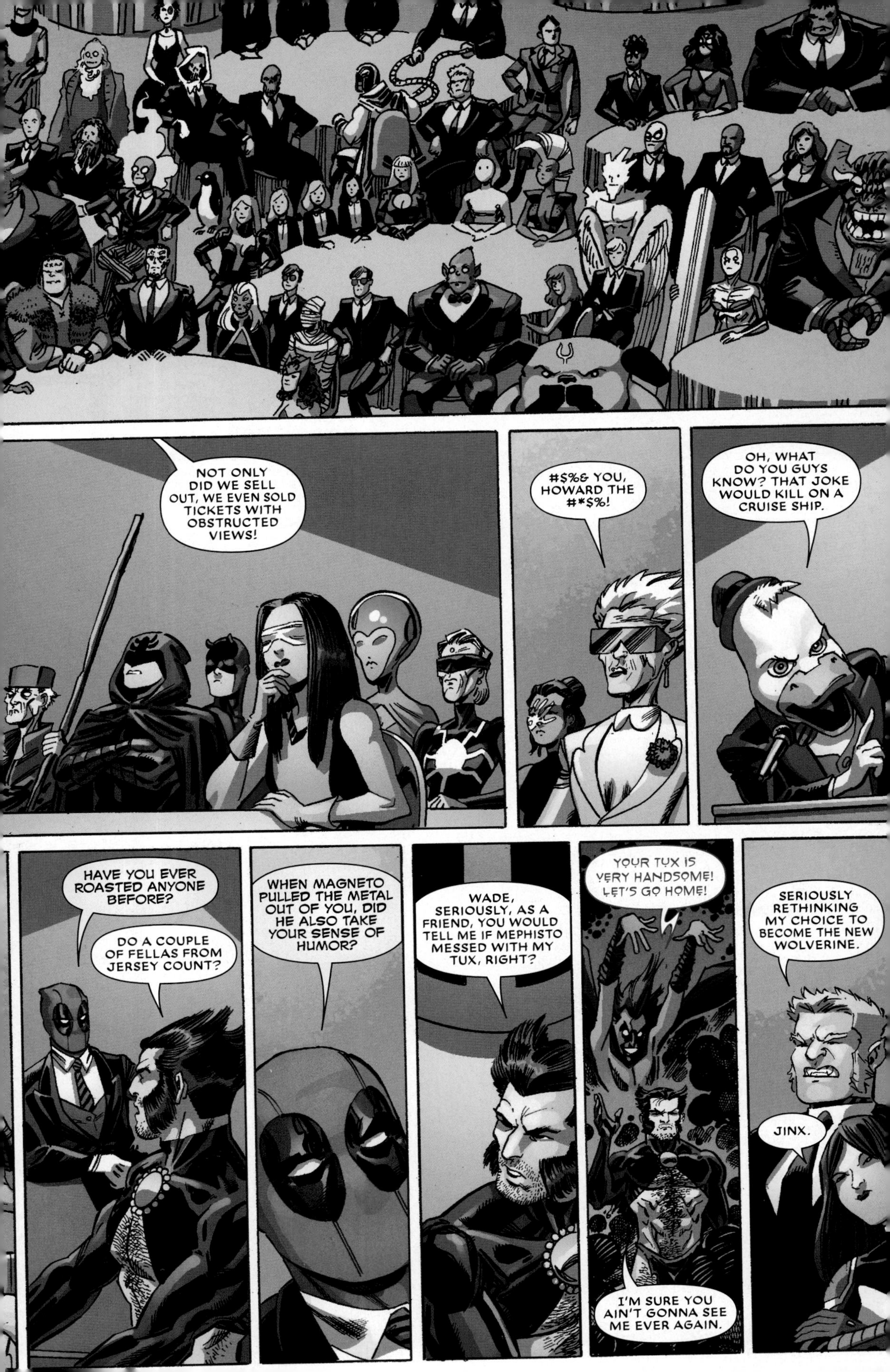
NOT ONLY DID WE SELL OUT, WE EVEN SOLD TICKETS WITH OBSTRUCTED VIEWS!
#$%& YOU, HOWARD THE #*$%!
OH, WHAT DO YOU GUYS KNOW? THAT JOKE WOULD KILL ON A CRUISE SHIP.
HAVE YOU EVER ROASTED ANYONE BEFORE?
DO A COUPLE OF FELLAS FROM JERSEY COUNT?
WHEN MAGNETO PULLED THE METAL OUT OF YOU, DID HE ALSO TAKE YOUR SENSE OF HUMOR?
WADE, SERIOUSLY, AS A FRIEND, YOU WOULD TELL ME IF MEPHISTO MESSED WITH MY TUX, RIGHT?
YOUR TUX IS VERY HANDSOME! LET'S GO HOME!
I'M SURE YOU AIN'T GONNA SEE ME EVER AGAIN.
SERIOUSLY RETHINKING MY CHOICE TO BECOME THE NEW WOLVERINE.
JINX.

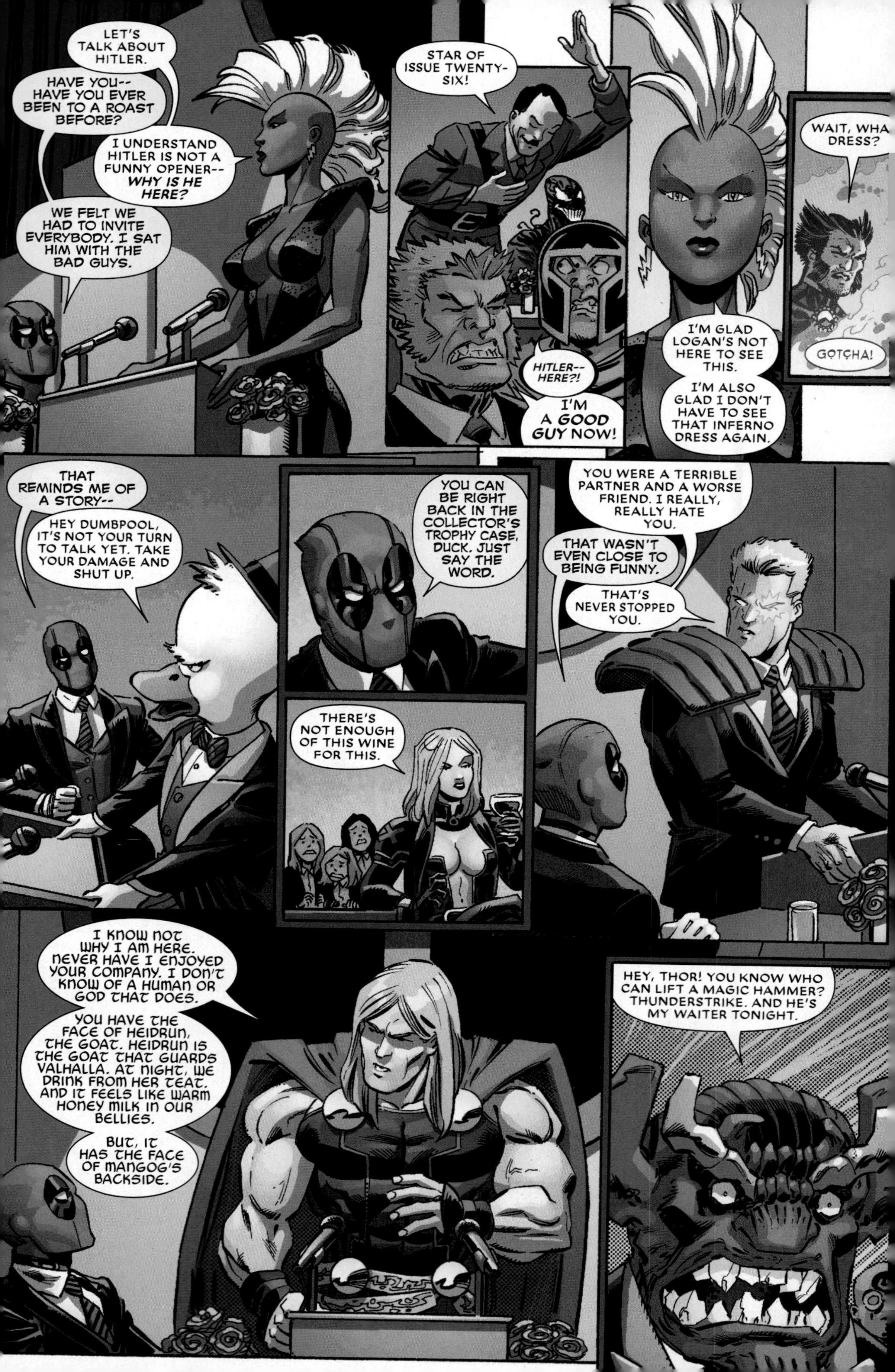
LET'S TALK ABOUT HITLER.
HAVE YOU-- HAVE YOU EVER BEEN TO A ROAST BEFORE?
I UNDERSTAND HITLER IS NOT A FUNNY OPENER-- WHY IS HE HERE?
WE FELT WE HAD TO INVITE EVERYBODY. I SAT HIM WITH THE BAD GUYS.
STAR OF ISSUE TWENTY-SIX!
HITLER-- HERE?!
I'M A GOOD GUY NOW!
I'M GLAD LOGAN'S NOT HERE TO SEE THIS.
I'M ALSO GLAD I DON'T HAVE TO SEE THAT INFERNO DRESS AGAIN.
WAIT, WHA DRESS?
GOTCHA!
THAT REMINDS ME OF A STORY--
HEY DUMBPOOL, IT'S NOT YOUR TURN TO TALK YET. TAKE YOUR DAMAGE AND SHUT UP.
YOU CAN BE RIGHT BACK IN THE COLLECTOR'S TROPHY CASE, DUCK. JUST SAY THE WORD.
THERE'S NOT ENOUGH OF THIS WINE FOR THIS.
YOU WERE A TERRIBLE PARTNER AND A WORSE FRIEND. I REALLY, REALLY HATE YOU.
THAT WASN'T EVEN CLOSE TO BEING FUNNY.
THAT'S NEVER STOPPED YOU.
I KNOW NOT WHY I AM HERE. NEVER HAVE I ENJOYED YOUR COMPANY. I DON'T KNOW OF A HUMAN OR GOD THAT DOES.
YOU HAVE THE FACE OF HEIDRUN, THE GOAT. HEIDRUN IS THE GOAT THAT GUARDS VALHALLA. AT NIGHT, WE DRINK FROM HER TEAT. AND IT FEELS LIKE WARM HONEY MILK IN OUR BELLIES.
BUT, IT HAS THE FACE OF MANGOG'S BACKSIDE.
HEY, THOR! YOU KNOW WHO CAN LIFT A MAGIC HAMMER? THUNDERSTRIKE. AND HE'S MY WAITER TONIGHT.

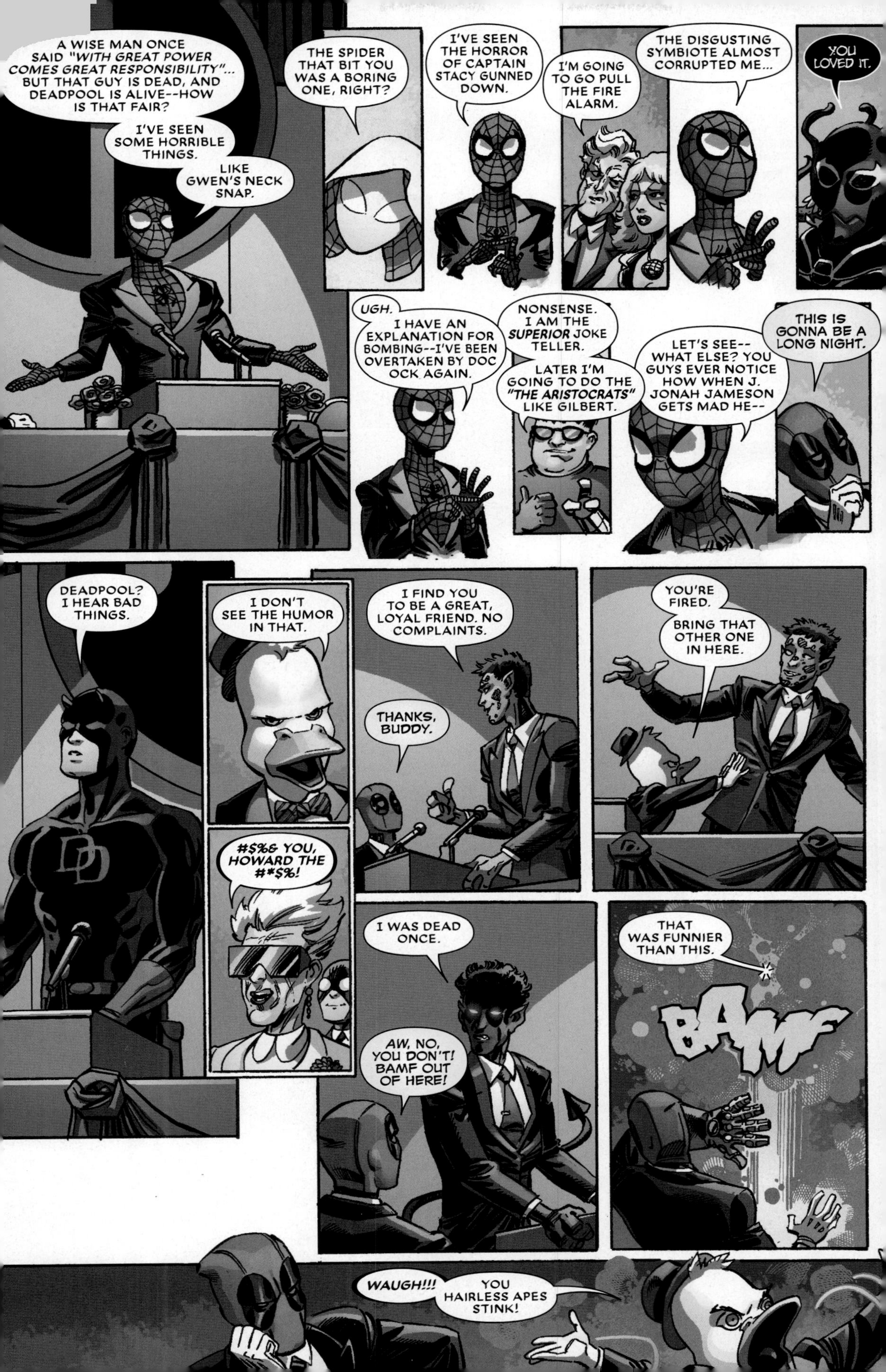
A WISE MAN ONCE SAID "WITH GREAT POWER COMES GREAT RESPONSIBILITY"... BUT THAT GUY IS DEAD, AND DEADPOOL IS ALIVE--HOW IS THAT FAIR?
I'VE SEEN SOME HORRIBLE THINGS.
LIKE GWEN'S NECK SNAP.
THE SPIDER THAT BIT YOU WAS A BORING ONE, RIGHT?
I'VE SEEN THE HORROR OF CAPTAIN STACY GUNNED DOWN.
I'M GOING TO GO PULL THE FIRE ALARM.
THE DISGUSTING SYMBIOTE ALMOST CORRUPTED ME...
YOU LOVED IT.
UGH.
I HAVE AN EXPLANATION FOR BOMBING--I'VE BEEN OVERTAKEN BY DOC OCK AGAIN.
NONSENSE. I AM THE SUPERIOR JOKE TELLER.
LATER I'M GOING TO DO THE "THE ARISTOCRATS" LIKE GILBERT.
LET'S SEE-- WHAT ELSE? YOU GUYS EVER NOTICE HOW WHEN J. JONAH JAMESON GETS MAD HE--
THIS IS GONNA BE A LONG NIGHT.
DEADPOOL? I HEAR BAD THINGS.
I DON'T SEE THE HUMOR IN THAT.
#$%& YOU, HOWARD THE #*$%!
I FIND YOU TO BE A GREAT, LOYAL FRIEND. NO COMPLAINTS.
THANKS, BUDDY.
YOU'RE FIRED.
BRING THAT OTHER ONE IN HERE.
I WAS DEAD ONCE.
AW, NO, YOU DON'T! BAMF OUT OF HERE!
THAT WAS FUNNIER THAN THIS.
BAMF
WAUGH!!!
YOU HAIRLESS APES STINK!

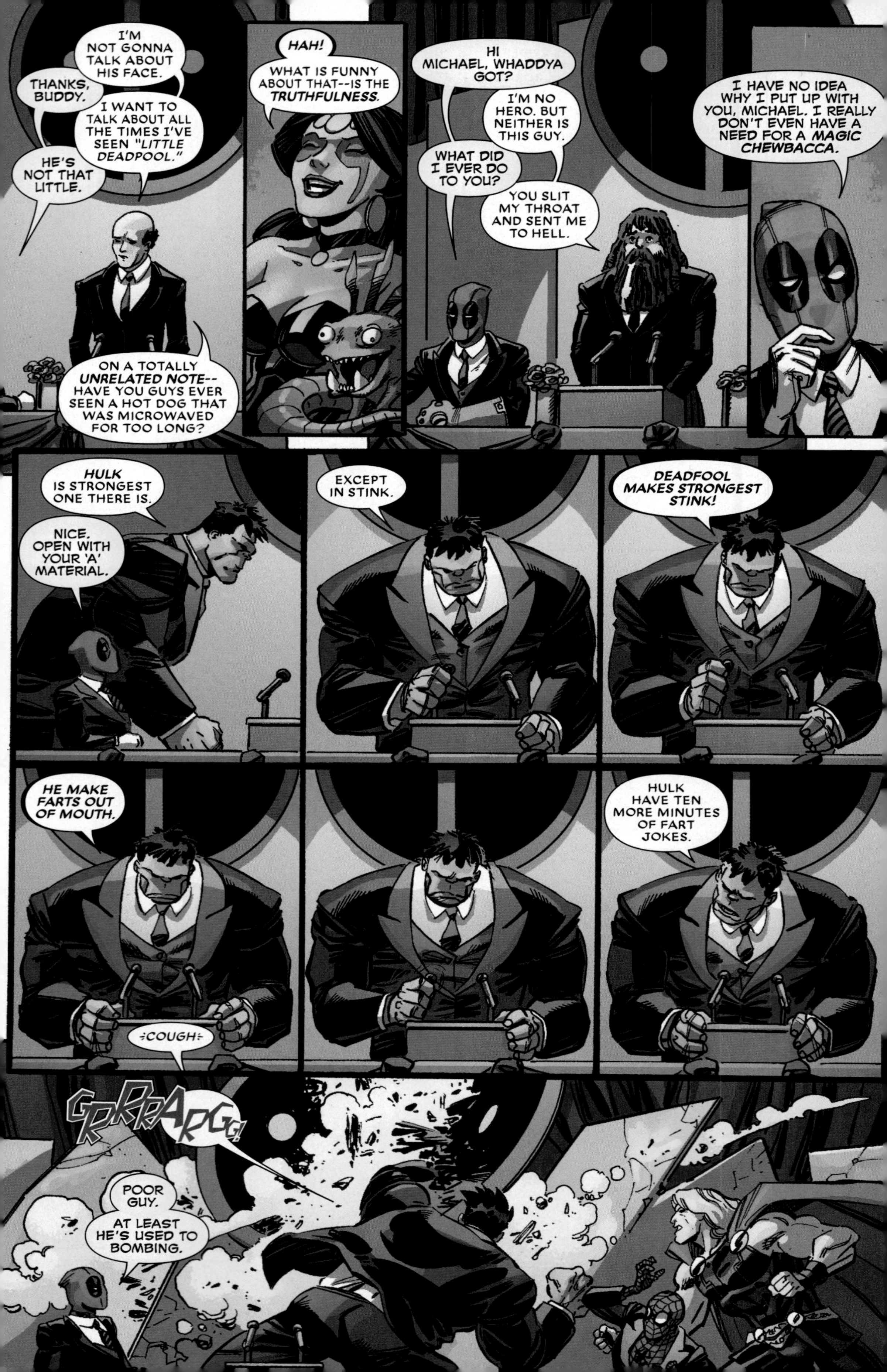
THANKS, BUDDY.
I'M NOT GONNA TALK ABOUT HIS FACE.
I WANT TO TALK ABOUT ALL THE TIMES I'VE SEEN "LITTLE DEADPOOL."
HE'S NOT THAT LITTLE.
ON A TOTALLY UNRELATED NOTE-- HAVE YOU GUYS EVER SEEN A HOT DOG THAT WAS MICROWAVED FOR TOO LONG?
HAH!
WHAT IS FUNNY ABOUT THAT--IS THE TRUTHFULNESS.
HI MICHAEL, WHADDYA GOT?
I'M NO HERO. BUT NEITHER IS THIS GUY.
WHAT DID I EVER DO TO YOU?
YOU SLIT MY THROAT AND SENT ME TO HELL.
I HAVE NO IDEA WHY I PUT UP WITH YOU, MICHAEL. I REALLY DON'T EVEN HAVE A NEED FOR A MAGIC CHEWBACCA.
HULK IS STRONGEST ONE THERE IS.
NICE. OPEN WITH YOUR 'A' MATERIAL.
EXCEPT IN STINK.
DEADFOOL MAKES STRONGEST STINK!
HE MAKE FARTS OUT OF MOUTH.
COUGH
HULK HAVE TEN MORE MINUTES OF FART JOKES.
GRRRRARGG!
POOR GUY.
AT LEAST HE'S USED TO BOMBING.

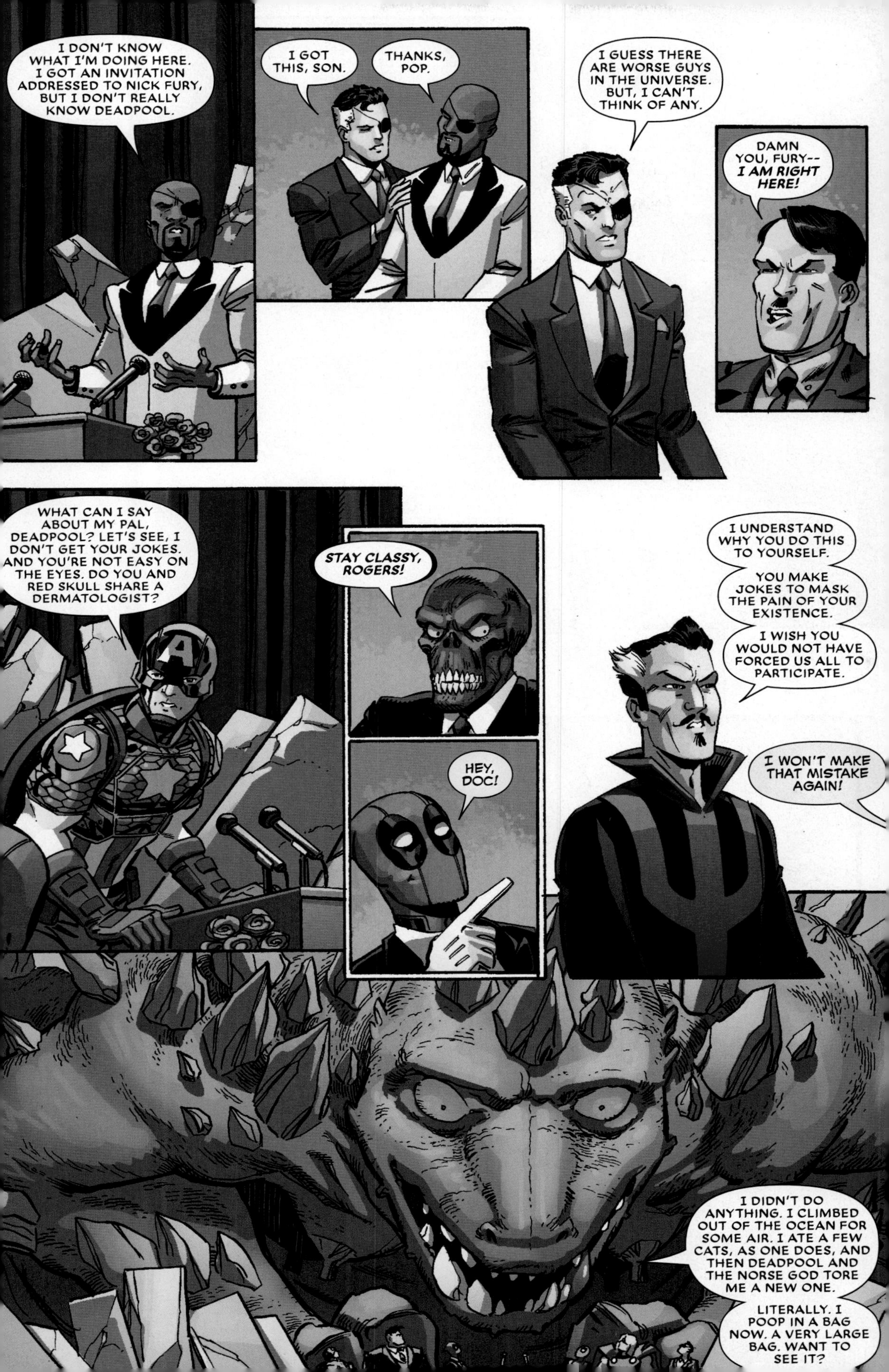
I DON'T KNOW WHAT I'M DOING HERE. I GOT AN INVITATION ADDRESSED TO NICK FURY, BUT I DON'T REALLY KNOW DEADPOOL.
I GOT THIS, SON.
THANKS, POP.
I GUESS THERE ARE WORSE GUYS IN THE UNIVERSE. BUT, I CAN'T THINK OF ANY.
DAMN YOU, FURY-- *I AM RIGHT HERE!*
WHAT CAN I SAY ABOUT MY PAL, DEADPOOL? LET'S SEE, I DON'T GET YOUR JOKES. AND YOU'RE NOT EASY ON THE EYES. DO YOU AND RED SKULL SHARE A DERMATOLOGIST?
STAY CLASSY, ROGERS!
HEY, DOC!
I UNDERSTAND WHY YOU DO THIS TO YOURSELF.
YOU MAKE JOKES TO MASK THE PAIN OF YOUR EXISTENCE.
I WISH YOU WOULD NOT HAVE FORCED US ALL TO PARTICIPATE.
I WON'T MAKE THAT MISTAKE AGAIN!
I DIDN'T DO ANYTHING. I CLIMBED OUT OF THE OCEAN FOR SOME AIR. I ATE A FEW CATS, AS ONE DOES, AND THEN DEADPOOL AND THE NORSE GOD TORE ME A NEW ONE.
LITERALLY. I POOP IN A BAG NOW. A VERY LARGE BAG. WANT TO SEE IT?

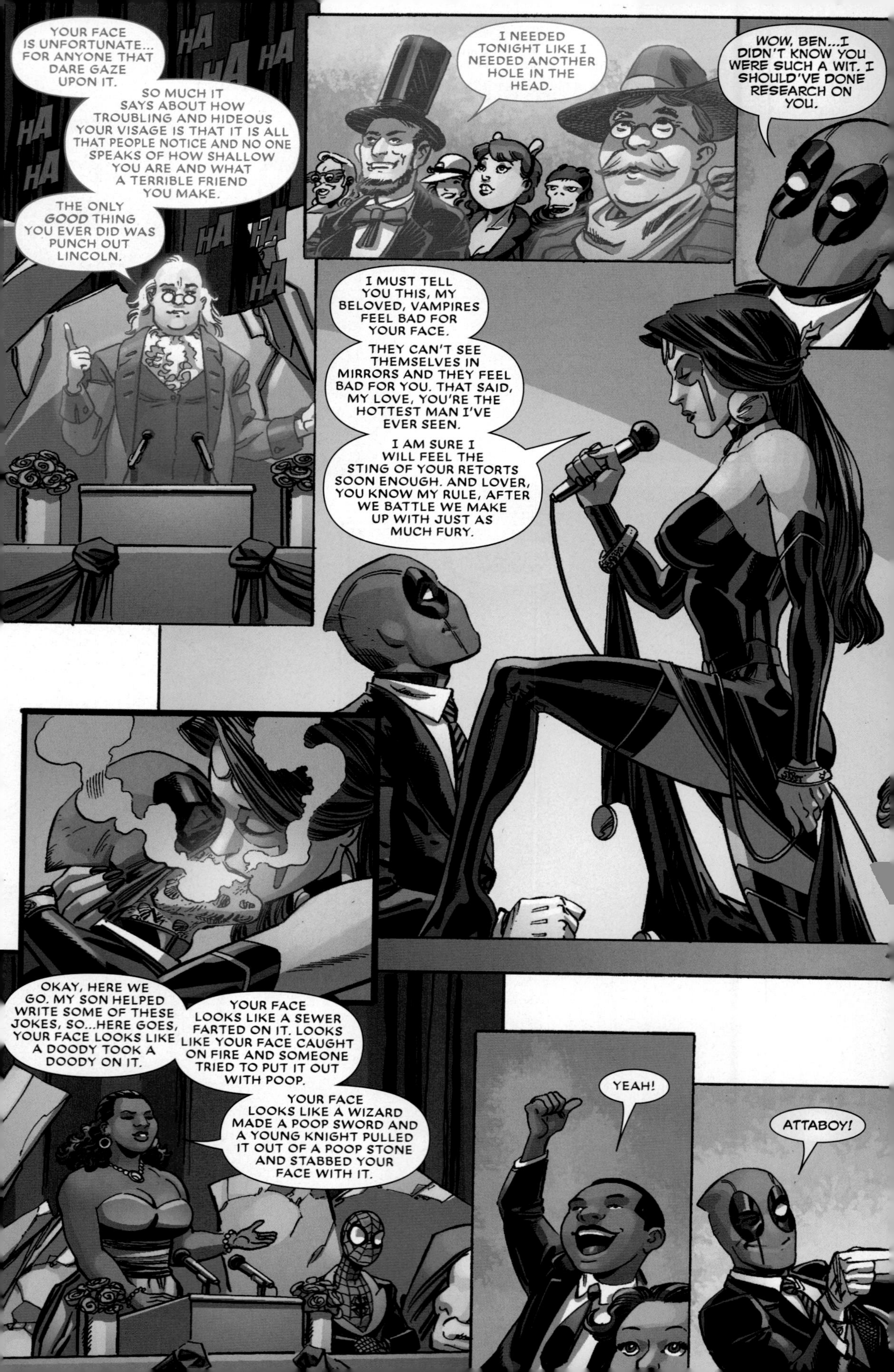
YOUR FACE IS UNFORTUNATE... FOR ANYONE THAT DARE GAZE UPON IT.
SO MUCH IT SAYS ABOUT HOW TROUBLING AND HIDEOUS YOUR VISAGE IS THAT IT IS ALL THAT PEOPLE NOTICE AND NO ONE SPEAKS OF HOW SHALLOW YOU ARE AND WHAT A TERRIBLE FRIEND YOU MAKE.
THE ONLY *GOOD* THING YOU EVER DID WAS PUNCH OUT LINCOLN.
HA HA HA HA HA HA HA HA HA HA
I NEEDED TONIGHT LIKE I NEEDED ANOTHER HOLE IN THE HEAD.
WOW, BEN...I DIDN'T KNOW YOU WERE SUCH A WIT. I SHOULD'VE DONE RESEARCH ON YOU.
I MUST TELL YOU THIS, MY BELOVED, VAMPIRES FEEL BAD FOR YOUR FACE.
THEY CAN'T SEE THEMSELVES IN MIRRORS AND THEY FEEL BAD FOR YOU. THAT SAID, MY LOVE, YOU'RE THE HOTTEST MAN I'VE EVER SEEN.
I AM SURE I WILL FEEL THE STING OF YOUR RETORTS SOON ENOUGH. AND LOVER, YOU KNOW MY RULE, AFTER WE BATTLE WE MAKE UP WITH JUST AS MUCH FURY.
OKAY, HERE WE GO. MY SON HELPED WRITE SOME OF THESE JOKES, SO...HERE GOES, YOUR FACE LOOKS LIKE A DOODY TOOK A DOODY ON IT.
YOUR FACE LOOKS LIKE A SEWER FARTED ON IT. LOOKS LIKE YOUR FACE CAUGHT ON FIRE AND SOMEONE TRIED TO PUT IT OUT WITH POOP.
YOUR FACE LOOKS LIKE A WIZARD MADE A POOP SWORD AND A YOUNG KNIGHT PULLED IT OUT OF A POOP STONE AND STABBED YOUR FACE WITH IT.
YEAH!
ATTABOY!

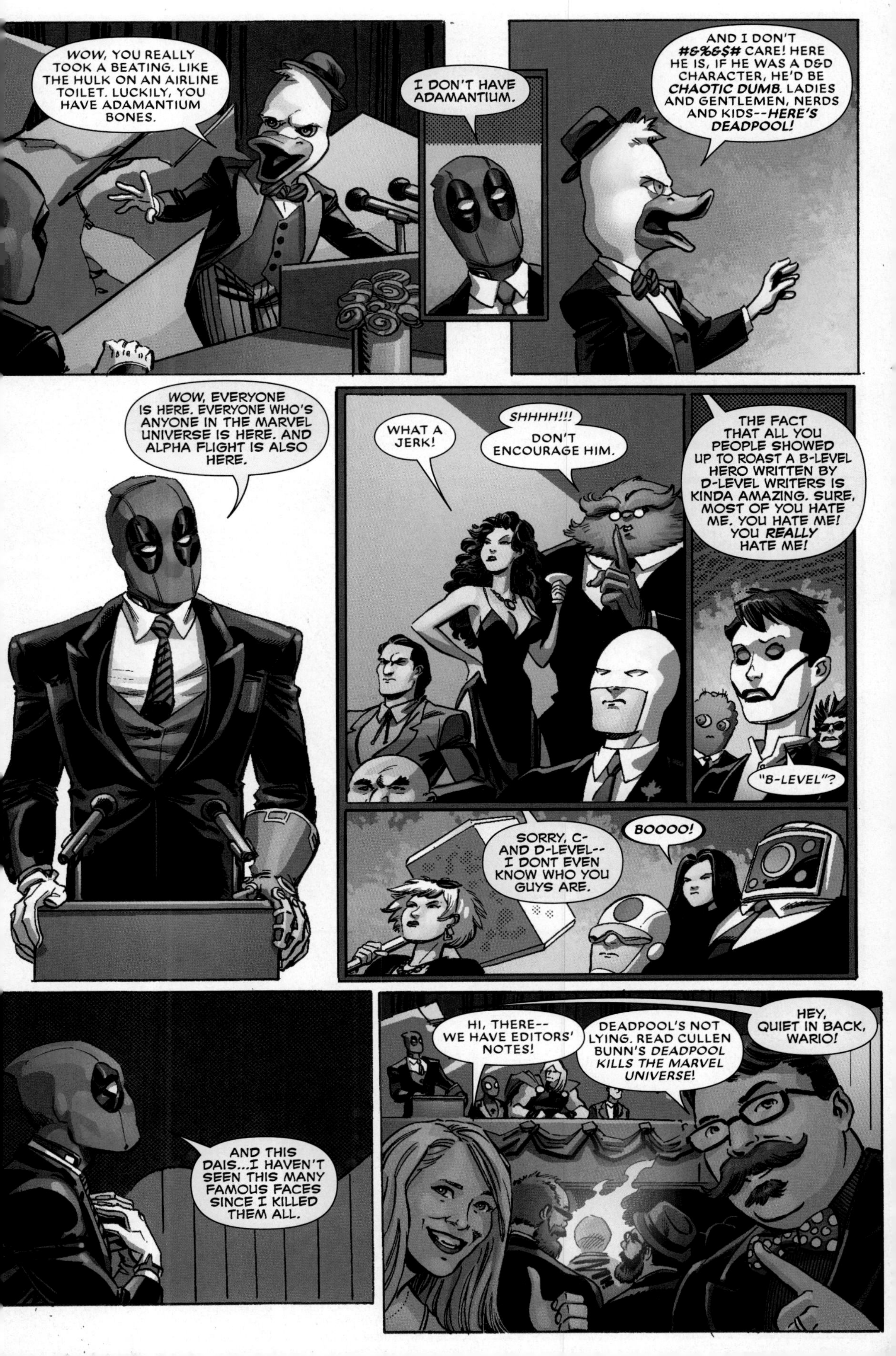
WOW, YOU REALLY TOOK A BEATING. LIKE THE HULK ON AN AIRLINE TOILET. LUCKILY, YOU HAVE ADAMANTIUM BONES.
I DON'T HAVE ADAMANTIUM.
AND I DON'T #&%&$# CARE! HERE HE IS, IF HE WAS A D&D CHARACTER, HE'D BE CHAOTIC DUMB. LADIES AND GENTLEMEN, NERDS AND KIDS--HERE'S DEADPOOL!
WOW, EVERYONE IS HERE. EVERYONE WHO'S ANYONE IN THE MARVEL UNIVERSE IS HERE. AND ALPHA FLIGHT IS ALSO HERE.
WHAT A JERK!
SHHHH!!! DON'T ENCOURAGE HIM.
THE FACT THAT ALL YOU PEOPLE SHOWED UP TO ROAST A B-LEVEL HERO WRITTEN BY D-LEVEL WRITERS IS KINDA AMAZING. SURE, MOST OF YOU HATE ME. YOU HATE ME! YOU REALLY HATE ME!
"B-LEVEL"?
SORRY, C- AND D-LEVEL-- I DONT EVEN KNOW WHO YOU GUYS ARE.
BOOOO!
AND THIS DAIS...I HAVEN'T SEEN THIS MANY FAMOUS FACES SINCE I KILLED THEM ALL.
HI, THERE-- WE HAVE EDITORS' NOTES!
DEADPOOL'S NOT LYING. READ CULLEN BUNN'S DEADPOOL KILLS THE MARVEL UNIVERSE!
HEY, QUIET IN BACK, WARIO!

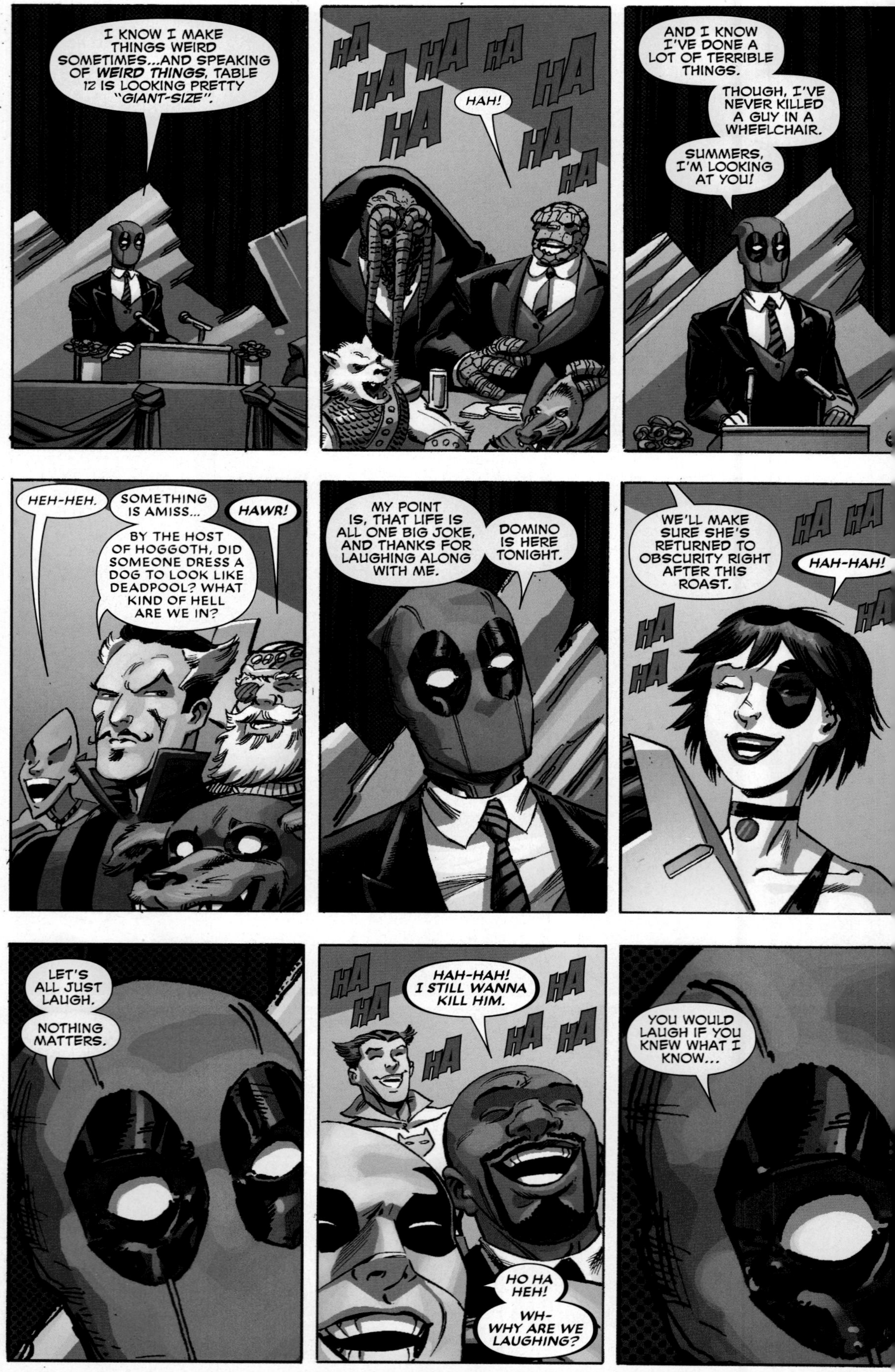
I KNOW I MAKE THINGS WEIRD SOMETIMES...AND SPEAKING OF *WEIRD THINGS*, TABLE 12 IS LOOKING PRETTY "*GIANT-SIZE*".
HA HA HA HA HA HA HA HA HA HA
HAH!
AND I KNOW I'VE DONE A LOT OF TERRIBLE THINGS.
THOUGH, I'VE NEVER KILLED A GUY IN A WHEELCHAIR.
SUMMERS, I'M LOOKING AT YOU!
HEH-HEH.
SOMETHING IS AMISS...
BY THE HOST OF HOGGOTH, DID SOMEONE DRESS A DOG TO LOOK LIKE DEADPOOL? WHAT KIND OF HELL ARE WE IN?
HAWR!
MY POINT IS, THAT LIFE IS ALL ONE BIG JOKE, AND THANKS FOR LAUGHING ALONG WITH ME.
DOMINO IS HERE TONIGHT.
WE'LL MAKE SURE SHE'S RETURNED TO OBSCURITY RIGHT AFTER THIS ROAST.
HA HA
HAH-HAH!
HA HA
LET'S ALL JUST LAUGH.
NOTHING MATTERS.
HA HA
HAH-HAH! I STILL WANNA KILL HIM.
HA HA HA HA
HO HA HEH!
WH- WHY ARE WE LAUGHING?
YOU WOULD LAUGH IF YOU KNEW WHAT I KNOW...

HA HA HA HAHA HA HA HA HA

HAH!

YOU GOT ME!

DON'T LAUGH, KID-CLOPS, YOU'RE GONNA GROW INTO THAT JERK.

LADY THOR SENDS HER REGARDS, SHE'S AT A DIFFERENT ROAST TONIGHT. SHE'S COOKING SOME FROST GIANTS WITH LIGHTNING.

HEY, ODINSON, THANKS FOR CLEARING YOUR CALENDAR.

HEH.

IT IS GOOD FOR YOU THAT I AM VERY DRUNK ON THIS MEAD.

HA HA HA HA HA

YOU KNOW GROOT ISN'T THE FIRST WOODEN MEMBER OF A TEAM--BEFORE HIM THE BLACK KNIGHT WAS AN AVENGER FOR YEARS.

OH BOY-- IS IT MY TURN?

NO, JORDAN D. WHITE WON'T LET ME MAKE FUN OF THE HANDICAPPED.

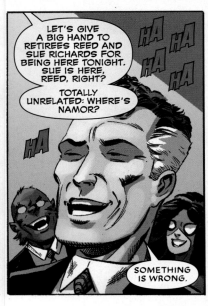

LET'S GIVE A BIG HAND TO RETIREES REED AND SUE RICHARDS FOR BEING HERE TONIGHT. SUE IS HERE, REED, RIGHT?

TOTALLY UNRELATED: WHERE'S NAMOR?

HA HA HA HA

HA

SOMETHING IS WRONG.

HAH-HAH!

I TRIED TELEPORTING AWAY, BUT I JUST END UP BACK HERE!

HAH!

I WISH I WAS DEAF AND NOT BLIND!

HA HA HA

STRANGE--DO SOMETHING.

KNOCK! KNOCK!

WHO'S THERE?

THE VISHANTI!

THE VISHANTI WHO?

THE VISHANTI WHO HAVE FORSAKEN US!

WE'RE DYING!

HA HA HA

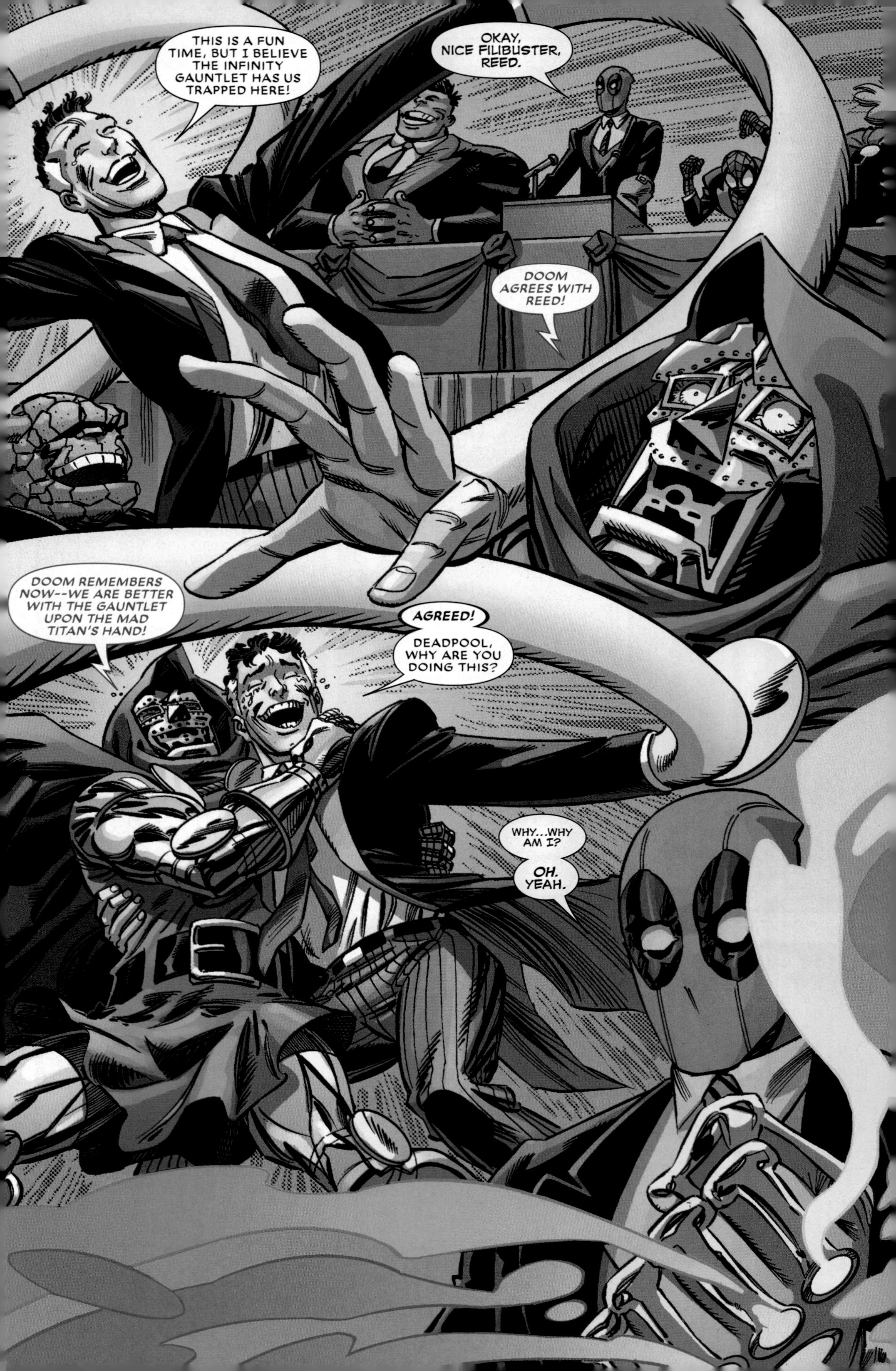
THIS IS A FUN TIME, BUT I BELIEVE THE INFINITY GAUNTLET HAS US TRAPPED HERE!
OKAY, NICE FILIBUSTER, REED.
DOOM AGREES WITH REED!
DOOM REMEMBERS NOW--WE ARE BETTER WITH THE GAUNTLET UPON THE MAD TITAN'S HAND!
AGREED!
DEADPOOL, WHY ARE YOU DOING THIS?
WHY...WHY AM I?
OH. YEAH.

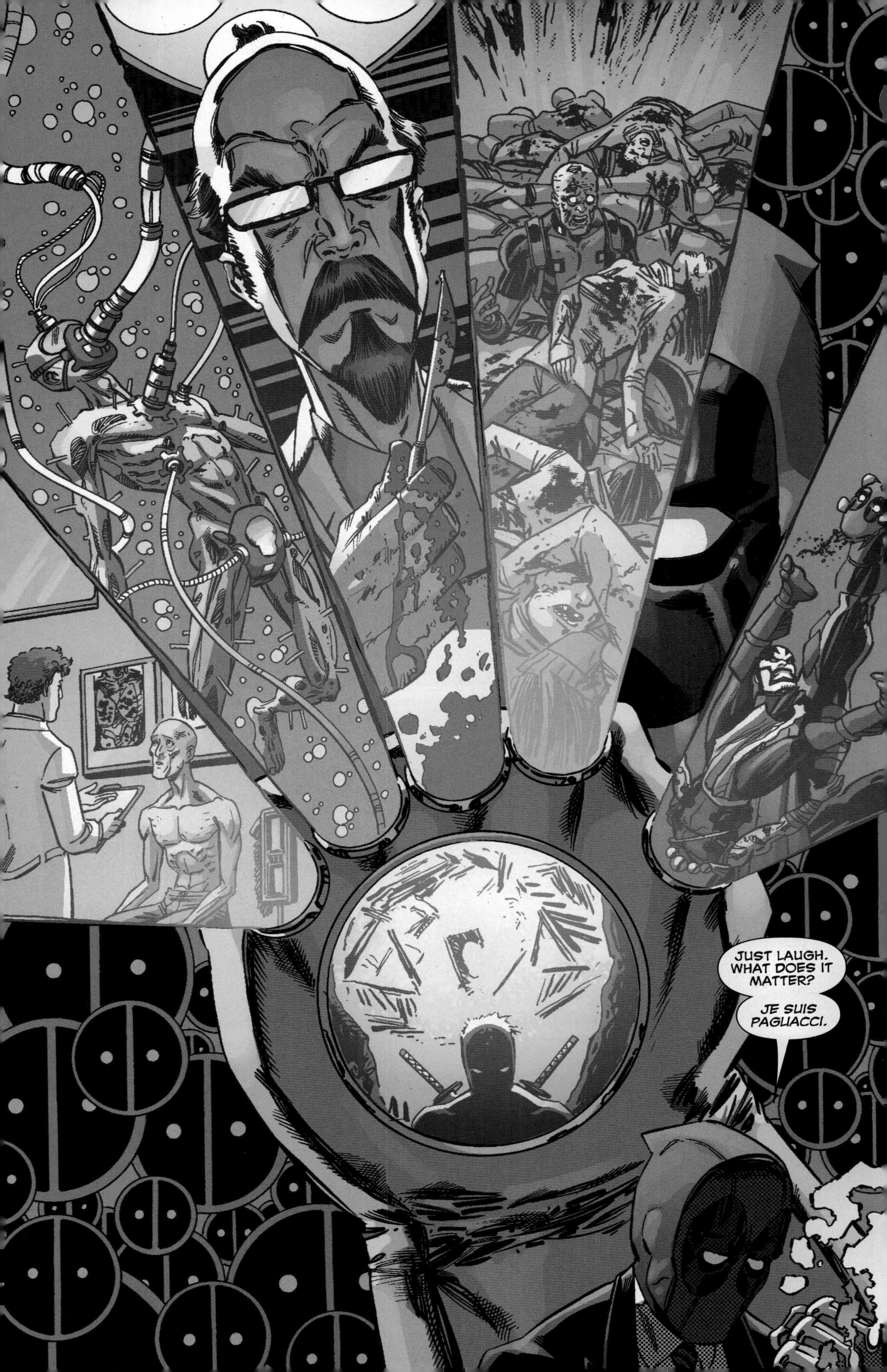
JUST LAUGH. WHAT DOES IT MATTER?
JE SUIS PAGLIACCI.

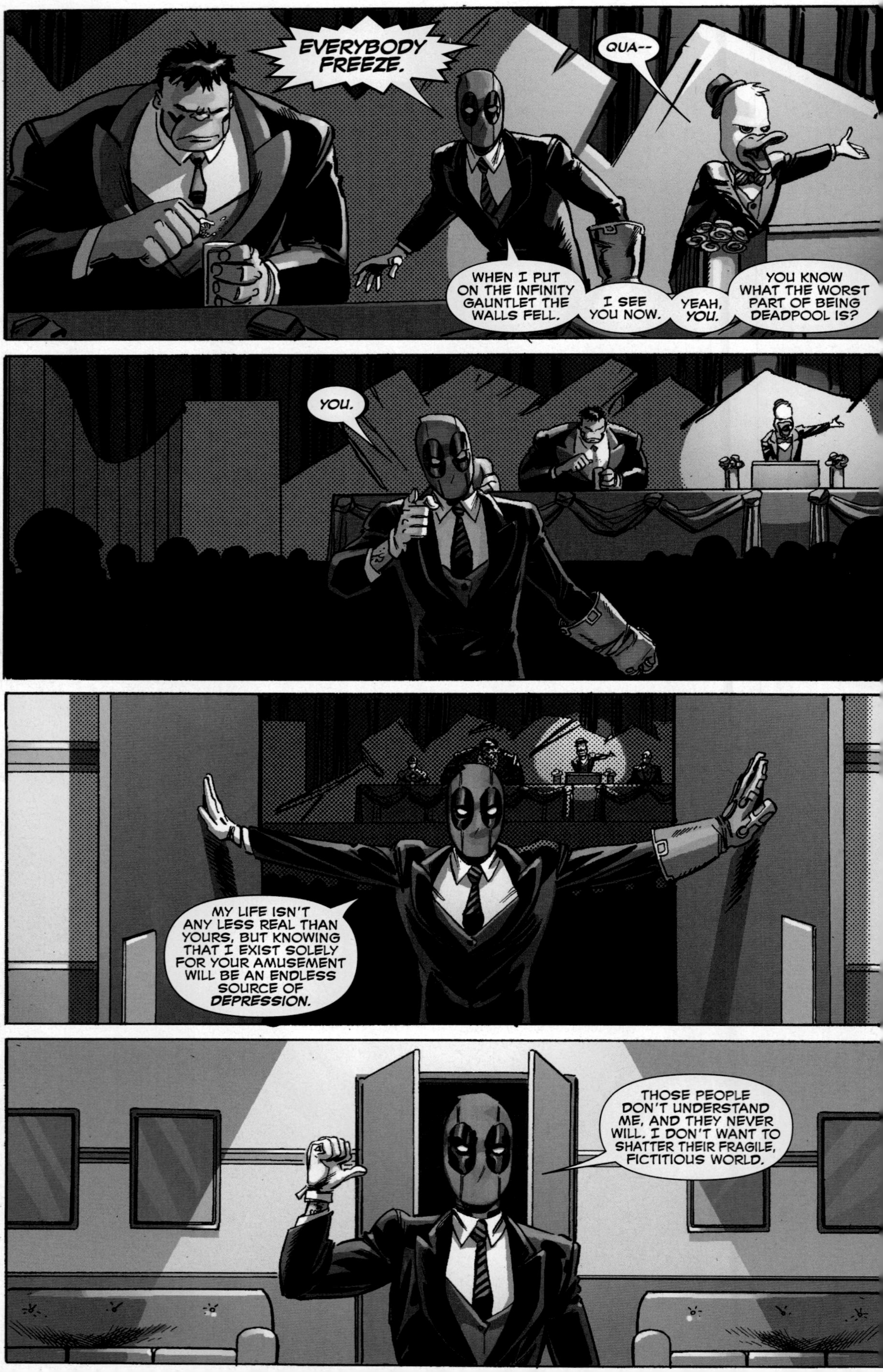
EVERYBODY FREEZE.
QUA--
WHEN I PUT ON THE INFINITY GAUNTLET THE WALLS FELL.
I SEE YOU NOW.
YEAH, YOU.
YOU KNOW WHAT THE WORST PART OF BEING DEADPOOL IS?
YOU.
MY LIFE ISN'T ANY LESS REAL THAN YOURS, BUT KNOWING THAT I EXIST SOLELY FOR YOUR AMUSEMENT WILL BE AN ENDLESS SOURCE OF DEPRESSION.
THOSE PEOPLE DON'T UNDERSTAND ME, AND THEY NEVER WILL. I DON'T WANT TO SHATTER THEIR FRAGILE, FICTITIOUS WORLD.

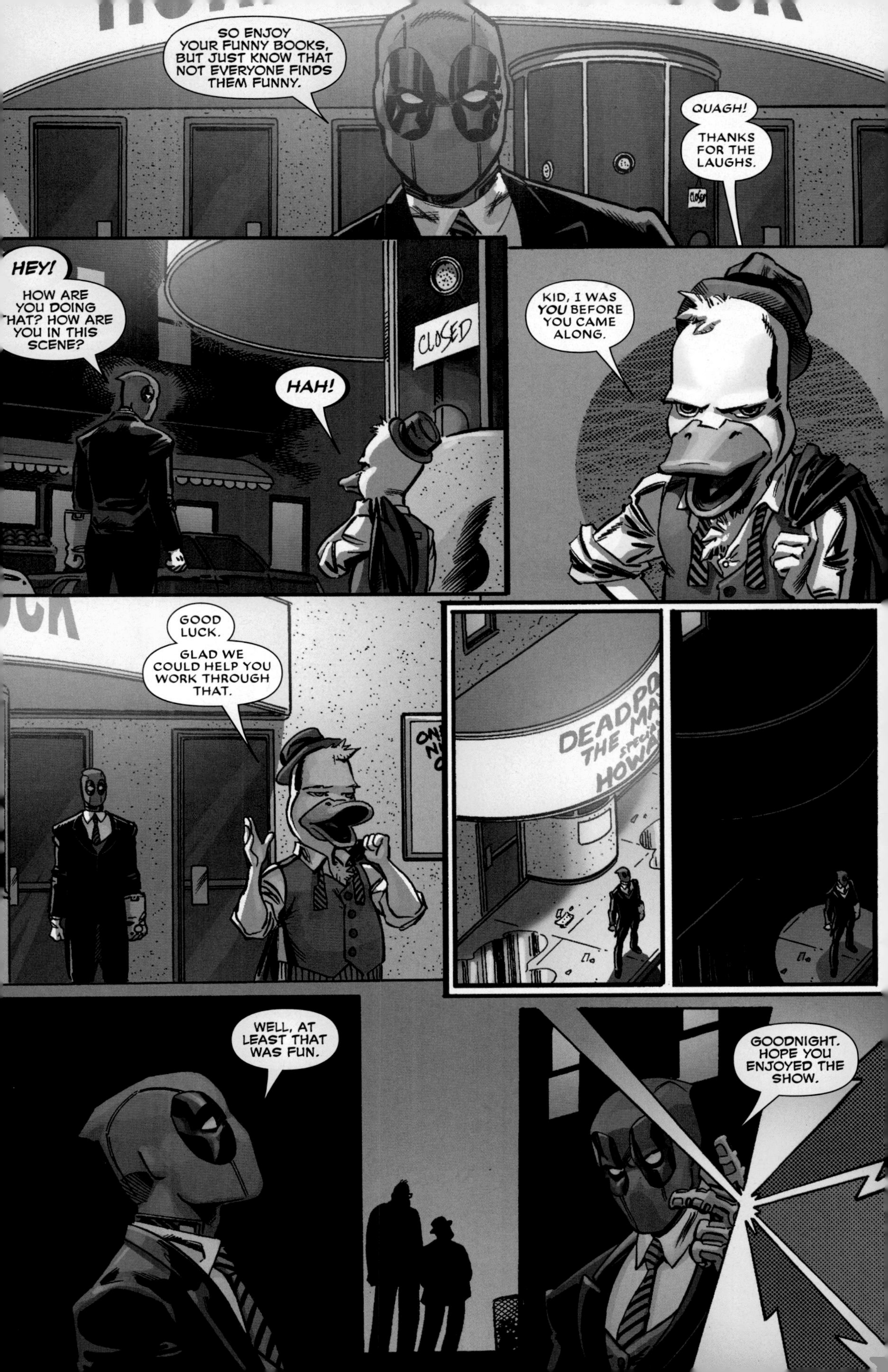
SO ENJOY YOUR FUNNY BOOKS, BUT JUST KNOW THAT NOT EVERYONE FINDS THEM FUNNY.
QUAGH!
THANKS FOR THE LAUGHS.
CLOSED
HEY!
HOW ARE YOU DOING THAT? HOW ARE YOU IN THIS SCENE?
HAH!
KID, I WAS YOU BEFORE YOU CAME ALONG.
GOOD LUCK.
GLAD WE COULD HELP YOU WORK THROUGH THAT.
WELL, AT LEAST THAT WAS FUN.
GOODNIGHT. HOPE YOU ENJOYED THE SHOW.

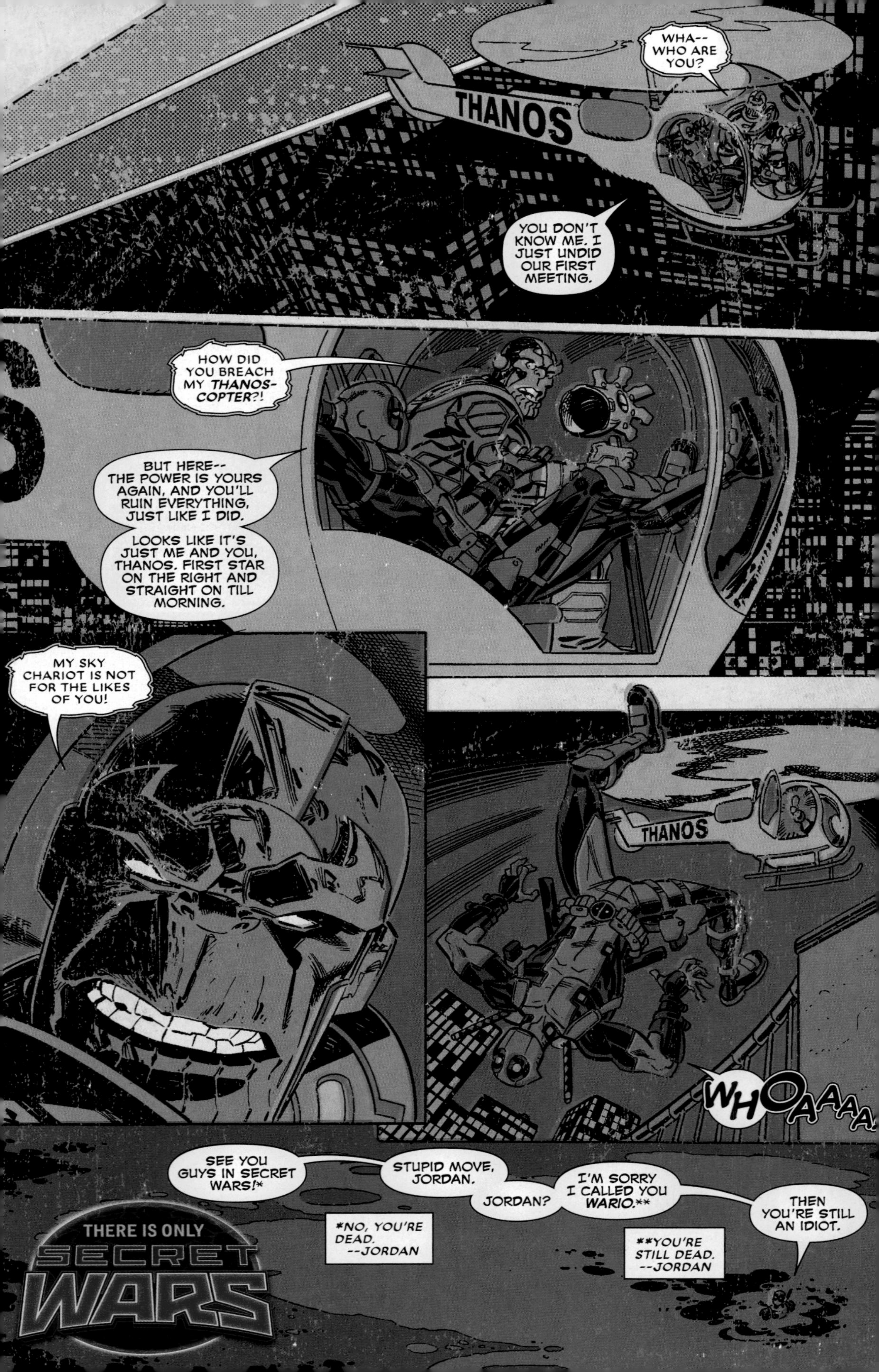
WHA-- WHO ARE YOU?
THANOS
YOU DON'T KNOW ME. I JUST UNDID OUR FIRST MEETING.
HOW DID YOU BREACH MY THANOS-COPTER?!
BUT HERE-- THE POWER IS YOURS AGAIN, AND YOU'LL RUIN EVERYTHING, JUST LIKE I DID.
LOOKS LIKE IT'S JUST ME AND YOU, THANOS. FIRST STAR ON THE RIGHT AND STRAIGHT ON TILL MORNING.
MY SKY CHARIOT IS NOT FOR THE LIKES OF YOU!
THANOS
WHOAAAAA
SEE YOU GUYS IN SECRET WARS!*
STUPID MOVE, JORDAN.
JORDAN?
I'M SORRY I CALLED YOU WARIO.**
THEN YOU'RE STILL AN IDIOT.
*NO, YOU'RE DEAD. --JORDAN
**YOU'RE STILL DEAD. --JORDAN
THERE IS ONLY SECRET WARS

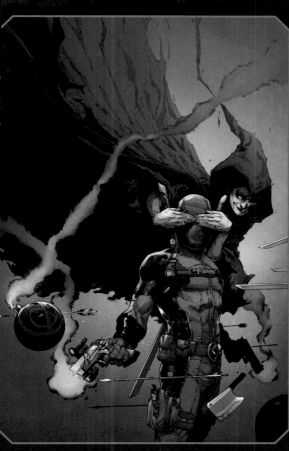

#250 VARIANT BY
JEROME OPEÑA & JASON KEITH

ONE MINUTE LATER
AVENGERS
EARTH'S MIGHTIEST SUPER-HEROES!
DEADPOOL
MARVEL
COMICS
GROUP
I GOT THIS!
PANOSIAN

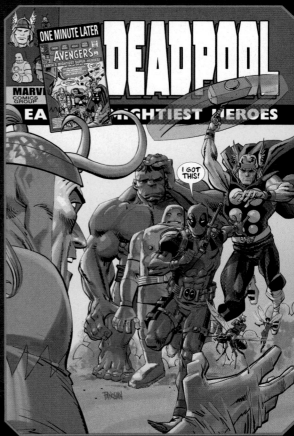

#250 AVENGERS VARIANT BY
DAN PANOSIAN

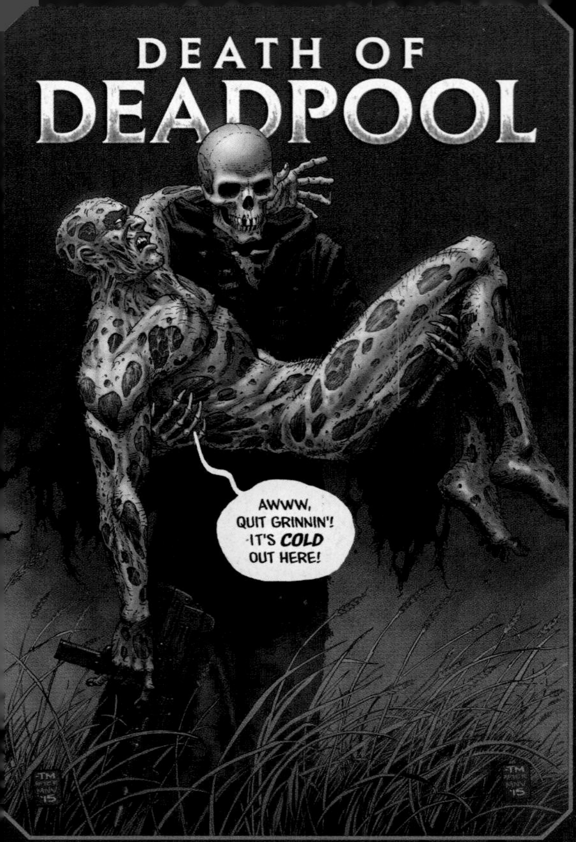
DEATH OF
DEADPOOL
AWWW, QUIT GRINNIN'! IT'S *COLD* OUT HERE!

#250 DEATH OF DEADPOOL VARIANT BY TONY MOORE

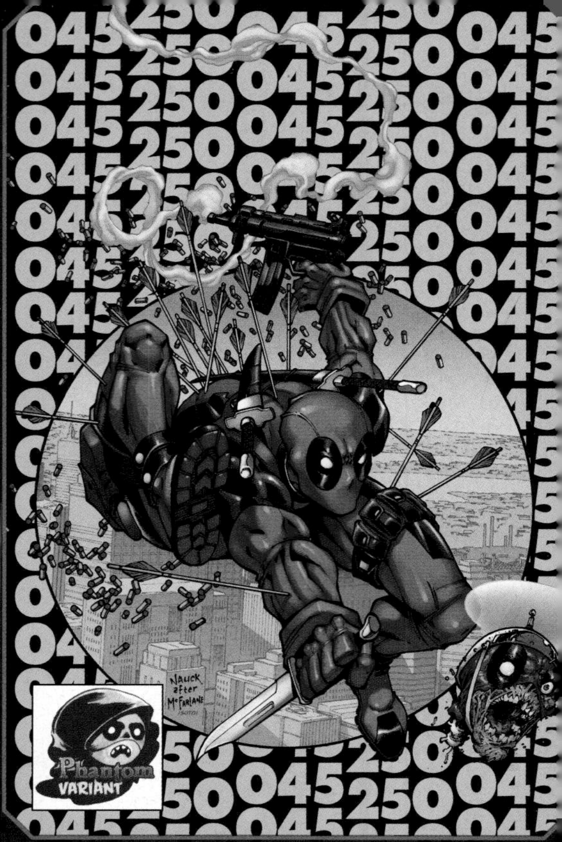
NAUCK after McFARLANE
Phantom
VARIANT

#250 VARIANT BY TODD NAUCK & CHRIS SOTOMAYOR

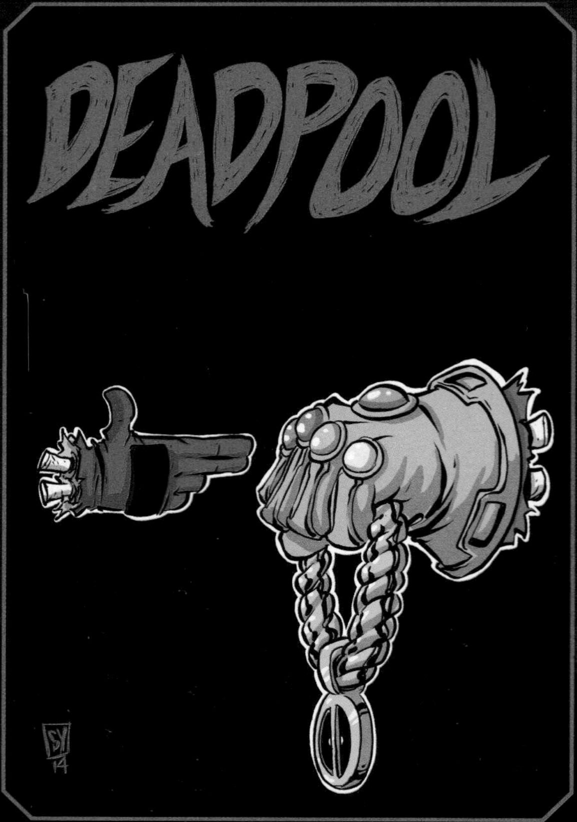
DEADPOOL

#250 VARIANT BY SKOTTIE YOUNG